TEACHING AS DECISION MAKING

Instructional Practices for the Successful Teacher

Marvin Pasch
Georgea Sparks-Langer
Trevor G. Gardner
Alane J. Starko
Christella D. Moody
Eastern Michigan University

Longman
New York & London

Teaching as Decision Making

Longman, 95 Church Street, White Plains, N.Y. 10601

Associated companies:
Longman Group Ltd., London
Longman Cheshire Pty., Melbourne
Longman Paul Pty., Auckland
Copp Clark Pitman, Toronto

Few books are completed by the authors alone. We appreciate the contributions of Tom Tobias, the talented Ypsilanti teacher whose cartoons brighten our writing, and of EMU photographer Dick Schwarze.

We are indebted to the Ypsilanti, Michigan, school board and to Superintendent James Hawkins for permission to photograph George School principal Leo Clark and teachers Grace Aaron, Elaine Bortz, Kay Brown, Deloris Butler, Donna Carpenter, Mary Williams, and C. J. Wysocki, as well as the student teachers and students who appear in the photographs. Our thanks to EMU administrators for their financial and emotional encouragement; also to the many faculty and students who took time to reflect upon and comment on our work.

We owe an enormous debt of gratitude to our spouses—Judy, Peter, Patricia, Bob, and Charles—and to other family members who were willing to elevate the writing of *Teaching as Decision Making* to a family priority. That debt never can be sufficiently repaid.

Executive editor: Raymond T. O'Connell
Development editor: Virginia Blanford
Production editor: Halley Gatenby
Cover design: Anne Pompeo
Photos: Dick Schwarze
Cartoon art: Thomas Tobias
Text art: Pencil Point Studio
Production supervisor: Anne Armeny

Library of Congress Cataloging-in-Publication Data

Teaching as decision-making / Marvin Pasch . . . [et al.].
        p.   cm.
    Includes bibliographical references.
    ISBN 0-8013-0157-2
    1. Teaching. 2. Lesson planning. 3. Classroom management.
I. Pasch, Marvin.
LB1025.2.T4156   1990   90-31117
371.1'02—dc20   CIP

ABCDEFGHIJ—DO—99 98 97 96 95 94 93 92 91 90

Contents

CHAPTER 1

Teaching as Decision Making

Chapter Overview

In this book, the nature of decision making is explored as it relates to the empowerment of teachers. Empowerment involves a feeling of self-efficacy—the knowledge that you are in control of your work environment and that what you do as a teacher makes a difference with students. An empowered teacher has assumed the responsibility to become a *designer* of instruction and to reflect on teaching practices to improve instruction. Contrast the designer teacher to the less active, less involved *consumer* teacher, who implements someone else's philosophy, materials, and methods. The chapters that follow expand on this theme and will enhance your understanding of the decision-making process while improving your teaching capability and performance.

THE FUNDAMENTAL THEORY THAT ORGANIZES THIS TEXT

Consider two alternative conceptions of teachers today. The first conception, the teacher *consumer*, through preference or circumstance permits the curriculum—the content of what is taught—to be determined and organized by others. Typically, the teacher consumer has surrendered to the textbook the responsibility to define, analyze, and develop the curriculum. Although teacher consumers retain the responsibility to teach from the textbook, they do not participate in the creative process that brings it to life and thus have no significant stake in its success.

Contrast the consumer teacher with the teacher *designer*, an able professional who helps develop district and/or grade-level goals, creates units of study, writes instructional objectives, and makes decisions about instructional materials. In effect, the teacher, not the textbook, is the major curriculum designer. As teacher designers plan their teaching sequences, they adjust the scope, depth, and complexity of their teaching plans to match the needs, abilities, interests, and prior knowledge of their students. After completing instruction, they evaluate and revise their teaching plans in response to student performance and feedback. Teacher designers are interested in more than just what goes on within their classrooms. They take an active interest in their own professional development, the growth of their profession, and the recurring need for educational change and improvement.

Teacher designers have the fullest opportunity to flex and stretch their decision-making powers. They make *planning* decisions—choosing and analyzing content, writing objectives, selecting learning activities, and evaluating instruction. They make *implementation* decisions as they design and teach units and lessons, make adjustments for individual student needs, and enhance their students' thinking skills. Finally, they make decisions about *classroom management*, applying their beliefs and principles about individual human beings and communities to create and maintain a positive learning environment.

Teacher designers make a full range of decisions about planning, implementation, and management. These decisions are ongoing but may be thought of as occurring before, during, and after teaching:

Decisions before Teaching—Planning for Action
Decisions during Teaching—Action, Observation, Modifications
Decisions after Teaching—Reflection, Predictions, Redesign

Before teaching, the teacher designer asks these questions: What objective(s) do I want to achieve? What type of lesson will I need in order to teach the necessary content? Through what activities will the students achieve the objective(s)? What problems may arise during the lesson? What strategies have I planned to confront problems if they arise? *During* teaching, the teacher designer is conscious of how well the lesson is being received by students and is ready to make adjustments as needed in the pace, depth, and complexity of the lesson. Such decisions may even require shifting to a different activity or, in unusual circumstances, changing to a different lesson and objective(s). *After* teaching, the teacher designer evaluates the success of the lesson by asking how well the students attained the objective(s). Why was the lesson successful or unsuccessful? What could I have done differently?

The purpose of this text is to explore a wide range of issues and topics teacher designers must consider as we approach the 21st century. But how do we define decision making? What are the characteristics of an effective decision maker? These questions have helped shape this textbook. Before presenting the theory, however, we would like to share with you some background information about us, the authors.

During the period 1985–1988, we were involved as teachers, administrators, and researchers in a teacher education project at Eastern Michigan University. This project, *Collaboration for the Improvement of Teacher Education*, (CITE), was based on contemporary research on (1) the nature and impact of the surrounding society on schools, school personnel, and children; (2) the effects of human development and learning principles on schooling; and (3) promising research-based teaching practices (Sparks, Simmons, & Pasch, 1988).

Soon after the CITE project objectives were conceived, it became necessary to assess instructional decision making—that is, changes in teachers' thinking about educational methods and practices. In educators' language the study of teaching methods and practices is referred to as *pedagogy*. We soon realized that little is known about how educators think about pedagogical decisions and how this thinking can be identified, classified, analyzed, and evaluated. Since then, a number of contemporary teacher educators have coalesced around the term *teacher reflection* to describe a teacher's instructional decision making (Spring, 1985; Schon, 1987; Parsons, 1983; Zeichner & Liston, 1987). There are many views of teacher reflection (Grimmett & Erickson, 1988), ranging from the technical view (e.g., "How well are the techniques I'm using working?") to the ethical/moral view (e.g., "What are the long-term effects on society of this content or this technique?"). A common definition consistent with the approach taken in this book is "the teacher's ability to make rational [educational] choices and to assume responsibility for one's choices" (Ross, 1987)—in other words, to make thoughtful instructional decisions.

Researchers on classroom behavior have concluded that the practice of teaching is complex and uncertain (e.g., Clark, 1988). The demands on teachers have been characterized as "more complex than that of the physician during a diagnostic consultation with a patient" (Shulman, 1984, p. 3).

Our work has focused on the question "What do teachers think about when making a teaching decision?" (Simmons, Sparks, Starko, Pasch, Colton, & Grinberg, 1989). We have come to the conclusion that, while teachers need to be able to use educational ideas and language to describe or label classroom events, such tasks are not sufficient for full professional functioning. Therefore, this book does not simply provide you with rules and techniques. The following "Belief Statements" describe more fully our view of reflective professional decision making.

Belief 1. Success in Teaching Results from More Than Just "Good Technique"

We feel it is essential that teachers not only think about technique but also ask *why* a certain technique works or does not work. Further, teachers should ask themselves about conditions—students, physical factors, or social context—that may influence the outcome of a technique. Finally, teachers should consider the long-term political and social effects of their classroom practices. Thus a true professional considers a wide range of factors when making a teaching decision.

Think of all the factors, issues, and knowledge a teacher needs to consider when making a teaching decision. Make a list of as many as you can.

Figure 1.1 shows the factors we think contribute to successful and responsible teaching decisions. The first factor is teacher characteristics and beliefs. Teacher traits such as self-confidence, enthusiasm, intelligence, and commitment affect what a teacher will do on a particular day. Personal beliefs about students' ability to learn, the purposes of schools, and social values will also influence a teacher's choice of actions. For example, a teacher with

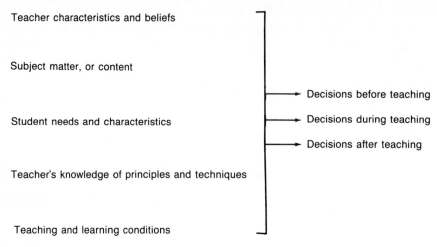

Figure 1.1. Factors Influencing Teaching Decisions

students labeled as "slow learners" may believe that he or she has little potential influence on their learning and give up prematurely.

The subject matter, or content, also influences teaching decisions. Teaching science may call for certain techniques, while teaching literature may require different techniques. After a while, a teacher begins to see how to represent a complex idea.

The students certainly have an important impact on our decisions. If learners are poorly motivated or discouraged, we may need to be especially enthusiastic and active in our teaching. Students' learning styles may also influence our choice of activities. We need to take into consideration home background when trying to relate new ideas to students' prior experiences. For example, referring to water skiing as an illustration in a science explanation may totally confuse a student who has never seen that sport.

A significant influence on teaching decisions is how much we know about teaching, learning, and classroom management. We need a professional knowledge base of concepts, principles, and techniques to draw upon. These ideas include knowledge of human development, learning theory, and teaching methods.

Finally, we cannot ignore the other conditions that influence everyday classroom life. The social and political forces in the school, district, and community help determine what we teach and, sometimes, how we teach. We also should remember that we exert a powerful influence on our students' values—an influence that may become apparent only later on, in their adult lives, as they imitate the models we have provided for them.

As you progress in your teacher education, you will learn how to become sensitive to all these factors. In your field experiences and early years of teaching, you will begin to see how these ideas can be woven together into the wonderful complexity of teaching.

Belief 2. The Standard of Success in Teaching Is Student School Performance

A number of standards can be used to measure teaching success. A generation ago, infrequent observations by supervisors were combined with student or parental complaints to make judgments about a teacher's success. Some educators have argued that the results of teaching become apparent only years later; thus conclusions based on what teachers and students do in classrooms can be misleading. Finally, others argue that the proper standard of teaching success is student behavior outside the classroom, in the real world. We believe, however, that the only standard of teaching performance that is both reasonable and practical is the learning achieved by students, as demonstrated by their attitudes and behavior in the school and classroom. This learning should include students' academic knowledge and skills in addition to their emotional and social development.

Belief 3. Teaching Is Both an Art and a Science

Just as there is a range of raw talent in any field, there are teachers whose students outperform their peers in other classrooms. Often, these teachers cannot describe what they do or explain how and why they do it. Some naive observers point to these naturally successful teachers and argue that their existence proves that teaching is an art. Therefore, they say, scientific analysis of teaching behavior is a waste of time. The reality is that the majority of us possess no exceptional characteristics that, in and of themselves, will make us unusually effective with young people. Thus it is our view that informed reflection based on insightful, practical, scientific theory will improve the teaching performance of *all* teachers. We cannot rely on artistry alone.

Belief 4. Teachers Who Reflect on Their Teaching Methods and Practices Are Better Teachers Than Those Who Do Not

You should not be surprised that we believe that knowledge about teacher behavior as it affects student performance is essential for successful teaching. This knowledge, however, must be presented in a format that will not only communicate information but will lead to insights and to positive changes in teaching performance. We have included topics and information in this text to enhance your ability to become a thoughtful and successful teacher. We have also presented ideas in such a way as to highlight what is especially important, to provide practice exercises for you to expand and sharpen your understanding, and to allow you to apply and assess your growing capabilities.

HOW IS THE TEXT CONTENT ORGANIZED?

> Topic I. Planning for Instruction: Setting the Stage
> Topic II. Implementation: Getting Out There and Teaching
> Topic III. Classroom Management: Establishing a Positive Environment

Planning for instruction is accomplished prior to teaching. It may be a solitary activity for the teacher or may involve a small group of teachers and, in some cases, students. Planning is best done in a supportive environment where the teacher has both time and tranquility to reflect on past and future teaching lessons. Implementation is usually accomplished in face-to-face contact with one student, a small group of students, or a classroom group. We should not forget, however, that mediated lessons—those taught by media such as a movie, field trip, or computer-managed instruction—do not require that the classroom teacher be present. Classroom management includes a set of common expectations for the teacher and the students. It also helps establish procedures and positive and negative consequences for student

performance and behavior. In contrast to the previous topics, classroom management issues will be considered during both the planning and implementation phases.

The topic "Planning for Instruction" follows this introductory chapter. It consists of three chapters: Chapter 2, "Choosing and Analyzing Classroom Goals"; Chapter 3, "Writing Instructional Objectives/Evaluating Results"; and Chapter 4, "Principles of Selecting and Implementing Learning Activities." The content of these three chapters completes what is often called the *instructional planning cycle*, shown in Figure 1.2.

Although the text divides the planning cycle into three chapters and thus implies a sequence as shown in Figure 1.2, the reality is that planning is not a rigidly sequenced process. Some successful teachers do indeed plan according to that sequence. Other equally successful teachers begin planning by conceiving of an activity they wish to implement and then work back to goals and objectives (Clark and Yinger, 1987). Others may think of an outcome they wish to achieve and then create an evaluation procedure. Only when they are sure they can create that procedure will they return to the goal/objective and activity phases.

Regardless of how the sequence is initiated, successful planners consider and define each step before implementing an instructional lesson or unit. Key ideas in the planning phase are the relationship between educational philosophy and teaching practices; the nature of educational content, with special attention to the central place of generalizations and concepts; the integration of content and learning process; the transformation of broad educational goals into specific instructional objectives; a review of major constructs in educational evaluation;

principles for selecting learning activities; and a focus on learning activities such as lecture, discussion, role playing, and simulation.

The topic "Implementation" includes three chapters: Chapter 5, "Unit and Lesson Design"; Chapter 6, "Teaching to Enhance Thinking"; and Chapter 7, "Teaching for Individual Needs." Of special note is the explanation of different types of lessons (i.e., direct, inductive, and social lessons), research principles related to successful teaching, and examples of each lesson type. We also present strategies and techniques for enhancing student thinking, with special attention to the design and delivery of classroom questions. Finally, we discuss teaching gifted and talented children; children with intellectual, emotional, or physical disabilities; and children from multicultural and bilingual home environments.

The topic "Classroom Management" is dealt with in two chapters: Chapter 8, "Classroom Management: Traditions, Programs, and Research," and Chapter 9, "A Rational Approach to Classroom Management." In Chapter 8, we consider three traditions from which classroom management philosophies emerge—commonsense, behavior management, and humanistic. We outline several programs identified with the latter two traditions. Finally, in Chapter 9, the rational approach to classroom management is described and recommended as an effective way to combine the best features from the other traditions.

In the final chapter, Chapter 10, "Looking Back and Ahead," we provide an opportunity to review the content presented in previous chapters, to revisit some of the key instructional objectives you have achieved in your journey through the content, and to examine again the model of instructional decision making presented in this introductory chapter. Finally, we take a look forward to your development as an educational professional and as a positive force for educational change.

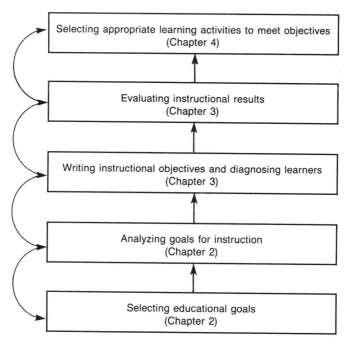

Figure 1.2. Instructional Planning Cycle

HOW IS THE TEXT CONTENT PRESENTED?

The presentation of content is as important as the content itself. We are conscious of our responsibility to follow our own principles for the effective design of instruction. Consequently, each chapter contains the following features:

Overview: The overview previews the content of the chapter or the section and, often, provides a justification of its importance. It serves, along with the objectives, as an organizer for the content. It also relates the content to material in previous chapters or sections. Occasionally there are overviews for sections within chapters.

Set activity: A set activity is found in the introductory pages of each chapter and in many of the sections. The purpose is to prepare you for the content by placing you in a realistic situation that illustrates the content in the chapter. The set activity provides an opportunity to respond to questions that highlight the issues involved.

Objectives: The objectives are written in terms of what you will be expected to know and/or do when you have completed the section or chapter material. Thus you will be able to evaluate your success in achieving the objectives. The objectives follow the format we expect you to use when you write learning objectives. That format will be presented in Chapter 3.

Check for understanding: Check-for-understanding exercises are interspersed throughout the chapters and require your response, as a means of reviewing content just presented. Often, the check-for-understanding exercise is followed by a key that includes the correct answers.

Summary: A chapter summary reviews the content presented and refers to the chapter overview to establish a relationship between what was promised and what was delivered. The summary may introduce content to follow in later chapters. Occasionally there are summaries for sections within chapters.

Guided practice: At the end of most chapters there are exercises that require you to apply the knowledge or skills you have just gained. The correct answers follow the exercise to help you see how well you are doing. Occasionally there are guided practice exercises at the end of sections within chapters.

Independent practice: At the end of most chapters there are suggested activities for you to do on your own. These are usually in the form of projects for you to complete with your own content and/or grade level curriculum in mind. Independent practice exercises assume that you are knowledgeable and skilled and can be successful as an independent performer. Occasionally there are independent practice activities for sections within chapters.

CHAPTER SUMMARY

As you explore the chapters that follow, examine the information in a careful and systematic way and respond to the exercises provided. We have written this book because we believe the information can help you to be the best teacher possible. We hope that you will find the information both practical and thought-provoking. It is our vision for you to become a teacher designer capable of making thoughtful and appropriate instructional decisions. Good luck!

REFERENCES

Clark, C. M. (1988, March). Asking the right questions about teacher preparation: Contributions of research on teacher thinking. *Educational Researcher*, pp. 5–12.

Clark, C. M., & Yinger, R. J. (1987). Teacher planning. In D. C. Berliner & B. V. Rosenshine (Eds.), *Talks to Teachers* (pp. 342–368). New York: Random House.

Grimmett, P. P., & Erickson, G. L. (Eds.) (1988). *Reflection in teacher education*. New York: Teachers College Press.

Parsons, J. S. (1983). Toward understanding the roots of reflective inquiry. *The Social Studies, 74*(2), 67–70.

Ross, D. R. (1987). Teaching teacher effectiveness research to students: First steps in developing a reflective approach to teaching. Paper presented at the annual meeting of the American Educational Research Association, Washington, D.C.

Schon, D. A. (1987). *Educating the reflective practitioner*. San Francisco: Jossey Bass.

Shulman, L. S. (1984). It's harder to teach in class than to be a physician. *Stanford School of Education News*, Palo Alto, CA: Stanford University, pp. 1–5.

Simmons, J. M., Sparks, G. M., Starko, A., Pasch, M., Colton, A. B., & Grinberg, J. (1989). Exploring the structure of reflective pedagogical thinking in novice and expert teachers: The birth of a developmental taxonomy. Paper presented at the annual meeting of the American Educational Research Association, San Francisco.

Sparks, G., Simmons, J., & Pasch, M. (1988). *Collaboration for the improvement of teacher education*. Final Report, Office of Educational Research and Improvement. Washington: DC: U.S. Department of Education.

Spring, H. T. (1985). Teacher decision-making: A meta-cognitive approach. *The Reading Teacher, 39*, 290–295.

Zeichner, K. M., Liston, D. P. (1987). Teaching student teachers to reflect. *Harvard Educational Review, 57*(1), 23–48.

TOPIC ONE

Planning for Instruction: Setting the Stage

CHAPTER **2**

Choosing and Analyzing
Classroom Goals

Chapter Overview

Why is there so much debate and disagreement about the goals and
achievements of American education? From where does a
successful teacher derive educational goals? How does the
successful teacher choose from the bewildering variety of goals
those that are best for the children in the classroom? After selecting
the goals, how does the teacher transform them into instructional
objectives that can guide teaching and learning and can be assessed
when instruction ends? These are the major questions to be
addressed and answered in this chapter.

The chapter consists of two sections. In Section 1, the focus is
on educational philosophy and the selection of educational goals. In
Section 2, the focus shifts to the process of analysis for
transforming a broad educational goal into a specific instructional
objective.

Section 1. Choosing Worthwhile
Educational Goals

Set Activity

Read the following scenario. Try to determine the different curriculum philosophies expressed by
the various speakers:

It was a warm evening in early May as the sun filtered into the school board room of the
Landstown, Maryland, schools. Marvin Pancett, the school board president, tried to remain calm
in the midst of an angry exchange between two members of the community task force, which was
examining the topic "The School Curriculum in the 21st Century." The task force chair, Maude
Jones, was completing her majority group report on the place of economics education in the school
curriculum:

"The majority members are in agreement that an understanding of how our economy
functions is a necessary ingredient in what we are calling "consumer education," but that is
not the entire story. We want high school graduates to have survival skills so that they can be
smart consumers—so that they can use credit wisely, avoid the crooks and cheats in the
marketplace, and get their money's worth from the purchases they make."

The chair of the task force minority group, Paul Garcia, was visibly angry as he rose to speak:

"This business about consumer education is nothing more than nonsense! Schoolchildren need more reading, and math and history. They do not need consumer newsletters and checklists that are not only antibusiness but take away precious class time from learning the essentials. There already is too much time being given to stuff that should be taught at home and not in school—all this sex education and career education, and now you want to add consumer education! Enough is enough!"

In response, Carla Martinez, a member of the task force majority, responded:

"Mr. Garcia lives in a different world that is insulated from the problems faced every day in our public schools. If he spent time in the schools, he would see that many of the kids in this town come from families in trouble—divorces, desertions, where both parents are working and the teenagers are working too, and still there is not enough money to make the family feel secure. Teachers don't have the luxury to teach content separate from the problems of everyday life. It's the problems that make the content meaningful for the children."

The board members listened in growing frustration to the debate between the advocates of the minority and majority reports. Finally, school board president Pancett, distressed because the hour had reached midnight, adjourned the meeting for one week to cool tempers. The next morning Mr. Pancett showed up at the door of the school superintendent, Dr. Ruth Borkman, to discuss the confusing series of events at the school board meeting the previous evening:

"Dr. Borkman, what in the world happened last night? I have to admit that the arguments between the two segments of the task force overwhelmed me. Why is the committee so split?"

"Marv, what happened last night is not so surprising to me. There are wide differences of opinion about what should be taught in the schools both among educators and in the larger community. These differences obviously are present in the task force."

Dr. Borkman then proceeded to explain the educational philosophies that one might expect to find in a public school in the United States and how the philosophies affect the school curriculum and the teachers' instructional approaches.

The positions taken by members of the curriculum task force reflect the two most common educational philosophies found in American schools today. Can you describe the two educational philosophies expressed by the two community spokespersons? In the space provided below, write a paragraph describing each one.

Philosophy 1

Description _____

_____

_____

Philosophy 2

Description _____

_____

_____

Section 1 Objectives

After you have completed this section, you will be able to:
1. classify examples of educational statements that reflect progressive, essentialist, and reconstructionist philosophies
2. define an educational goal
3. create educational goals using Tyler's Curriculum Rationale
4. list the steps in the educational planning process

THREE VIEWS OF EDUCATIONAL PHILOSOPHY

Progressivism: Social and Personal

As Dr. Borkman explained to school board president Pancett, the majority group members of the curriculum task force were defending a *progressive* educational philosophy. Educational progressivism developed as the United States was transformed from a rural, small-town, slow-paced, and personal society into the urban, large-city, fast-paced, and relatively impersonal society we recognize today. Although the transformation of American society occurred over generations, social scientists and historians label the period 1880–1914 as the major era of change.

As the pace of industrialization quickened, millions of immigrants thronged into the United States, and America soon became an urban society. The surge in population—with many new Americans living in crowded, squalid homes in big-city neighborhoods—changed forever the clarity and simplicity of the one-room schoolhouse, where children aged 6 to 14 were taught by a teacher whose mission extended not much further than instruction in reading, writing, and arithmetic and the inculcation of a few moral imperatives. Such schools were replaced—immediately in urban areas, more slowly in the countryside—by multiroom and multigrade comprehensive schools that housed hundreds, even thousands of students. With rapid and massive changes in the size and composition of the schools, together with similar changes in the society at large, advocates of progressivism believed that education beyond the three R's was also required.

Although it is difficult to identify what beliefs and values were shared by all educational progressives, most favored curriculum experimentation and flexibility rather than a prescribed program for the transmission of subject matter. Thus a major focus of the progressive curriculum was on learning to think rather than on learning particular subject matter. In addition, progressives were committed to a child-centered educational program in schools that exemplified democratic values and processes. Ironically, progressive teachers found themselves in situations in which they had to choose between supporting the educational and social choices made by an individual child and a desire to support democratic values in the classroom. In its most common form this dilemma is illustrated by the decision made by a large majority of the students to pursue a particular unit of study and the unyielding refusal of a small group to abide by the decision. What is the teacher to do? Ultimately, it was this recurring dilemma that led to a split in the progressive movement.

One group of progressives—let's call them "social progressives"—retained the belief that social development is the primary function of modern education. Known also as "life adjustment" educators, social progressives see schooling as a process of preparing young people to be successful adults in a democratic society. They view curriculum in terms of the knowledge, skills, and attitudes that assist young people to confront and master the tasks they will face as adults. In the contemporary educational area, social progressives can be seen leading the fight for an increased emphasis on citizenship education: nutrition, health, and family issues; career education; dropout prevention; and emotional, moral, and character development.

One version of a social progressive curriculum plan was centered on what was called "persistent life situations." As described by one of its developers, persistent life situations are those that

> recur in the life of the individual in many different ways as he grows from infancy to maturity. Each individual is concerned to some degree with some fundamentals as keeping well, understanding himself, making a living, getting along with others, adjusting to the natural environment, dealing with social and political structures and forces, developing a sustaining philosophy or set of values. (Stratemeyer, 1970, p. 57)

A more recent example of a social progressive's conception of curriculum may be found in the "Functional Life Curriculum" (Klein, Pasch, & Frew, 1979). The focus of the Functional Life Curriculum was to prepare students to assume full roles in the adult society. The developers of the Functional Life Curriculum determined that school content should be organized within four clusters:

1. *Gaining Insight into Contemporary Life:* Examining persistent themes that affect contemporary life such as science, morals and values, the environment, the need for communication, and the appreciation of human existence
2. *Understanding Oneself and Others:* Developing a positive self-concept, understanding human growth and development, building social relationships, exploring cultural differences

3. *Becoming a Responsible Adult:* Exploring careers, becoming politically mature, learning effective family behaviors
4. *Education for Independence:* Mastering basic skills and problem-solving techniques, developing leisure-time activities, appreciating one's individuality, maintaining a home. (Klein, Pasch, & Frew, 1979, pp. 142–143)

Although many members of "The School Curriculum in the 21st Century" task force support a social progressive view of the curriculum, a second group of progressives is also represented on the task force. Let's call them "personal progressives." Personal progressives argue that instruction must be tailored to meet the needs and interests of the many kinds of children who enter the public schools. They are opposed to a predetermined curriculum that rigidly organizes and structures what all children are expected to learn. Many progressive teachers in the period 1930–1960 were influenced by the ideas of William Heard Kilpatrick, who espoused the "project method." According to this view, the child's experiences formed the basis for curriculum decisions rather than "subject matter fixed-in-advance." Understandably, Kilpatrick argued that "subject matter was useful only when it could be combined with the child's interests (Ravitch, 1983, p. 52).

One of the best-known contemporary personal progressives, John Holt, was influential in the 1960s through his books *How Children Fail* (1964) and *How Children Learn* (1970). Holt derided what he believed was the authoritarian climate in many schools where control and docility were prized and freedom and spontaneity extinguished (1964, p. xiii). He was a leading proponent of the movement that became known as "open or informal education." In such an approach, learning is individualized, teaching is informal, content is based on student expressions of needs or interests, play is valued, children are active, and learning takes place in a noisy and joyful setting.

Essentialism

A second educational philosophy, espoused by the members of the task force minority group, is *essentialism*. Essentialism is a belief that the purpose of schooling is to impart necessary knowledge, skills, and attitudes to enable young people to function as fully developed human beings. To achieve maturity, the learner must understand the external world of observable reality and abstract ideas. Some essentialists focus their attention on what has been called the "basic skills"—reading, writing, and arithmetic. Others have a more extensive list of essentials. Still others argue that the essentials are contained in the school subjects that have been generated through disciplinary study—literature, English and other languages, history, the social sciences, chemistry, physics, biology, mathematics, and the fine arts. These essentialists argue that disciplinary knowledge has stood the test of time. Because it has been examined, refined, and revised over the centuries, the knowledge gained from disciplinary study is more valuable than knowledge gained from any other source of educational content.

A recent example of the essentialist position can be found in the book *Cultural Literacy: What Every American Needs to Know*, by E. D. Hirsch, Jr. (1987b). Hirsch maintained that "no modern society can think of becoming a classless society except on the basis of universal literacy. . . . To be truly literate, a high school graduate must be able to grasp the meaning of written materials in any field or subject provided that those materials are addressed to a general audience" (p. 129). Hirsch continued his analysis of productive schooling to argue that the curriculum should impart intensive knowledge, consisting of "mental models"—what we commonly label as concepts or ideas. However, Hirsch believed that extensive knowledge is also necessary. Extensive knowledge is background information in the form of essential facts, names, places, terms, dates, and events.

Pursuing a military analogy, Hirsch quoted the delightful monologue by the major-general in Gilbert and Sullivan's operetta *Pirates of Penzance*. Through the monologue, Gilbert poked fun at a 19th-century educational system that produced adults who possessed a catalogue of shared extensive knowledge but too few mental models into which to place the knowledge.

> *I am the very model of the modern Major-General,*
> *I've information vegetable, animal, and mineral,*
> *I know the kings of England, and I quote the fights historical,*
> *From Marathon to Waterloo, in order categorical;*
> *I'm very well acquainted too with matters mathematical,*
> *I understand equations, both simple and quadratical,*
> *About binomial theorem I'm teeming with a lot o' news—*
> *With many cheerful facts about the square of the hypotenuse.*
>
> *(Gilbert, 1932, pp. 155–157)*

Hirsch argued that in contemporary schools the problem is reversed. According to Hirsch, the dominant concern for relevance and pluralism so prevalent in most schools results in a fragmented curriculum and youngsters who learn few topics, such as literary and historical works, in common. Thus he concluded that U.S. youngsters share little knowledge of the culture that has shaped and enriched the Western world.[1]

Support for Hirsch's position came from a study, *American Memory: A Report on the Humanities in the Nation's Public Schools*, by Lynne Cheney, chair of the National Endowment for the Humanities (1987). Cheney drew on the data from an NEH study to reveal that two-thirds of U.S. 17-year-olds who were tested did not know when the Civil War was fought (even granting them a 50-year margin of error), could not correctly identify the Reformation and the Magna Carta, and were unable to identify such literary giants as Nathaniel Hawthorne, Jane Austen, Geoffrey Chaucer, and Walt Whitman. In general, students were able to answer only 50 percent of the questions in the literature and history test categories— "Shakespeare," "Short Stories," "Novels and Novelists," "Civil Rights," "The Constitution," and "Chronology: When It Happened" (Ravitch & Finn, 1987).

Entering the growing debate, Nancy McHugh, a former president of the National Council of Teachers of English, agreed that the gaps in student knowledge are appalling but disagreed that the remedy is to "pour facts into students' heads. . . . Trivial pursuit-minded kids can answer all the questions [on an assessment] and still not be educated" (McHugh 1987, p. 23). Patrick Welsh, an English teacher at T. C. Williams High School, Alexandria, Virginia, and author of the book *Tales Out of School*, cautioned that "we have, if anything, too much of the historical approach to literature where you have one of these boring textbooks where kids memorize historical dates and link them to literary dates and names. . . . there's so much memorization in school that the game is to memorize the stuff, get the grade on the test, and then forget it" (Welsh, 1987).

---

[1]For an in-depth exploration of the concept of cultural literacy and its application in schooling, consult Estes, Gutman, & Harrison, 1988; Hirsch, 1988; Worsham, 1988.

Reconstructionism

The two educational philosophies progressivism and esssentialism were at war within the Landstown schools curriculum task force and are at war in the general society, as reflected by the various reactions to the cultural literacy argument. However, there is a third philosophy that should not be overlooked. This philosophy, known as *reconstructionism*, is characterized by a belief that schools should prepare the future adults of society to work for and to demand societal change. Reconstructionists maintain that the present society is seriously flawed and/or corrupt and must be thoroughly reformed. In contrast to progressives and essentialists, reconstructionists look to the future and describe their vision of a more just society, and they attempt to persuade children to accept that image of the future. George Counts, a noted educational reconstructionist in the 1930s, wrote:

> There can be no good individual apart from some conception of the character of a good society; and the good society is not something that is given by nature: it must be fashioned by the hand and brain of man. This process of building a good society is to a very large degree an educational process." (Counts, 1932, p. 26)

Many reconstructionists are political and social activists who blur the lines that separate the schools from the society. They often seek to engage young people in political activity and social action projects in the community. When times are good and the society is at peace with itself and with other nations, reconstructionist views of the curriculum (when expressed) are often ignored by the general public. However, when the nation is uneasy, reconstructionism gains many advocates both within the educational establishment and outside it.

Two such periods in 20th-century U.S. history come easily to mind. During the bleak economic times of the 1930s, many reconstructionists argued that the market economy of the United States, at that time virtually unregulated by the government, had failed. They blamed the economic collapse on ruthless capitalists who had grown rich at the expense of workers and consumers.

A second period of intense reconstructionist activity occurred in the late 1960s. At that time, a values and life-style gap widened to create a serious identity crisis between the leaders of the nation, many in their 50s and 60s, and political activists, the majority in their teens and 20s. With the war in Vietnam adding to the ferment, reconstructionists called for disarmament and noninterference in the affairs of other countries. They also supported the aspirations of individuals and groups who had received inequitable treatment in the political and economic life of the nation. During this period the needs of women and minorities, the poor, and the handicapped received greater attention in schools and in the larger society than at any previous time in U.S. history.

Reconstructionist pressure during this period brought about a number of educational changes, including the replacement of required disciplinary courses in world and U.S. history and American and British literature with optional mini-courses such as War and Revolution, Readings in Justice, Nonviolent Civil Disobedience, Sexism and Racism in 20th-Century America, Black Voices, and Parenting Today. Graduation requirements were reduced, even totally eliminated; standardized-testing programs were changed after scrutiny for racial, ethnic, and gender biases; grading practices based on letter grades were deemphasized, especially for young children; instructional grouping practices based on abilities were eliminated; academic credit was given for off-campus activities; and school-and-community relationships were enhanced. Finally, a number of alternative, free, or community schools were created. What was distinctive about these schools was the social purpose established for

them that influenced the teachers and students who worked in them, the building of bridges between activities in the school and the outside community and the desire to create a "new model of cooperative social life" (Ravitch, 1983; p. 253).

Let's assume a reconstructionist had been active on the "School Curriculum in the 21st Century" task force. What might that advocate have written as a minority report? Think about what that report might sound like before continuing.

The remarks of the reconstructionist would probably be similar to the following:

> Teaching children about how the economy functions will guarantee the perpetuation of an economic system that has failed to deliver an equitable share of the wealth to all our people. We should be teaching young people to question whether taxes are apportioned fairly and to examine the way decisions are made about what is produced and how it is distributed. The school curriculum in the 21st century should be organized around such questions as "In this land of abundance, why are there so many homeless people?" "Why are milk and grain destroyed by farmers or distributors, when so many people go to sleep hungry each night?" "Why are so many people unemployed when many jobs listed in the classified ads of the local newspapers go unfilled?" and "Why is the United States so rich while so many countries in Asia, Africa, and Latin America are so poor?"

CHECK FOR UNDERSTANDING

1. Define the progressive, essentialist, and reconstructionist educational philosophies.

_____

_____

2.   Which of the three educational philosophies do you support? If you were a member of the community task force examining the topic "The School Curriculum in the 21st Century," what would your report on economic education look like? Would your report have a progressive, essentialist, or reconstructionist emphasis? Write a paragraph from that report.

_____

_____

_____

_____

_____

_____

_____

_____

A SHORT COURSE ON RECENT EDUCATIONAL HISTORY

Prior to World War I, education above the elementary school years was available only to a minority of young people. Those who went on to the secondary school, generally the children of the well-to-do, pursued an essentialist curriculum. The subjects taken in secondary school were designed as a preparation for collegiate study—mathematics, Latin, literature, history, rhetoric, and science. During the 1920s, John Dewey's progressive ideas—that the school curriculum should include experiences that appealed to the natural interests of children and meet practical needs—gained the ascendancy. In the 1930s, the Great Depression generated the first widespread support for reconstructionist curriculum.

In 1957, the Soviets launched Sputnik, and the race to hurl the first human into space began. Many Americans sided with essentialist critics who blamed U.S. schools for the failure of scientists and engineers to beat the Soviets in the space race. In addition, schools were found guilty of teaching children out-of-date and/or inaccurate scientific material as well as the manipulation of mathematical symbols without an understanding of their meaning. In the 1960s, the focus of criticism shifted to a concern expressed by reconstructionists and progressives that classroom content was irrelevant both to the upheavals occurring in society (the rebellion of America's youth, the fragmentation of society, the civil rights and antiwar movements) and to the desire of young people to gain knowledge and skills that were of immediate and/or clear value to them.

In the following decade, another group of essentialists accused the schools of failure to teach the basics of education—written and numerical literacy and the ability to communicate effectively when speaking. Since the mid-1970s, criticism has been raised about the poor performance of U.S. students in science and mathematics as compared to Japanese students. There have also been calls to make classrooms more interesting, even exciting, to concentrate on character development, to focus on youngsters' thinking skills, to lower the dropout rate in urban schools, to improve students' reading comprehension and lower the rate of functional illiteracy, to provide more classroom time to the fine arts—and so on.

A summary of the relative influence of the educational philosophies at various times in the 20th century is shown in the following chart.

1900–1920   Essentialists are dominant. However, progressive influence increases in strength particularly in later period.

The authors of the *Committee of Ten Report* (1893) uphold liberal education and study in the academic disciplines.

John Dewey, the founder of educational progressivism, argues that the child should be the focus of the curriculum.

The Cardinal Principles of Secondary Education (1918) centers on "life adjustment" curriculum topics such as health, citizenship, and vocation.

1920–1960   Progressivism is dominant, with reconstructionists influential during the Great Depression and essentialist criticism growing strong in the late 1950s.

School textbooks and curriculum guides implore teachers to shift attention from subject matter to the child's experience.

William Heard Kilpatrick's "project method" and progressive educators spread the message across the land.

George Counts argues in the 1930s that schools must lead society toward a more peaceful, harmonious, equitable, and just society.

In the 1950s, the first period of conservative attack on progressive schools gains support as the Soviets become the first to place satellites into orbit. Critics attack progressives for their alleged inattention to science and mathematics education.

1960–1965   Revival of essentialist curriculum occurs.

Educators and scholars work together to create school units and courses of study that emphasize the principles and concepts that organize each discipline.

Government programs such as those authorized by National Defense Education Act (1958) and the National Science Foundation support the training of educators to teach the new curricula.

1965–1975   Progressives and reconstructionists make dramatic changes in the school curriculum.

Attacks on schools as being stifling and repressive increase. Dozens of influential books critical of schools are published.

	Racial, ethnic, gender, class, and generational differences affect the schools as the war in Vietnam further reduces educational consensus.
1975–1990	Curriculum moves in an essentialist direction.
	Second period of conservative criticism of schools takes place.
	Politicians hear calls for a more basic education with a concentration on reading, writing, and mathematics.
	Nation at Risk report (1983) attacks schools for reducing graduation requirements and required courses and permitting students to select mostly soft elective courses.
	Competency testing movement, to ensure that students have a minimal level of performance when they complete schooling, expands.
	Schools and teachers are increasingly held accountable for the students they pass and/or graduate.

CLASSIFICATION OF EDUCATIONAL GOALS

Given the complexity and diversity of potential educational content and with a philosophical perspective as a backdrop, how does a knowledgeable teacher go about the task of creating broad educational goals? When you have finished this portion of Chapter 2, you should be able to recognize and write educational goals that reflect essentialist, progressive, and reconstructionist content.

What are *educational goals? Educational goals* are statements of educational intent that provide general direction to the teacher in developing instruction. Educational goals are often written to describe large blocks of content such as a course of study or a unit of study. Although a goal may be written in specific and precise language, most goals are general in form. Thus they must undergo further analysis before they can be useful as guideposts in the design of teaching lessons.

Educational goals should be written in terms of *student behavior and activity*, rather than in terms of what the teacher is expected to do. For example, the two statements below would not be acceptable educational goals:

The teacher will explain the differences between complete sentences and sentence fragments.

The teacher will post the rules for student behavior in small-group activities.

until they were rewritten as follows:

The students will describe the differences between complete sentences and sentence fragments.

The students will participate in small-group work activities.

The following are examples of educational goals in the area of economic education appropriate for school children. We have chosen them to reflect essentialist, progressive, and reconstructionist philosophies. Note that some of the goals represent a blending of educational philosophies. For the purpose of illustration, we have identified the philosophic source(s) of each goal. Students will be able to

1. understand the nature of a contract (essentialist, progressive)
2. identify examples of economic resources (essentialist)
3. know the difference between a want and a need (essentialist)
4. make correct change (essentialist, progressive)
5. explain the economizing problem (essentialist)
6. design a way to allocate resources for individuals and groups (reconstructionist, progressive)
7. be wise and efficient shoppers (progressive)
8. know the function of a bank in a market economy (essentialist)
9. be responsible money managers (progressive)
10. know the difference between a luxury and a necessity (essentialist)[2]

How does a successful teacher identify and select these goals? Although there are dozens of models to assist teachers to select educational goals, we shall base our work on the curriculum analysis model developed by Ralph Tyler, one of the major figures in curriculum development in the 20th century. In the 1930s, Tyler developed a systematic framework that has since been popularly referred to as "Tyler's Curriculum Rationale" (1969). The rationale appears as Figure 2.1. In Tyler's conception of the process of curriculum design, you as the teacher begin by examining a range of available materials on the subject matter you wish to teach. Such materials include textbooks, books written on the topic, curriculum guides, magazines and newspapers, and information gained through interviews with knowledgeable educators, students, parents, and other resource people in the community. When your examination has been completed, you list all the possible goals that emerged.

To utilize the rationale, you divide the goals into three groups based on their philosophic source: (1) goals that assist the student to master important subject matter, (2) goals that relate to contemporary societal needs, and (3) goals that relate to the students' personal needs and/or interests. Do you recognize in Tyler's three sources of goals the educational philosophies discussed previously in the chapter? Subject matter mastery is consistent with an essentialist philosophy. Societal needs can be confronted from either a progressive or a reconstructionist perspective. Attention to student needs or interests is progressive in nature.

Tyler suggested that teachers gather a wide range of goals, identify and list goals from each of the three sources, and then use their educational philosophy and knowledge of child development and instructional theory to filter out those goals that are most appropriate to be taught in the classroom. Tyler's Curriculum Rationale, then, is a process to generate educational goals, classify them, and then select those that will serve as the content organizers for curriculum and instruction. To clarify the three sources, we will examine them in greater detail.

---

[2]For additional information about consumer education for youngsters in grades 3–6, consult Kourilsky, *Mini-Society: Experiencing Real World Economics in the Elementary School Classroom* (1983). The "mini-society" is a simulation of an economic system, complete with money, banks, businesses, and other institutions. It permits students to confront and engage many problems of contemporary society.

Examination of curriculum materials, and discussions with students, teachers, parents, and others to gather topics from which curriculum goals are generated

Ensuring that goals have been generated that fit in each of the three philosophic groupings

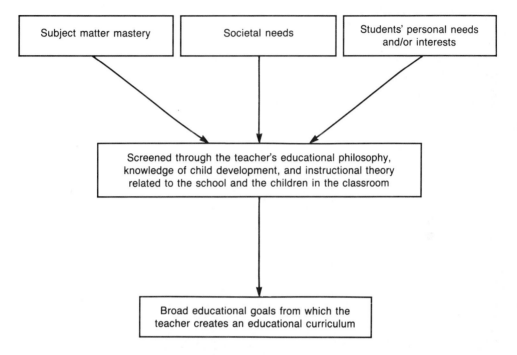

Figure 2.1. Tyler's Curriculum Rationale. (*Basic Principles of Curriculum and Instruction*, by Ralph Tyler. Published by University of Chicago Press, Copyright 1969.)

Subject Matter Mastery

Few argue the importance of effective written and oral communication. The ability to read well enough to understand instructions, to analyze political and social opinions expressed in writing, to gain information and enjoyment from newspapers, magazines, and books, and to write complete and comprehensible sentences and paragraphs is a prerequisite for a full life. Through science we learn how living things adapt and reproduce, how motion can be generated and transformed in direction, how airplanes fly, how submarines go below the surface and rise, and how new substances are produced from the chemical synthesis of other substances. The study of mathematics enables us to measure, estimate, and predict and serves as the tool of other disciplines. Through history and the social sciences we learn of our past and gain insights into human behavior both as individuals and as members of social groups and other types of organizations. Exposure to the fine arts helps us appreciate beauty and grace as we experience enjoyment and aesthetic richness.

Responding to Societal Needs

The mass media bombard us with the difficulties and concerns facing many members of our society. Consider the last month's news. There were probably stories of crime, epidemics, economic distress, family problems, government crises, racism and sexism, small towns and big cities in trouble, AIDS, runaway children, sex and violence on television or in the movies, families unable to afford a home, adult illiteracy, corruption, pollution, drought or flood, destruction of forests and endangered animal species. This list of serious societal problems suggests needs that must be met and that, as solutions are explored, can lead to the development of educational goals. Those goals can be both progressive or reconstructionist, preparing the child to assume an adult role or preparing the young to be activists in remedying the ills of our present society.

Personal Needs and Interests

Establishing goals for a curriculum based on student needs and interests prior to meeting with a particular classroom of students would be inappropriate. However, mastery of skills such as reading, listening, writing, respecting others, analyzing, and evaluating is essential for all educated persons. Assisting youngsters to be skeptical consumers of information could represent content on which to build personal goals. Investigation by students of a topic of interest is an excellent way to enhance personal growth. Developing a healthy self-concept and caring for others could be seen as worthwhile personal goals. The use of learning centers and free-time activities suggests a personal approach to curriculum planning.

The wise teacher is aware of the particular characteristics of the children in the class. Some children come to school having had a rich and varied diet of experiences that are well correlated with the school curriculum. They have traveled a good deal and been to museums and other cultural institutions; they learned to read as preschoolers and continue to do so at a brisk pace when they began school. Correct and sophisticated standard English is spoken in the home. Parents are willing and able to assist the child with homework and are supportive of the school's homework policy.

Other children come to school without these advantages. They have not traveled outside the immediate neighborhood, have rarely been read to at home, hear languages other than English spoken at home, or hear English spoken haltingly or incorrectly. Thus children will come to the classroom from a wide variety of backgrounds, with a wide variety of needs and interests. Sensitive teachers are aware of these diverse conditions and plan their educational programs to respond to them.

CHECK FOR UNDERSTANDING

Review the process recommended by Tyler for selecting content goals. Write two examples of goals in a content area of your choice.

Subject matter _____

_____

_____

Societal needs _____

_____

_____

Personal needs and/or interests _____

_____

_____

_____

Section 2. Analyzing Content Goals

Section 2 Objectives

After you have completed this section, you will be able to:
1. classify examples of affective, psychomotor, and cognitive goals
2. relate concepts, generalizations, and facts in a content area of your choice
3. sort examples of concrete and abstract concepts
4. break down a content area into a generalization, concept, and facts network
5. construct a learning hierarchy in a content area of your choice

MILLICENT STEPHENS'S PUZZLE

Fairhill Elementary School, a K–6 school in Landstown, Maryland, was charged with the responsibility from the Board of Education to begin the revision of the curriculum by acting on one of the central recommendations of the task force assigned to explore the subject "School Curriculum in the 21st Century." The task force recommended that the school system develop a unit of study titled "Learning to Spend and Save Money Wisely" and find a place for it within the fourth-grade social studies course of study.

Millicent Stephens, a fourth grade teacher at Fairhill, stared out the window of her classroom on a warm June morning and recalled the meeting three weeks ago with her principal, Janet Martin. Ms. Martin had asked Millicent to lead the curriculum team of five fourth-grade teachers to develop the curriculum unit on money management. On the positive side, Millicent realized that she had been a social studies major in college and had studied economics; moreover, she surely could use the three weeks' salary she would earn during the summer for the curriculum development project. On the negative side, Millicent recognized that she lacked sufficient knowledge of curriculum design and analysis to give her confidence that she could lead a team of teachers to develop the unit. She thought back to her teacher education preparation and wished that more class time had been spent on transforming broad educational goals into specific instructional objectives. She stared at a partial set of goals for the unit.

Students will:

1. understand the nature of a contract
2. show regard for people regardless of their income or occupation
3. know the difference between a want and a need
4. make correct change from different amounts of money
5. explain the economizing problem facing individuals and societies
6. create a way to allocate resources for individuals and groups
7. learn to avoid borrowing beyond their means
8. write legibly on such forms as receipts, orders, and checks
9. respect the value of money
10. know the difference between a luxury and a necessity

THREE DOMAINS OF EDUCATIONAL CONTENT

Educational goals can be classified in a number of ways. In the previous section we learned that goals can be classified according to philosophic positions—progressivism, essentialism, and reconstructionism. Another way to classify goals is to subdivide them into knowledge, skills, and attitudes. In this book, we will use a classification scheme that organizes goals into *affective, psychomotor*, and *cognitive* groupings or domains.

Some goals are clearly classified in one of the three domains. Other goals have characteristics that suggest they reside in more than one domain. That fact will become clearer as we examine various goals. In any event, a teacher should be able to determine into which domain a goal is most appropriately classified.

The *affective* domain involves emotional behavior—that is, feelings, attitudes, preferences, and values. Whereas cognitive goals involve the learning of both subject matter and learning processes, affective objectives involve process learning almost exclusively. The range of possible behaviors around which affective goals can be written is quite large. For example, an affective goal might be expressed as the awareness that differences exist in the expected behavior of people in various ethnic and racial groups. A more specific, and significant, goal would be to expect students to respond to classmates from a different ethnic, racial, or cultural group in ways that are appropriate and supportive.

In Millicent's list of goals, numbers 2, 7, and 9 are affective. Goal 2 indicates that the child will have respect for all people irrespective of their lack of wealth or status. In goals 7 and 9, the concern is for students' appreciation of thoughtful and careful consumption.

The *psychomotor* domain consists of learning that is sensory in nature, ranging from involuntary, reflexive movements to complex chains of skillful and purposeful behavior, such as dancing and playing quarterback. Any physical skill that requires repeated practice to perfect is psychomotor—for example, playing the piano or pronouncing words in an unfamiliar language. Observing, listening, speaking, and small- and large-muscle control are the most common skills on which psychomotor goals are constructed. Among the school courses of study, sports and the practical and fine arts play a special role in the physical development of learners, as does "readiness" instruction in the primary grades that emphasizes play and motor development. In Millicent's list of goals, number 8 is properly classified as psychomotor, since it involves coordination between the eye and the hands in producing legibly written financial forms.

Cognitive (intellectual) goals require students to memorize and recall information or to use their intellectual skills to determine meaning and to relate new information to previous learning. Higher level cognitive goals require the learner to disassemble information or to assemble it in new forms, to judge its worth and merit, and to apply it in complex ways to solve everyday problems and those in the workplace. A majority of school tasks involve cognitive goals. These goals often entail learning the answers to questions for which there is an agreed-upon correct answer. However, a less obvious but potentially more fruitful direction for cognitive teaching is to prepare youngsters to take informed risks and to be confident in confronting questions and issues where there is no known or agreed-upon answer.

Which of Millicent's goals are cognitive? Numbers 1, 3, 4, 5, 6, and 10 are best classified as cognitive. Although goal 4 has the psychomotor component of recognizing and organizing money combinations, the intent of the goal writer is clearly to assess the learner's knowledge of coins and bills of different values.

CHECK FOR UNDERSTANDING

To assess your capability to classify educational goals into the cognitive, affective, and psychomotor domains, place C for *cognitive*, A for *affective*, or P for *psychomotor* in the blank preceding each of the following goals.

_____ 1. Students will recognize the importance of proper nutrition in diet.

_____ 2. Students will be able to serve a volleyball successfully.

_____ 3. Students will show respect for the rights of other people.

_____ 4. Students will expand sentences by adding adjectives and adverbs to simple noun–verb sequences.

_____ 5. Students will create a useful map legend and grid.

_____ 6. Students will construct a papier-mâché object that hangs together properly.

_____ 7. Students will swim various distances in the pool using the backstroke.

_____ 8. Students will identify the vowels.

_____ 9.   Students will do their seat work without disturbing their neighbors.

_____ 10.   Students will appreciate the value of honesty.

If you classified examples 1, 4, 5, and 8 as cognitive goals, you were correct. Example 1 may have led you astray if you indicated it as affective. "Proper nutrition" is a value, but the process of recognition of what constitutes a healthy diet is a cognitive decision based on knowledge of the relationship of calories, protein, carbohydrates, and fats, as well as vitamins and minerals. If the goal had been for students to "choose to eat a healthful diet," the affective domain would have been the correct response, because the goal is to encourage students to value healthful foods. Examples 2, 6, and 7 are psychomotor goals, while examples 3, 9, and 10 are affective goals.

THE STRUCTURE OF SUBJECT MATTER

Content goals are selected by the teacher to identify the depth and breadth of the particular subject that will be taught. For example, as seen in the outline below, the appropriate breadth and depth of the "Learning to Spend and Save Money Wisely" unit might break down into the following content outline:

Content Outline: Learning to Spend and Save Money Wisely

   I.   Choices have to be made by individuals, families, businesses, and governments.
       A.   Resources are scarce in relation to wants, since resources are finite and wants are unlimited.
       B.   Wants are goods and services that people would like to acquire or services they would like to use.
       C.   A benefit is given up when a choice is made (opportunity cost).
  II.   Resources are used to produce goods and services.
       A.   Natural resources include such things as farmland, water, air, animals, mineral deposits, climate.
       B.   Human beings are resources.
       C.   Abilities and traits are resources.
       D.   Things built by human beings are resources; tools, machinery, equipment are resources.
 III.   All economies must reconcile the differing priorities of sellers who supply goods and services and buyers who demand the goods and services.
       A.   Supply is the total amount of a good or service that sellers are willing and able to supply at different prices in a given market at a particular time.
       B.   Demand is the total amount of a good or service that buyers are willing and able to purchase at different prices in a given market at a particular time.
       C.   Price is the amount of money the seller receives and the buyer pays for one unit of the given good or service.
       D.   A market is the arrangement or place where buyers and sellers come together to buy and sell goods and services.

    E.   In a market economy such as in the United States, decisions about what to produce and to buy and the price set for goods and services are made in markets through the interaction of supply and demand.

 IV.   Wealth is the accumulated possessions of persons, groups, businesses, and governments (things or services owned by one person or group that can be sold to another person or group).

  V.   Money is anything that is commonly accepted in exchange for goods and services within a given society.

    A.   Money is a medium of exchange.

    B.   Different items have been used as money throughout history.

    C.   Money can be spent for goods or services, saved, or invested.

    D.   Saving requires that consumption in the present be postponed.

    E.   Investment is savings for the purpose of increasing wealth.

 VI.   Banks are needed in a market economy to operate and facilitate the growth of the economy.

    A.   Some banks are government-owned; others are privately owned.

    B.   Banks create money, extend credit, help people save, provide loans, and accrue interest.

    C.   Through these functions, banks assist a market economy to grow.

While the creation of a content outline is a necessary task in the development of a curriculum unit, it is only one task in a long process. The curriculum developer must also have an understanding of the nature of cognitive knowledge so that the content does not become merely a list of unconnected information. When a content outline is tempered by an understanding of the nature of subject matter, the logical chunks—the groupings and relationships that organize the content—will become apparent. To understand the nature of subject matter, we shall turn our attention to the work of Jerome Bruner, an internationally acclaimed psychologist.

In 1960, Bruner's influential book *The Process of Education* was published. Soon the book became a best seller in educational circles, and key ideas from the book have since been adopted by teachers in the United States and many other countries. One of these ideas focused educators' attention on the nature of subject matter and the way that subject matter ought to be organized for teaching purposes. Bruner supported the notion that every subject taught in schools has a structure and that structure has a particular form composed of three elements—*concepts, generalizations*, and *facts*. He considered all three elements as appropriate for student learning. However, Bruner's central position was that the school "curriculum of a subject should be determined by the most fundamental understanding that can be achieved of the underlying generalizations that give structure to that subject" (p. 31). He argued that instruction should center on the "fundamentals"—the generalizations and concepts of the subject rather than the individual facts. To illustrate his belief (see Figure 2.2), he used the analogy of the fully blooming shade tree: its trunk and branches represent the subject's organizing generalizations and major concepts, and the leaves represent the multitude of specific facts that describe the nature, history, and scope of the subject and provide examples of its application.

Bruner argued that understanding the structure of subject matter assists learners to make the subject more understandable. It increases retention and transfer of learning, enhances the capability of the learner to relate newly introduced content to previously learned content, and it provides a path for learning additional content within the same subject.

Figure 2.2. Bruner's Concept of the Structure of Knowledge

Philip Phenix, a philosopher and educator, summarized the advantages of teaching through a structured approach by noting that

> one of the secrets of good teaching is the practice of clearly charting a way through the subject of instruction so that the students know how each topic as it comes along fits into the whole scheme of the course and of the discipline to which it belongs. They understand where they are in relation to what has gone before and to what is to be studied subsequently. The effect of such teaching is a growing appreciation of the inner logic of the subject, resulting at length in a grasp of its spirit and method which will be proof against the erosions of detailed forgetting. (1960, p. 307)

An example of a fundamental generalization comes from the study of history. The student who examines unfamiliar cultures after first understanding that "regardless of when or where they lived, regardless of their race, nationality, or religion, all people possess many characteristics in common" will be a more accurate, reliable, and productive investigator than will one who has not understood this concept. In the hands of a creative and knowledgeable teacher, this idea can be a connecting thread that is applied as students learn about new peoples and cultures.

Research underway to identify effective history and mathematics teachers indicates that a cognitively rich representation of the central ideas in these subjects is a crucial ingredient in their profiles (Shulman, 1986). Finally, recent support for the use of a structural framework in

the development of teaching units and lessons as a vehicle to facilitate the understanding and communication of subject matter was expressed by Chambers (1988):

> What we require are teachers who know their disciplines in depth, good teachers of math and good teachers of history and good teachers of literature, who understand the structure of their particular discipline and how it is different from that of other disciplines and who can pass on such awareness to their students. (p. 5)

CONCEPT LEARNING

What does the foregoing discussion about concepts, generalizations, and facts have to do with the puzzle facing Millicent Stephens as she attempts to lead her team of teachers in the development of the unit "Learning to Spend and Save Money Wisely"? Refer to the content outline on pages 31–32. The first outlined area for study was the following:

I. Choices have to be made by individuals, families, businesses, and governments.
   A. Resources are scarce in relation to wants, since resources are finite and wants are unlimited.
   B. Wants are goods that people would like to acquire or services they would like to use.
   C. A benefit is given up when a choice is made (opportunity cost).

The outline is a first step in developing a structured analysis of cognitive content. However, before proceeding further, it is necessary to analyze the three elements of that content—concepts, generalizations, and facts. Let's first examine the concept.

What are concepts? How can we tell a concept when we see one? *Concepts* are categories or classes of things or ideas that share a common set of critical characteristics. In the topical outline, *scarce resources, unlimited wants, finite resources, goods,* and *services* are concepts. Concepts are like lenses or road maps that human beings use to examine the world as identified by the five senses. They permit us to use previous experience and knowledge to place new information in a context, to associate the present with the past, and to recognize new information as a variation of what we have learned previously.

We learn many concepts through direct experience, outside of school. In fact, preschoolers and primary-age youngsters often learn to use concepts to classify new experiences prior to learning the verbal labels, or names, they will later use to identify the concepts to others. However, the learning of concepts, together with the words used to label and describe them, is an essential element in successful school instruction. In fact, many learning psychologists and instructional planners believe that concepts are the essential building blocks in a quality curriculum.

To illustrate how concept learning aids us in understanding what may at first seem like a novel experience, imagine disembarking from a train in a place you have never been before, in a country where you do not speak or understand the language—on the surface a frightening prospect! However, the more you analyze the problem, the lower is your level of fear. Safely stored in your long-term memory are the concepts of *hotel, restaurant, bank.* Train stations typically have tourist information centers where it is likely that someone will speak English and provide you with a simplified dictionary that can help you to interpret the unfamiliar language. You know that the bank can exchange your U.S. dollars for the local currency. You can expect to find taxi cabs or public transportation. All in all, the concepts you have learned make it possible for you to function in what appears at first to be a totally alien environment.

Concepts have characteristics, often called *attributes.* Attributes allow us to distinguish between examples of the concept and nonexamples. Nonexamples are not members of the concept class but are similar enough to confuse the unwary observer. For example, a particular table may look something like a chair but it is not a chair. In making the distinction, it is important to distinguish between *critical* and *noncritical* concept attributes. Only critical attributes can be used to determine whether a given item is an example of the concept. From the list of concepts in the "Learning to Spend and Save Money Wisely" unit, let's examine the concept *goods.* There are many examples of goods, from automobiles to silver watches to thumbtacks. All these examples share the critical attribute of being things that people would like to acquire. They also are made primarily of metal. However, the fact that these items are made of metal is not a critical attribute of a good, since we know that a lace scarf is also a good. What about the concept *scarcity*? Examples of scarcity are oil, gold, and clean air, all of which share the critical attribute of being in short supply.

There are a number of ways in which concepts can be organized. For our purposes, we will classify concepts as *concrete* or *abstract.* A *concrete* concept is one that can be described in terms of its observable attributes. That is, examples exist in the physical world, and from observation a decision can be made as to whether a given example fits within the concept or not. For example, *chair* is a concrete concept, as are *yellow, dog,* and *girl.* The critical attributes that determine whether something is a chair are that (1) it is used to sit on, (2) it stands on four legs, (3) it has a back rest, and (4) it is built to seat only one person (*Webster's New Collegiate Dictionary*, 1981). Using these attributes to guide us, we can distinguish among chairs, tables, couches, stools, and so on. We can distinguish between examples and nonexamples that are presented to us.

Concrete concepts are most commonly taught in the lower elementary grades. In the later grades, teachers must teach the more difficult-to-learn idea of abstract concepts. An *abstract* concept is one that cannot be observed either because it does not possess physical dimensions or because its physical dimensions are not critical in distinguishing between examples and nonexamples. Let us examine two abstract concepts to illustrate this. First, consider the concept *citizen*. Although citizens have physical attributes, in that all citizens are human beings and can be observed, you can't tell a citizen from a noncitizen by physical appearance. The physical attributes are not critical in identifying examples. Thus the concept *citizen* is abstract. As a rule, the preparation for teaching an abstract concept such as *citizen* is more extensive and detailed than the preparation needed to teach a concrete concept, such as *chair*.

As complicated as it is, *citizen* is an example of an abstract concept that has a clear definition and attributes that together can be used to distinguish examples from nonexamples. In the unit "Learning to Spend and Save Money Wisely," most of the abstract concepts have clear definitions and attributes. These include *businesses, governments, choices, resources, goods and services, wants, needs, market, price, demand*, and *supply*.

The teaching and learning of concepts whose attributes and/or definitions cannot be used to distinguish all examples from all nonexamples are more difficult. Examples of such concepts are *freedom, honesty, trust, value, democracy, beauty, good citizenship*. Although these concepts have definitions and attributes, neither can be used to distinguish all examples from all nonexamples. For example, the dictionary definition of *political freedom* is the "absence of necessity, coercion, or constraint in choice or action" (*Webster's New Collegiate Dictionary*, 1981). Are we free in the United States? Reasonable people would agree that we are. Yet there are restrictions on our freedom. There are traffic regulations that control how fast we drive. In some communities, smoking is forbidden in public buildings or restricted to a designated location. Individuals wanting to get married, own a dog, or carry a gun must obtain a license. In all these cases, our freedom of choice and action is limited.

CHECK FOR UNDERSTANDING

To assess your understanding of different concepts, create two groups of five concepts in a subject area of your choice. The first group should contain concrete concepts; the second group should contain abstract concepts. In your group of abstract concepts, include concepts with clear definitions and/or attributes and concepts with unclear definitions and/or attributes. Check your groupings with a colleague.

Concrete Concepts	**Abstract Concepts**
_____	_____
_____	_____
_____	_____
_____	_____
_____	_____

What does this explanation of the different kinds of concepts have to do with teaching? A teacher must know that a concept has a definition and a set of critical attributes and be able to teach both to students. A teacher should be able to determine whether a concept is concrete or abstract and thus whether examples and nonexamples can be presented to students in visual form or only through words. Finally, as we shall learn in Chapter 5, there is more than one way to teach a concept, and knowing the type of concept you intend to teach can help you teach it successfully.

GENERALIZATION LEARNING

If concepts are the road maps for teaching and learning, then generalizations are the destinations good teachers attempt to reach. A *generalization* is a statement that expresses a relationship between two or more concepts.[3] Whereas a concept is usually expressed in a word or two, a generalization is always expressed as a statement, often as a complete sentence.

The following examples are generalizations:

Metals expand when they are heated.
The pace of life in small towns is slower than it is in large cities.
Retired people tend to vote in greater numbers than do voters from ages 18 to 21.
Division is the reverse of multiplication.
The more plant life there is in a region, the less room there is for other living things.

A second way to distinguish a generalization from the other elements of subject matter is to contrast it with a *fact*. Both generalizations and facts have the attribute of being statements. However, facts subsume information about particulars—people, things, places, time, events. In addition, a fact is typically verified by making a single observation, by conducting a simple experiment, or by consulting a credible reference. The following examples are facts:

Henry Ford was the father of the modern assembly line.
Count Basie played the piano in his orchestra.
Whales are the largest mammals.
The U.S. Constitution can be changed through the passage of amendments.
Gold is more malleable than iron.

A generalization cannot be checked through a single observation: experimentation through repeated trials is required. In some cases, many references must be consulted and compared before we can feel confident that a particular generalization is an accurate description of reality. Even then, we would not be surprised that some knowledgeable people would disagree about the accuracy of that generalization. We know, after all, that generalizations are constructed from concepts. Abstract concepts with unclear definitions and/or attributes, as we have learned, are difficult to apply to all cases we may encounter.

---

[3]In the scientific literature, such statements are labeled as *principles, theories,* or *laws,* depending on the scope of the statement and the degree of confidence that it will stand repeated testing. However, for our purposes in planning instruction, the term *generalization* will suffice.

The following chart shows the differences between facts and generalizations:

Fact	**Generalization**
Is concrete, definite, with no reasonable doubt	Is not absolute (contains some "wiggle")
Is usually verified by a single observation or reference	Verification requires a good deal of experimentation
	Expresses relationship between two or more concepts
Usually referwsd to one person, event, or thing	Applies to many examples
Applies to a single example	

CHECK FOR UNDERSTANDING

Examine the following examples. Identify those that are *generalizations* by writing **G** and those that are *facts* by writing **F** in the space to the left of each example.

_____ 1. In a democracy, the decision-making power is placed in the hands of the majority while at the same time the rights of the minority are protected.

_____ 2. Teaching is both a science and an art.

_____ 3. The color green is a combination of yellow and blue.

_____ 4. The number of seconds in one month (30 days) is 2,592,000.

_____ 5. Radio waves transmitted from one city can be received in a city half way around the world because they are reflected by the ionosphere layer of the atmosphere.

_____ 6. If there are x ways of doing one thing and y ways of doing another thing, then there are x plus y ways of doing both.

_____ 7. The term *Karma* is associated with Hinduism.

_____ 8. The earliest alphabet originated in the Middle East.

_____ 9. Paul Bunyan was the subject of tall tales.

_____ 10. Residents of Washington, D.C., began voting for president in 1964.

Examples 3, 4, 7, 8, 9, and 10 are facts; examples 1, 2, 5, and 6 are generalizations.

Although generalizations are powerful tools in understanding the past, present, and future, they must not be interpreted mindlessly. In the spirit of scientific investigation, the generalization is valid only if there is no external intervention that changes the relationship between the concepts. For instance, consider the following generalization about past and future educational performance:

> The best single predictor of a young child's educational performance in high school and college is the number of years of schooling (8, 12, 16, 16+) of the child's parents.

That prediction is accurate if nothing intervenes to alter the relationship between the level of education of the child's parents and his or her predicted school performance. However, that is precisely what we expect a good teacher to do—to make it possible for the child to prosper intellectually and emotionally as a consequence of schooling. Good teachers do intervene and alter, for the better, the expected result. Thus a generalization has to be interpreted as a general truth that will prove to be an accurate prediction in a majority of cases. It doesn't guarantee that a particular child will fit the pattern or that intervention from the home or the school or from another significant person in the child's life will not alter the balance in some dramatic way.

What follows are other generalizations about schooling and education that have been adapted from a U.S. Department of Education booklet *What Works: Research about Teaching and Learning* (1986).

Generalizations Related to General Educational Issues

1. The better record a school has had in implementing previous change, the more likely the school is to implement a proposed educational change.
2. If the time students are engaged in work directly related to the goals of instruction is increased, then greater learning gains will result.
3. If teachers set and communicate high expectations for students, then they will elicit greater academic performance from students.
4. In respect to deductive lessons, if teachers explain exactly what students are expected to learn and demonstrate the steps needed to accomplish a particular academic task, students will learn more.
5. Student achievement rises when teachers ask classroom questions that require their students to interpret, analyze, synthesize, and evaluate information, rather than simply memorize and recall that information.

Generalizations Related to Specific Content Issues

1. *Mathematics*—The use of physical objects as an element in lessons improves the learning of mathematics in the primary grades.
2. *Science*—The use of application lessons in the form of experiments improves the learning of science concepts.
3. *Learning to write*—Effective writing teachers use a creative process approach of conception, composition, revision, and editing. The computer has proven its worth as a tool in the development of writing skill.
4. *Reading comprehension*—Students achieve better results when teachers precede reading assignments with a structured overview of what they will encounter in their reading and then complete the reading exercise with a summary discussion.
5. *History*—Approaching history through personal or group investigation is an effective way of learning about the past and motivates students to appreciate history as a school subject.

Moving from a general understanding of the nature and importance of generalizations back to Millicent Stephens's problem as she attempts to analyze the content in the "Learning to Spend and Save Money Wisely" unit, let's examine a key economic generalization that would be taught in the content outline on pages 31–32.

> Assuming no change in the quantity demanded by consumers, if producers increase the supply of a given good or service to the marketplace, then the price of that good or service can be expected to fall.

This generalization expressing the relationship between price and supply is a universal theme in economics and has enormous potential to assist school children to understand everyday life. Curriculum developers have used it along with the companion generalization of demand (see below) to organize units and lessons on the nature and function of the marketplace in the U.S. economy, in which the government plays a limited role in the determination of what is produced and consumed.

> Assuming no change in the willingness of producers to supply a given good or service, if consumers increase the quantity demanded of the good or service, then the price of that good or service in the marketplace can be expected to rise.

The two generalizations with their associated concepts are shown in Figure 2.3.

Generalizations

Assuming no change in the quantity demanded by consumers, if producers increase the supply of a given good or service to the marketplace, then the price of that good or service can be expected to fall.	Assuming no change in the willingness of producers to supply a given good or service, if consumers increase the quantity demanded of the good or service, then the price of that good or service in the marketplace can be expected to rise.

Concepts

supply   quantity demanded   price
producers   consumers   good or service   marketplace

Facts

The price of oil has dropped in the world market as compared to the price in 1980 as more oil has been discovered or has become available.	During the 1970s the price of oil rose substantially as demand for oil increased in relation to available supply.
The average price of a personal computer has declined as compared to 1980 as more companies have entered the market as producers of computers.	During the 1970s the price of food rose as worldwide demand increased faster than did the output of the world's farms.
The average prices of products sold in supermarkets in large cities are lower then they are in small towns because of the competition of many stores attempting to draw consumers' business.	As the number of workers covered by employer-paid medical insurance has increased since 1970, so has the cost of their medical care.

Figure 2.3. A Concept, Generalization, and Fact Analysis

FACTUAL LEARNING

The analysis of the three elements of content concludes with the third element—*facts*. As indicated in the discussion of generalizations, a *fact*, for purposes of instruction, is a statement about particulars (people, things, places, times, or events) and is typically verified by making a single observation, by conducting a simple experiment, or by consulting a credible authority.

Don't underestimate the importance of facts in learning and living. To illustrate their importance, imagine that you begin reading an article in a newsmagazine about the stock market collapse on October 19, 1987, in which the stock market dropped over 500 points in one day, a fifth of its total value. You read the following sentence:

> Wall Street remembers the shantytowns and bread lines of the 1930s caused by the "Great Crash of 1929."

Assume you do not know that the major financial institutions in the United States, as well as the New York Stock Exchange, are located in and around Wall Street in New York City. You do not remember that in the Great Depression of the 1930s many unemployed people lost their homes or could not afford to pay rent and buy food. Thus they were forced to live in temporary shacks made of scrap, wood, tin, or cardboard known as "shanties." They also stood for hours in long "bread lines" to receive food donated by the government or by private charities. You do not know that the "Crash" referred to the stock market collapse that led to the widespread failure of banks, businesses, and farms and then to a worldwide depression. If you know none of these facts, what sense can you make of the sentence from the article?

Collectively, the facts that we possess add to our reputation as educated persons. However, if facts are to be useful in increasing our understanding and capability to interpret the environment, they must be related to generalizations and concepts. For example, being able to list the names of the U.S. presidents has little meaning unless the list is organized under concepts such as effectiveness, political party affiliation, and philosophy. A child's ability to recall the scientific names of all mammals would be of little value unless the child could identify animals that were mammals and could recognize the critical attributes of a mammal. In the stock market example, you would read with optimum understanding if you were able, mentally, to place the facts into an existing structural network. That structure includes knowledge of how the stock market functions, together with generalizations that relate the stock market to the U.S. economy and the banking and monetary system. Finally, it includes the capability to evaluate the likelihood that a stock market collapse would initiate a catastrophic depression similar to the one that occurred in the 1930s.

CONTENT ANALYSIS

Having analyzed educational content and identified the three elements of that content— concepts, generalizations, and facts—we can return to Bruner's prescription to teach content in the form of a fully blooming tree with the trunk and major branches representing the generalizations and concepts and the leaves representing the specific facts. Millicent Stephens and her fourth-grade teacher planning group would be well to organize their content analysis of the "Learning to Spend and Save Money Wisely" unit using the fully blooming tree scheme. They would create an analysis of each unit of instruction after developing their instructional tree for the unit. Let's see how that might look. Look again at the first topic in the unit—we'll call it "Making Choices":

I.   Choices have to be made by individuals, families, businesses, and governments.
   A.   Resources are scarce in relation to wants, since resources are finite and wants are unlimited.
   B.   Wants are goods people would like to acquire or services they would like to use.
   C.   A benefit is given up when a choice is made (opportunity cost).

Generalization

Since resources are scarce and human wants are unlimited, if purchases have to be made by individuals, families, businesses, and governments, then some alternative purchases will have to be foregone.

Concepts: resources, scarcity, wants, choices

Concept definitions
Resources are the means used to produce goods and services.
Scarcity is a deficiency in quantity compared with demand.
Wants are desires or wishes.
Choices are alternative purchases of desired goods or services.

Concept Examples Leading to Factual Statements

Resources—Natural resources, human beings, things created by humans such as tools and money, human capabilities and traits
Scarcity—Clean air, diamonds, talent
Wants—Wealth, fancy cars, fame, good health, big house
Choices—New bike rather than clothes, one music tape rather than another, admission to one movie rather than another

Using Bruner's "fully blooming tree" illustration, the "Making Choices" topic is shown in Figure 2.4.

THE ANALYSIS OF LEARNING PROCESS

When the content of a particular unit or lesson is analyzed and the concepts, concept examples, generalizations, and facts are identified, half the task of organizing content for instruction is completed. To complete the job, we must determine what students are to do with that content. That requires, first, an understanding of the developmental needs and capabilities of children at differing chronological and performance ages. The teacher must be aware that children develop and mature at different rates. A task that someone claims is appropriate for a 5-year-old may be an accurate barometer of what some 5-year-olds can be expected to do, but a substantial number of actual 5-year-olds in a kindergarten classroom may have previously learned the lesson planned by the teacher or may not be intellectually or developmentally prepared to learn it at the time the teacher wishes to introduce it. For example, many

Since resources are scarce and human wants are unlimited,
alternative purchases will have to be forgone.

Figure 2.4. Bruner's Concept of the Structure of Knowledge Applied to the "Making Choices" Topic

5-year-olds are able to write their given and family names on work papers. A quick diagnosis might reveal that half the children can do this prior to instruction. Another 40 percent are ready to learn the skill. The remaining 10 percent lack the necessary small-motor development to write legibly enough to justify the time the teacher would have to devote to the task. Consequently, the teacher would be wise to postpone the attempt for this group in the class. We will return to the issue of diagnostic preassessment again in greater detail in Chapter 3.

The second requirement for the analysis of learning processes is an understanding of the knowledge and skill necessary to accomplish a given learning task. A *learning task* is defined as a planned sequence of steps to move someone from "ignorance of some specified fact or concept to knowledge or understanding of it, or of proceeding from incapability of performing some specific act to capability of performing it" (Carroll, 1963, p. 724).

The process of breaking down a task into its component subtasks and arranging them in a hierarchical pattern, from simple to complex, is known as *task analysis*. Task analysis is similar to the procedure we will employ to assist Millicent Stephens and her colleagues on the fourth-grade development team. In task analysis, we have two elements to consider—(1) the components that make up the item being analyzed and (2) the breakdown of the components into smaller pieces.

Consider the example of a task analysis that is appropriate for an elementary education classroom, shown in Figure 2.5.

Lesson Objective: Each child will be able to write an upper case letter A correctly.

Entry level prerequisite: The student can hold and manipulate a pencil in proper writing position.
1. The student can hold a pencil correctly.
2. The student can draw a straight line.

The teacher presents the child with a sharpened pencil and a piece of paper on which a 1–2 inch rectangle or square is drawn

1. The student can draw a line from the middle of the top line to the right-hand lower corner of the figure.

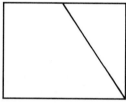

2. The student can draw a line from the middle of the top line to the left-hand corner of the figure.

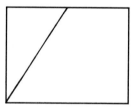

3. The student can place the pencil in the middle of the left line and draw a line to the middle of the right line.

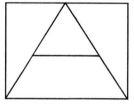

Mastery of goal: The student can make an A under the supervision of the teacher and then independently.

Figure 2.5. Drawing the Letter A: A Task Analysis Example (*Curriculum Analysis and Design for Retarded Learners,* by N. Klein, M. Pasch, and T. Frew. Merrill Publishing, 1979, pp. 174–175).

CHECK FOR UNDERSTANDING

It's your turn to practice the skill of task analysis. Assume you are a third-grade teacher and are planning a lesson on the topic "Following Directions." In the space at left below, write a task analysis of the required directions to teach a novice to make a properly constructed peanut butter and jelly sandwich.

Entry level prerequisites:

Psychomotor: The student can manipulate a butter knife and spread peanut butter on a slice of bread without tearing the bread.
Cognitive: The student can list characteristics of a successful set of directions, sequence a series of steps, use clear language, and recognize when the task is completed.

Correct sequence: The student is able to

1. take two pieces of bread out of the package
2. open the peanut butter and jelly jars
3. select a butter knife
4. spread peanut butter on one slice
5. spread jelly on the peanut butter
6. close the sandwich

The student can now enjoy the sandwich.

Now that you have practiced a task analysis involving a physical process and also are familiar with subject matter analysis to generate concepts, generalizations, and specific facts, we will turn our attention to the analysis of intellectual (cognitive) learning processes. By *intellectual learning process*, we refer to what the human mind does with the subject matter to be learned. Before we introduce the approach to analyzing learning processes that we will use in this chapter, let's consider what we wish the outcome of our analysis to be. We wish to create a classification framework, commonly referred to as a *taxonomy*, that can accomplish all of the following:

1. structure and order instructional objectives
2. structure and order testing procedures and items
3. assist teachers to plan and implement lessons at higher thinking levels
4. be more precise in planning objectives and learning activities
5. enable the teacher to decide when to pursue an alternative objective that is suggested by students

There are two widely known taxonomies of learning processes. One was developed by Robert Gagne and published in his book *The Conditions of Learning* (1965). The other was created by Benjamin Bloom and others, first presented in *Taxonomy of Educational Objectives. Handbook I: Cognitive Domain* (1956). The two writers took different directions to arrive at the same goal—the ability to identify categories of instructional objectives on the basis of their underlying intellectual learning processes and to organize them into a classification system that orders them from simplest to most complex. Although the empirical support for their efforts is uneven, strong in some areas, weaker in others, we believe that teachers can derive benefit from using either of their classification systems. (See page 49 for a chart comparing the two approaches.)

We use the Gagne approach to classifying learning processes in this chapter and in the next chapter. That will enable us to utilize what we have learned about the analysis of subject matter into concepts, generalizations, and facts as we consider learning processes. In Chapter 6, the Bloom approach will be used to explore the important area of "levels of thinking" as you develop classroom questions and other approaches to the improvement of thinking.

The label we will attach to Gagne's perspective on learning processes is the *learning hierarchy* classification system. A learning hierarchy is a flow chart that orders intellectual learning tasks from the most complex, at the apex of the hierarchy (superordinate), to the simplest tasks (subordinate), which are displayed at the base of the hierarchy. Within the hierarchy, tasks that are at the same level of complexity (coordinate) are shown at the same vertical level of the hierarchy, as in Figure 2.6. The form of a hierarchy is a pyramid, with the learning of a generalization at the apex of the pyramid. The pyramid spreads out horizontally to include concepts and, finally, concept attributes and specific facts.

For example, let us use the content outline "Making Choices" from pages 31–32. Content included in or suggested by the outline can be shown in the form of a hierarchy like the following.

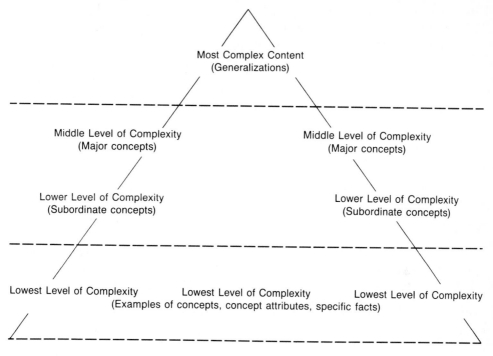

Figure 2.6. A Learning Hierarchy

Generalization

Since resources are scarce and human wants are unlimited, if purchases have to be
made by individuals, families, businesses, and governments, then some alternative
purchases will have to be foregone.

Concepts

Resources   Scarcity   Wants   Purchases (Choices)

Concept Examples, Concept Attributes, Specific Facts
(Using *Resources* as an Example)

Definition of Resources	Examples of Resources	Specific Facts about Resources

Resources are the means used to produce goods and services.	Natural resources
	    coal
	    oil
	    water
		Oil-producing nations have increased their wealth since the 1970s at the expense of oil-consuming nations.

continued

Definition of Resources	Examples of Resources	Specific Facts about Resources
	Human resources talents energy commitment good health Facilities and equipment machinery tools factories Financial resources money credit	The Soviet Union claimed that it restricted emigration because it feared a "brain drain." The Japanese auto makers abandoned the inexpensive auto market to companies in Korea and Yugoslavia because of increasing labor costs.

The remaining step in developing a learning hierarchy is to integrate the subject matter analysis with the learning processes we expect students to use in demonstrating that they have mastered the content. The learning processes we will use were originally conceived by Gagne (1965) and then refined by Merrill (1971). They consist of four major learning categories: *emotional, psychomotor, memorization* (recall of previously learned information), and *complex cognitive* (intellectual skills). In the form of a hierarchy, the categories are shown in Figure 2.7. (The emotional category is similar to the affective domain we discussed earlier.)

Merrill added a new level of sophistication by dividing complex cognitive into three sublevels, from simplest to most complex—*concept learning, principle learning*, and *problem solving*. Shown in hierarchical form, the analysis of intellectual functioning is displayed in Figure 2.8.

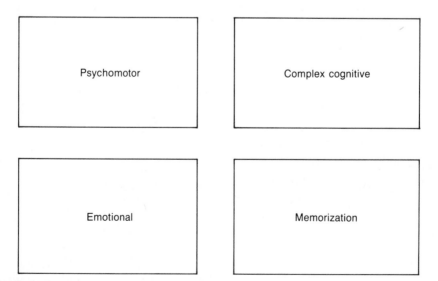

Figure 2.7. Four Major Learning Categories

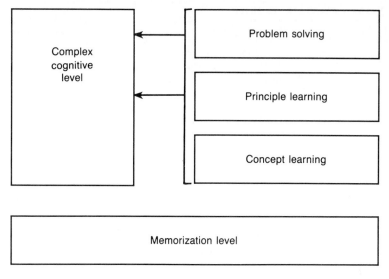

Figure 2.8. Levels of Intellectual Functioning

As we noted earlier, Bloom's taxonomy is discussed in Chapter 6. For those who have learned it previously or wish to compare the two approaches, the following chart may prove helpful.

Bloom Level

Evaluation: Making critical judgments using predetermined criteria.

Synthesis: Combining information to form a whole that did not previously exist.

Analysis: Breaking down complex information into its essential elements.

Application: Learning concepts and applying them to specific examples encountered in unfamiliar situations.

Comprehension: Interpreting information by expressing it in your own words.

Knowledge: Recalling previously learned information.

Gagne Level

(No direct reference. Best advice is to include evaluation tasks in the problem-solving category.)

Problem solving: Using concepts and generalizations to solve complex real-world problems.

Principle learning: Explaining the relationships among concepts to form a generalization.

Concept learning: Learning concepts and applying them to specific examples encountered in unfamiliar situations.

(Gagne includes this in the memorization category.)

Memorization: Recalling previously learned information.

The levels and sublevels of intellectual functioning and a description of each are combined with appropriate "action verbs" in Table 2.1. The action verbs will be used to represent the desired learning processes when instructional objectives are written.

TABLE 2.1. The Learning Process Hierarchy

Level	Description	Action Verbs
Problem Solving Sublevel	If the student is presented with an unfamiliar problem involving a combination of concepts and generalizations that may be organized into alternative solutions and is able to select among the relevant concepts and generalizations and creatively solve the problem, then problem solving can be inferred to have taken place.	solve, construct, build, justify, prove, evaluate, attack, criticize, defend and/or reject, argue, conclude, perform, judge, create, synthesize, establish
Principle Learning Sublevel	If the student is presented with an unfamiliar situation involving two or more concepts and correctly relates them through the application of the relevant generalization, then principle learning can be inferred to have taken place.	explain, predict, relate, break down, compare and contrast, show how, assess, use, infer, determine cause and/or effect, draw a diagram, rank according to some standard, analyze
Concept Learning Sublevel	If the student is presented with an unfamiliar example of a concept and correctly identifies the example as a member of the concept class, then concept learning can be inferred to have taken place.	classify, apply, find, choose, compute, sort
Complex Cognitive (Level II)	If the student is presented with an unfamiliar stimulus—for instance, a new example of a concept—and makes the appropriate response, then complex cognitive learning can be inferred to have taken place.	
Memorization (Level I)	If the student is presented with a familiar stimulus, such as a series of objects, and is asked to identify their names, and the student makes the correct response, then memorization learning can be inferred to have taken place.	select, distinguish, underline, recognize, identify, list, place in order, define, state, name, describe, recall, label, reproduce, indicate

The final hierarchy example, using the "Making Choices" topic, is shown in Figure 2.9. It combines all the elements of an appropriately constructed learning hierarchy—subject matter analysis, learning process analysis, and relevant action verbs.

Generalization Sublevel

Given your knowledge of economic principles, explain why a family making $25,000 a year might choose to save $3,000 a year for a down payment on a home rather than place it as a down payment on a new car.

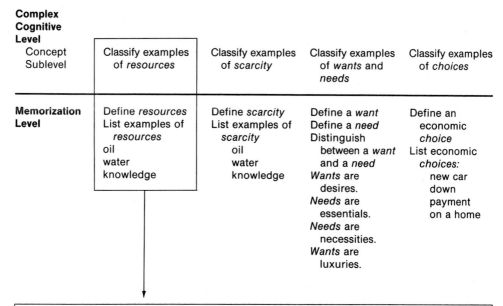

Complex Cognitive Level

Concept Sublevel	Classify examples of *resources*	Classify examples of *scarcity*	Classify examples of *wants* and *needs*	Classify examples of *choices*

Memorization Level

	Define *resources* List examples of *resources* oil water knowledge	Define *scarcity* List examples of *scarcity* oil water knowledge	Define a *want* Define a *need* Distinguish between a *want* and a *need* *Wants* are desires. *Needs* are essentials. *Needs* are necessities. *Wants* are luxuries.	Define an economic *choice* List economic *choices:* new car down payment on a home

---

Additional Hierarchy Detail for Concept *Resources*

Concept Definition	Concept Examples	Specific Facts
Students will be able to recall definitions, attributes and specific facts as follows:		
Resources are the means used to produce goods and services.	Natural resources coal oil water Human resources talents energy commitment good health Facilities and equipment machinery tools factories Financial resources money credit	Oil-producing nations have increased their wealth since the 1970s at the expense of oil-consuming nations. The Soviet Union claimed that it restricted emigration because it feared a "brain drain." The Japanese auto makers abandoned the inexpensive auto market to companies in Korea and Yugoslavia because of increasing labor costs.

Figure 2.9. Learning Hierarchy for "Making Choices" Topic

FINAL THOUGHTS ON CONTENT AND THE ANALYSIS OF LEARNING PROCESS

After teaching about content and learning process analysis to hundreds of students over the past decade, we have encountered many student questions. What follows are three of the most common concerns expressed by students, followed by our responses, responses that we hope will reduce any anxiety about your capability to analyze content and learning processes.

Question 1

"I can't identify generalizations in the subject matter I am expected to teach. The textbooks don't identify them. I don't know how to find them. I feel like Millicent Stephens did before she began her curriculum development task. Can you help me?"

Unfortunately, too few subject matter textbooks are organized in a structural way so that the fundamental generalizations and concepts are identified and highlighted and then related to factual information. Many textbooks, especially in social studies, provide information without any mention of the concepts and generalizations that help to classify and explain the information. For example, a sixth grade textbook in history might allocate two pages of text to World War II, listing the nations at war and their leaders, mentioning the major battles and generals, and so on. However, the historical concepts of related events, chronology, and cause and effect, the political concepts of militarism, institutional racism, fascism, communism, and democracy, the geographic concepts of continents, islands, and oceans, site, location, and space, the economic concepts of markets, raw materials, and industrialization, and similar topics are nowhere to be found. If the teacher does not organize the text material into a structural outline, much of what will be read and discussed related to World War II will probably be forgotten.

As bleak as the situation appears, there are some strategies you can use to increase your capability to identify key generalizations and concepts in the subjects you teach. First, the professional journals and conference programs of such associations as the International Reading Association (IRA), National Council for the Social Studies (NCSS), National Council of Teachers of English (NCTE), National Council of Teachers of Mathematics (NCTM), National Science Teachers Association (NSTA), and other organizations, and their state affiliates, provide articles, papers, and presentations focused on the organization of content for teaching purposes. Some of these associations publish monographs containing lesson and unit plans grounded in fundamental generalizations and concepts. In addition, there are specialized curriculum resource and development centers in some subject areas, such as the *Joint Council on Economic Education*, and instructional journals for elementary and secondary teachers, such as *Learning* and *Instructor*, that publish lesson and unit plans and produce special issues on curriculum. To use magazines and journals productively, you can consult specialized reference guides to published material organized by topics, titles, and author names.

School district curriculum guides are a second useful source for structural lesson plans. Most include sample lesson plans and are oriented toward the teaching of generalizations and concepts. Often the unit or lesson you want to develop has been prepared by someone in some other school district and you can adapt it for your use.

A third source is textbooks and other works on the topic written for adults or for students at a higher or lower grade level than your class. Someone may have organized the topic in a structural way, and you can use the organizing framework while increasing or reducing the level of complexity of the reading material and other activities.

A final source consists of other educators with whom you come into contact. Teachers who are active members of the profession, attend meetings and conferences, and take inservice and graduate course work can be expected to gain more insights into the structure of subject matter than will those who do not.

Question 2

"Just as soon as I think I can classify tasks and objectives at some level of Gagne's learning hierarchy, I come across one that I can't classify. Or a group of us get together and we have three different answers. Even the instructor is unable to persuasively justify why an objective is at the concept level or the principle level. Why does this happen?"

Bear in mind that you are attempting to accomplish one of the most complex intellectual tasks in teaching. In terms of learning process, creating a learning hierarchy is at the problem-solving level, requiring you to select and organize a set of related concepts, generalizations, and facts into a meaningful network of content. You may not be knowledgeable enough about the topic you must teach to be able to analyze its structure quickly. Furthermore, the content and learning process frameworks are composed of abstract concepts, and it may be difficult to define them, to identify critical attributes, and to classify examples and nonexamples. Finally, because you are likely to be teaching abstract concepts, it is understandable that you find it difficult to determine whether some element of the content is a generalization or a fact or whether a given instructional objective is at the concept level or the principle level.

Question 3

"The learning process hierarchy is too complex. There are too many levels and it's too difficult to keep the levels straight in my mind. Can't you simplify it further?"

Good question! There is a simplified version of the hierarchy for you to consider. It is based on the generalization that most of the advantages gained from the hierarchy can be achieved by discriminating between

Complex Cognitive Learning
and
Memorization

These become the two levels of the hierarchy.

Level 1, *memorization*, consists of familiar tasks where the student is asked to remember or recall information such as names, dates, definitions, items, numbers, labels, statements, that has been taught previously. No learning process other than memorization is involved. For example, the question "What happened in the 1970s to the price of gasoline when the supply of oil was drastically reduced?" is at the memorization level. For appropriate verbs to use in creating instructional objectives at the memorization level, consult Table 2.1.

Level 2, *complex cognitive learning*, consists of tasks that are triggered by an unfamiliar example, a novel situation, or a problem that the student must classify, explain, or solve. Remember that in order for the task to be at this level the testing question must contain an unfamiliar element—for instance, "If you were a wheat farmer in the United States and you knew that there would be a severe drought in wheat-growing regions of Canada and the Soviet Union in the coming year, would you plan to plant more or less wheat next year? Why or why not?" For appropriate verbs to use in creating instructional objectives at the complex cognitive level, consult Table 2.1. You are free to use any of the verbs from the concept, principle, or problem-solving sublevels.

CHAPTER SUMMARY

This chapter opened at a school board meeting in the Landstown, Maryland, school system, during which the approval of an economics education program became entangled in the continuing debate over the nature and mission of public schools in the United States. A review of the three major educational philosophies—progressivism, essentialism, and reconstructionism—and the recommended process for generating educational goals using Tyler's Curriculum Rationale were presented. The central problem of Chapter 2 was introduced as fourth-grade teacher Millicent Stephens pondered her challenge to lead a team of teachers to design and to develop a curriculum unit called "Learning to Spend and Save Money Wisely." She was concerned that her teacher preparation had not given her sufficient insights into the process of curriculum design and development. We trust that your study of Chapter 2 will substantially reduce or eliminate your concern if you find yourself in the role of Millicent Stephens.

When you face the challenge of analyzing educational content, you will be aided by your understanding of the distinctions between cognitive, affective, and psychomotor content, especially the breakdown of cognitive content into concepts, generalizations, and facts. You should be able to analyze cognitive content of a topic and develop a subject matter hierarchy of that topic. Finally, you should be able to integrate the analysis of subject matter into an analysis of learning process, using the learning hierarchy approach as conceived by the psychologist Robert Gagné.

To gain guided practice and independent practice, you may wish to complete the following activities.

Guided Practice Activity A. Identifying Concepts, Generalizations, and Specific Facts

Write *C* for *concept*, *G* for *generalization*, or *SF* for *specific fact* in the space to the left of each example.

_____ **1.** inflation

_____ **2.** impulse buying

_____ **3.** If a country has a budget deficit, it can be eliminated by either reducing expenses or increasing revenue.

_____ **4.** The United States had a deficit balance of trade in the period 1980–1988.

_____ **5.** consumer

_____ **6.** If the government attempts to reduce a large deficit by borrowing from citizens and other countries, the value of its currency is likely to decline.

_____ **7.** The Joint Council on Economic Education is a source for information for educators who wish to integrate economic education into their courses of study.

_____ **8.** command economy

_____ **9.** An economic generalization is a statement expressing the relationship between two or more economic concepts.

_____ **10.** The major purpose of the General Agreement on Tariffs and Trade (GATT) is to reduce trade restrictions and promote the freedom of commerce.

Guided Practice Activity A. Answer Key

1. Concept or principle
2. Concept
3. Generalization
4. Specific fact
5. Concept
6. Generalization
7. Specific fact
8. Concept
9. Tricky one! This reads like a generalization but it's actually a definition of the concept *economic generalization*. A generalization has to relate two or more concepts. What we label as a definition is another way of denoting a concept. The correct answer then to Number 9 is *concept*.
10. Specific fact

Guided Practice Activity B. Classifying Examples of Learning Processes

Indicate which type of learning process each item represents. Write *M* for *memorization*, *CL* for *concept learning*, *PL* for *principle learning*, or *PS* for *problem solving* in the space to the left of each example.

_____ 1. After practicing simple interest calculations, complete unfamiliar problems for homework.

_____ 2. Recall the definition of the concept *impulse buying*.

_____ 3. Explain why the United States and the Soviet Union both face the economizing problem.

_____ 4. Comprehend the definition of *balance of trade* when it appears in a newspaper story.

_____ 5. Identify the three characteristics of a consumer.

_____ 6. Defend or reject the thesis "The Soviet Union has more to gain if trade with the United States is substantially increased."

_____ 7. List a source of economic information of use to educators.

_____ 8. When given an example of a particular country's economy, apply your knowledge of command economies to decide if it is one or not.

_____ 9. Sort a group of unfamiliar statements into a group consisting of economic generalizations.

_____ 10. Assume you live in one of the countries that was on the list of those with a severe balance of trade problem—a country that we did not discuss in class. Create a solution to the balance of trade problem that takes into account the country's resources and other key characteristics.

Guided Practice Activity B. Answer Key

1. Concept learning or principle learning (Math objectives are often difficult to classify unless you are able to examine the actual problems. The complexity of the task is the key to whether to classify it at the concept, principle or problem-solving level.)

2. Memorization
3. Principle learning
4. Memorization
5. Memorization
6. Problem solving

7. Memorization
8. Concept learning
9. Concept learning
10. Problem solving

Independent Practice Activity A. Planning a Content Outline for a Topic of Your Choice

1. Assume that you are teaching in a school, with grade level and subject area of your choice. Create a generalization that would be a worthy learning outcome for your students. Write it below.

   _____

   _____

2. List two or more concepts that are related through your generalization. Write them below.

   _____

   _____

3. Write two concept examples or specific facts that are related to your subject matter hierarchy.

   _____

   _____

Independent Practice Activity B. Creating a Complete Learning Hierarchy for the Topic of Your Choice

Using the content outline from Independent Practice Activity A, construct a flow chart learning hierarchy that integrates the concepts, generalizations, and specific facts with the appropriate learning process levels. Use a separate sheet of paper. Your completed hierarchy should be similar in form to the "Making Choices" example on page 51.

REFERENCES

Bloom, B. (Ed.). (1956). *Taxonomy of Educational Objectives: Handbook I. Cognitive Domain*. White Plains, NY: Longman.

Bruner, J. E. (1960). *The Process of Education*. Cambridge: Harvard University Press.

Carroll, J. (1963). A model of school learning. *Teachers College Record, 64,* 723–733.

Chambers, J. H. (1988, April). Teaching thinking throughout the curriculum. *Educational Leadership, 45* (7), 4–6.

Cheney, L. V. (1987). *American Memory: A Report on the Humanities in the Nation's Public Schools*. Washington, DC: National Endowment for the Humanities.

Counts, G. S. (1932). Dare schools build a new social order? New York: *John Day, 7,* 9–10.

Estes, T. H., Gutman, C. J., & Harrison, E. K. (1988, September). Cultural literacy: What every educator needs to know. *Educational Leadership, 46* (1), 14–17.

Gagné, R. M. (1965). *The Conditions of Learning*. New York: Holt Rinehart & Winston.

Gagné, R. M. (1968). Learning hierarchies. In M. D. Merrill (Ed.), *Instructional design: Readings* (pp. 118–131). Englewood Cliffs, NJ: Prentice-Hall.

Gilbert, W. S. (1932). *Plays and Poems of W. S. Gilbert*, New York: Random House.

Goodlad, J. I. (1985, September). The great American schooling experiment. *Phi Delta Kappan, 67,* 266–271.

Hirsch, E. D., Jr. (1987a, Summer). Cultural literacy and the schools. *American Education*, pp. 8–15.

Hirsch, E. D., Jr. (1987b). *Cultural Literacy: What Every American Needs to Know*. Boston: Houghton Mifflin.

Hirsch, E. D., Jr. (1988, September). Hirsch responds: The best answer to a caricature is a practical program. *Educational Leadership, 46* (1), 18–19.

Holt, J. (1964). *How Children Fail*. New York: Pitman.

Holt, J. (1970). *How Children Learn*. New York: Pitman.

Klein, N., Pasch, M., Frew, T. (1979). *Curriculum Analysis and Design for Retarded Learners*. Columbus, OH: Merrill, 142–143.

Kourilsky, M. L. (1983). *Mini-Society: Experiencing Real World Economics in the Elementary School Classroom*. Menlo Park, CA: Addison Wesley.

Mager, Robert F. (1984). *Goal Analysis*. Belmont, CA: David S. Lake.

Merrill, M. D. (1971). Necessary conditions for defining instructional outcomes. In M. D. Merrill (Ed.), *Instructional design: Readings* (pp. 173–184). Englewood Cliffs: NJ: Prentice-Hall.

McHugh, N. (1987, September 16). Quoted in *Education Week*. Washington, DC: Editorial Projects in Education, *7* (2), 1, 23.

Nation at Risk. (1983). Washington, D.C.: U.S. Department of Education.

Phenix, P. H. (1960, April). The topography of higher liberal learning. *Phi Delta Kappan, 41,* 307.

Ravitch, D. (1983). *The Troubled Crusade: American Education 1945–1980*. New York: Basic Books.

Ravitch, D. E., & Finn, C. E. Jr. (1987). *What Do Our 17-Year-Olds Know?* Washington, DC: National Endowment for the Humanities.

Shulman, L. S. (1986, February). Those who understand: Knowledge growth in teaching. *Educational Researcher*, pp. 4–14.

Stratemeyer, F. (1970). Developing a curriculum for modern living. In R. T. Hyman, *Approaches in curriculum* (pp. 53–72). Englewood Cliffs, N.J.: Prentice-Hall.

Tyler, R. (1969). *Basic Principles of Curriculum and Instruction*. Chicago: University of Chicago Press.

U.S. Department of Education. (1986). *What Works: Research about Teaching and Learning.* Washington, DC: U.S. Government Printing Office. Available from the Consumer Information Center, Pueblo, CO 81009.

Webster's New Collegiate Dictionary. (1981). Springfield, MA: G. & C. Merriam.

Welsh, P. (1987, November). *Update.* Alexandria, VA: Association for Supervision and Curriculum Development, *29* (8).

Worsham, T. (1988, September). From cultural literacy to cultural thoughtfulness. *Educational Leadership*, 46 (1), 20–21.

CHAPTER 3

Writing Instructional Objectives and Evaluating Results

Section 1. Writing Clearly Stated Objectives

Section 1 Overview

The Sea Horse Fable[1]

Once upon a time a Sea Horse gathered up his seven pieces of eight and cantered out to find his fortune. Before he had traveled very far he met an Eel who said,

"Psst. Hey bud. Where 'ya goin'?"

"I'm going out to find my fortune," replied the Sea Horse, proudly.

"You're in luck," said the Eel. "For four pieces of eight you can have this speedy flipper, and then you'll be able to get there a lot faster."

"Get, that's swell" said the Sea Horse, and paid the money and put on the flipper and slithered off at twice the speed. Soon he came upon a Sponge, who said,

"Psst. Hey bud. Where 'ya goin'?"

---

[1]From *Preparing Instructional Objectives*, by Robert F. Mager. Copyright © 1984 by David S. Lake Publishers, Belmont, CA 94002.

"I'm going out to find my fortune," replied the Sea Horse, proudly.

"You're in luck," said the Sponge. "For a small fee I will let you have this jet-propelled scooter so that you will be able to travel a lot faster." So the Sea Horse bought the scooter with his remaining money and went zooming thru the sea five times as fast. Soon he came upon a Shark who said,

"Psst. Hey bud. Where 'ya goin'?"

"I'm going out to find my fortune," replied the Sea Horse.

"You're in luck. If you take this short cut," said the Shark, pointing to his open mouth, "you'll save yourself a lot of time."

"Gee, thanks," said the Sea Horse, and zoomed off into the interior of the Shark, and was never heard from again.

The moral of this fable is that if you're not sure where you're going, you're liable to wind up someplace else.

The "Sea Horse Fable," which first appeared in *Preparing Instructional Objectives*, by Robert Mager, provides whimsical support to those who value clearly written instructional objectives. Furthermore, it introduces you to the content of Section 1, the transformation of curriculum goals into clearly stated instructional objectives. In Chapter 2 you learned how to select and analyze educational goals. Without being aware of it, you also created the framework upon which you will write instructional objectives as well as procedures you will use to evaluate whether students have achieved the objectives. In this section, you will learn the characteristics of a properly written instructional objective and how to recognize "good" from "not so good" objectives and, finally, how to write the "good" ones. (In Section 2 of this chapter, the focus will be on the evaluation of instructional results as promised in the objectives.)

Set Activity

It's early October and time for the families of the children who attend the Martin Luther King Elementary School in the Landstown, Maryland, school district to participate in the annual open house. The evening begins with remarks by school officials, who request parent participation on district committees and task forces. The principal closes the general session by reporting on school progress as well as the opportunities and challenges of the coming year. Finally, the parents disperse to meet with their youngster's teachers and to form a personal impression to place alongside the verbal reviews of the teacher provided by their children. As a result of their children's enthusiasm, many of the parents come expecting to be impressed. Only a few anticipate being bored or irritated. Most parents have a "Give the teacher credit, it's a difficult job" attitude. They arrive hoping to be informed about the work their children have done and will do in the subject(s) for which the teacher is responsible. A substantial number of parents seek guidance from the teacher concerning the role of the parents in reinforcing school goals and tasks.

Imagine yourself as an invisible observer able to flit from room to room, listening to the teachers introducing their educational plans and programs for the coming year to groups of parents. Specifically, you attend the sessions in two fourth-grade classrooms where the focus of attention is on the insertion of a new unit titled "Learning to Spend and Save Money Wisely," developed by Millicent Stephens and her team of fourth grade teachers.

Below is a partial transcript of the sessions in these classrooms, in the form of two case studies. After reading the two case studies, answer the questions that follow them.

Fourth-Grade Class   Room 214   Mr. Abrams

MR. ABRAMS: A school district curriculum group led by Miss Stephens of Fairhill Elementary School developed this unit last year and we are expected to teach it at Martin Luther King. So that's what we will be doing in social studies this marking period.

MR. VASQUEZ (PARENT): Mr. Abrams, what are the goals you hope to achieve as you teach the unit to our children?

MR. ABRAMS: I would have to reexamine the teacher's guide that came with the unit to describe the specific goals, but, in general, I expect to teach students about the nature and value of money and how to use it wisely.

MRS. WASHINGTON (PARENT): That sounds O.K. to me, but can you tell me a little more about what my daughter will know when she completes this unit?

MR. ABRAMS: I really am not prepared to do that at this time. Remember, some of the responsibility for learning rests with the student and also with the parents. My responsibility is to provide general direction for the students and give them the materials from which they will learn.

MR. LASSIVER (PARENT): I believe in assisting the teachers by knowing what's expected of my child and encouraging and helping my child to study at home. Under your approach it will be difficult for me to do that.

MR. ABRAMS: Possibly we should discuss that at the parent–teacher conference scheduled between us. Thank you all for coming tonight, and I look forward to meeting individually with you on conference day in November to discuss your child's progress.

Fourth-Grade Class   Room 212   Mrs. Calzone

MRS. CALZONE: One of the highlights of this year's social studies course of study is the new unit "Learning to Spend and Save Money Wisely," developed last year by a school district curriculum group led by Miss Stephens of Fairhill Elementary School. I have examined the unit and am prepared to teach it. I have added some features to the unit that makes it especially useful for my students.

MR. SARASON (PARENT): Mrs. Calzone, what are the goals you hope to achieve as you teach the unit to our children?

MRS. CALZONE: That's a good question. In fact, I have prepared a handout to give to each of you. The handout includes the goals as well as some recommended activities that you can do at home to assist your youngster to achieve the goals.

MRS. RODRIQUEZ (PARENT): I'm glad these are written clearly! I also appreciate the fact that the goals are written directly to students. The goal "to know the difference between a want and a need" is of special interest to me. I hope you succeed in getting my son, Tony, to learn the difference." (general laughter erupts)

MRS. CALZONE: Thanks for the expression of support, Mrs. Rodriquez! Actually, I was hoping that the adults and older brothers and sisters at home would help me. I have two instructional objectives for that goal; one is to have the students recognize examples of wants and needs from a list of goods and services they have not seen previously, and the other is, together with family members, to generate a list that would be appropriate for persons ages 10 to 13. I hope you will all participate in the activity that will accompany the objective. In fact, we will be doing that activity next Thursday or Friday. May I have your participation?

ALL PARENTS IN UNISON: Yes. (enthusiastic applause)

MRS. CALZONE: Thank you all for coming tonight, and I look forward to meeting individually with you on conference day in November to discuss your child's progress.

1. Which teacher do you think was more effective in developing a positive relationship with

   parents? _____

2. Why was this teacher more effective? _____

   _____

   _____

3. Explain the relationship between "The Sea Horse Fable" and the two case studies.

   _____

   _____

   _____

   _____

4. Are there any issues or concerns that surfaced as you read the two case studies? If so, what

are they? _____

_____

_____

Section 1 Objectives

After you have completed this section, you will be able to:
1. defend or reject the position that teachers who use instructional objectives are more successful in generating student learning than are those who do not
2. explain the advantages and disadvantages of using instructional objectives
3. define the A, B, C, and D characteristics of a clearly stated objective
4. classify examples of educational statements as clearly stated objectives
5. create clearly stated objectives at the memorization, concept learning, principle learning, and problem-solving levels

THE CONTROVERSY OVER THE USE OF INSTRUCTIONAL OBJECTIVES

There has long been a controversy about the value of instructional objectives. Those who support them argue that if teachers expect to achieve success, they must be able to define success, and then assess students' progress in reaching it. To advocates, the success of teaching is measured by student learning. They also believe that learning, from the simplest and/or most trivial outcome to the most complex and/or most worthy outcome, can be measured.

Some advocates of the use of instructional objectives believe that all learning outcomes can be measured in some useful way. Other, more pragmatic proponents are willing to concede that some outcomes are beyond easy measurement by the teacher. However, all advocates agree that teachers who utilize clearly stated instructional objectives are more successful in enhancing the learning of their students than are teachers who do not use them.

Employing a fanciful style, William Strong wrote "A Didactic (and Somewhat Moral) Fable,"[2] focused, in part, on arguments over the worth of instructional objectives (Strong, 1975). In his article, Strong transported the reader to a "not too distant land" where two educational reformers lead their zealous armies of supporters. The Ant, leader of the behavioral educators, offers a spirited defense of the use of instructional objectives. Opposing

---

[2]"A Didactic (and Somewhat Moral) Fable," by W. Strong, from *Media and Methods*. Published by the American Society of Educators, March 1975.

the Ant and her forces stands the Grasshopper, leader of the progressive educators, who advocates self-initiated learning and inquiry. On one special occasion, the teachers in the land gather for a "Great Debate" between the two spokespersons over the value of objectives-based instruction. After the Grasshopper claims that spontaneity and creativity are lost when objectives guide instruction, the Ant responds:

> I'm interested enough in creativity, for example, to ask a question that you're afraid to ask—namely, the question of what behaviors go into it. You see creativity and solving quadratic equations and analyzing propaganda and valuing one painting over another aren't just abstractions. They're complex behaviors. Now if we're interested in teaching those behaviors, it's helpful to look at what they involve—in other words, to do a systematic task analysis. You see this puts the focus on the *process*, not on the product. And if you're a teacher, you can begin by specifying behavioral criteria that will provide you with feedback on whether the learners are really getting what you want them to get. (p. 51)

Critics claim that there is no persuasive evidence that instructional objectives enhance student learning, especially the learning of higher order thinking skills. Many critics have taken issue with the methodology of studies that demonstrate increased learning in classes in which teachers use objectives-based instruction. Furthermore, these critics assert that the outcomes from these studies were too narrow, shallow, or trivial and that important learning outcomes cannot be measured by commonly used testing instruments and procedures. As a result, they say the focus of these evaluation studies was on recall and on "yes-or-no" answers rather than on responses that required students to make distinctions and choices among alternative answers. In addition, as expressed by the Grasshopper, a focus on predetermined outcomes in the classroom is more effective in analyzing the past than in encouraging young people to prepare for the future. The Grasshopper believes that, in respect to the future, the Ant's technology

> can't tell us what it's going to be like. So doesn't it make more sense to give learners *practice* in coping with problems than to give them ready-made, packaged answers? Our future's going to need people who are psychologically whole, independent, creative, thoughtful, and behaviorally *active*—but not in the trivial sense of activity that comes from doing a mind-sapping, step-by-step learning sequence. The kingdom's going to need people who can articulate problems, plan approaches to them, ask answerable questions, gather data, make hypotheses, and test out their conclusions. Do you follow? People who are fully *involved* in the business of living and learning. (p. 52)

CHECK FOR UNDERSTANDING

1. Which speaker do you think had the more persuasive arguments? _____

Why? _____

_____

_____

_____

2.   If you were in the audience, what questions would you ask of either or both speakers?

_____

_____

_____

3.   Do you have a position on the value of instructional objectives as a strategy to enhance

student learning? If so, what is it? _____

_____

_____

_____

Not surprisingly, we have our position on the value of instructional objectives in classroom teaching. We have used objectives to organize this book, and we use them to structure the classes we teach. Consequently, we are on the side of the Ant on this issue.

Used wisely, instructional objectives make planning clearer, more efficient, and more productive. They provide a continuing focus on learning expectations for both the teacher and the student. Without doubt, the use of instructional objectives improves the accuracy and consistency of testing and increases student performance on academic tests. Finally, using instructional objectives boosts teachers' confidence in diagnosing both student performance and the instructional program.

We are also mindful of three dangers in the use of instructional objectives. First, there is a tendency to concentrate one's teaching on cognitive objectives, because they are easier to write and assess and take less class time to produce measurable outcomes. Worthy personal and social objectives in the affective domain may be cast aside. Second, there is a tendency, as well, to write instructional objectives at the memorization and concept-learning levels and not at the principle-learning and problem-solving levels. If that tendency is permitted to govern our behavior, higher level teaching and learning will be minimized. Third, instructional objectives may sometimes diminish the flexibility and responsiveness that allow us to take advantage of that special "teachable moment." When it arrives, often unexpectedly, we have to be prepared to set the instructional objective aside.

With full awareness of these dangers, and weighing the dangers against the benefits to be gained from using instructional objectives, we recommend them to you. The remainder of the book will demonstrate our commitment to their continuing role in classroom teaching.

THE NATURE OF AN INSTRUCTIONAL OBJECTIVE

In Chapter 2, we explained that an educational goal provides general direction to the teacher in developing instruction. Although both goals and objectives describe student rather than teacher behavior, a goal generally covers more content than an objective does and thus is phrased more broadly. For example, a goal might encompass the content that will be taught in a semester or year-long course, whereas an instructional objective might cover the content for a week-long unit or for a single-day's lesson plan.

An *instructional objective* is defined as a specific statement of what the student will know or be able to do after the unit or lesson ends. Instructional objectives can be developed for all types of content, whether affective, psychomotor, or cognitive, in all subject areas and across all grade levels. They can be conceived and written at all levels of subject matter, from facts to concepts to generalizations, and all levels of learning process, from memorization through problem solving. When prepared properly, instructional objectives can be used to plan learning activities that will teach the content as well as provide evaluation procedures to assess student learning of that content.

RECOGNIZING INSTRUCTIONAL OBJECTIVES

Given what you know about educational goals and instructional objectives, can you recognize examples of each? To assess your capability, tell whether each of the following is an *educational goal* or an *instructional objective*.

Students will be able to:

1. recognize the importance of a contract
2. appreciate the value of honesty
3. understand potential conflicts among economic goals
4. compute correctly by making change from a dollar bill
5. recognize the relationship between government and the economy
6. when given a list of goods, classify, by listing in writing, examples of luxuries
7. identify deceptive sales techniques and practices
8. appreciate the need to conserve energy
9. demonstrate that they understand that one cannot long continue to borrow beyond one's income
10. write legibly on business forms

If you decided that items 4, 6, and 10 are instructional objectives, you were correct. Why are they classified as instructional objectives while the other items are not? Using the language of instructional designers, we say that they pass the *behavior* test that distinguishes an educational goal from an instructional objective; that is, both the content to be learned and the expected learning process and level are described. Let's examine item 4 and determine what elements contained within it make it an acceptable instructional objective:

Students will be able to compute correctly by making change from a dollar bill.

Element 1. *What is to be learned?* What is to be learned is the knowledge and skill involved in computing number combinations adding up to and subtracting from 100 (clear content description).

Element 2.   *Learning process and level.* The learning process is to compute (clearly understood process). The learning level is concept learning, since the verb *compute* refers to tasks at that level.[3] (See Table 2.1, Chapter 2, page 50.)

In writing instructional objectives, we must describe how the student is to demonstrate achievement of the objective. In item 4 it is "by making change from a dollar bill." In item 6 it is "by listing in writing, examples of luxuries." In item 10 it is "write legibly on business forms." These examples illustrate what we call the *"by clause"* of an instructional objective. Sometimes the "by clause" adds clarity to the verb that identifies the learning process, as in item 4, in which the learning process is "to compute" and the "by clause" is "by making change from a dollar bill." Another approach is illustrated in item 10, in which the "by clause" is implicit in the action verb "write."

Let's turn our attention to items in the list that are not instructional objectives.

Item 3: Students will be able to understand potential conflicts among economic goals.

Item 8: Students will be able to appreciate the need to conserve energy.

CHECK FOR UNDERSTANDING

Why are items 3 and 8 *not* instructional objectives? Write your answer below.

_____

_____

_____

_____

_____

The justification for not classifying item 3 as an instructional objective is as follows:

Students will be able to understand potential conflicts among economic goals.

Element 1.   *What is to be learned?* What is to be learned is the generalization that "economic goals are often in conflict" (clear content description).

Element 2.   *Learning process and level.* The learning process is "to understand." How does one demonstrate understanding? The verb *to understand* is not included in the action verb list in Table 2.1 because "understanding" is an inherently unclear process. Does the writer wish the student to memorize

---

[3]The assumption is that the task is unfamiliar, since the concepts of addition and subtraction must be applied to make change. There is little likelihood that a student could correctly make change by memorizing all the change combinations without applying the relevant concepts.

the generalization that "economic goals are often in conflict"? If so, then it should be so stated. However, if the task is at the complex cognitive level, then a different verb is needed. In any case, the verb must be followed by an appropriate "by clause." (The level of learning is very unclear.)

An example of a rewritten item 3 that conforms to the behavior requirement of an instructional objective follows:

When given a written description of a previously presented case study, students will be able to identify it as an example of the conflict of economic goals.

Let's turn our attention to the second unacceptable example of an instructional objective, item 8:

Students will be able to appreciate the need to conserve energy.

Element 1.   *What is to be learned?* What is to be learned is energy conservation. The topic *conserving energy* is somewhat broad. What kind of energy is to be conserved? Where is the energy to be conserved?)

Element 2.   *Learning process and level.* Since this is an affective objective, we are most concerned with an appropriate "by clause" to follow the verb (unclear learning process).

An example of a rewritten item 8 that conforms to the behavior requirement of an instructional objective follows:

Students will be able to appreciate the need to conserve energy by voluntarily participating in the house energy audit project.

WRITING CLEARLY STATED INSTRUCTIONAL OBJECTIVES

A clearly stated instructional objective must contain a behavior statement as well as three other characteristics. A helpful way to remember the four characteristics is to use the *A, B, C, D* mnemonic aid, or memory device. The letter *B*, of course, stands for *behavior*. What do the others represent?

Let us begin with *A*, for *audience*. Since clearly stated instructional objectives are developed from educational goals to be achieved by a particular student or students, the student or students are identified in the *audience statement*. The following examples are acceptable audience statements:

Sixth-grade students will be able to
Art students in the elementary grades will be able to
Students who complete their other assignments will be able to
Students in the Tiger math group will be able to
Students in the social studies group studying the Constitution will be able to

Often the audience statement precedes and becomes the stem for a set of instructional objectives, as in the following example:

After completing this unit, sixth-grade students will be able to

That concludes the audience (A) requirement of a clearly stated objective. Since the behavior (B) requirement has been completed earlier, let's move on to the conditions (C) requirement.

A *conditions (C) statement* is included when special circumstances are present during testing that may affect student performance. Conditions may be equipment or materials to be used by the student, a time requirement, or some other limitations within which the student is expected to perform. If there are not special circumstances, then a conditions statement may be omitted from the objective. The following are five examples of condition statements:

Using the outline map provided
In pen
Given a protractor
Keeping within the lines
As a volunteer

Conditions often describe a requirement that must be met by the student if the product or performance is to be accepted by the teacher. Referring to the examples above, there is an assumption that if the student in the second example does not "use a pen," the assignment would not be acceptable. In the same spirit, other condition requirements suggest that points will be subtracted from the product or performance if the student violates a condition, as in the fourth example, in which a student is warned to keep "within the lines." The fifth example is used with an affective objective that aims to increase student participation in voluntary social improvement projects.

A *degree statement (D)* describes the criteria or standards that will be used by the instructor to determine whether the student has achieved the instructional objective being tested. The degree statement explains how the student product (i.e., written exam, model, painting, essay, research paper) or performance (i.e., speech, teaching demonstration, sprint, debate) will be graded.

There are two ways that a degree statement may be expressed. The first is in quantitative terms. *Quantitative* degree statements are typically associated with teaching lessons in which the subject matter yields "right" answers rather than "best" answers. Quantitative degree statements also are associated with the lower level learning processes of memorization and concept learning rather than the higher level processes of principle learning and problem solving. The following five examples are quantitative degree statements:

achieving 7 out of 10 correct
with 75 percent accuracy
listing at least 3 reasons
using 10 of the week's spelling words
making 5 of 10 free throws

Qualitative degree statements refer to the teacher's assessment of a complex student behavior. Often qualitative degree statements are difficult to construct because they require teachers to determine the form and substance of the minimally acceptable student product or performance, as well as to guide students in the preparation of their assignments.

Five examples of qualitative degree statements follow:

Essays will be judged on the accuracy of factual statements, relevance to the topic, persuasive appeal, mechanics (sentence structure, spelling, word usage, organization and coherence).

Radio commercials will be judged on how appealing they make the product to potential customers, clarity, and proper use of language.

Art projects will be graded on whether they show three or more colors, and present a street scene as described in the assignment.

Travel brochures will be graded according to the following criteria:

1. accurate information on costs, mileage, and other details
2. attractive pictures and drawings
3. interest and appeal for the potential customer
4. correct use of the language

That concludes the description of the four elements of a clearly stated objective:

(A) for Audience, (B) for Behavior, (C) for Conditions, and (D) for Degree.

To provide you with additional examples of clearly stated objectives, we have brought back for your attention the "Making Choices" topic, presented in learning hierarchy form in Chapter 2, Figure 2.9 (page 52). Recall that the hierarchy was derived from the "Learning to Spend and Save Money Wisely" unit title suggested by the curriculum task force. It was then to be analyzed and developed by Millicent Stephens and her fourth-grade teacher colleagues. Following are (1) a unit rationale that describes the content to the student and justifies its importance, and (2) clearly stated instructional objectives that the fourth-grade teacher/developers created to guide student learning.

Unit Rationale: Making Choices

Do you get everything you want from the important adults in your life—father, mother, grandparents? Do they ever say "no" to you? Do you sometimes think that adults get everything they want? Or do you know that every person and every group has to make choices? No matter how wealthy a person is, there are too many things to buy and to do for anyone to have all his or her wishes satisfied. The same is true for families and for countries. In this unit, you will learn why choices about what to buy must be made and about the difference between what we need and what we want.

Unit Objectives

When the unit is completed, you will be able to:

1. write a story of a family that must make a choice among three purchases. The story must be between 250 and 500 words and must include reasons why a particular choice is made. These reasons must be based on what you have learned in this unit.
2. choose 10 resources from a list of items given to you. To be successful, you must make fewer than three errors.
3. find wants and needs when given a list of goods and services. To be successful, you must make fewer than three errors.

4.   write a definition for the following ideas: *good, service, want, need, luxury, necessity, resource, scarcity*, economic *choice*. For your response to be successful, two of three classmates must be able to identify the idea when given your definition.

5.   find an example of an economic choice that the United States government has made or must make between what the people need and what resources are available. The example should come from either a newspaper or magazine article that appeared in the past 12 months. The example must be written, with pen, in your own words. Length should be between 200 and 300 words. The source of your example must be listed.

SECTION 1 SUMMARY

The section began with the parable "The Sea Horse Fable," whose theme supports the use of instructional objectives in the classroom. Further arguments were presented by the Ant, as the leader of the educators who advocate the use of instructional objectives, and the Grasshopper, leading the opposition to their use. The text provided two arguments in favor of the use of instructional objectives: (1) they assist the teacher in focusing student attention on what is expected in the lesson and unit; (2) they increase the likelihood that assignments and tests will be related to what was actually taught. The section then listed two arguments against the use of instructional objectives: (1) since lower level instructional objectives are easier to construct, important higher level outcomes may be lost; and (2) some spontaneity may be lost when the classroom is focused on predetermined outcomes.

The remainder of the section was devoted to preparing you to write clearly stated objectives using the A—audience, B—behavior, C—conditions, and D—degree statement format. An example of a unit rationale and objectives focused on the "Learning to Spend and Save Money Wisely" unit, to illustrate the concept of clearly stated objectives in a concrete way. In our view, the use of clearly stated objectives is an important element in successful instruction. We hope that you will develop the same regard for them. The following activities will provide you with guided and then independent practice.

Guided Practice Activity. Identifying Audience, Behavior, Conditions, and Degree Elements of a Clearly Stated Objective

Write *A* for *audience*, *B* for *behavior*, *C* for *conditions*, or *D* for *degree* above the sections that illustrate one of those elements in the following clearly stated objectives.

After completing this unit, fourth grade students will be able to:

1.   explain, in a story that you write, why a family that you will create and describe must make

a choice among three purchases. The story must be between 250 and 500 words and must

include reasons why a particular choice is made. These reasons must be based on what you

have learned in this unit.

2.   choose 10 resources from a list of items given to you. To be successful, you must make

fewer than three errors.

3. find wants and needs when given a list of goods and services. To be successful, you must make fewer than three errors.

4. write a definition for the following ideas: *good, service, want, need, luxury, necessity, resource, scarcity*, economic *choice*. For your response to be successful, two of three classmates must be able to identify the idea when given your definition.

5. find an example of an economic choice that the United States government has made or must make between what the people need and what resources are available. The example should come from either a newspaper or magazine article that appeared in the past 12 months. The example must be written, with pen, in your own words. Length should be between 200 and 300 words. The source of your example must be listed.

Guided Practice Activity. Answer Key

Audience

After completing this unit, fourth grade students will be able to:

Behavior

1. explain, in a story that you write, why a family that you will create and describe must make a choice among three purchases.

Conditions

The story must be between 250 and 500 words

Degree

and must include reasons why a particular choice is made. These reasons must be based on what you have learned in this unit.

Behavior

2. choose 10 resources from a list of items given to you.

Degree

To be successful, you must make fewer than three errors.

Behavior

3. find wants and needs when given a list of goods and services.

Degree

To be successful, you must make fewer than three errors.

Behavior

4. write a definition for the following ideas: *good, service, want, need, luxury, necessity, resource, scarcity*, economic *choice*.

Degree

For your response to be successful, two of three classmates must be able to identify the idea when given your definition.

Behavior

5. find an example of an economic choice that the United States government has made or must make between what the people need and what resources are available.

Conditions

The example should come from either a newspaper or magazine article that appeared in the past 12 months. The example must be written, with pen, in your own words. Length should be between 200 and 300 words. The source of your example must be listed.

Independent Practice Activity A. Writing Clearly Stated Instructional Objectives

Write three clearly stated instructional objectives for a teaching lesson or unit of your choice. Each objective should include the *behavior* requirement and either or both the *conditions* and *degree* requirements. Label the requirements as we have done in the answer key to the Guided Practice Activity. _____

_____

_____

_____

_____

Independent Practice Activity B. Writing Clearly Stated Instructional Objectives at Three Levels of Learning Process

Using the three clearly stated instructional objectives you wrote in Independent Practice Activity A, revise, if necessary, so that one is at the *memorization* level, a second at the *concept* level, and a third at either the *principle* or *problem-solving* level. Write your revised objectives below.

1. _____

_____

2. _____

_____

3. _____

_____

Section 2. Evaluating Instructional Results

Section 2 Overview

There is a natural relationship between writing objectives and evaluating instructional success. The two processes can be considered as a two-step sequence. After the objectives are written, it is time to consider how you will determine whether they have been achieved when instruction terminates. The evaluation of instruction involves evaluating both students and how well you as the teacher planned and implemented what you stated in the objectives.

We will begin this section by looking at the evaluation of a particular student's performance. When you have completed your work on the section, you should be able to define key terms of importance in education evaluation and make decisions about the kinds of assessment and grading system you will use in your teaching.

Set Activity

Read the following classroom dialogue between a teacher and a parent. Then answer the questions that follow:

MRS. CAMPISON (PARENT OF A FIFTH GRADER): Mrs. Samson, my daughter, Loretta, is in your fifth-grade class this year. I'm afraid that she is very upset about the grade she received from you in social studies this marking period. She has cried herself to sleep since she received her report card the day before yesterday.

MRS. SAMSON (FIFTH-GRADE TEACHER): Mrs. Campison, I'm sorry about Loretta's reaction to the grade she received. My purpose in teaching is to assist students to be more confident and knowledgeable persons rather than to make them unhappy.

MRS. CAMPISON: Mrs. Samson, is it true that you are a harder grader than Mr. Carson? Loretta told me that students in your class do more work than their friends in Mr. Carson's classroom.

MRS. SAMSON: I won't compare my requirements to another teacher's requirements. However, it is true that I expect students to do their best work. I have found that if I have high expectations for my students, they will make more learning progress than if I were less demanding.

MRS. CAMPISON: But what about the students who are frightened by your approach to teaching, as Loretta is? What do you say to these students?

MRS. SAMSON: First, there are very few students who do not benefit from my approach. Consider that we are at the end of the first marking period. Some students need more time to understand that I am serious. Second, I believe that it is the teacher's responsibility to motivate students and to provide the best instruction possible. However, it is also the teacher's responsibility to judge how well the students have learned what has been taught and to assign a grade to that judgment. I appreciate the concerns you express about Loretta's schoolwork and hope you will encourage her to respond positively to the challenge to do better in school.

MRS. CAMPISON: Where is the place for effort in your scheme of things? Loretta tells me that she tries as hard as she can but she still fails to satisfy you.

MRS. SAMSON: Effort, if it is strong and persistent, results in improvement. I am absolutely convinced of that.

MRS. CAMPISON: I see that we are not getting anywhere with this discussion. I do intend to speak with Loretta and to offer her additional assistance and to encourage her to pay more attention in class and to ask for help from you when she needs it. However, I must say that I find your approach to teaching children unduly threatening and unbending. After all, these children are only 10 and 11 years old. I believe they ought to enjoy their childhood and be encouraged to cooperate with each other rather than to compete for your approval and for grades.

MRS. SAMSON: Mrs. Campison, if you and I support each other and motivate Loretta to do her best work in my classroom, I am confident that we can make a significant contribution to her educational development.

What is your reaction to the two persons featured in the dialogue? Do you find yourself more in agreement with the ideas expressed by Mrs. Campison or Mrs. Samson? Why? Write your responses below.

_____

_____

_____

_____

_____

_____

Section 2 Objectives

After you have completed this section, you will be able to:
1. compare and contrast common educational terms such as *diagnosis, norm and criterion evaluation, formative and summative evaluation, assessment,* and *grading*
2. list common assessment procedures on a continuum from "most controlled" to "most natural"
3. explain the importance of validity when conducting an educational evaluation
4. define alternative evaluation approaches such as mastery learning and contracting

EDUCATIONAL EVALUATION

What do we mean by educational evaluation? *Educational evaluation* is a systematic process that leads to a judgment about the worth or merit exhibited by a person or persons, or by an instructional program.[4] Educational evaluation is considered systematic because it is planned, organized, and completed periodically and its judgments are subject to revision or redress through established review procedures. Compare this systematic process to the evaluations we make in everyday life. How often we decide whether something is attractive or unattractive, fair or unfair, good or bad! Normally, we are not called upon to defend our evaluative decisions. However, in our role as teachers, the evaluations we make will be fair game for public scrutiny.

Often an educational evaluation entails judgments about both the learner and the instructional program that produced the learning. The conversation between Mrs. Campison and Mrs. Samson involved the evaluation of a student's performance. However, the parent implied that the teacher's instructional approach was a factor affecting the student's performance. Parents have the right to demand that when we make educational evaluations, we can defend them with appropriate reasoning and evidence using language that a noneducator will understand.

Educational evaluations can be made at any time for a variety of purposes. Two of these purposes are labeled *formative* and *summative*. *Formative evaluation* provides information for improvement while the person or program has the time and/or opportunity to improve. Thus formative evaluation helps a teacher make better decisions about student performance and instructional success. Examples of evaluation procedures used for formative evaluation of learners are pre-tests and self-tests, quizzes, drafts of assignments that are reviewed and returned for revision, practice exercises, and so forth. Examples of formative evaluation of instruction include exercises to check for understanding, and short questionnaires in which students are asked to identify what objectives they have achieved and what objectives remain to be learned.

Summative evaluation is used to make educational decisions about persons and/or programs after instruction terminates. Examples of procedures used for summative evaluation of learners include unit tests, final exams, term papers, student teaching evaluations, report cards, decisions to retain or promote a student, and the like. Examples of summative evaluation of instruction are student evaluations of courses and teachers, formal evaluations of teachers by supervisors, tenure reviews, and other procedures. Remember that it is the purpose of the evaluation that determines whether it is formative or summative. In reality, a given evaluation procedure may serve both purposes. Think for a moment about a unit test that is designed as a summative evaluation of students' performance after the completion of one unit and also serves a formative purpose to guide students toward improved performance in the next unit.

If educational evaluation is a decision about worth or merit, how do we define terms such as *assessment* and *grading*? We shall examine the issue of assessment first. *Assessment* is the process of measuring the quantity and/or quality of a behavior or the indicator of that behavior.

---

[4]An instructional program may be as large as the program offered by an entire school district or as small as an element in a lesson plan, such as a learning activity.

It is the foundation information upon which an educational evaluation decision is based. When we assess, we determine what students know about some content and/or their level of skill in performing some task. We might also assess students' motivation to engage in further study of that content. Assessments can be placed on a continuum between *controlled* and *natural*. A *highly controlled assessment* suggests the use of a special testing environment—chairs arranged to discourage copying from neighbors, no books or papers on desks, the requirement that the test be completed within a given time period, and so on. In a controlled assessment, the learners are always aware they are being assessed. The most common form of controlled assessment is a standardized or teacher-made paper and pencil test, typically administered in the classroom. Nevertheless, there are other kinds of controlled assessments that a wise teacher should include in his or her repertoire. For example, the observation of student product or presentation offers a somewhat different view of student skill or achievement than does a paper and pencil test.

Written homework assignments, interviews, questionnaires and checklists, observations and examination of existing records are types of less controlled assessments. Finally, at the far end of the spectrum are *natural assessment* procedures. Natural assessment requires no artificially constructed testing environment, and the learners are not aware that they are being assessed—for instance, the teacher might observe play during recess, check the kind and number of library books students choose, and so on. A continuum of assessment procedures from "most controlled" to "most natural" is shown in Figure 3.1.

DIAGNOSING LEARNERS

For an example of learner diagnosis, let us return to Mrs. Samson's fifth-grade classroom. Imagine that she has decided to develop an instructional unit in science on the topic "Mammals." She has outlined the objectives and activities she will teach in the unit. At this point she should think about two kinds of assessment—*pre-assessment* (diagnosis) and *post-assessment*. When educators pre-assess student performance, *prior to instruction*, it is to diagnose a student's *entry level*. Specifically, the teacher determines what the student knows or is able to do before instruction begins or whether the student has any emotional reactions to the content—that is, whether the student's feelings are positive, neutral, or negative. When we assess student performance *after instruction*, the concern shifts to determine what students have learned as a result of instruction.

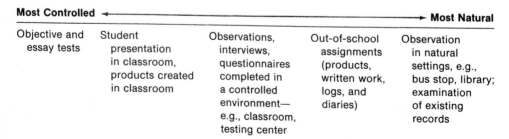

Most Controlled ←――――――――――――――――――――――――――――――→ **Most Natural**

Objective and essay tests	Student presentation in classroom, products created in classroom	Observations, interviews, questionnaires completed in a controlled environment— e.g., classroom, testing center	Out-of-school assignments (products, written work, logs, and diaries)	Observation in natural settings, e.g., bus stop, library; examination of existing records

Figure 3.1. Assessment Continuum: Most Controlled to Most Natural

CHECK FOR UNDERSTANDING

If you were Mrs. Samson, what would you wish to know about the fifth-grade students' entry level competence before you develop the instructional unit "Mammals"? Write your response below.

_____

_____

_____

_____

_____

There are two related issues involved in the diagnosis of students' entry level competence through pre-testing—what methods to use to gather the information and what content and skills to assess. Let's examine the methodology of pre-testing. Pre-testing can be accomplished through both *formal* and *informal* methods. An example of a *formal method* would be a written test, similar in style, length, and degree of difficulty to the post-test that you will administer when the lesson or unit instruction has ended. An example of an *informal method* would be for students to write down three animals that they believe are mammals and to explain why they are mammals. Formal methods take more time to develop and administer but yield more precise information about student entry level competence. However, as a general rule, you will want to use an informal method, spending as little classroom time as necessary to secure the necessary information.

In regard to the content of a pre-test, think of it in two different ways. First, consider some general knowledge and skills issues. What knowledge and skills do students need to be successful in achieving the objectives in this unit? (see Chapter 2). Do students have the necessary background knowledge to read successfully the written material about mammals that you have gathered? Can they comprehend the words and sentences? Can they identify the main idea in each of the reading selections? Can they distinguish the essential core of the reading from the detail that surrounds it?

Second, pre-testing is done in a unit-specific way to explore the particular content. You might pre-test by asking students if they can identify examples of mammals when given pictures or names of a variety of animals, some being mammals and others nonmammals. You might ask students to list the characteristics that make an animal a mammal. You might ask for students to list the names of animal groups other than mammals.

A task analysis and/or a learning hierarchy, both discussed in Chapter 2, is a helpful foundation for unit-specific pre-testing. After completing your task analysis, you would know that mammals are vertebrate animals and that they share five critical attributes.

MAMMALS

All mammals:

1. nurse their offspring during the early stages of life
2. give their young protection and training to survive and to grow strong
3. have hair at some time in their life cycle
4. are warm-blooded (their body temperature must remain within a specified range, regardless of external conditions)
5. have a more highly developed brain than other animals

As a result of your task analysis, you would have listed a variety of mammals in your notes from which to draw and compare examples. Your list includes various orders of mammals, among them primates, marsupials, carnivores, and rodents. In addition, you are prepared to explore some interesting and unusual facts about mammals. For instance, the largest mammal that ever lived is the blue whale, which measures up to 100 feet. A bat from Thailand, the Kitti, is the smallest mammal, about the size of a bumblebee. Bats are the only mammals that fly. Most mammals are herbivorous—that is, they eat plants; some mammals are carnivorous; they eat the flesh of other animals.

Your unit-specific pre-testing will determine if the students' prior knowledge is sufficient to begin the unit at the entry level you had expected. With a typical group of fifth graders, you can expect that a few students will need some review material to study before beginning the unit. You may also discover through the pre-test that some students have already learned what you planned to teach. As you have anticipated this, you will have planned independent projects for these students. In any event, the responses you receive from students on a pre-test can be used to determine the complexity of the content to be taught in the unit, the nature of the set activity you will use to initiate study of the unit, and other planned activities.

Now let's return to the terms *assessment, evaluation,* and *grading.* Mrs. Samson uses a pre-test as an *assessment* in order to *evaluate* how well students are prepared to study the proposed unit on mammals. Using the pre-test helps to customize the unit to meet the particular needs of the students in the class. When the assessment results have been gathered and examined, the teacher makes a judgment (*evaluation*) of the worth or merit of the results. In the case of the pre-test prior to the mammal unit, Mrs. Samson has to judge whether students are ready to proceed to study her proposed unit as tentatively planned, or whether adjustments need to be made.

Finally, at the end of the unit, she will assess and evaluate the students on what they have learned and will assign a *grade* to communicate her judgment to the student, to parents, to other educators, and to interested and appropriate others. Bear in mind that a grade is a label that our society uses to represent value earned. It is a kind of certificate that communicates earned achievement to educators, employers, and the general public. If they are to be useful to society, grades have to be sufficiently accurate so that they can predict future performance. Thus a student who receives nothing but A's in elementary school mathematics should expect to receive similar grades in junior high.

No doubt you are aware of the intense debate about the relative worth and/or utility of the grading process. The decision whether to assign grades, the process used to determine the value represented by the grades, and the particular symbols used as grades are political decisions as much as educational decisions. In most school settings, these decisions are only partially under the control of the teacher. Remember that the value of a grade as an indicator is only as good as the evaluation decisions upon which the grade is based. If grades are not given, the teacher must evaluate student performance and communicate the judgments about that performance in some other form.

VALIDITY

The grading controversy illustrates the most important criterion on which the field of educational evaluation rests—validity. *Educational validity* can be defined as the property of an assessment that makes it an accurate measure of what it purports to measure. Although there are several kinds of validity of interest to the classroom teacher, only *content validity* is directly under his or her control and responsibility. Content validity is best described by the following teaching prescription

> Tell them what they will learn, teach them what you told them, and test them on what you taught.

However, achieving a high level of content validity is more complex than the simple prescription suggests. Fortunately, your analysis of the content you will teach and the use of clearly stated objectives are the foundations on which valid tests are developed.

There are two dimensions of content validity. First, *a valid assessment is one that provides an adequate coverage of the content taught in the unit.* In the case of the "Mammal" unit, adequate assessment must include questions on lower and higher order mammals, on the critical characteristics of mammals compared to other animals, and on other specific information taught in the unit. If some aspect of the content is missing from the assessment, students can rightfully argue that too much emphasis was placed on some portion of the unit and too little on other portions. Another common violation of validity occurs when students are assessed on skills or knowledge that was not taught in class but instead had been acquired previously—material learned in earlier courses or through students' personal experiences. For example, consider the injustice that is created when a social studies teacher permits a student to submit a unit project on colonial America that was the result of last summer's family excursion through the original thirteen colonies. Obviously, one family provided a child with opportunities for cultural enrichment that were far beyond the capacity of other families. Thus, while we do not wish to belittle the value of the excursion (wouldn't we all have enjoyed the trip?), we believe that to give substantial credit to the student for a project based on an outside experience compounds the effects of economic and class inequity.

The second dimension extends the issue of educational validity into learning process. *It is necessary not only to "test on what you taught" but to test at the appropriate level of learning.* Thus the match between objectives, activities, and evaluation procedures includes the requirement that objectives written at any given learning level, such as concept level, be matched with activities and evaluation procedures at the same level. We all are familiar with instructors in elementary and secondary school and in college who promise lofty aims such as "enhancing thinking skills," "learning to make informed judgments," and "exploring ways to solve problems" and then test for the recall of bits and pieces of information.

SHARING RESPONSIBILITY FOR EVALUATION

Until now, we have implied that the teacher has worked alone to design, administer, interpret, and evaluate student learning. There is an alternative approach, one that transfers some evaluation responsibility to the learners. Such an evaluation process is more natural and less

controlled. For example, student pairs can test and assess each other's spelling or math work and record the scores they achieved. As they enhance their sense of responsibility, the students can be expected to grow more self-reliant.

Some teachers have been successful in creating a natural atmosphere for evaluation that emphasizes both peer evaluation and self-evaluation. They use self-reports, logs, and journals, small group and class meetings as assessment procedures. Often these teachers permit students to evaluate themselves, other students, the instructional program, and the teacher. Unfortunately, the more natural the evaluation, the less control the teacher has over the environment. For such evaluation to work, teachers must provide clear sets of directions and rules and must be specific about the consequences of violating the rules. Natural evaluation procedures that transfer responsibility from the teacher to the students are successful only in those classrooms in which a high level of trust, encouragement, and community spirit exists.

EVALUATION AND GRADING

Another alternative evaluation approach derives from a different way of viewing students in the classroom and develops further the concept of grading. A classroom of youngsters is typically viewed as a group of 20–35 students. Our backgrounds as students prepare us to think of a classroom as a group. After all, we have competed against our classmates for grades, awards, scholarships, and admission to college. In college we may have become accustomed to see the instructor put a grade distribution on the chalkboard showing how many students received A, B, C, D, F. Often the instructor explains how the grade distribution was developed—how many correct answers were required in order to receive which grades and what curve the instructor developed to ground and defend the evaluation. Although the concept of "normal distribution" may remain mysterious, we know that the instructor arranged all the grades in a row and then established cutoff scores between grades—for instance, 92–100=A, 85–91=B, and so on.

This view of evaluation is referred to as *norm-referenced*. That is, the evaluator examines all the scores and determines where each individual's score fits within the distribution. The average score and other scores that deviate from the average as computed through a statistical procedure become critical determinants of an individual's grade. Scores that deviate well above the average get A's and B's; scores that deviate well below the average get D's and F's. Scores that cluster around the average get C's.

One major disadvantage of norm-referenced evaluation is that, as student performance increases, the teacher is likely to raise the curve to retain a similar proportion of A's, B's, and C's. Thus students experience the phenomenon of working harder or better without seeing any grade change. A second major disadvantage is that the value of the grade is difficult to interpret from one group to the next. Since the grade is determined by the performance of students in a particular group, a grade in social studies in one fifth grade classroom, taught by teacher A, may represent much more or much less educational value than an identical grade in a fifth grade classroom taught by teacher B. Consequently, well-known testing programs such as the National Assessment of Educational Progress (NAEP), Scholastic Aptitude Test (SAT), and American College Testing (ACT) programs compare an individual's score against standards determined through the analysis of scores from a national sample group.

The alternative view of evaluation considers each student as an individual, and the

individual's performance is assessed against predetermined performance standards or criteria, known in the evaluation literature as *criterion-referenced*. An assessment that is criterion-referenced enables the teacher to determine with confidence whether a child's response reaches a predetermined standard. Using standards as the definition of success rather than child-to-child comparison makes it theoretically possible for all students to be successful and receive A's.

One example of a teaching/learning model based on criterion-referenced evaluation is called *contract learning*. In such a model, the standards for receiving a given grade are described to all students. Each student contracts with the teacher to perform certain tasks at a given quality level in order to receive the agreed-on grade. Objectives and activities are identified, requirements determined, and deadlines established. Contract learning has the advantage of permitting a student to concentrate on certain subject areas or units within a subject and not on others. It also helps prevent the teacher from labeling students, for instance, as A or C students, since students can choose the grade they will seek to achieve.

A second example of a criterion-referenced evaluation is known as *mastery learning* (Carroll, 1963; Bloom, 1984; Guskey & Gates, 1984). It is an individualized instruction approach for use in a structured, Ant-style instructional program. It is based on the belief that all students can be successful in achieving all objectives if additional learning time is allowed for those who may need it. Mastery learning, if it is to be successful, requires that teachers use clearly stated objectives, including all elements (A, B, C, D statements), employ pre-assessment and other kinds of formative evaluation procedures, and use alternative strategies and learning activities. Finally, they must be prepared to reteach lessons when necessary, using alternative methods and materials. Advocates claim that if these assumptions are met and if a sufficient time for learning is provided, all students can "master" all objectives. Theoretically, they claim, the only distinctions among students would be in the time required to achieve mastery. The quality of the work produced would be similar.

CHAPTER SUMMARY

This chapter began with the parable "The Sea Horse Fable," which illustrates how important it is for teachers and students to know where the educational program is headed. The parable served as an introduction to the first section of the chapter, focusing on the rationale for and the skills needed to write clearly stated instructional objectives. Well-written objectives contain three elements—*audience, behavior*, and *degree* statements—and may also include a *conditions* statement.

The second section of the chapter focused on educational evaluation. The section began with a confrontation between a teacher and a parent over a child's academic performance. The confrontation brought to the surface the complex and difficult issues involved in assessing and judging academic learning. Often evaluation problems occur because the evaluator has made a validity error, either (1) testing what was not taught or failing to test adequately what was taught; or (2) testing at a different level of learning from what the student had practiced. Finally, there are alternative approaches to educational evaluation based on premises other than competition among learners. Whatever the evaluative method used, thoughtful educational evaluation will enable the teacher to make wise judgments about the performance of students and about the quality of the educational program.

Independent Practice Activity C. Reviewing Your Educational Evaluation Philosophy

In the beginning of this section of Chapter 3, you read about a confrontation between a teacher, Mrs. Samson, and a parent, Mrs. Campison, involving the grade her daughter, Loretta, received in social studies. Given what you have learned in this chapter, how would you have responded to the parent's concerns if you were Mrs. Samson? Write your answer below.

_____

_____

_____

_____

_____

Independent Practice Activity D. Classifying Clearly Stated Objectives

In the following exercise you are to classify examples of clearly stated objectives and to rewrite incomplete objectives to make them clearly stated. In addition, you are to identify examples of *audience, behavior, condition*, and *degree* statements.

1. Place *x* next to each objective that has a *behavior* statement. (Disregard whether the objective also has *audience, conditions*, and/or *degree* statements.)
2. Rewrite objectives that are incomplete by adding a *behavior* statement. Do your work in the space below each incomplete example.
3. Where you find a clearly stated objective, label the *audience, behavior, conditions*, and *degree* statements by writing *A, B, C*, or *D* above the appropriate sections.

_____   1. The student will learn the important generalizations about the concept *fiction.*

_____   2. Students will be able to express themselves creatively.

_____   3. Given 10 fractions, sixth grade students will be able to express each in decimal form with 80 percent accuracy.

_____   4. Given several unfamiliar statements made by political leaders, 10th grade Honors Humanities students will classify those that reflect ideas expressed by Thomas Paine in *Common Sense.*

_____ 5. Students will be able to define, in writing, the following trigonometric functions: *sine, cosine*, and *tangent*.

_____ 6. Each student will be able to appreciate the need for safety in the operation of hand tools.

_____ 7. The student will be able to recognize the unique qualities of the visual arts.

_____ 8. Students will demonstrate their capability to use the "lay-up" by scoring four out of six baskets in the gym while showing proper technique.

_____ 9. Eleventh grade American history students will defend or reject the thesis that "the conquistadores were nothing more than cruel and greedy pirates" by writing a five-page essay on the topic. All papers must be typed and double-spaced. The essay will be judged on factual accuracy, organization, and the quality of five references used in the essay.

_____ 10. Each student will be familiar with the major parts of the plant.

Independent Practice Activity E. Culminating Exercise ("Cipher in the Snow")

Assume you are considering the article "Cipher in the Snow," which concludes this chapter, as a reading in your seventh grade classroom.

1. What entry level pre-assessment questions would you ask in order to be confident that the article was appropriate for your students? In your answer consider both general and content-specific concerns.

_____

_____

_____

_____

_____

2. In respect to the concept of "background knowledge" as expressed by Hirsch in *Cultural Literacy: What Americans Need to Know* (see Chapter 2), what concepts and facts would someone have to know that might affect comprehension of the article? Are there any that you might need to assess prior to discussion of the article?

_____

_____

_____

_____

_____

3. Assume your lesson objective is for students to explain in a one-to-three-page, double-spaced essay what they would do if they were the teacher in the story to prevent a repeat of the tragedy depicted in "Cipher in the Snow."
   a. Write three objective test questions that assess student achievement of the objective. Write each at a different level of learning process (for instance, memorization, concept learning, or principle learning).

Item 1. _____

_____

_____

Item 2. _____

_____

_____

Item 3. _____

_____

_____

   b. Write one essay test question that assesses student achievement of the objective. Write it at the principle learning level.

_____

_____

_____

_____

_____

CIPHER IN THE SNOW

It started with tragedy on a biting cold February morning. I was driving behind the Milford Corners bus, as I did most snowy mornings on my way to school. It veered and stopped short at the hotel, which it had no business doing, and I was annoyed as I had to come to an unexpected stop. A boy lurched out of the bus, reeled, stumbled, and collapsed on the snowbank at the curb. The bus driver and I reached him at the same moment. His thin, hollow face was white even against the snow.

"He's dead," the driver whispered.

It didn't register for a minute. I glanced quickly at the scared young faces staring down at us from the school bus. "A doctor! Quick! I'll phone from the hotel . . ."

"No use, I tell you he's dead." The driver looked down at the boy's still form. "He never even said he felt bad," he muttered, "just tapped me on the shoulder and said real quiet, 'I'm sorry. I have to get off at the hotel.' That's all. Polite and apologizing like."

At school, the giggling, shuffling morning noise quieted as the news went down the halls. I passed a huddle of girls. "Who was it? Who dropped dead on the way to school?" I heard one of them half-whisper.

"Don't know his name, some kid from Milford Corners," was the reply.

It was like that in the faculty room and the principal's office. "I'd appreciate your going out to tell the parents," the principal told me. "They haven't a phone and, anyway, somebody from school should go there in person. I'll cover your classes."

"Why me?" I asked. "Wouldn't it be better if you did it?"

"I didn't know the boy," the principal admitted. "And in last year's sophomore personalities column I note that you were listed as his favorite teacher."

I drove through the snow and cold down the bad canyon road to the Evans place and thought about the boy, Cliff Evans. "His favorite teacher!" I thought. "He hasn't spoken two words to me in two years!" I could see him in my afternoon literature class. He came into the room by himself and left by himself. "Cliff Evans," I muttered to myself, "a boy who never talked." I thought a minute. "A boy who never smiled. I never saw him smile once."

The big ranch kitchen was clean and warm. I blurted out my news somehow. Mrs. Evans reached blindly toward a chair. "He never said anything about being ailing."

His stepfather snorted, "He ain't said nothin' about anything since I moved in here."

Mrs. Evans pushed a pan to the back of the stove and began to untie her apron. "Now hold on," her husband snapped, "I got to have breakfast before I go to town. Nothin' we can do now anyway. If Cliff hadn't been so dumb, he'd have told us he didn't feel good."

After school I sat in the office and stared bleakly at the records spread out before me. I was to close the file and write the obituary for the school paper. The almost bare sheets mocked the effort. Cliff Evans, white, never legally adopted by his stepfather, five young half-brothers and sisters. These meager strands of information and the list of D grades were all the records had to offer.

Cliff Evans had silently come in the school door in the morning and gone out the school door in the evening, and that was all. He had never belonged to a club. He had never played on a team. He had never held an office. As far as I could tell, he had never done one happy, noisy kid thing. He had never been anybody at all.

How do you go about making a boy into a zero? The grade school records showed me. The first- and second-grade teachers' comments read, "Sweet, shy child, timid but eager." Then the third-grade note had opened the attack. Some teacher had written in a good, firm hand, "Cliff won't talk. Uncooperative. Slow learner." The other academic sheep had followed with "dull"; "slow-witted"; "low I.Q." They became correct. They boy's I.Q. score in the ninth grade was listed as 83. But his I.Q. in the third grade had been 106. The score didn't go under 100 until the seventh grade. Even shy, timid, sweet children have resilience. It takes time to break them.

I stomped to the typewriter and wrote a savage report pointing out what education had done to Cliff Evans. I slapped a copy on the principal's desk and another in the sad, dog-eared file. I banged the typewriter and slammed the file and crashed the door shut, but I didn't feel much better. A little boy kept walking after me, a little boy with a peaked, pale face, a skinny body in faded jeans, and big eyes that had looked and searched for a long time and then had become veiled.

I could guess how many times he'd been chosen last to play sides in a game, how many whispered child conversations had excluded him, how many times he hadn't been asked. I could see and hear the faces and voices that said over and over, "You're dumb. You're dumb. You're a nothing, Cliff Evans."

A child is a believing creature. Cliff undoubtedly believed them. Suddenly it seemed clear to me: When finally there was nothing left at all for Cliff Evans, he collapsed on a snowbank and went away. The doctor might list "heart failure" as the cause of death, but that wouldn't change my mind.

We couldn't find ten students in the school who had known Cliff well enough to attend the funeral as his friends. So the student body officers and a committee from the junior class went as a group to the church, being politely sad. I attended the service with them and sat through it with a lump of cold lead in my chest and a big resolve growing through me.

I've never forgotten Cliff Evans or that resolve. He has been my challenge year after year, class after class. I look up and down the rows carefully each September at the unfamiliar faces. I look for veiled eyes or bodies forced down into a seat in an alien world.

"Look, kids," I say silently, "I may not do anything else for you this year, but not one of you is going to come out of here a nobody. I'll work or fight to the bitter end doing battle with society and the school board, but I won't have one of you coming out of here thinking himself into a zero."

Most of the time—not always, but most of the time—I've succeeded.

The story is true, but the names of the characters and the location have been changed.

"Cipher in the Snow" by Jean Mizer Todhunter, from *Today's Education*, November 1964. Published by the National Education Association, 1964.

REFERENCES

Bloom, B. S. (1984). The search for methods for group instruction as effective as one-to-one tutoring. *Educational Leadership, 41*(8), 4–18.

Carroll, J. (1963). A model of school learning. *Teachers College Record, 64,* 723–733.

Guskey, T. R., & Gates, S. L. (1984). Synthesis of research on the effects of mastery learning in elementary and secondary classrooms. *Educational Leadership, 43*(8), 73–80.

Mager, R. F. (1962). *Preparing Instructional Objectives.* Belmont, CA: Fearon.

Strong, W. (1975, March). A didactic (and somewhat moral) fable. *Media and Methods,* pp. 27, 28, 50–55.

Todhunter, Jean M. (1964, November). Cipher in the snow. *NEA Journal, 53*(8), 8–10.

CHAPTER 4

Principles of Selecting and Implementing Learning Activities

Chapter Overview

In Chapters 2 and 3, we analyzed content structures and wrote objectives. We used Millicent Stephens's unit "Learning to Spend and Save Money Wisely" as an example. Now assume that Millicent has completed her learning hierarchy, objectives, and diagnosis of learners, and has written an objective for her first lesson: Students will be able to identify resources in their communities and homes. Now Millicent needs to plan activities to meet this objective. She knows that a book chapter on resources is available, but she wonders if that material will hold students' interest. She needs some activities that will help students see that the awareness of resources is a daily concern. She consults other teachers, unit guides, and community facilities to find ideas for interesting real-life activities that will help her students meet the objective. Finally, Millicent chooses a variety of activities, including lecture, role playing, and field trips, to accomplish her objective.

Many times we implement activities for our students because they are in the teacher's guide, because we have used the same activity for many years, or because, as inexperienced teachers, we could not think of any other way to present the material to students. This chapter will explore principles and guidelines to help you select the most appropriate learning activities for your students. You will also find suggestions for using several "bread-and butter" teaching techniques, including lecture, discussion, questioning, and experience-building activities such as projects and field trips.

Set Activity

Assume that Millicent decided to use a textbook reading and a lecture to inform her students about resources. As she is teaching, she is getting little response from her students. They seem to be bored. Suzie is staring out the window, and three children in the back are whispering. Millicent has planned her lecture carefully and provided much detail about the locations of resources within the community. But the children seem uninterested.

What is going on here? Consider some of the factors that might be contributing to the students' lack of attention. Think about what influences your own learning. List as many factors as you can below.

_____

_____

_____

_____

_____

You may have thought of some of the following possibilities: The teacher never got the students' attention at the beginning of the lesson, she did not make the material relevant to their everyday lives, or the material was too abstract and complex for the students. Perhaps they were sleepy because it was right after lunch, or the content was presented in a disorganized and confusing way, the lecture lasted too long, no visual aids were used, students were not directly involved through interaction with the teacher or with others, the presentation lacked variety, and so on.

As you can see, there are many reasons that might explain why students are inattentive during a learning activity. If Millicent wants to redesign this activity so that it will be more effective the next time she uses it, she will need to know why it did not work very well. This chapter will present many of the factors and principles that can help you with such decisions.

As you read, you may wish to outline the information presented in this chapter. Use the outline provided for that purpose on pages 151–152.

Chapter Objectives

After you have completed this chapter, you will be able to:

1. describe the social/political/community, school, and physical factors that may influence the choice of activities
2. describe characteristics of students that may influence teaching decisions
3. describe types of content knowledge important for teaching
4. explain how the different components of memory work and the implications for teaching
5. apply principles of learning and teaching to select, implement, and evaluate learning activities
6. describe effective ways to conduct lecture, discussion, questioning, and meaning-building activities

Section 1. Factors to Consider When Selecting Activities

Recall our discussion of the factors involved in teaching decisions in Chapter 2. We considered the subject matter content, social and political factors, students' needs and interests, the teacher's philosophy, and the teacher's knowledge of learning principles and teaching techniques. We take those same factors into consideration when we are selecting learning activities to meet our instructional objectives. These factors are presented in Figure 4.1.

Notice the arrows labeled "reflection" surrounding the terms "instructional decisions" and "actions." Figure 4.1 should remind you to think carefully about your teaching decisions and the results of those decisions. Before making a decision, you will reflect on the five factors listed in the figure. After your decision leads to an action, you will observe the results and reflect on the action—what worked and what didn't. During your reflections, you will use these factors and the principles presented in the chapter to determine why particular activities were or were not successful. You can then use this information to revise your lessons as necessary.

Before we go into a discussion of each of the factors, let us clarify one of the realities of teaching that makes it a complex endeavor. There is no one learning activity that will work with all children, in all circumstances, or for all types of content and objectives. The teacher must make a conscious decision about what to do. Such decisions, based on a great deal of information, must often be made in a split second. In other situations you will have more time to reflect on the complexities of teaching and learning—for example, when you are preparing lesson plans and redesigning lessons.

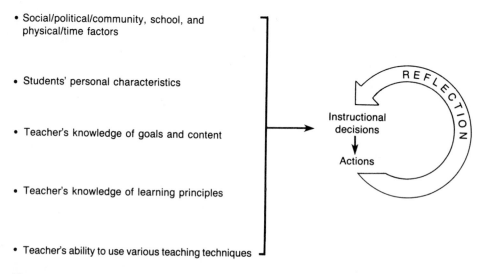

- Social/political/community, school, and physical/time factors

- Students' personal characteristics

- Teacher's knowledge of goals and content

- Teacher's knowledge of learning principles

- Teacher's ability to use various teaching techniques

Instructional decisions

Actions

REFLECTION

Figure 4.1. Factors Influencing Teaching Decisions

Thus teaching is not merely a set of behaviors and skills that you learn to perform. While good technique is important, an even more important factor is to know *when to use* the techniques and skills we have acquired. The better the choices we make, the better will be our students' learning and enjoyment.

SOCIAL/POLITICAL/COMMUNITY, SCHOOL, AND PHYSICAL/TIME FACTORS

Most teachers work for a school system that is governed by a school board, a group of elected citizens or appointed officials. Members of the board reflect the attitudes, values, and philosophy of the community served by the schools. Thus board members exercise an important influence on school programs, policies, regulations, and curriculum. While the school board members rarely spend large amounts of time examining the actual teaching activities used, they do have a vested interest in what happens in classrooms. As representatives of the community, they want to be sure that students are learning appropriate skills and attitudes.

Imagine yourself teaching in an ethnically diverse community that has experienced conflict between the Hispanic and Anglo cultures. The school board has expressed concern over this conflict and has made "conflict resolution" a goal for the year. You, as a teacher, would then strive to select classroom activities that would enable students to deal with conflict and learn how to resolve it. When deciding how to teach about natural resources, for instance, you might select a learning activity in which teams of students work together to solve a problem. You would teach, model, and give feedback on the social skills needed for students to work constructively together. This type of activity would more likely meet the district goal than would a straight lecture that offers little opportunity for interaction or conflict resolution.

Sometimes you will find yourself selecting activities based on school factors. One such factor might be schoolwide goals. Such goals, which are often developed through discussions with school staff, will influence what you choose to do in your classroom. For example, a school planning team might set a goal to improve students' reading scores. You would then emphasize reading, especially the kinds of tasks given on the reading tests. Or the team might plan to work on students' self-esteem. Your response might be to give more specific positive feedback to students as they show progress in their work, or you might set up a weekly game that many of the lower achieving students could play successfully.

Other school factors that may influence the choice of activities include the size of the school, the grade levels served, and the physical facility. Some schools are designed for open-space learning, reflecting a progressive orientation. In such schools, classes can be easily combined for joint activities, offering greater flexibility for team teaching and sharing of resources.

Time factors can also influence your choice of activities. We mentioned earlier that the time of day might explain why Millicent's students were so bored. Often students come in from recess or lunch "high as kites," only to become drowsy a few minutes later. Some teachers attribute the low energy to sugar in the foods eaten at lunch. As a teacher, you should anticipate an energy ebb and plan an activity that is especially active and novel to keep students' attention.

Finally, many unanticipated classroom events will require an on-the-spot decision to change an activity. An example would be a fire drill, student illness, or the arrival of a new student. One of the authors was teaching a first-grade math lesson one day when a cat walked in through the window. Of course, the students' minds were no longer on math. So she took advantage of this teachable moment and turned to a prior objective in creative writing, by listing descriptive words about cats and having the class create a variety of cat poems and stories.

CHECK FOR UNDERSTANDING

Think of other examples of the three types of factors that may influence the choice of classroom activities: *social/political/community, school,* and *physical/time.* Write them below and compare them with a partner's list.

Social/Political/Community Factors   **School Factors**   **Physical/Time Factors**

_____

_____

_____

_____

_____

_____

STUDENTS' PERSONAL CHARACTERISTICS

All instructional decisions involve students. The most carefully conceived objectives or well-designed lessons have meaning only when they affect particular students. Just as you considered your students' needs when planning goals and objectives in Chapters 2 and 3, you should think carefully about your students when choosing learning activities. You will have to consider the ways the students' strengths, weaknesses, needs, desires, and interests will affect the teaching and learning process. The more you know about the individual differences among your students, the more effectively you can adapt instruction to your particular class and to each new group of students you encounter throughout your teaching career.

Intellectual Abilities

Students differ in many ways. In every class you will find a range of general and specific intellectual abilities. Traditionally, general intellectual ability has been measured by IQ, scores derived from a test originally developed to predict success in school. While IQ tests frequently provide information on the ease with which individuals approach school tasks, they have been called into question as measures of total intellectual potential. Since the early 20th century, psychologists have debated the importance of general intelligence versus sets of specific academic abilities. Are individuals generally either "smart" or "less smart" or do they differ in more complex ways? Might a person be intelligent in math and less intelligent in language? What kinds of important intellectual abilities might not be measured by paper and pencil tests, or a test given in one day? In addition, cultural and language differences have a significant impact on test performance. Students who have been exposed to key test vocabulary words clearly have an advantage over those who have not or those for whom the English language is unfamiliar. Students who have played with blocks before are likely to be more comfortable in a testing task involving blocks than those for whom manipulating blocks is a new experience. Are those students less "smart" than students whose previous experiences have enabled them to be more successful test takers? We think not.

While the roles of general and specific ability or the validity of test scores will continue to be debated, from a practical standpoint several things are clear. Some students learn quickly and easily—they can solve problems, think abstractly, and remember information more readily than others. It is important to provide appropriate instruction for such students, challenging their abilities with a depth and pace of instruction beyond those that other students can absorb. Other students need more assistance in learning, extended opportunities for practice, and a careful linking of new and prior experience. Still other students demonstrate strengths in specific areas but weaknesses in others. If a student shows advanced ability in language but difficulty in math, it is important to investigate such patterns and to vary instruction to meet them.

Finally, we must be cautious about interpreting any test that attempts to assess intellectual ability. While a thorough examination of testing issues is beyond the scope of this text, we can remind you that any score represents performance on a particular day. Such a score may be influenced by factors as diverse as illness on the day of the test, familiarity with the language of the test, and prior experience with the vocabulary and materials of testing. In providing instruction that is appropriate to student needs and abilities, we must take into account not just IQ and standardized test information but also observations of performance under a wide range of circumstances.

Prior Knowledge and Experience

Students' prior experiences at home, at school, and in the community affect not just test scores but students' responses and performance in many areas. Cognitive psychology has informed us that learning is not a passive event, like filling a cup, but an active process in which each individual builds knowledge, linking new bits of information or experience to internal "circuits" called *schemata*. You might think of the knowledge and skills in your objectives as pieces of a Tinker Toy set. You may pass out the pieces, but students have to fit them into their own structures, and each structure is different.

In what ways might students' prior experiences affect their learning? If, for example, students have never seen a cow or a picture of a cow, they will probably have difficulty understanding lessons on Jack and the Beanstalk (remember that Jack traded the cow for a handful of beans?), dairy farming, or mammals. Students who have never traveled outside their home town have fewer schemata available to provide the basis for a discussion on variation in climates. Students who have not experienced segregation or seen or heard about its effects are less prepared for meaningful learning regarding civil rights than those whose experiences provide ties to the subject. It is important to assess your students' familiarity with major concepts that underly your instruction. For example, you might begin a lesson on sea life by having students brainstorm all the plants and animals they have seen living in water.

Some students' prior experiences, either at home or in school, have not provided them with the expected prerequisite skills for their grade level. Effective instructional planning must include careful diagnosis of prior knowledge, experience, and skills related to your topic. Your learning hierarchy and task analysis can provide a framework for identifying needed skills.

If some students lack important knowledge and skills, you must decide whether *remediation* or *compensation* would be more appropriate. A *remedial* approach entails teaching prerequisite knowledge and skills before proceeding with planned instruction. For example, before teaching a unit on long division, Ms. Brown identified several students unable to multiply one-place numbers. Based on this finding, she divided the class into two groups and allowed one group to concentrate on multiplication before she introduced long division. Since understanding long division would be impossible without knowing multiplication, she believed that instruction in multiplication was necessary before the group could be successful in long division. If the necessary knowledge and skills can be attained in a reasonable length of time, remediation is the logical approach.

Sometimes, however, remediation is not possible or would represent an unreasonable use of class time. In such cases, a teacher may choose compensatory instruction instead. *Compensation* involves choosing an instructional approach that circumvents areas of weakness. In remediation, we fill in the "potholes" before proceeding down the road; in a compensatory approach, we drive around them. If, for example, Mr. Fidler was teaching an urban class with little experience outside the city, he might choose to alter a lesson on the characteristics of mammals to focus on squirrels, dogs, and cats, rather than the farm animals emphasized in the text. This would allow him to proceed with the content (mammals) without spending time elaborately developing the concept *farm animals*. (He may, of course, choose to teach about farm animals at another time.) If a student was strong in math but had weak reading skills, the teacher might provide reading assistance to the student in interpreting a math story problem rather than delaying instruction in problem solving until the student's reading skills could be remediated. In each case, a compensatory approach would allow meaningful instruction to take place, despite weaknesses in prerequisite experiences or skills.

In addition to experiences, knowledge, and skills, students bring attitudes, values, and social patterns that have been shaped by prior experiences. Some students come from homes in which school success is highly valued. In other home environments students may be encouraged to value "street smarts," athletic success, or social status. Some families reward problem solving or independent thinking, while some emphasize conformity and the memorization of facts. Some homes are language-rich and encourage a variety of expression, while other homes prefer children to be seen and not heard.

Children who come from homes that support the types of learning emphasized in school have intellectual and emotional advantages. It is our responsibility as teachers to model both skills and attitudes that will support all children in their learning. High expectations for all children, rewards for varied accomplishments, ties to personal experiences, and family involvement all set a classroom tone that balances recognition of the variety of values students bring to school with the encouragement of attitudes likely to promote achievement. Careful observation and attention to student and parent comments can help you identify students who need extra support in balancing values from home and school. Such observations can also make you aware of areas of student interests, allowing you to tap those interests through lesson planning or in suggestions for individual activities.

CHECK FOR UNDERSTANDING

List at least four ways in which students in a fourth-grade class might differ from one another. How might each of these differences affect Millicent Stephens's unit "Learning to Spend and

Save Money Wisely"? _____

_____

_____

_____

_____

_____

_____

Learning Styles

In addition to intellectual strengths and weaknesses, students vary in the ways they learn best. The way a student learns can be defined as his or her *learning style*. Hunt (1979) has said that learning style "describes a student in terms of those educational conditions under which he is most likely to learn. Learning style describes *how* a student learns, not *what* he has learned" (p. 27).

There are many theories of learning styles, but one principle underlies them all: Individuals do not all learn best in the same way. Circumstances or methods that may promote learning for one individual may not be helpful for others. Some learning styles are not better or stronger than others, merely different. As teachers, it is important to recognize that students not only learn in different ways but may learn in different ways from the way *we* do. An approach may seem logical to a teacher and work well for some students—the students whose styles are similar to that of the teacher—and not be effective for other, equally intelligent students whose styles are different.

Perhaps the simplest variation in learning styles may be found along sensory channels. Some individuals learn best through visual information; they process information best if it comes to them through their eyes. Others learn best auditorily, processing information most efficiently if it comes to them through their ears. Still others benefit most from information presented kinesthetically, involving the sense of touch or whole body movement. These differences do not reflect the relative acuity of eyes, ears, or other senses. While a student with poor eyesight would certainly have trouble with information presented only visually, it is possible to have 20/20 eyesight and still not process visual information well. The connection between the eyes and the brain may simply not function as well as that between the ears and the brain. For example, a student who is a strong auditory learner may best experience the story of the first Thanksgiving by listening to the teacher tell the story. A strong visual learner would absorb the lesson most successfully if the story were accompanied by pictures or text, and a kinesthetic learner would benefit from opportunities to role-play a dramatization of the holiday (Barbe & Swassing, 1979).

Gregorc (1982) developed a theory of learning styles that was not derived from the functioning of the individual senses but from the ways individuals organize and process information from all the senses. The theory is based on two dimensions, *perception* and *organization*. *Perception* refers to the means by which an individual takes in information. While most people have the ability to perceive both concrete information (accessible to the

A concrete sequential person

An abstract sequential person

senses) and abstract information (ideas, feelings), some people grasp information best when it is presented concretely, while others are most comfortable taking in and manipulating information in abstract form.

Individuals also vary in the ways they *organize* information. Some individuals organize information best in a sequential, or linear, way, with each bit of information leading to the next in a straight-line manner. Others are more comfortable with an organization Gregorc calls *random*, a nonlinear, holistic approach characterized by leaps of logic and the processing of several bits of information simultaneously.

Gregorc combines the perceptual and organizational abilities into four learning styles associated with particular behaviors and characteristics. Each style has a unique and organized view of the world and operates from a particular point of view. While no individual operates in only one style, many people have strong preferences for one or more channels. Such preferences can be identified through a learning styles inventory, or more informal observations of behavior, language, and habits.

A *concrete sequential (CS)* individual prefers concrete information processed in a sequential manner. Such an individual might be characterized as practical, structured, down-to-earth, and organized. A CS adult balances the checkbook carefully, organizes closets, and rarely forgets an appointment. A CS teacher is a natural at keeping complete records, arranging classroom materials, and developing logical units of study. A CS child learns best when information is presented in a systematic fashion, with practical applications and hands-on activity.

A person with a dominant *abstract sequential (AS)* channel prefers learning abstract information and organizing it sequentially. Such a person may be seen as studious and intellectual. An AS adult is happiest when searching for new knowledge, analyzing problems, or evaluating issues through logic and reason. He or she may not be concerned with such concrete issues as whether the two socks match or what the outdoor temperature is. An AS teacher may present brilliant lectures or carefully structured research projects, while an AS child may debate logically, analyze literature critically, and forget her lunch.

An *abstract random (AR)* individual prefers abstract information, but processes it in a holistic, nonlinear fashion. This person may be seen as sensitive, emotional, and artistic. An AR individual may write poetry, counsel friends, and be an expert at relationships, whether between individuals or academic disciplines. He may have moments of personal or professional insight without being able to explain them. An AR teacher loves interdisciplinary teaching, thematic units, and a classroom full of art (including on the ceilings). An AR student may be the life of the class, have an eye for beauty, and possess a wonderful imagination but have little idea how to transfer his or her ideas into concrete reality.

Finally, a *concrete random (CR)* individual processes concrete information in nonlinear ways. CR individuals are natural problem solvers, explorers, and inventors. CR individuals love to tinker with gadgets, appliances, or ideas. Their garages and cupboards may overflow with spare parts and unusual tools for future experimentation. As teachers, they have

An abstract random at studio

CONCRETE RANDOM

classrooms full of experiments and emphasize creative problem solving and independence. CR students flourish in such an atmosphere, often finding solutions to problems through intuitive leaps they cannot explain. Like AR learners, CR students have trouble when asked to show their work (Butler, 1986; Gregorc, 1982).

In this brief overview, you may have caught a glimpse of yourself or someone you know. In examining how these characteristics might affect teaching and learning, let us consider several questions. What would happen to a child with a strong AR preference in a CS teacher's classroom, or vice versa? In either case, the mismatch between teaching style and learning style could create difficulties for both student and teacher. Neither style is "right," but the two styles are different.

Does this mean we should try to match teachers' and students' styles in assigning classrooms? Probably not. Aside from the logistical difficulties of such a proposal, we do students a disservice if we allow them to function in only their preferred mode. As adults, we need to flex our styles for given situations, taking on preferred or less preferred styles as needed. (For example, in filling out income tax forms, it is highly desirable to function in a CS manner—or hire a CS accountant!) However, we can make sure that at least some of our activities for each topic or unit allow students to function in preferred ways. We can also provide special support to students when assigning work outside their preferred styles.

Dunn & Dunn (1975) have described learning styles as "the manner in which 18 different elements of four basic stimuli affect a person's ability to absorb and to retain information, values, facts or concepts" (p. 74). The four types of stimuli are environmental, emotional, sociological, and physical. For example, under environmental stimuli, students may prefer bright or dim places, warm or cool places, a specific noise level, or a particular physical arrangement. Emotional stimuli include variation in motivation, persistence, responsibility, and amount of structure preferred. Sociological variables include preferences for working individually, in pairs, teams, or groups, whereas physical variables include perceptual (sensory modalities) differences, and preferences for food and time of day. While we cannot examine each scale individually, the fact that students vary in their responses to such a large number of variables provides additional evidence for the number of individual differences found in each classroom.

CHECK FOR UNDERSTANDING

Imagine you are teaching a unit on plants. List five activities that would appeal to varying learning styles. You may use any of the learning-style frameworks presented. Label each with the learning style(s) to which it would appeal—for example, "Drawing a leaf—visual." Write your answers below.

1. _____

2. _____

3. _____

4. _____

5. _____

TEACHER'S KNOWLEDGE OF GOALS AND CONTENT

Recall our discussion of the structure of content in Chapter 2. It is important that we think about the material to be taught as more than a collection of random facts. We should go back through the material and mine it for its essential concepts and generalizations. A useful question to ask ourselves is: "If my students were using this information in real life, what facts, concepts, and generalizations would they need to know? How would I expect them to use this information in everyday life?"

Your work in preparing a content outline, learning hierarchy, and unit objectives will help you immensely here. As you come to understand more fully the structure of the content and your objectives for student learning, you can visualize the activities that may help students learn it best.

Take science as an example. You want students to be able to recognize a given weather pattern and predict the weather for the next few days. You have organized your content and decided on the topics and the level of detail for each topic. In your learning hierarchy, you have identified the facts, concepts (e.g., pressure), and generalizations (e.g., direction of air in low- and high-pressure zones). You have broken the content into clearly stated instructional objectives and diagnosed students' readiness and prior knowledge.

Now you have to select the activities that will best help your students meet the objectives. If there are many important facts and examples, you may decide to use readings, peer teaching, or lecture. If there are fewer details but more generalizations you want to stress, then you might try experiential and discovery activities.

This brings us to an important point: Not all goals and objectives are best taught by means of the same activities. Some activities work better for some objectives than for others. You will want to take into consideration the level of thinking, the learning domain and level, and content difficulty.

One important aspect of an objective is the level of learning required. If you want students to be able to recite multiplication tables (memorization), then one set of activities may be appropriate—for example, drill with flash cards, use of manipulative materials such as rods or blocks, group oral games, and so on. However, if your objective is that students be able to solve word problems involving multiplication, then your activities might include small-group problem solving—for instance, you might demonstrate the thinking strategies by explaining as you solve a problem on the board—or an inquiry task in which students discover that the area of a rectangle can be determined by multiplying the length by the width. Thus lower level and higher level objectives may require different types of activities.

Whether the objective is affective, psychomotor, or cognitive will also influence your choice of activities. Affective outcomes usually take a longer time to develop and are often best taught through direct experience—for example, role playing. Imagine that you are helping students learn to be supportive and uncritical of one another. You might discuss and demonstrate the supportive words and actions you desire and the "put-down" words and actions you want to discourage. Then you could observe students in groups in the hallway and on the playground and give feedback on their treatment of their classmates. You may want to bring two students to the front to act out both types of behavior and discuss the reactions. This objective is one that you might address periodically throughout several weeks or months.

A final consideration regarding objectives is the difficulty of the content you want to teach. As most experienced teachers can tell you, some topics and skills are easier to teach than others. One famous difficult topic for elementary teachers is fractions. After a few years of practice, many teachers have been able to represent fractions in a way that makes sense. That is, teachers discover visual aids, examples, or sequences for teaching that work to help students understand.

The first time you teach any new content, it is difficult to know what will make it meaningful to students. You can get ideas from textbooks, other teachers, curriculum specialists, workshops, teachers' magazines, college courses, or even trial and error. When you find an approach that clarifies a difficult concept, skill, or generalization quickly and thoroughly, you stick with it.

TEACHER'S KNOWLEDGE OF LEARNING PRINCIPLES AND ABILITY TO USE INSTRUCTIONAL TECHNIQUES

Like other professionals, a teacher has a knowledge base from which to draw when making decisions for action. This knowledge can be organized into three categories: (1) human growth and development, (2) learning principles, and (3) instructional strategies. The first area, while extremely important, is not discussed as a separate topic here, because most of you will, at some time, take a course in educational psychology that deals with human cognitive, social, emotional, and physical development. The latter two areas—learning and instructional strategies—will make up the next two sections of this chapter.

SECTION 1 SUMMARY

In this section, we considered several factors that influence the choice of learning activities: social/political/community, school, and physical issues; students' personal characteristics, including learning styles; teacher's knowledge of the goals and content; teacher's knowledge of learning principles; and teacher's ability to use various teaching techniques.

While the last two factors will be examined closely in the next section, we hope you will ask yourself the following questions when designing learning activities: What do I know about this community, school, and physical environment that might influence the effectiveness of activities? What individual needs of students (intelligence, prior knowledge, or learning style) might influence the success of the activities I select? What information (facts, concepts, generalizations) is most important to teach? Are the activities appropriate for the level of learning and content difficulty?

Asking these questions can help you plan activities and anticipate any difficulties. Research and theory on teaching and learning tell us that your teaching will be more successful in promoting the student outcomes you value if you take into account the factors discussed in this chapter as you develop appropriate learning activities.

Guided Practice Activity A. A Review of Factors to Be Considered in Planning Learning Activities

This exercise deals with three of the factors involved in selecting activities: (1) social/political/community, school, and physical factors; (2) students' personal characteristics; (3) teacher's knowledge of goals and content. First, write down the key ideas for each factor. Then, for each factor, think of an example from your own experience (observation, reading, etc.) that illustrates how this factor either was or was not considered in selecting a learning activity. For example, you might remember a teacher who only lectured and was ineffective because the visual learner's needs were not considered.

1. Social/political/community, school, physical factors

   a. Key ideas: _____

   _____

   _____

   b. Examples: _____

   _____

   _____

2. Students' personal characteristics

    a. Key ideas: _____

    _____

    _____

    b. Examples: _____

    _____

    _____

3. Teacher's knowledge of goals and content

    a. Key ideas: _____

    _____

    _____

    b. Examples: _____

    _____

    _____

Section 2. Learning Principles

MEMORY AND LEARNING THEORY

First, let's look at what is known about learning. Since education is what we're about as teachers, we need to pay attention to what researchers have discovered about learning. We will draw on the *information processing model* of memory, based on many years of research on memory and decision making (Gage & Berliner, 1984). This is not the only theory of learning; specialists will always disagree regarding exactly how the mind works. There are physiological models and intuitive models, among others. The information processing model, however, is well respected and is most useful for the purpose of this book.

Processing info

To make instructional decisions, we need to understand the three parts of memory (1) *sensory memory*, (2) *short-term memory*, and (3) *long-term memory*. These elements are shown in Figure 4.2. We'll examine each one in turn.

Sensory Memory

Our *sensory memory* receives all the signals from the world around us through sight, hearing, smell, taste, and touch. Everything we perceive becomes a part of the sensory memory. That's billions of pieces of information! Can you imagine what would happen if we attempted to

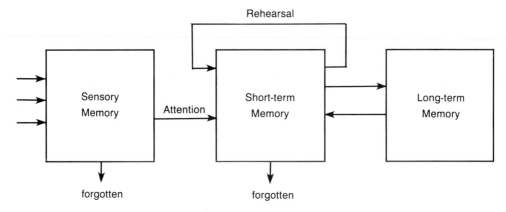

Figure 4.2. The Information-Processing Model of Memory

process all this information at once? We would suffer from severe information overload. Therefore, the sensory memory has a safety valve—forgetting. If we have no need to remember something, the sensory information remains in our memory for only a split second—roughly 0.75 second.

What if we do want to remember something taken in by sensory memory? How do we hold onto it before it's forgotten? We pay attention to it. Attention will always be conscious, or deliberate. Of all the sights, smells, and sounds around us, only those that capture our attention are taken into our short-term memory for processing. The only way to make sure that a piece of sensory information remains in our memory is to pay attention to it.

severe informational overload

Have you ever been talking with a friend at a party or in a restaurant when you hear a bit of a very interesting conversation behind you? Perhaps you heard your own name or a good friend's name. You began to listen in to that conversation. Unfortunately, you were also expected to remain attentive to your current conversation. So you tried to listen to both conversations. Could you do it? Could you fully attend to two conversations at once? Probably not. Only what we attend to can be processed, and our ability to attend to more than one thing at a time is limited.

Now you can see why it's so important to have your students' attention when you are teaching. No attention, no memory! It's as simple as that. The only way for information not to be ignored or forgotten is to pay attention to it long enough for it to be transferred to short-term memory.

How can we focus students' attention on learning? There are several ways. First, we should start out lessons with something that gets students actively involved and interested in the topic. An excellent way to capture students' attention is to ask them to describe what they know about the topic, either in writing or with a partner. This task enables students to recall their prior knowledge of the topic and, at the same time, focuses their attention on the content. In addition, it gives you good diagnostic information about what students know or remember about your topic.

What about during lessons? We can focus students' attention by "verbal markers," statements such as "This is important" or "I want you to remember this." Telling the students the objective of the lesson and how they will use the information in the future can also help. Varying the tone of our voice, moving around the room, and using gestures are other ways to focus students on the topic. Many teachers introduce novelty, emotion, and humor into their lessons to capture students' attention. Other teachers use jokes, personal (but relevant) stories, and games to change the pace and keep students interested.

Short-Term Memory

The *short-term memory (STM)* is sometimes called the "working memory" because it is where conscious thinking occurs. It has two characteristics: (1) it has a limited capacity—about seven items at a time—and (2) it can "hold" information only for a limited amount of time—up to 15 to 30 seconds.

The limited capacity of the STM means that any information that comes in after all the spaces are filled will be lost unless it is somehow integrated with the rest of the information. Think about the fact that only about seven bits of information can be held at once. How many digits are in a telephone number? Right, seven. When a commonly used number is longer than seven digits, it is often "chunked" into sections—for example, Social Security numbers are nine digits in three chunks: 123-45-6789.

Just to test this idea out, see if you can remember this list of terms. Look at the terms for 10 seconds and then cover them. Try to jot them down from memory. The words do not have to be remembered in the same order.

jogs
team
injury
baseball
hits

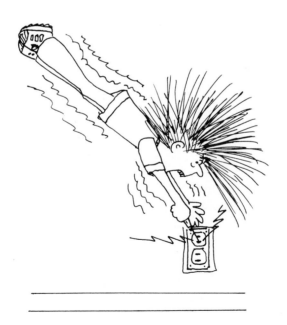

_____

_____

short-term memory

How many did you remember? Ask a friend to do this task and see how many of the words he or she could remember. Discuss the strategies you used to remember the items on the list.

As we noted, one common way of memorizing lists is to "chunk" the items into meaningful groups. Since the five words are all on the subject of sports, they can be organized into a sentence. Then that whole group takes up only one space in STM, leaving room for more incoming information. Figure 4.3 illustrates this idea.

You also may have used *rehearsal* to remember the list, by repeating the words over and over. Rehearsal is an effective tool for keeping information in working memory long enough to use it or move it into long-term memory. This relates in part to the second characteristic of STM—short duration.

The STM is limited in the amount of time the information is remembered—only up to 15 to 30 seconds. Unless we do something to transfer the information into long-term memory, we will probably forget it after these few seconds. What do you do when you want to remember a phone number and you can't write it down? You usually just keep repeating it until you don't need it anymore. Have you noticed that you remember for a long time things you repeated many times? Think about advertising slogans, like "Reach out and touch someone," "You deserve a break today." Because of constant repetition, we tend to remember these slogans a long time.

In addition to repetition (rehearsal), there are many other strategies we use to retain information by transferring it into our long-term memory. Many of these strategies are presented under "Long-Term Memory," on page 113.

Now what does this information about STM have to do with teaching? There are two important principles to be used here. First, when presenting complex information, it should be "chunked" into logical bits and processed only a few pieces at a time. When students are told a long string of unrelated facts, their memories can't organize them and it is difficult to transfer them into LTM. Well-organized information is easiest for our brains to process.

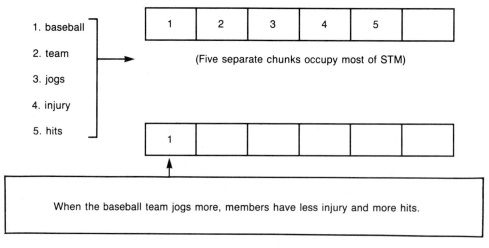

1. baseball
2. team
3. jogs
4. injury
5. hits

| 1 | 2 | 3 | 4 | 5 | |

(Five separate chunks occupy most of STM)

| 1 | | | | | |

When the baseball team jogs more, members have less injury and more hits.

This chunk occupies only one space and leaves space for more information to be processed.

Figure 4.3. Chunking in Short-term Memory

Another key to teaching relates to the amount of time the information stays in STM. Since information is forgotten so quickly, students need to have time either to take note of the ideas or to discuss and practice the information so it can be stored in LTM. When we just throw information at students with no chance for them to digest it by actively processing it, it tends to be forgotten as they turn to new information. Rehearsal through active processing should always accompany the introduction of new information, so that students' memories do not get overloaded and lose valuable material.

CHECK FOR UNDERSTANDING

Look at the diagram below. See if you can explain to yourself or a friend in your own words how the sensory memory and STM work. Also discuss the role of rehearsal in STM. Reread the sections on sensory memory and short-term memory to see if you explained them correctly.

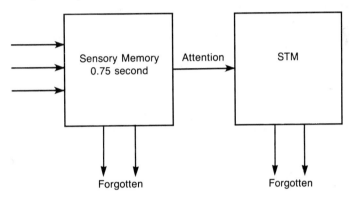

Long-Term Memory

Long-term memory (LTM) is the storehouse of information, facts, emotions, feelings, memories, and so on. Over 100 million bits of information are stored in LTM, but they are not stored randomly. In fact, it is the organization of information into networks (or *schemata;* singular, *schema*) in LTM that makes it possible to retrieve ideas that we want to remember.

Facts, concepts, generalizations, emotions, and other pieces of information are stored in networks of related meaning. These networks (schemata) help with the storage and retrieval of information. Consider this example. Have you ever smelled a sweet scent that reminded you of someone or of a particular incident? How do you think your memory retrieved that scene or person based only on that special scent? The memory of that scent was probably stored along with the memory of the person or experience associated with the scent in a schema, or network, in your LTM. When you smelled the scent, the memory was triggered and recalled.

LTM and STM have a productive partnership. LTM has a huge amount of information that we have stored through learning and experience. But we are not always conscious of that information. Recall that the STM is where we consciously work with information that is (1) retrieved from LTM or (2) brought in through sensory memory. But STM has a limited capacity—it can deal with only a certain amount of information at any given time. Therefore, we need a system of accessing manageable pieces of information from LTM for use in STM (see Figure 4.2).

Let's use an example from math to illustrate this system. If I am solving a word problem involving proportions, I will need to bring into working memory the information in the problem and the information I have stored in LTM about similar problems. But I can't manage everything at once. I will first deal with the measurements, work on them in STM, and store that information in LTM (or on paper). Then I will consider the equivalencies in STM, and store that information. Then, to solve the problem, I will put together what I have learned. In this way the STM serves as a temporary storage area while I work with information. The LTM is the permanent storage place for what I have learned through my work in STM.

It is interesting to consider how the information stored in LTM might influence our ability to make meaning out of our experiences. Someone who is watching a baseball game and has no idea what a "change-up" is (a slow pitch thrown with the same motion as a fastball) would probably not notice when the pitcher throws a change-up, and might conclude that the batter missed the ball because he just wasn't having a good day. Those of us who know about change-ups would observe the great job the pitcher did of fooling the batter by suddenly altering the speed of the ball.

Because we have a network of meaning in LTM, we are able to attend to the pitching speed, label it, and process it consciously in STM. Then we store it in our network of meaning for baseball, which is now enriched by the experience. The person with little prior knowledge of baseball did not even attend to the pitching speed and, therefore, did not receive the information in STM for processing. In short, it was forgotten because it was never noticed.

It is similiar with our students. Sometimes we are trying to make an analogy with something we think is common experience. Yet the students do not share that experience and so the comparison falls on deaf ears. One of us was introducing a lesson on *Romeo and Juliet* to a group of sixth graders. We tried to make Shakespeare's play meaningful to them by comparing it with *West Side Story*. Little did we realize that few of the students had seen the movie or the play! We had missed in our attempt to hook into the students' prior knowledge.

Why is it that some facts or ideas or impressions are so much easier to remember than others? Learning psychologists would say that the number and richness of connections among the pieces of information determine retrieval from LTM. In other words, if I have been exposed to something only once and had little opportunity to discuss it or use it, it will be harder for me to remember because it has few connections with other information in my LTM. However, when I have rehearsed, discussed, experienced, and seen something in action over a period of time, I am more likely to remember it because these experiences have enriched the many connections among the pieces of information in my LTM.

In a sense, then, how meaningful something is to us is determined by the amount of experience we have had with it. The more experience, the more connections. The more connections, the more meaning. It is our job to help students see relationships between new and old information and to help them organize the new information we present.

One final note on LTM involves the idea of *automaticity*. Not everything has to be transferred from LTM to STM for it to be functional. For example, as you are reading these words, you are looking at many letters and immediately, with very little conscious processing, understanding their meaning. Your decoding of these words is automatic, and therefore takes little processing in STM. Because of automaticity, your STM is freed up to consider how what you are reading relates to what you read before and the overall meaning.

Beginning readers often have to spend a great deal of conscious "space" in STM for merely figuring out the pronunciation and meaning of words, with little attention to meaning.

Reading is not automatic for these students. How did your reading become automatic? Yes, through many hundreds of hours of practice. For a skill to become automatic, we must practice and practice. But there is a payoff. Once a task becomes automatic, we can perform it (e.g., decode words) and process other aspects of information (e.g., related ideas and concepts) at the same time. Thus, developing automaticity is an excellent way to increase brain capacity so we can operate at higher levels of thinking.

CHECK FOR UNDERSTANDING

1. Explain how the long-term memory works. Don't forget to describe how LTM and STM

   work together and the idea of *automaticity* (refer to Figure 4.2). _____

   _____

   _____

   _____

2. Explain why the arrows between LTM and STM in Figure 4.2 go in *both* directions.

   _____

   _____

   _____

   Check your answers with the information presented in this section.

PRINCIPLES OF LEARNING

We have described briefly how memory works—it is limited in how long and how much information it can handle at one time, and it seeks to find and make connections among pieces of information. But how does this knowledge help us as teachers?

In this section we list and explain six principles that can help you select learning activities. These ideas have been culled from research on learning and memory and are useful for planning activities, for making decisions during lessons, and for analyzing and redesigning lessons. The principles are *congruence, organization, variety, active processing, experience-based learning,* and *higher level thinking.*

Congruence Principle: Make Sure There's a Match among Objectives, Activities, and Evaluation

Have you ever sat through a college lecture course and then taken a test on the material, only to learn that the test had little relationship to the lecture or the course textbook? This is an extreme example of lack of congruence. The concept of *congruence* is the same as *content validity,* as discussed in Chapter 3. If we are going to go to the trouble to analyze our content structure and write objectives, then we should make an effort to teach lessons that lead to these objectives and to test whether the objectives have been achieved. Such teaching is *congruent.* That is, all the pieces fit together—the objectives, the activities, and the evaluation procedures.

One of us had a chemistry teacher in high school who started every class with a story about football. As we continued to ask questions, he would go on and on, until the bell rang, about his experiences as a football star. There was no congruence between his chemistry-instruction objectives and his football-story activities. Even worse, when it came time to give the test, he used tests from the teacher's manual, even though he had spent only a fraction of class time on the content covered by the test. His teaching method was clearly an infraction of the congruence principle.

Simply put, when you select activities, you should make sure they lead to your objectives. You will also want to be certain that your tests assess the skills and ideas you have developed through your learning activities. For instance, if you want students to be able to solve word problems, they will need adequate demonstration and practice activities on solving word problems. Finally, when you evaluate your objectives, your test should include word problems.

Congruence can be a bit tricky with higher level objectives. For example, if we want students to be able to compare and contrast the characteristics of a mammal and a reptile, we may discuss in class the similarities and differences between a cat and a snake. On the test, however, if we included a question about a cat and a snake, we would only be testing memory of a prior lesson. To see whether students can engage in higher level thinking, we need to test

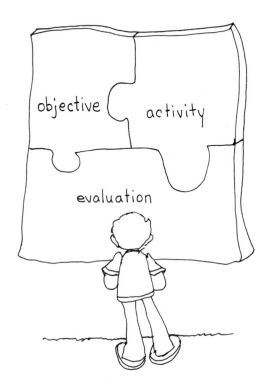

them with *new* information. In this case, students would be asked to compare a mammal and a reptile not previously discussed in class, perhaps a dog and a lizard. This task would require students to apply their ability to compare and contrast to a situation not previously encountered.

In addition, we must make sure that, if we are teaching to a higher level objective, our class activities provide opportunities to practice functioning at those higher levels of learning. Too often, we teach to memory-level and understanding-level objectives and then expect students to be able to apply the knowledge at higher levels on a test, without ever having been asked to do so before.

CHECK FOR UNDERSTANDING

Mrs. Zarett is teaching limericks, and her objective is for students to be able to write a limerick. She shows them examples, and describes the characteristics of a limerick. She practices to make sure they can describe the characteristics and points them out in examples. Then, for her evaluation of their learning, Mrs. Zarett asks students to write a limerick. Determine whether the principle of congruence has been followed, by comparing the objective with the activities and evaluation. On the lines below, write your comments about the congruence of these activities.

The evaluation was at the higher level (problem solving or application), while the activities took the students only to the lower levels of concept understanding. There is a mismatch here, a lack of congruence. Mrs. Zarett should have provided practice on the actual writing of limericks before testing the students' ability to do so.

One way to help yourself provide congruent activities is to restate frequently to students the instructional objective you want them to attain and to remind them periodically of how they'll be expected to demonstrate what they have learned. In this way, you remind yourself and the students of where the lesson is heading and how the classroom activities relate to the objective. An excellent teacher we know kept showing his fourth-grade students the final project on community services that his last year's class had done. Seeing the project kept students motivated and focused on the outcome while they were learning the content and skills required for the project.

Organization and Clarity Principle: Make the Organization of the Information Obvious to Students

Since the brain naturally wants to organize information into meaningful networks, or schemata, the teacher can capitalize on this inclination by helping students see the patterns and structure in new information. How can this be done? Many teachers use an overhead projector, blackboard, or poster to display information as they explain it. When deciding how to show the organization of the material, remember that your learning style may not match your learners' styles. You may prefer lists and outlines, while some of your students may need to see the information displayed spatially. The outline on pages 31–32 and Figure 2.9 are our attempts to show how the information in the "Making Choices" topic is organized. The list is a sequential one; the figure is more abstract and spatial. Concept maps and webbing are also ways to show the interconnections among ideas. Examples of these will be provided in the next chapter.

Many people have trouble making sense of information when it is unclear how one piece relates to another. Such people like to see the big picture first and then fit the details in later. Other people can't find the big picture until they have understood all the details. You will have both types of learners in your classes. Therefore, you can show the structure before, during, and after providing information so that all learning preferences are taken into account. In any case, be sure to focus students' attention on the structure and organization often during presentation of information. Statements such as "This next point relates to the one we just discussed in this way . . ." or "We've been talking about mammals. Now look up here and see how our next topic, reptiles, relates to . . ." help students focus on the relevant information.

Not all information lends itself to easy organization. For example, when there are many disparate facts to be memorized (e.g., the names of the notes on a scale), it may be hard to find any meaningful way of categorizing them. In such cases, you may wish to use a mnemonic device—a memory aid. You have probably used such devices at one time or another, especially when cramming for a test. In Chapter 3 we used the mnemonic *A B C D* to help you remember the characteristics of a clearly stated objective: *audience, behavior, conditions,* and *degree*. A mnemonic device we use in Michigan to remember the names of the Great Lakes is HOMES: Huron, Ontario, Michigan, Erie, and Superior. Other mnemonic devices include making up a story or sentence using the first word or letter of items in a list (e.g., "Every Good Boy Does Fine" for the notes of the scale) and creating an image for each item on the list.

To illustrate the latter idea, try memorizing the following pairs of words:

bell	boy	candy	paper
paint	shoe	car	dog

What memory aid did you use to recall these pairs? Many people find it helpful to create an image for each pair—for example, a person painting a giant bell, or a boy with a big shoe. Such imaginary pictures are especially useful for visual learners. You can help students recall important information by sharing memory aids and by encouraging students to make them up in class.

CHECK FOR UNDERSTANDING

Think of the two principles we have presented so far, congruence and organization. For each, create three examples that illustrate how these principles can be used in teaching. The example may be a technique you have seen a teacher use or something you have tried yourself. List them below.

Congruence	Organization
1. _____	_____
_____	_____

2. _____   _____

   _____   _____

3. _____   _____

   _____   _____

Variety Principle: Appeal to the Different Styles, Needs, and Preferences of Students

Having read the discussion, earlier in the chapter, of students' learning needs and styles, you are probably not surprised by the need for variety. We do not all learn in the same way, and, as teachers, we should acknowledge this in our planning and teaching. We also know that students must attend to information in order to learn it. Young children especially have trouble attending to one topic for any length of time. In light of these facts, we can plan a variety of activities that will appeal to each learner and hold his or her attention throughout the lesson.

Take the lesson on resources that Millicent Stephens was teaching (page 92). She might start out with students brainstorming in small groups all the "things" their parents buy and list on paper the materials these items are made of. Then Millicent might focus the learners' attention on the outcome of the lesson—their projects showing community resources. Using a map, she might explain where many of the major resources are located, and she could structure the information by grouping different types of resources according to geographic region. Students then might draw maps and illustrate the different resources on the maps.

Millicent used visual, auditory, and kinesthetic learning modes. The organization of her lecture may have appealed to *sequential* learners, while those who prefer a more *random* style would probably feel comfortable brainstorming. The fact that students worked in groups and individually also allowed for different learning preferences. Because Millicent included a variety of activities that appealed to different learning styles and needs, more students are likely to achieve success. Their brains will accept and process the information more easily when they are tuned in and when their particular strengths are appealed to. The guideline to follow is to have a good deal of variety in your lessons, not only to maintain students' attention but also to "hook into" your learners' particular styles.

There is one aspect of this principle that deserves greater attention—modeling. To *model* is to show, demonstrate, or illustrate something as you explain it. Most educators suggest that lectures or other verbal lessons be illustrated visually. Modeling is not always easy to do, but it is worth making an effort to reach the visual learners in your class.

What techniques might you use? One second-grade teacher we know put on a "costume" each Friday to illustrate a different idea the class had been studying. In a unit on careers, for instance, she dressed up as a business executive one Friday and as a police officer on another day. It is not necessary to go to such extremes, of course. You can draw pictures on the board to illustrate how a bill becomes a law, or fill a tank with water to show how different weights and densities of materials float and sink. You can have students role-play the digits in a number to illustrate place value in math. Colored chalk can be used to highlight different words and ideas you want students to notice. For example, if students are working on recognizing adjectives, a story on the board might have all adjectives highlighted in red.

Finally, don't forget that humor, novelty, and emotion are excellent ways of providing variety—something a little different. Dare to be a little outrageous occasionally. We think you'll be pleasantly surprised with the results.

There are many ways to add variety to your lessons. Talk to other teachers, read teachers' magazines, and be creative. It's fun to try new approaches, and it's rewarding when you finally see a hard-to-reach student tune in.

Active Processing Principle: Help Students Make New Information More Meaningful

This principle has two parts. One, *linkage to prior knowledge,* refers to the process by which teachers make sure students understand new information by relating it to what is already in long-term memory. The other, *active involvement,* is the technique of encouraging student participation, to help students digest or process the information so it goes into LTM.

Linking new information to prior knowledge is an important key to learning. Remember our example, in the discussion of LTM, of the "change-up" in baseball? If you know little about baseball, you probably started to feel a bit lost; a piece of information was not meaningful to you. Similarly, much of what we teach students is new to them, so we have to present it in such a way that it is easily understood. One very effective way is to "hook" the new idea(s) to something the students already know. For example, when teaching about fractions, use a pizza pie cut into slices. Let the students see that fractions are indeed not as mysterious as they might seem. The students have been dealing with fractions at the dinner table for years!

Often teachers begin a lesson in a way that will show what prior knowledge or experience students have about the topic. One teacher we know began a lesson on the sea by having students write for three minutes what they knew that related to the sea. As the teacher walked around and read students' responses, she found that most students had little idea of what the sea is. So she asked them to think about the lake near the school and imagine it getting so big that their school was on an island. Then she related the concept *island* to the continents. If she had found that the students were familiar with the concept of *sea, ocean,* and other related ideas, she would not have had to develop the background knowledge for the students and she could have begun at a higher level of instruction. Even if only a few students had prior knowledge of the sea, she could have asked these students to share their experiences and build a knowledge base for the others.

Active participation is the second important aspect of teaching for long-term learning. If students are provided information as they sit passively, they are less likely to remember it than if they have some direct involvement with the material. This is why it is so important for teachers to include a variety of activities that enable students to touch, speak, write, act out, explain, draw, and create.

Do you remember we mentioned that information is more easily stored and recalled when it is embedded in a rich network of experiences, facts, ideas, concepts, and so on? Such a meaningful network is created through direct experience of the ideas, concepts, and generalizations to be learned. Take Millicent Stephens's money management unit as an example. Millicent's objective was for students to be able to distinguish between wanted items and needed items. Rather than just lecture or assign workbook pages on the topic, she could have students go to their kitchen at home and list 10 items on the shelf. Or the students could cut out pictures from advertisements in magazines. Then they would put their pictures in one of two piles, one labeled "necessary items" and one "luxury items." As they argued over which items might be necessary for survival, students would develop a rich web of meaning around

the two concepts *wants* and *needs*. Their direct experience and active involvement could help promote a significant understanding of the topic.

There are many ways to encourage students to participate, even during a lecture. The only requirement is that students, not just the teacher, actively work with facts and concepts. When presenting or demonstrating information, the teacher can pause after each one or two main ideas and ask students to answer a question or write down a summary. Or the teacher can ask true–false questions and have students vote. These techniques force students to work with the information in their short-term memories so that it can be transferred to long-term memory.

Practice and rehearsal (see page 113) are other strategies to help students remember new information and skills. The most active ways of practicing include peer teaching, perhaps with flash cards or a game; oral games and drills; and activities that require manipulation of concrete materials (e.g., blocks or cuisinaire rods). Such active participation may be combined with written activities in workbooks and dittos. Remember that individual written work may not appeal to every student's need for active, oral, kinesthetic involvement. Thus teachers should avoid overreliance on written exercises.

Experience-Based Learning Principle:
Relate the Material to Everyday Life

Imagine you are planning a lesson on the care and feeding of large mammals in a zoo. If you had to choose between reading about it in a book and visiting a zoo to discuss the subject with a staff member, which would you choose? Most likely you'd prefer the visit to the zoo. This example illustrates the principle that, wherever possible and appropriate, teachers should select experience-based activities that are close to real life.

Over a generation ago, Dale (1963) introduced the idea of the "Cone of Experience," as shown in Figure 4.4. The cone portrays a continuum of activities, with "direct purposeful experiences" at the base. Such experiences involve students in concrete, real-world problem-solving activities such as learning to ride public transportation, writing a school newspaper, or removing trash from a neighboring yard. At the top of the cone is "verbal symbols," referring to activities in which students work with abstract words and numbers—for example, by reading or doing multiplication tables.

An explanation of each "layer" from the base to the top follows.

Direct purposeful experiences involve students in activities in the world outside the classroom and outside school. Examples include participating in community clean-up projects, establishing a working banking system in the school, managing and staffing a school store, and assuming the duties of school crossing guard.

Contrived experiences approximate real-life situations. They are an "edited" version of reality. For example, kindergarten children may be introduced to pedestrian safety by simulating a street and crossing zone in the school yard. In this case the simulated situation is preferred over the real-life one because of safety concerns. In other cases, simulation may be used because of a need for simplification—for example, when using a model of the solar system to illustrate the orbits and rotation of planets.

Dramatized experiences include role playing and dramatic re-creations of actual or fictional events—for example, of scenes from history or literature.

Demonstrations, study trips, exhibits, educational television, motion pictures, recordings, radio, and *still pictures* all represent gradations from more concrete to more abstract learning activities.

The layer *visual symbols* includes activities where students work with maps, games, and other kinds of diagrams.

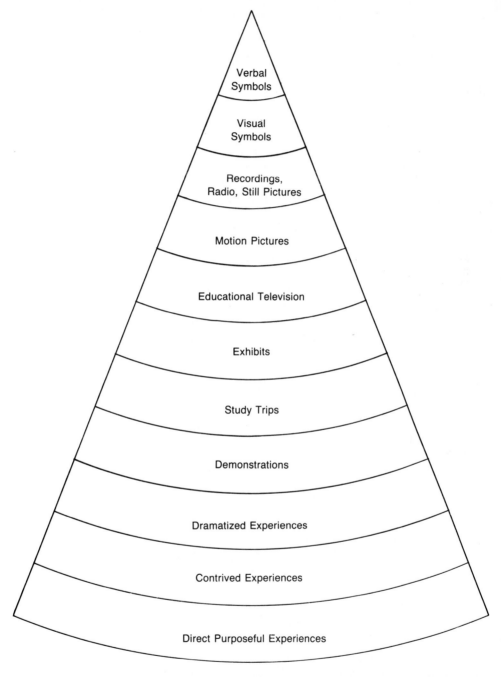

Figure 4.4. The Cone of Experience. (Illustration from *Audio-Visual Methods in Teaching*, Third Edition, by Edgar Dale, copyright ©1969 by Holt, Rinehart and Winston, Inc. Reprinted by permission of the publisher.)

Verbal symbols, the top layer, refers to activities, such as writing, speaking, and reading, in which students work with symbols (e.g., words and numbers) that do not look like the objects they represent. That is, the symbols, in and of themselves, do not provide any visual clue to assist in meaning. In these cases, students are working with abstract concepts.

The simplest way to think about the Cone of Experience is to organize activities into three subgroups, as shown below.

Learning by doing: Direct purposeful experiences
                              Contrived experiences
                              Dramatic experiences
Learning through observation: Demonstrations
                                    Study trips
                                    Exhibits
                                    Educational television
                                    Motion pictures
                                    Recordings
                                    Radio
                                    Still pictures
Learning through abstractions: Visual Symbols (letters, numbers, notes, etc.)
                                    Verbal symbols (sounds)

One implication of the Cone of Experience is that teachers should think about whether they are providing enough "learning by doing" activities. In most classrooms, there are too many abstract reading, writing, and listening activities and too few direct-experience activities. Too often, we rush students through the concrete activities so they can function at the abstract level. However, many students are not developmentally ready to learn from abstract activities. They need more time with concrete experiences.

It is important to remember, however, that one goal of schooling is to allow students to function at the higher, more abstract levels. Thus, as students mature, they need to be weaned away from a predominance of concrete experiences. Even among older students, however, concepts are often best introduced through concrete, real-life activities.

We suggest that you use the cone to help you plan a balance among learning activities. In general, you would emphasize "learning by doing" at the lower grades and "learning through abstractions" in the middle school years. However, all levels of the cone should be used at all levels of education.

CHECK FOR UNDERSTANDING

Assume you are teaching students about bird migration. Label the following activities according to the type of learning. On the line after each item, write *D* for *doing,* *O* for *observation,* or *A* for *abstraction.*

1. Teacher lecturing from a textbook on migration _____

2. Field trip to a bird sanctuary, including an interview with guide _____

3. Reading and then completing a workbook exercise on the topic _____

4. Seeing a filmstrip about bird migrations _____

5. Groups of students role-playing movements of birds on a map _____

We labeled items 2 and 5 as *doing,* 4 as *observation,* and 1 and 3 as *abstraction.*

Higher Level Thinking Principle: Encourage Higher Level Thinking in All Students

Our sixth principle is slightly different from the others. Each of the previous principles uses information about students, teaching, and learning to provide a guideline for planning lessons that will help students learn more effectively. That is also true for the principle of higher level learning. The rehearsal of information and complex processing necessary in promoting higher level thinking will help students learn. But beyond that, the principle of higher level thinking represents our value judgment about the kinds of learning that will be necessary for students entering the 21st century. We believe that higher level thinking is not only helpful in assisting students to learn now but is essential for their future success. In fact, we believe it is so important that we have devoted all of Chapter 6 to techniques for promoting higher level thinking.

Briefly summarized, *higher level thinking* requires students to use information rather than merely recall it. They may be asked to compare one concept or generalization with another; to use a skill in a new situation; to analyze the causes, effects, motivations, or other aspects of an event; to make judgments; to apply logic; or to combine information and prior experience in new and creative ways. Higher level thinking also includes the use of processes such as problem solving and decision making in real or simulated situations.

This type of learning is in marked contrast to rote learning or memorization of facts in which the facts are not used in a meaningful way. We are not implying that "lower level learning"—recalling and understanding basic facts, concepts, or generalizations—is unimportant. We are merely saying that it is only one step in a larger process. Good higher level thinking is built on a solid foundation of understanding. It is our hope that all students will have the opportunity and encouragement they need to build on that foundation.

In selecting learning activities, note that some have greater potential for enhancing higher level thinking than others. Role playing and simulations, and writing assignments that require students to relate a number of generalizations to one another in an essay or to solve a complex problem, are especially good for this purpose. Student projects that extend beyond description to include explanation and problem solving are also excellent vehicles for developing thinking skills.

SECTION 2 SUMMARY

The section began with a discussion of the three parts of memory: sensory memory, short-term memory, and long-term memory. We then presented six principles for selecting learning activities: congruence, organization, variety, active processing, experience-based learning, and higher level thinking. As you develop plans for teaching, keep these principles in mind. You can ask yourself these questions: Is there a match among my objectives, activities, and evaluation methods? How will I make the organization of key ideas explicit? How can I provide variety to maintain interest and appeal to different learning styles and needs? How and when will I get students actively involved in their learning? How can I relate this material to real-life experiences? How can I extend this lesson to higher level learning?

Guided Practice Activity B. Remembering the Learning Principles

First review the six principles of learning and make notes for yourself. Then create a mnemonic device, or memory aid, that will help you remember the six principles. Practice saying them from memory until you know they are in your long-term memory. Write or draw your mnemonic device in the space below.

Guided Practice Activity C. Applying the Learning Principles

Use the six principles of learning to analyze the actions taken in the scenario that follows. In the right-hand margin, write the name of the principle that is illustrated by the activity described in the scenario. Be ready to explain why this principle aids learning.

Mr. Jones is working with a group of fourth graders on a unit on local government. One objective of his lessons is for students to be able to create a news report based on interviews with two public officials (mayor, city clerk, comptroller, or city council member).

First, Mr. Jones focuses students on the lesson by telling them what he expects them to learn and that they will be seeing the impact of local government in their everyday lives. He shows a diagram of the structure of local government and a list of city workers. To convey information about each job, he has small groups of students research the responsibilities of each official and then he assigns these "experts" to new teams so they can teach each other about the jobs. He appoints a coach for each team and has them quiz the other team members on descriptions of workers' roles. Then the students play a game in which the teams compete against one another in answering questions about the local government officials. Students then complete a brief worksheet so the teacher can see how much each student has learned.

To move to the higher level of using and applying the information, Mr. Jones has each student write down two questions to ask one of the officials. Together, the class chooses two officials to invite to their class for group interviews. Interview techniques are studied, and students practice in pairs. They are also given an outline for recording their findings, and they analyze examples of news reports.

After the interviews are conducted, students work in small groups to prepare reports for the school paper.

Your responses may resemble the following. Mr. Jones used the learning principles in a variety of ways. For example, he demonstrated congruence by carefully planning activities leading to his objective, a news report based on interviews with public officials. Each planned activity served to assist students in reaching this goal. He demonstrated organization and clarity by providing students with written examples of content organization, such as the diagram of the structure of local government or the outline for recording interview findings. He certainly used the principles of variety and active processing in these activities. Students were involved in researching in small groups, coaching one another, playing a game, completing a worksheet, planning, practicing, and conducting interviews. The opportunity to interview actual public officials is a good example of the principle of experience-based learning. The selection mentions that Mr. Jones uses the principle of higher level thinking in having students write interview questions. In what other activities was higher level thinking demonstrated? As you discuss this lesson with a colleague, you may find other ways in which the six principles of learning enhanced Mr. Jones's lessons.

Section 3. Using Various Teaching Techniques

Section Overview

You may be thinking, "All this theory is great, but what do I actually *do* with the kids?" Your question is a good one. Having knowledge of learning theory and principles is of little value unless you have techniques for putting those ideas into practice. In this section we describe ways to structure the learning environment and then discuss several commonly used teaching techniques: lecture, questioning, discussion, and meaning-building activities. At this point we should again warn you that there is no research that conclusively proves which learning activities work best. As we have said before, when choosing an activity, it is important to consider the students, the community, the content, the goals, and your own philosophy. Another source to consider, however, is research on teacher effectiveness. This body of research has highlighted various teaching techniques that help students learn.

RESEARCH ON TEACHING

During the 1970s and 1980s, billions of federal dollars were spent on studies of how teachers could help students learn. Teaching behaviors were measured and correlated with student gains on achievement test scores so that researchers could make statements like, "Teachers who spend more time sitting at their desks have students who gain less on standardized tests" or "Teachers who keep students actively involved have students who gain more" (Stallings, Needels, & Stayrook, 1979).

More than 10 experiments (Gage, 1978) have shown that students whose teachers applied specific techniques (e.g., active involvement of learners, monitoring, and so on) in their classrooms scored higher on reading and math tests than students whose teachers did not use such strategies. We must interpret this research with caution, however, because the main student outcome examined was standardized test scores. Such tests do not measure everything that we value in education—for example, self-esteem, social skills, and many higher level learning skills.

In spite of our concerns, we find the research on effective teaching to be a valuable source of information on instructional techniques. See, for example, Berliner & Rosenshine, (1987). In fact, we refer to this research continually throughout this textbook. However, the research is not sufficient to be used as an "over the counter knowledge pill" that will guarantee success each day. Not one of the effective teaching practices will work every time with every teacher in every classroom. Techniques must be selected for their appropriateness to a particular lesson, class, and situation.

The strategy we recommend, therefore, is to plan your lessons using what you can glean from research, teaching principles, your experience, and your intuition, while also considering your classroom conditions. After you teach the lesson, take a few minutes to reflect on it. Note

what went well and what did not. Try to figure out *why* things turned out as they did. Think of changes you could make that might improve the lesson; share your thoughts with colleagues and ask for their suggestions. Using your notes, redesign the lesson and try again; revise again, and so on. With this approach you will find that teaching will be ever fresh—and always a learning experience.

STRUCTURING THE ENVIRONMENT

Before describing each technique, we should discuss an important consideration in planning learning activities—how to structure the environment. In other words, you must decide what group sizes to work with and whether to plan more student-directed or more teacher-directed activities.

Group Size

You have basically three choices for organizing your students: as a whole group, into small groups (usually six or fewer per group), and individually. We recommend that a mixture of class grouping patterns be used.

As in other aspects of teaching, the decision should be based on the teacher's knowledge of the community, students, content, and principles of instruction and learning. While whole-group teaching is efficient for presenting information (e.g., in the form of lecture/demonstration) and giving directions, it should not be the only form of instruction. In large groups, many students can tune out without being detected, and it is harder to keep every student actively involved.

The advantage of small groups is that they are versatile and that more students have the opportunity to participate. Students in pairs can discuss a question or solve a problem; groups of four can quiz each other on a particular skill or set of facts; groups of five or six can work together on a project, with each student having a clearly assigned role. In each case, students will be actively involved most of the time, rather than waiting for their turn to be called on, as so often occurs in large-group settings. By varying the activities of small groups, you can also provide instruction at differing levels of complexity simultaneously.

Individual work is appropriate when students are practicing for automaticity, are reviewing work previously studied, or are reading or writing. It is also useful when your diagnosis indicates that goals or activities that are appropriate for a particular student differ from those planned for others. Individual work is usually quiet time; this means that students are probably not vocalizing or sharing aloud, yet such sharing is a valuable form of processing.

Our suggestion is not to rely on any one group size too much. Students need to learn to listen in a large group, to interact in small groups, and to work independently. Such skills carry over into many real-life situations—for example, family living.

Please don't get the idea that you can use only one group size at a time—that, for instance, the whole class must be in small groups, or that the entire class has to work independently at the same time. On the contrary, you can use combinations of groupings at once. For example, you may be reteaching a small group of students who need more practice on a topic while the rest of the class works independently. Or you may be working with a reading group while three other groups work at centers cooperatively and four students work independently on projects.

Teacher-directed   Student - directed

Figure 4.5. Continuum of Teacher-directed and Student-directed Activities

Degree of Teacher Direction

Another decision is whether the activities you choose should be primarily teacher-directed or student-directed. Think of a continuum ranging from more to less teacher control, as in Figure 4.5. At one end of the continuum (the left side), the teacher sets the goals, chooses the activities, sets schedules for completion of each activity, and carefully monitors students' progress. Such an approach may be useful for teaching content that every student must master—for example, math facts.

At the other end of the continuum (on the right), imagine a classroom in which the students set their own goals, select their learning activities, and progress at their own pace. Students who are highly motivated to learn about a topic will flourish in such an environment. For example, two fifth-grade students we knew were so fascinated by a spelling lesson on words derived from the names of Greek and Roman gods that they sought out books on mythology in the library. Their teacher encouraged them to work together to gather information on Greek and Roman mythology and present their findings to the class. They even prepared a series of games and puzzles to teach the myths to younger children. This activity allowed the students to pursue their interest and develop independence. Of course, they still needed to show that they were keeping up with other important learning!

Does this example remind you of any of the curriculum philosophies we discussed in Chapter 2? We hope you are thinking of John Dewey and progressivism. Open, progressive classrooms tend to be more student-directed.

There is a middle position on this continuum, in which the teacher sets the goals and objectives but the students are allowed to choose from among a range of activities. Such an approach allows students to select those activities that match their own learning preferences. Many classes provide a mix of teacher-directed and student-directed activities; the teacher plans activities for the presentation of important content, but also encourages students to select topics or activities of interest for independent study. Such a mix is not only motivating but helps students develop the skills and attitudes of independent learning.

A Note to the Beginning Teacher

We know that as a beginning teacher, you will probably feel more secure if you organize your classroom using a large-group, teacher-directed format. Many experts recommend that at the beginning of the year, teachers keep students in a large group and have clearly designed teacher-led lessons (see Chapter 8). Such high structure helps the students see the classroom as a friendly but businesslike place where learning and progress are important. You will also want to plan activities early in the year to teach students the skills of small-group or individual work. Think carefully about how you want groups to operate, what individuals working alone should do if they need help, what the acceptable noise levels will be, and similar matters. You will have to spend time teaching and practicing these mechanics.

We encourage you to begin experimenting with small-group activities and student-directed learning during your student teaching. Observe several teachers who are skillful at using groups or self-directed work projects. In your first year of teaching, you may want to begin varying your classroom group sizes and the amount of teacher-directed work as soon as you feel you have created a well-structured class environment.

CHECK FOR UNDERSTANDING

What are two advantages and two disadvantages of each of the following ways of structuring the environment? Write your answers on the lines indicated.

Whole-group

Advantages: _____

_____

Disadvantages: _____

_____

Small-group

Advantages: _____

_____

Disadvantages: _____

_____

Individual/independent work

Advantages: _____

_____

Disadvantages: _____

_____

Highly teacher-directed

Advantages: _____

_____

Disadvantages: _____

_____

Highly student-directed

Advantages: _____

_____

Disadvantages: _____

_____

Check your answers against those of another student.

INTERACTING WITH STUDENTS

In this section we describe three commonly used teaching techniques: questioning, conducting discussions, and providing meaning-building activities.

Questioning

If students' learning and retention require that they interact with and rehearse information, how will you provide the opportunity? Think about your answer.

Just as we have attempted to engage you in rehearsing material through this question, you will frequently want to engage your students through effective questioning techniques. Questioning is one of the most powerful tools of any teacher. Questioning can serve many purposes: focusing student attention, helping students to interact with content, encouraging students to express values or opinions, and facilitating classroom management. In this section we will consider techniques for phrasing questions effectively and strategies to promote interaction with all your students: planning questions, pacing and phrasing questions, distributing questions, responding to student answers.

Planning Questions.   A carefully planned sequence of questions can lend clarity and structure to a lesson, leading students from one important idea to the next. Although it is important to maintain the flexibility to respond to students' ideas, needs, interests, and opinions, it is equally important to begin questioning with a road map or plan for your questioning. A series of questions that are prepared in advance is more likely to focus on lesson objectives and provide for both higher level and lower level thinking than questions produced on the spot.

There is no one correct way to sequence questions. Sometimes you may wish to begin with an open-ended (divergent) focusing question, and narrow the topic down through questions that involve descriptions and comparisons for answers. At other times you may prefer to proceed from lower level to higher level questioning. It is important to select the sequence of questions that corresponds best to your lesson objectives.

It is also wise to plan ahead of time the manner in which you will ask the questions. Will you ask the whole group and select random students to respond? Will you raise a question, then ask students to tell the answer to a partner? Will you pose a question to be discussed in small groups before calling for a response? If you note these ideas in your plans, you will be more

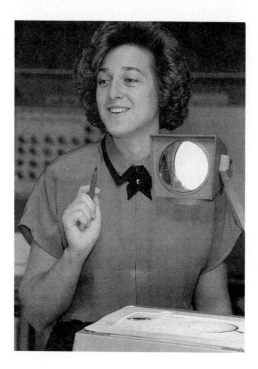

likely to provide variety in your questioning techniques. The following list contains a variety of questioning strategies that can be used with small and large groups.

Suggestions for Increasing Student Participation[1]

Small-Group Activities

1. *Discuss with a Partner*
   Examples:
   - In your own words, explain to your partner how the pistons in a car engine work.
   - Share with your partner the guidelines to keep in mind when writing an expository paragraph.
   - Discuss with your partner the meanings of these ten terms from our anatomy unit.
2. *Discussion in Small Groups*
   - Keep the group size to four or five so that each student can participate. Appoint a recorder to summarize the findings of the discussion.
3. *Write Questions*
   Examples:
   - Write one question about what we have just been studying. Try it out on a person near you. If that person can't answer the question, pass it to me. At the end of the period, I'll answer all questions that have been turned in.

---

[1]This list was derived from the ideas of Pam Robbins and Pat Wolfe of the Napa County Office of Education, Napa, California; and Priscilla Logan, Santa Fe Public Schools, Santa Fe, New Mexico.

- Write two questions based on the topic, "Planning Nutritional Meals." We'll use them tomorrow for a review of the unit.
4. *Brainstorm*
   - Brainstorming can be done as a group or with a partner. Define the topic or problem.
   - For example, the topic may be questions students think will be covered on an exam.
   Examples:
   - On your scratch paper, jot down as many terms as you can think of that are related to the topic we began studying yesterday. In 5 minutes we'll discuss these terms.
   - Repeat the same process as in the previous example, but share the ideas with a partner.
5. *Debate*
   - Discussion and examination of both sides of a question involves more students when done in small groups. In teaching debate techniques, first explain the structure. Then, with the help of a student, demonstrate a debate for the group. This gives students the guidelines of debating.
6. *Peer Group Teaching*
   - Using students as tutors is an effective learning device for both the tutor and tutored.
7. *Role Playing*
   - Simulating an event brings new perspectives to any lesson. Role playing involves more students when done in small groups, as it reduces the risk factor.

Whole-Group Activities
8. *Oral Reading*
   - Oral reading can be done in two ways.
     a. One student can read while the rest of the class follows with markers, their eyes, or their fingers.
     b. The entire class can read aloud together. For special dramatic effects, the boys and girls can alternate reading, etc.
9. *Whisper Answer in Teacher's Ear*
   - The teacher can select random students to whisper the answer to him or her.
10. *Provide Wait Time for Covert Rehearsal of Responses*
    - Waiting at least 3 seconds for an answer is a critical element in effective questioning of an entire class. Ask the students who have arrived at an idea to do something overt, such as put their right hand on the table, fold their arms, etc.
    - Promote even greater participation by telling the class how many have given the signal. For example, say, "Well, already 12 people have signaled that they know the answer." Wait until a sufficient response number is obtained. Then call on one randomly selected student to answer the question.
    Examples:
    - Which were the three Axis countries during World War II? (Pause) I can tell you're thinking. I see five hands, six, eight, lots more. Let's see, I think I'll call on Ted.
    - I want you to think about whether this blueprint would be practical for a house in an area that has a climate like Southern California's. I'll call upon someone in about 1 minute.

11. *Unison Response*
    - A teacher signal will indicate when the class should respond. For example, the slow raising of the teacher's hand means preparation. The abrupt lowering signals the point for the class response.

    Examples:
    - I'll point to a word and say a definition. If the definition I give is correct, please reply all together, "Yes." If it's incorrect, all say, "No."
    - I'll read some statements about the digestive process. If the statement is true, everyone respond together, "True," etc.
    - We'll check the answers to this worksheet together. I'll say the number of the question, then all of you respond with the answer on your paper. If the response is clear, we won't need to discuss that question. If it's garbled, we'll stop to clarify. (This obviously will work only with short-answer responses.)

12. *Consecutive Response*
    - Each student is responsible for recalling the previous student's response.

13. *Polling by Raised Hands*
    - Casting votes or canvassing for information—the data can be recorded on a chart visible to the entire class.

14. *Pointing*
    - Using an individual pictorial representation (map, diagram, picture), the students can point to the correct answer.

15. *Cross/Uncross Arms*

    Examples:
    - I'll read a series of statements about different kinds of angles. If you agree with the statement, cross your arms; if you don't agree, don't cross your arms. If you agree with Toby's opinion, cross your arms, etc.

16. *Flash Answers in Groups*
    - Flash cards made by students can be used in a variety of ways: true/false cards (color-coded for ease of reading), numerical multiplication-table answers, vocabulary review, and color-coded classifying.

    Examples:
    - We've talked about the three branches of our federal government. Students are divided into groups, and each group has three cards, each one stating a different governmental branch. I'll read a government duty (such as making laws). As a group, decide which branch of government would be responsible for that duty, and then hold up the correct card.
    - There are three animal classifications listed on the board, and they are color-coded. Each group has three pieces of paper, each a different color. I'll read the name of an animal, and as a group you decide which category that animal belongs to. Then hold up the appropriate piece of paper.

17. *Flashers*
    - A short answer can be written either on a laminated notebook with a water-soluble pen or on an individual chalkboard.

18. *Thumb Signals (Done at chest level in a personal, low-key manner)*

    Examples:
    - I'll read several statements about how to make a collar for a blouse. If the statement is true, put your thumb up. If it is false, put your thumb down. If you're not sure, put your thumb to the side.

> • If you agree with Jim's explanation of a zone defense, put your thumb up, etc.

19. *Finger Signals (Done at chest level in a personal, low-key manner)*
     Examples:
     • The three kinds of rock formations are listed on the board by number. I'll say a characteristic of a certain rock formation; you put up the appropriate number of fingers for the one that is being described.
     • The five main characters from the novel are listed on the board by number, etc.
     • I'll play several chords on the piano. If it's a major chord, put up one finger; if it's a minor chord, put up two fingers.

20. *Flash Cards*
     Examples:
     • You've made flash cards for your new Spanish vocabulary. Study them alone for 5 minutes. Then we'll do some "spot checking."
     • You've made flash cards for this week's vocabulary words. Practice them with a partner for 10 minutes. Then we'll have our quiz.

21. *Cross/Uncross Arms or Legs, Look Up or Down, Thumbs Up or Down, Pencils Up or Down*
     • The opposite positions can indicate positive/negative, higher/lower, or any two-part test of opposites.

Pacing and Phrasing Questions.   It is also important to consider how you will pace and phrase your questions. One of the most important concepts in pacing questions is *wait time*, which refers to the period between the time a teacher asks a question and the time he or she asks another question, questions another student, or, instead, answers the question. Rowe (1974) discovered that the average wait time for each teacher was less than 1 second. No wonder students sometimes have trouble finding time to think! In studies in which wait time was increased to 3 seconds or longer, numerous changes were observed:

> Length of responses increased.
> Number of voluntary responses increased.
> Complexity of response increased.
> Student questions increased.
> Student confidence increased.
> Student failure to respond decreased.
> (Tobin, 1980; Tobin & Campie, 1982)

There is no one perfect amount of wait time. In quickly paced recall questions, short amounts of wait time are appropriate. In divergent questioning, or questions requiring higher level thinking or evaluation, longer wait time allows students sufficient time to formulate answers, consider more than one perspective, or reflect on other students' responses. In general, however, you will probably do best pacing your questions more slowly than feels natural at first, allowing "think time" before asking for responses.

It is also important to consider the phrasing of your questions. In general, it is best not to start a question with a student's name, such as, "Gina, why did Lafayette agree to help the colonists?" All the other students know immediately that they are not being questioned and can ignore both the question and the answer. Improved classroom interaction by students at all levels can be achieved when questions are phrased so all students know they are responsible for considering a response. In this case, more students would have thought about Lafayette's motivation if the question had been phrased, "Everyone think about why Lafayette agreed to help the colonists. (Wait time) Gina? (Wait time)." It is also advisable to avoid the "Who can tell me . . ." habit of asking questions. Such phrasing invites students to call out the answer, thus depriving the others of valuable mental rehearsal of the material.

Distributing Questions.   Even when teachers call for responses after a question, students do not always have an equal chance for classroom interaction. Research has noted a variety of questioning patterns and numerous inequalities in the opportunities students have for responding to questions. Many teachers call on high-achieving students much more frequently than low-achieving students, boys more than girls, white students more than minority students, students at the front more than students at the back, or even students on one side of the classroom more than the other.

Any time an unequal pattern of questioning develops, some students have greater opportunity to process the material and transfer information to long-term memory than others. It also sends nonverbal messages to students about which youngsters in the classroom are considered capable or important. Research in classrooms that have implemented more equitable questioning patterns indicates that they lead to greater interaction by all students, more willingness to respond, and increased questioning by students (Cooper & Good, 1983).

How can you distribute questions equitably to your students? Some teachers like to use props to ensure that all students have an equal chance of being asked a question. Popsicle sticks or index cards with student names on them can be pulled at random, assuring that students have an equal chance of being chosen each time. Other teachers keep track of who they call on by making a mark on their seating chart each time they call on a student. Every day or two they check to see who is getting called on frequently enough and who needs to be called on more. In this way they can monitor their own distribution of questions. You may wish to ask a friend to observe a lesson you teach and note the students with whom you interact. Such observations can provide valuable information for improving questioning patterns.

Responding to Student Answers.   Once a student has responded to a question, you will need to decide whether to praise, acknowledge, redirect, probe, prompt, correct, or ask a new question.

While *praise* can be important in creating a positive classroom atmosphere and building self-esteem, it must be used selectively. Praise that is routine or repetitive quickly becomes meaningless. A response of "good" after every student answer is almost like no response at all. Praise that is global ("You are always such a good student") does not help students identify the characteristics of their work that led to their success ("You made excellent use of figurative language in your description of the forest") and has the potential to create or increase emotional problems. Youngsters who are led to believe that they are always expected to be "good students" may become fearful of challenging tasks or open-ended situations. Teachers must also be alert for students who are embarrassed by public praise. For many students, a private comment is more welcome than public praise given during class.

Finally, praise can be seen as a "terminal" response, frequently ending discussion or thought. If you ask a divergent question and give elaborate praise to the first answer, other students are less likely to respond, assuming the "right" answer has already been given. Some research has indicated that while routine, familiar procedures were not adversely affected by praise or rewards, early rewards may have a detrimental effect on problem solving or higher level thinking (Costa, 1985). While each teacher needs to be sensitive to the effects of praise in his or her classroom, in many cases praise is most appropriate for unmotivated or reluctant learners, lower grade students, lower level cognitive tasks, or practice of previously learned material (Costa, 1985). In other cases, silence or *acknowledgment* of responses ("I understand" or "That's one possibility") may be more appropriate, and lead to continued student efforts. You may also wish to accept the response nonverbally (perhaps through a nod) or *redirect* the question to another student: "What do you think, Ben?"

Sometimes student responses are unclear or incomplete. In such cases, it is important to *probe* for further clarification or information. In some cases a general probe such as "Please explain further" or "Can you elaborate on that?" can be used. In other cases it is best to be more specific, in order to be sure what the student is thinking. If, for example, a teacher had asked the class "How did Washington's troops feel at Valley Forge?" and a student responded, "Happy," it would be important to probe, "Why were they happy?" If the student replies, "Well, they were cold and hungry, but they knew they were fighting for an important cause and I think that would have made them happy," the teacher would plan a much different response than if the student had responded, "They were camping out, and camping is fun."

When probing, be aware of your responses to ethnic, achievement, and gender groups in the classroom. It is important that probing as well as questioning be equitable; teachers who seek responses from as many students as possible send the message that all students are considered capable and are expected to participate.

If a student answer is inaccurate or incomplete, you may wish to *prompt,* or cue the student toward a more complete response. It is important to help students understand which parts of an answer were correct and which were incorrect, while providing information that may lead to a completely correct response. The process of prompting students requires care and sensitivity, so that students have every opportunity for success without embarrassment. For example, if Mr. Holmes asked, "What are the characteristics of mammals?" and Suzanne replied, "They live in the water," Mr. Holmes might correct her and then provide a prompt to lead Suzanne to a correct response. A prompt often involves asking another question. "No. Although some mammals live in the water, *all* mammals don't live in the water. Remember yesterday when we talked about the cow being a mammal? What were some of the characteristics of the cow we said were shared by all mammals?"

Good teachers should not only question students but listen effectively to what students say. Garrett, Sadker, and Sadker (1986) suggest that teachers can improve their listening through attending behavior and active and reflective listening. *Attending behavior* refers to a variety of verbal and nonverbal responses that signal to students "I am listening to you. I believe that the things you have to say are valuable." Nonverbal signals include eye contact, an emphathetic facial expression (for example, nodding or smiling), relaxed body posture (signaling "I have time to listen to you"), and comfortable physical proximity (distance). Verbal signals can include silence, which is a chance for the teacher to reflect and the speaker to continue; brief verbal acknowledgments, such as "I see" or "Yes"; or brief summaries of the speaker's statements. In many cases attending behaviors can be viewed as common courtesy. Unfortunately, without conscious attention, they may be lost in the flurry of classroom activity, in which the critical moment of silence or careful eye contact may seem difficult to maintain. However, with care and practice, you will be able to signal to your students that, no matter how busy you are, you value the things they are saying.

You can also signal students that you are paying attention to them by *active and reflective listening*. *Active listening* entails identifying both the intellectual and emotional attitude of the speaker. If Jared says, "This is a dumb book," he is conveying an emotional as well as an intellectual message. You should carefully observe nonverbal cues and consider all you know about Jared to discern what the message might be. Jared might be saying, "I am upset because

I don't understand this book" or "I am offended by the stereotypes presented here" or "I read this three years ago and I am bored."

After actively listening to a student, you may reflect, or restate, the messages you thought you received. *Reflective listening* may involve paraphrasing the statements ("You don't like the book") or expressing both the statement and the inferred emotion ("You seem upset about reading this book"). Reflective listening is a powerful tool that must be used with care. It is particularly valuable when emotions are high and misunderstandings easy, or in situations in which clear understanding is critical. You will need to be sensitive to the amount of reflecting that is sufficient to elicit clarity without becoming monotonous or parrot-like.

CHECK FOR UNDERSTANDING

How might you use *reflective listening* to respond to the following students' comments? Write your answers on the lines as indicated.

Jane (looking at the floor): I hate recess.

You: _____

Miguel (smiling broadly): I'm going to be on the citywide Quiz Bowl team!

You: _____

CHECK FOR UNDERSTANDING

Select a topic that would take about 15 minutes to explain. Assume your objective is for students to be able to explain the main points of the lecture in their own words. In the space below, outline the *information you plan to teach* on the left. On the right, create a visual aid to *show the organization* of the information (e.g., a picture, graph, or outline).

Information   **How I'll show the organization**

Now, list the questions and questioning technique(s) you will use (see "Suggestions for Increasing Student Participation," pages 134 to 137 for ideas).

Questions   **Questioning technique**

_____

Finally, list two questions you can use to extend the content into higher level thinking.

1. _____

_____

2. _____

_____
_____

Conducting Discussions

What is the difference between asking questions and having a discussion? Think about the differences before you read on.

Some of the possible points you might have thought of are (1) the relative extent of participation by students and by the teacher, (2) the focus of communication, and (3) the classroom atmosphere. In questioning, the teacher is almost always the focus of attention. Communication travels from teacher to student, back to teacher, and is redirected to another student, forming a pattern like a many-armed spider, with the teacher at the center. In a discussion, the patterns of communication are much more diverse. While the initial stimulus may come from the teacher, additional comments may travel from student to student, with students adding questions or comments as desired. Figure 4.6 illustrates the difference between questioning and discussion. While questioning is sometimes directed at "quizzing" students, discussion is an open-ended exchange of ideas designed to share information and possibly to reach consensus, rather than to seek the "right" answer.

Questioning   Discussion

Figure 4.6. Interaction Patterns in Questioning and Discussion

A good classroom discussion is a valuable learning experience, full of opportunities for higher level thinking and ties to student interests and experiences. Like many worthwhile goals, however, it is a challenge requiring planning, patience, and practice. Many students spend years in school without participating in a real discussion. Their inexperience can sometimes turn "discussions" into questioning sessions in which all attention is focused on the teacher, and students attempt to discern exactly what the teacher "wants." Because they find it difficult to imagine that the teacher wants them to express opinions (to say nothing of asking questions of their own), they expend enormous energy trying to find the "right" answer.

In many classes it is useful to plan numerous experiences with paired or small group mini-discussions before attempting to share ideas with an entire class. You can think of the small-group sharing as a way of priming the pump for greater participation in the large group. Students may be asked to describe to a partner their favorite character in a story or to discuss in a group of five the items they would bring with them in a covered wagon; a pair of students might debate the pros and cons of proposed legislation in pairs, with a third student noting major arguments. Such activities accustom students to talking to one another without depending on the teacher to direct the conversation. They also provide needed variety, even in classes already adept at whole-group discussion.

If you want students to raise questions during class discussions, you may wish to structure activities to practice such behaviors. Students can be asked to write questions about stories they've read, current issues, historical dilemmas, or almost any other content. Some teachers even explain the levels of Bloom's taxonomy (see Chapter 6) to their students, to enable them to write higher level questions for class discussions. It is important to reinforce students' questioning behaviors, letting them know we are glad that they are seeking information, clarification, or opinions.

Key to a successful class discussion is an open-ended topic for discussion. There is little point in discussing the year the American Revolution started, or the sequence of events in *Johnny Tremain*. Facts, sequences, or issues on which there is already consensus do not make good discussion topics. Concepts that are fuzzy, issues generating a genuine difference of opinion, or opportunities to tie personal experiences to content provide more change for successful expression. During a discussion, the teacher (or other discussion leader) may serve several roles:

1. Provide the initial stimulus for discussion
2. Provide additional information, clarification, or correction of misinformation as needed
3. Paraphrase, summarize, or compare student positions to add clarity
4. Maintain the focus of the discussion. This role demands good judgment and a gentle hand. While it is important not to allow class discussions to stray far from the topic at hand (how many of you had a teacher who could be distracted from the day's topic by the mere mention of last night's big game?), occasional diversions can provide significant information about students' needs, wants, and values. In general, discussion leaders should try to keep discussion on the topic of concern.
5. Respond to student comments with acceptance, rather than praise or criticism. Remember that either praise or criticism can be viewed as a terminal response, cutting off further discussion. If one student's response is effusively praised, other students are apt to think that that response was the right one and hesitate to comment further. Of course, if students' comments are met with personal criticism or harassment, neither they nor others are apt to continue. Students will benefit from instruction on expressing disagreement without fear of being insulted.

6. Draw the discussion to a close through summarizing and/or seeking compromise or consensus.

As you conduct classroom discussions, be aware of the patterns of student interactions. You may want to ask an observer to keep track of student contributions during one class day. You can encourage contributions from all students by using small groups, and by teaching skills of discussion and cooperation. These topics are discussed further in the section on cooperative learning in Chapter 5.

Providing Meaning-Building Activities

There are many types of activities we can use to present content. However, we know from research on memory and learning that "presenting" content is not enough to ensure student learning. Each student must create meaning for himself or herself, tying new experiences into existing schemata in individual ways (recall the discussion on schemata in the section on long-term memory). Our task is to structure classroom activities to enable students to build meaning as powerfully as possible, with a rich network of links to previous experience.

How do students construct meaning from experience? Imagine for a moment that you are about to begin a unit on France. Think for a moment: If you had unlimited time and resources, what would be the best ways to help students develop a network of experiences about France?

Did you plan a field trip to France? Did you imagine students eating croissants in Paris, touring the countryside, speaking French to other children? Perhaps you were a little more cautious with your unlimited budget and imagined bringing French food, music, art, and guest speakers to your classroom. In either case, you probably wanted students to experience France as completely as possible. While few of us will ever teach in a situation with unlimited resources, we can use the principle of experience-based learning and the Cone of Experience, as described in Section 2 of this chapter, to come as close to this ideal as possible, through a variety of activities.

Field Trips.   It is unlikely that you will take many field trips to Europe. However, a field trip can be a powerful tool in helping students build meaning. Field trips are particularly appropriate when students do not have the prior experiences necessary to construct the concepts you are teaching. If students have not been exposed to farm animals, libraries, supermarkets, or cities, field trips can provide them with a basis from which to build these common concepts.

In other cases, field trips can provide experiences to build ideas that are new for most students. For example, few 20th-century students have seen a blacksmith or watched the process of candle making. A trip to a restored village can bring meaning to these concepts through a rich variety of multisensory experiences. Students who have never been exposed to Impressionist paintings will gain a deeper understanding of the interplay of light, paint, and canvas by viewing original works of art than is possible with most reproductions.

While there are many logistical considerations in planning a field trip (and we urge you to consult with several experienced teachers before embarking on your first one), from the perspective of building meaning, one point is key: Know the purpose of your trip. Many school districts have imposed severe limitations on field trips, in some cases because of budget concerns, but in others because of the perception that field trips are "fun and games," a day off for students and teachers. If you are to be successful in planning and implementing field trips, it is essential that you and the students both understand the purpose of the trip, the goals for the day, and the expectations for future study.

Like any other activity, a field trip needs to be focused. In some cases the focus may be expressed in a fairly general way, such as "While we are at the farm, try to remember all the different kinds of animals you see." In other cases students may be seeking highly specific information. "During our visit to the museum, use your hypothesis forms to check your group's hypotheses about occupations in ancient Egypt. Record any data that support or refute your hypothesis on the form. When we get back to class, we will compare notes." In either case, students have a focus for their observations that will assist in building important concepts.

Role Playing and Simulation.   It is not always possible to plan a field trip: The location may be impractical (e.g., Australia), unavailable (e.g., a robotics factory), or impossible (e.g., 18th-century Massachusetts). If the concept you are teaching does not center on a particular location but on a general issue, such as provisions for people with handicaps, it is possible to give students indirect experiences through role playing or simulation.

In *role playing,* students usually try to solve a problem by assuming a particular role—for example, making a decision about dolphins caught in tuna nets from the perspective of an environmentalist, a fisher, or a representative of a tuna company. A *simulation* involves students in longer, more complex situations that represent a simplified version of real life. While the tuna dilemma role play might entail a single discussion, a related simulation might require students to maintain the roles over several days and operate in "realistic" conditions. For example, the fisher might need to catch a certain number of tuna to support a family, or the tuna company might need a specific cost ratio to stay in operation.

Role playing and simulation can be used to provide students with experiences not possible in real life. They may take part in the tool making of the aborigines, the complex planning of robotic factories, or the challenges of physical handicaps in ways that provide complex and meaningful experiences. Simulation and role playing are discussed again in Chapter 5 as types of social lessons.

Media.   Filmstrips, movies, video and audio tapes, and other types of media can provide students with meaningful experiences that bring content to life. They enable students to travel to remote areas of the earth, see dramatic productions by famous performers, and take simulated journeys through time and space. Media can add variety to classroom activities while providing stimulating visual images that assist memory.

However, like any other input, media must be used in carefully planned and focused lessons. It is not enough to tell students, "We will see a movie on this topic." Students should be prepared ahead of time so that they can concentrate on important topics or aspects of the production. There should also be follow-up activities that reinforce concepts or that practice skills. Be aware that taking notes or gathering information from a movie, videotape, or filmstrip is a different task from obtaining the same information from text. In a book, there is always the opportunity to go back and reread a passage—a film just keeps on turning! Preview long movies to find stopping points. Again, activities conducted before the showing will alert students to the information you want them to learn from the film. For example, a fourth-grade class preparing to see a film on sharks can draw up a list of questions about sharks that might be answered by the film. With the questions in front of them, students can jot down brief relevant information during the film without having to take notes on everything presented. Any questions left unanswered provide impetus for further investigation.

Finally, remember that students can create, as well as watch, media. Slide shows, videotapes, audiotapes, photo essays, and filmstrips can all be produced by students in a wide

variety of settings. Your district media specialist or a good book on audiovisual production can provide the information you need to get started. Projects of this type not only help students develop technical, planning, sequencing, and decision-making skills but avoid the tedium of yet another report.

Demonstrations and Displays.   Would you rather read about the differences between physical and chemical changes, or watch a teacher tear a piece of paper and then combine baking soda and vinegar, the mixture resulting in great bubbling and fizzing? Are you more likely to remember that carbon dioxide is heavier than air after hearing a lecture on the subject or after watching carbon dioxide "poured" out of a cup to extinguish a candle? Certainly, the excitement and multisensory impact of *demonstrations* cannot be duplicated by either reading or lecturing alone.

Depending on the nature of the task and the availability of materials, demonstrations can be conducted by the teacher, a student, or groups of students. A task that is complex or involves fire or potentially dangerous chemicals is best left to the teacher at all but high school levels. Sometimes limitations in budget or facilities make it impossible for each student to conduct a demonstration or experiment. If it is possible in your school, the effort is worthwhile, because individual participation has greater learning impact than being a spectator. Do not become discouraged by the seemingly complex procedures involved in preparing for demonstrations or individual experiments. Sometimes in the busy pace of a teacher's life, looking for 30 paper cups in which to mix baking soda, or tracking down the only set of test tubes in the building,

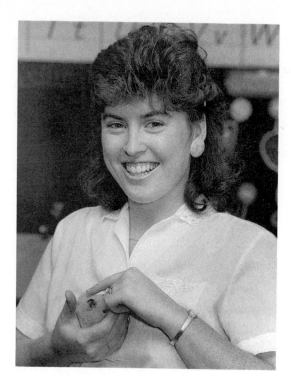

may seem like a daunting task. Remember that time spent creating powerful meaning-building experiences will pay enormous dividends in student learning—which is, of course, our goal.

In a similar fashion, *displays* can provide students with more interesting, varied, and stimulating experiences than talk or pictures alone. Some teachers create classroom displays from personal items, perhaps an arrangement of souvenirs from Mexico during a unit on that country. Others are able to locate traveling displays through district or interdistrict media centers or local museums. Many museums, especially those with collections devoted partially or entirely to children, provide interesting exhibits that can be borrowed at minimal cost. We have borrowed displays as varied as local rocks and minerals, skeletons of mammals, artifacts of 19th-century schools, and butter-making equipment of the last 150 years! Check with other teachers, parents, district media personnel, and local museums to see what is available in your area. You may also consider working with your students to create classroom displays or mini-museums. Not only do such activities, and the product created, reinforce the content you are teaching; they provide students with good opportunities to develop organizational skills.

Of course, like all other activities, demonstrations, experiments, and displays should not stand alone, but be focused, planned, and related to your instructional sequence. The most original displays or the most dramatic demonstrations are meaningless unless students understand how they fit in with previous experiences, what they mean, and why they are important.

CHECK FOR UNDERSTANDING

With another person in your class, discuss your experiences with field trips, simulation/role playing, media, and displays/demonstrations. To prepare yourself for this discussion, jot down activities you have seen that fit into the four categories. Write your answers in the spaces indicated.

Field Trips	Simulation/Role playing	Media	Displays/Demonstrations

Projects.   Projects, whether done in groups or individually, are an imaginative way to build meaning. You might think of a project as the creation of a real-life product that represents a synthesis of relevant learning. For example, students in Millicent's money management unit might collect data on how many televisions each family in their neighborhood owns, display the information on a graph, and present a written report relating the data to the concepts of *needs* and *wants*.

To complete projects successfully, students must integrate and apply a variety of skills and understandings. In the example above, such skills include graphing and averaging; the concepts to be understood include *necessities* and *wants*. A progressive-minded teacher, favoring student-directed learning, may encourage students to begin the project, let them discover the need for specific skills and concepts, and then enable them to seek out their own learning materials (actually prepared ahead by the teacher). An essentialist-oriented teacher might explain the information on money management directly.

Regardless of the teacher's educational philosophy, projects allow students to bring skills, concepts, and generalizations together in a product that is useful to them and is conducted in real-life settings. The TV survey gives students the opportunity to apply new ideas and gain a deeper understanding of how their neighbors' TV watching relates to the concepts of *needs* and *wants*. It also demonstrates to the students the real-life utility of data gathering and graphing.

Centers.   Not all meaning-building activities are teacher-directed. One means for facilitating student-directed learning is through the use of centers. A *center* is a part of the classroom organized for student investigation of a particular topic or area of study. It may be set up on a table in the corner, a cutting board, two or three desks near a bulletin board, an easel, or in any other location your creativity can devise. While there are many possible uses for centers, we will discuss two types: *learning centers* and *interest-development centers*.

A *learning center* is designed to help students master and/or practice a particular body of content. For example, a learning center on multiplication might contain numerous activities to help students learn rules of multiplication, practice multiplication facts, and solve word problems. The activities might take the form of worksheets, puzzles, projects, or games to be completed by individuals or small groups.

Because learning centers are student-directed, activities should generally provide opportunities for self-correction and record keeping. It is important that students practice the organizational skills and responsibility necessary to track their progress and that you have a ready means for determining which students have completed specific activities. Because a learning center is generally used to teach and/or provide practice in required content, you may choose to have students complete a specified number of activities and then check regularly on their progress.

Interest-development centers are not used to teach required content but to encourage students to explore topics in or outside the general curriculum. You may create such a center in an area of personal interest (e.g., a trip to Spain), as an extension of the regular curriculum (e.g., Japanese music), or in an area of interest to a particular group of students (e.g., rocketry). Activities in an interest-development center generally include suggestions for investigation, puzzling questions, ideas for projects, and keys to resources.

Because an interest-development center focuses and develops individual pursuits, such activities are frequently optional. Books on using teaching centers and conversations with experienced teachers can be helpful in planning centers for your classroom. You may even want to share ideas with someone at your grade level and swap center ideas to double your resources.

Reading and Writing.   Of course, students can build meaning and acquire information through the traditional activities of reading and writing. Bringing students into contact with a wide variety of print materials—books, magazines, pamphlets, newspapers—is an important goal of our educational system. While an extended discussion on strategies for deriving meaning from text is beyond the scope of this book, the general principles we have discussed hold true for reading in much the same way they do for other activities. "Take out your textbook and read pages 87 and 88" is not sufficient motivation to enable most students to derive the maximum meaning from the text. Like all other experiences, reading needs to be focused, tied to prior knowledge, and followed by related discussion and/or practice. A lesson that begins with students creating lists of items they want and items they need, then asks students to read pages 87 and 88 to see if the text's definition of *wants* and *needs* is the same as theirs, and includes a discussion on similarities and differences in the students' and text's ideas is more likely to facilitate student learning than one that merely requires students to read the text.

It should be clear by now that while we can provide information to students in many ways, our instructional principles remain constant. Students need a variety of meaningful, participatory activities presented in an organized manner, to tie their experiences together and enable them to acquire and process new information.

CHECK FOR UNDERSTANDING

Imagine that you are at a party and one of the guests discovers that you are a teacher. He begins complaining about his son's second-grade teacher, who "wastes the students' time playing games when they could be studying." Then he demands to know why his son spent time visiting the aquarium and building a life-size model of a shark when he had a perfectly good science book. After you take a deep breath, what will you say? Write your answers below.

_____

_____

_____

_____

SELECTING LEARNING ACTIVITIES AND REFLECTIVE DECISION MAKING

In this chapter we have described several factors to take into consideration when planning learning activities. These are

- Social, political, community, school, and physical factors
- Students' personal characteristics
- Teacher's knowledge of goals and content
- Teacher's knowledge of learning principles
- Teacher's ability to use a variety of instructional techniques

A key concept of this book is that teaching is a sophisticated process of decision making in which each of these factors is considered. We realize, however, that not all decisions are purely intellectual. Your own personal philosophy of teaching and learning will certainly come into play. Your emotions and health will influence your decisions; your personality and style will affect your teaching. While these factors cannot be ignored, we suggest that teaching can be an intelligent and purposeful activity, guided by cognitive reasoning.

Therefore, we hope you avoid a haphazard method of planning. Many teachers select activities only on the basis of convenience or student interest, without regard to whether they match the instructional objectives, relate to students' learning needs, and so on. In essence, then, we are asking you to develop a purposeful, analytical approach to teaching that will help you make the best decisions possible for the students, content, and conditions at the time.

We suggest that you see your growth as a decision maker as a gradual process. First, you will plan your activities to meet your objectives while taking into consideration community, content, students, learning principles, and teaching techniques. Then you will design a lesson or action plan for the teaching period. Finally, you will try it out, modifying it as necessary as you go.

The next step—reflection and redesign—is crucial to your development as a teacher, and we warn you, it will be hard to find time for it. The payoff, however, is worth it. We suggest that when you finish a lesson you spend a few moments reflecting on what went well and what did not go well. It is easiest to pick one successful and one less successful moment for analysis. For each moment, go back through the five factors, considering the community, students, content/objectives, learning theories, and techniques. Also consider the six learning principles. Ask yourself if any of these ideas can help explain why things went as they did. Then you can decide how to pursue or develop the successful parts of the lesson, emphasizing the factors or principles that made them work. You can also plan an alternative approach that might make the less successful parts of the lesson work better. Independent Practice B, at the end of this chapter, contains a Reflection Journal to be used for this purpose.

Your choice of an alternative is informed by your prior analysis, so it is likely to represent a real improvement. You try out your modification, rethink it, redesign it, and try again until you feel you have a sequence of activities that work reasonably well. But be prepared, because you may need to modify further when students, goals, or content change. Teaching is an ever-renewing process.

Guided Practice Activity D. Organizing the Information in the Chapter

To help you organize the information in the chapter and to deepen your understanding, prepare a brief outline of the main points made in each of the sections of the chapter. Below is a "starter outline" to assist you. Make sure that you can explain in your own words the ideas in each section. You may wish to do this task with a study partner, taking one section at a time. Write your outline on a separate sheet.

- **I.** Factors to consider when selecting activities
    - **A.** Community, school, and classroom factors
        - **1.** Social/political/community
        - **2.** School
        - **3.** Time/physical
    - **B.** Students' personal characteristics
        - **1.** Intelligence
        - **2.** Prior knowledge and experience
        - **3.** Learning styles
    - **C.** Teacher's knowledge of goals and content
- **II.** Teachers' knowledge of learning principles
    - **A.** Memory and learning theory
        - **1.** Sensory memory
        - **2.** Short-term memory (STM)
        - **3.** Long-term memory (LTM)
    - **B.** Principles of learning
        - **1.** Congruence
        - **2.** Organization and clarity
        - **3.** Variety
        - **4.** Active processing
        - **5.** Experience-based learning
        - **6.** Higher level thinking
- **III.** Teacher's ability to use a variety of instructional techniques
    - **A.** Structuring the learning environment
        - **1.** Group size
        - **2.** Degree of teacher direction

B. Interacting with students
  1. Lecturing
  2. Questioning
  3. Conducting discussions
  4. Providing meaning-building activities

Guided Practice Activity E. Applying Principles and Techniques

Assume you are teaching a unit on a topic of your choice. List the topic below and brainstorm the content and objectives. Be sure to include both affective and cognitive objectives. Do not forget to include real-life learning and objectives for higher level thinking.

_____

_____

_____

_____

Next, select one objective and list questions and questioning strategies you might use to accomplish the objective.

_____

_____

_____

_____

Pick another objective that would lend itself to a discussion activity. List potential discussion starters and reminders to yourself about conducting the discussion.

_____

_____

_____

For a higher level objective, brainstorm as many meaning-building activities as you can. List them below.

_____

_____

_____

Independent Practice Activity A. Self-Analysis Questions

Using the categories listed (I, A,B,C; II, A,B; III, A,B) in Guided Practice Activity D, create a list of questions to ask yourself as you are planning learning activities. For example, using the category *community,* you might ask, "Are there any special goals of the school I need to consider as I design my activities?" Brainstorm at least five questions you might ask yourself for each category. Write them down and bring them to class for a group comparison. This may serve as an excellent tool for later decisions when planning lessons.

Independent Practice Activity B. Reflection Journal

Observe a teacher or teach a short lesson yourself. Then fill in the following journal. (Use extra paper if you need more space.)

Reflection Journal

What I did:

How it worked:

One successful aspect of the lesson:

Why did this part go well? What do I know about teaching and learning that might explain why? What conditions were operating that might explain why?

One less successful aspect of the lesson:

Why did this part not go well? What do I know about teaching and learning that might explain why? What conditions were operating that might explain why?

Ideas for next time. What I learned from this experience:

REFERENCES

Barbe, W., & Swassing, R. (1979). *Teaching through Modality Strengths: Concepts and Practices.* Columbus, OH: Zaner Bloser.

Berliner, D. C., & Rosenshine, B. V. (Eds.). (1987). *Talks to Teachers.* New York: Random House.

Butler, K. (1986). *Learning and Teaching Style in Theory and Practice.* Columbia, CT: Learner's Dimension.

Cooper, H., & Good, T. (1983). *Pygmalion Grows Up: Studies in the Expectation Communication Process.* New York: Longman.

Costa, A. (1985). Teacher Behaviors That Enable Student Thinking. In A. Costa (Ed.), *Developing Minds: A Resource Book for Teaching Thinking* (pp. 125–137). Alexandria, VA: Association for Supervision and Curriculum and Development.

Dale, E. (1963). *Audiovisual Methods in Teaching.* New York: Holt, Rinehart & Winston.

Dunn, R., & Dunn, K. (1975). *Educator's Self-Teaching Guide to Individualizing Instructional Programs.* New York: Parker.

Gage, N. L. (1978). *The Scientific Basis of the Art of Teaching.* New York: Teachers College Press.

Gage, N. L., & Berliner, D. (1984). *Educational Psychology* (3rd ed.). Boston: Houghton Mifflin.

Garrett, S., Sadker, M., & Sadker, D. (1986). Interpersonal communication skills. In J. Cooper (Ed.), *Classroom Teaching Skills* (3rd ed., pp. 225–269). Lexington, MA: D. C. Heath.

Gregorc, A. (1982). *An Adult's Guide to Style.* Maynard, MA: Gabriel.

Hunt, D. E. (1979). Learning style and student needs: An introduction to conceptual level. In *Student Learning Styles: Diagnosing and Prescribing Programs* (pp. 27–38). Reston, VA: National Association of Secondary School Principals.

Rowe, M. (1974). Wait time and rewards as instructional variables: Their influence on language, logic, and fate control. *Journal of Research in Science Teaching, 11,* 81–94.

Stallings, J. A., Needels, M., & Stayrook, N. (1979). *How to Change the Process of Teaching Basic Reading Skills in Secondary Schools.* Final report to National Institute of Education, Menlo Park, CA: SRI International.

Tobin, K. (1980). The effect of an extended teacher wait time on science achievement. *Journal of Research in Science Teaching, 17,* 469–475.

Tobin, K., & Campie, W. (1982). Relationships between classroom process variables and middle-school science achievement. *Journal of Educational Psychology, 74,* 441–454.

TOPIC TWO

Implementation: Getting Out There and Teaching

CHAPTER 5

Unit and Lesson Design

Chapter Overview

In Chapter 4 we listed factors to consider when selecting learning activities. But we saved a major point until this chapter: Activities are not planned as isolated events to keep kids busy. Rather, activities should be the elements of well-designed, well-organized lessons that help students attain specific learning outcomes. These lessons should not be isolated events, either. When organized into units, they lead systematically to the accomplishment of long-range goals that reflect useful skills and ideas for daily living.

In this chapter we introduce a structure for unit design and three basic types of lessons. We emphasize that the choice of lesson types and activities is based on the teacher's style, the content, the outcomes, and the students.

Chapter Objectives

After you have completed this chapter, you will be able to:
1. explain each component of a unit
2. describe three categories of instructional lessons
3. describe the seven elements of direct lessons
4. design a direct (deductive) lesson consistent with the principles of such lessons
5. design an inductive lesson consistent with the principles of such lessons
6. design a social lesson consistent with the principles of such lessons
7. discuss the advantages and disadvantages of each type of lesson

Section 1. Unit Planning

Set Activity

Look over the headings of the prior chapters in this book. If you were asked to design a unit "Community Helpers," what steps would you take to help yourself plan? What would you need to do before you were ready to teach your first lesson? List steps below.

_____

_____

_____

_____

_____

     Check to see if you included selecting goals, analyzing content and creating a learning hierarchy (or task analysis), writing lesson objectives, making lesson plans, and planning diagnostic and evaluation procedures.

Many teachers and curriculum planners go through the steps listed in the set activity when preparing a unit of instruction. A *unit* is a series of lessons that lead to the accomplishment of a broad goal. The final product usually includes the following components:

    Rationale
    Content outline and learning hierarchy
    Objectives
    Lesson designs and plans
    Evaluation procedures
    Materials

Each of these components is described below.

RATIONALE

The unit *rationale* is a brief statement that explains the content and purposes of the unit. The rationale is written for the students and those who will be using the unit. It can be used to focus attention on key unit issues, to provide motivation, and to justify the importance of the content in terms of subject matter, societal needs, and needs or interests of learners (see Tyler's Curriculum Rationale in Chapter 2).

The rationale should be brief, no more than a paragraph or two in length. Two examples are provided below.

Road Map Skills (Grade 4)

Have you noticed how many people travel by car on summer vacations? Perhaps you have traveled with your family a long distance by car. How do people who travel such long distances know how to get to their destination? The traveler learns to depend on a road map, especially when the area is new. A road map reduces the danger of getting lost, thus making the trip more relaxing and enjoyable. In this unit, you will learn the secrets of a road map so you can plan your own vacation to any place on the map.

Pet Care (Grade 3)

Do you have a pet, maybe a dog, a cat, or a bird? Many third graders have to feed, clean, and bathe their pets. In this unit you will learn some useful things about caring for animals. Even if you do not have a pet, you can learn what to do if you find an injured animal. Finally, you will learn something about people who work with animals in pet shops and zoos. You should enjoy this unit and learn more about how humans and animals can live happily with one another.

CONTENT OUTLINE AND LEARNING HIERARCHY

The content outline and learning hierarchy help create a structure showing the main ideas, the concepts, generalizations, and facts that students are to learn. As you remember from Chapter 4, information must be structured in meaningful ways to be learned. That is, it is

organized into a logical pattern for learning. A teacher can present information in an orderly way only after a thorough and searching analysis of the content. Since we cannot teach everything about a subject, we must make decisions about essential ideas and then organize those ideas logically. This analysis allows the teacher to identify the most important concepts, generalizations, and facts. Chapter 2 presented several examples of content outlines and learning hierarchies for the "Making Choices" unit.

OBJECTIVES

After deciding on the most important ideas in the unit, we can turn them into clearly stated instructional outcomes to be achieved by students. These long-term objectives will include all cognitive, affective, and psychomotor outcomes relevant to the unit. Each long-term objective will need to be broken down into subobjectives—smaller, more specific objectives that lead to the long-term objective. For example, consider the topic "Needs and Wants" in the money management unit. A long-term higher level objective is

> The students will be able to correctly distinguish the concept *needs* from *wants* when given a list of items found in a variety store.

Two subobjectives leading to this objective are

> The students will be able to:
> 1.   describe in their own words the meaning of *needs* and *wants*
> 2.   give examples of *needs* and *wants*

After completing subobjectives 1 and 2, students are more likely to be able to do the higher level task of distinguishing needed items from wanted items in a variety store. Without such clear breakdowns of sublearnings, we may fail to provide the proper knowledge base for higher level tasks. Or worse, we may present content in a random order. In such a case, it is impossible for students to build upon prior lessons.

Your instructional objectives become the en route stopovers for what you hope to accomplish in your unit. They are valuable for two reasons. First, they indicate the logical progression of a lesson. As we saw in this example, without a lesson on understanding needs and wants, students are unlikely to be able to apply those concepts in a new situation.

A second reason for creating subobjectives is that it helps us diagnose the learners' readiness for the content and thinking required by the unit. Recall our discussion in Chapters 3 and 4 of the importance of diagnosing learners' prior knowledge, interests, and needs. Your list of objectives can help you design a diagnostic test or activity to assess which students have the required skills to succeed in the unit. For example, if we are going to set up a store as part of our money management unit, we have to check to see if students are able to add and subtract so they can make correct change. Having such information before we begin teaching allows us to fill any gaps for the few students lacking the essential skills required to begin the unit.

Early diagnosis also helps us determine which students have already met some of our unit's subobjectives. For example, imagine you are teaching a fifth-grade unit on the western United States. If some students had a fourth-grade teacher who devoted a good deal of time to the subject Native Americans, we would want to find out which objectives (those related to Indians) those students have already achieved. They may need more advanced activities—for example, presenting their knowledge to others through a skit or a small play. Or they could be encouraged to pursue their learning in another area.

After this process of writing objectives, arranging them in a logical order, and diagnosing students, you'll be ready to select an objective for your first lesson that is at the correct level of difficulty for most students. When you have completed this task, your instruction (and students' learning) is likely to be more successful.

LESSON DESIGNS

A *lesson* is a sequence of activities designed to help students achieve one or more objectives. At this point, you have an objective for your first lesson. You are ready to plan activities that will help students learn. What will these lessons look like? That's what the rest of this chapter is about: how to plan activities that systematically lead students to your objective. But before we get into the details of designing lessons, let's look at the final components of a unit.

EVALUATION OF LEARNING

In the evaluation component, you plan how well you will assess students' achievement of your objectives. Of course, you have not waited until the end of your teaching to find out if students have learned anything. In Chapter 3 we stressed the importance of continuous assessment of students' learning. By *continuous assessment*, we mean that you will want to find out how well students are learning throughout your teaching—before, during, and after learning activities.

At the end of your unit, however, you will plan a more comprehensive assessment that lets you know which students met which objectives. The final unit evaluation may be a test or it may be a project that combines many of the objectives. For example, in the money management unit, students might create a budget for a small business or a family. The monthly income would be fixed, the resources would be defined, and the wants and needs would be specified.

Regardless of the method of assessment, the unit evaluation procedures should provide adequate information about each student's mastery of the most important unit objectives. As a result of this information, the teacher may choose to reteach certain crucial content, especially if later learning is dependent on that content. It is important to remember that continuous assessment of each objective throughout the lessons has provided information on how to modify the activities for students' individual needs. Many teachers refer to this process as *monitoring* (assessing) and *adjusting* (making needed changes).

MATERIALS

What materials and resources do you need in order to teach the unit? Any books, visual aids, films, or other media or materials should be listed at the end of the unit. You should also include a copy of any worksheets, overheads, and other materials you plan to use. Organizing your material helps you stay on top of the logistical planning for each day's lessons. Often a film or special materials must be ordered well ahead of time. The long-range planning is crucial to smooth-running lessons.

CHECK FOR UNDERSTANDING

Review the unit components. Imagine that you are asked to develop a unit in a particular subject or topic that you might teach soon. Below, list the components of the unit planning process and briefly describe how you would apply each component to your subject or topic.

1. _____

2. _____

3. _____

4. _____

5. _____

6. _____

Section 2. Terminology and Lesson Types

Let's assume that you are about to plan a lesson to fit into the money management unit. You must decide what learning activities you will select to lead students from where they are to where you expect them to be (as stated in your objective). As we said in Chapter 4, there is no one activity or single lesson that will work with all objectives, classroom environments, and students. In our view, teaching involves not only planning but also day-by-day experimentation and responsive adjustments as you discover what works best for you and your students. Consequently, an effective teacher must possess a wide repertoire of skills, methods, and learning activities and be willing to employ them in the classroom. Such a teacher then observes and reflects on the impact of the activities on the students' learning and self-esteem. The principles presented in Chapter 4 are helpful for such analysis of what worked well, what did not, and why.

The remainder of this chapter presents three categories of lessons: *direct, inductive*, and *social*. First, however, we will define some terms.

TERMINOLOGY

What is the definition of a *lesson*? How does it differ from a *learning activity* or a *teaching method*? How do these terms relate to a *teaching unit*?

A *learning activity* is a task students perform in order to achieve the objective—for example, reading, listening, working at learning centers, and so on. A *teaching method* is a mix of learning activities that, together, over a period of time, help students achieve the objectives. Examples of teaching methods include teacher-directed classroom and student-directed classroom, and activity-oriented, formal, informal, content-oriented and process-oriented teaching.

Now that we have clarified the terms *activities* and *method*, what is the definition of a lesson? A *lesson* is a set of learning activities that teach to and measure the achievement of one or more instructional objectives. Most lessons include readiness activities, information activities, and practice and assessment activities. Lessons are the building blocks for an instructional unit.

Units consist of a series of lessons whose specific objectives and activities work together to achieve a broader set of goals. Recall the objectives in the "Making Choices" unit in Chapter 3 (see pages 71–72). Each of the stated objectives could be the organizer for a lesson. The lessons build on each other to form a unit that meets the broader goal(s). Figure 5.1 illustrates how activities are combined to form a lesson and how lessons are combined to form a unit.

We will also be using the terms *lesson design* and *lesson plan* in this book. A *lesson design* includes all the activities required to teach and assess a particular instructional objective, regardless of the time it may take. It is not true that every objective can be achieved in one class session. In fact, most objectives take more than one day before we have finished adequate practice, review, and testing. We contrast the term *lesson design* with the more commonly used term *lesson plan*, which describes what the teacher intends to do on a particular day.

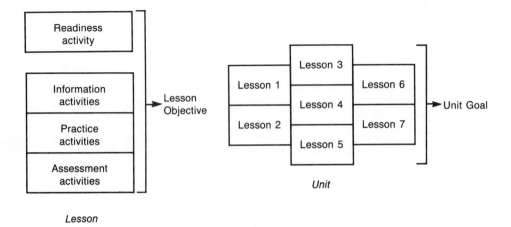

Figure 5.1. Lessons and Units

To make the distinction more meaningful, consider that a lesson plan for Wednesday might include elements from lesson designs for two or three objectives. Figure 5.2 illustrates the difference between a lesson design and a lesson plan.

Bear in mind that a lesson design could be for a cognitive, affective, or psychomotor objective. Affective lesson designs are typically more complex and less tidy than cognitive or psychomotor lesson designs. For instance, an objective dealing with students' respect for one anothers' property may stretch over a longer period of time and may require monitoring and feedback on the playground, in the hallways, and in the lunchroom. Often, too, one activity can help us teach more than one objective.

Just as there are many alternative learning activities, there are several alternative lesson types. We shall focus our attention on three types.

1. Direct (deductive) lessons
2. Inductive lessons
3. Social lessons

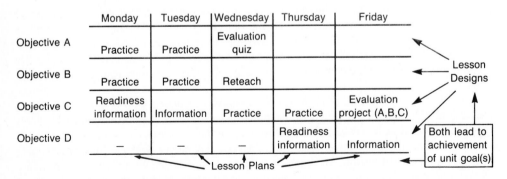

Figure 5.2. Lesson Design versus Lesson Plan

Figure 5.3. A Direct (Deductive) Lesson

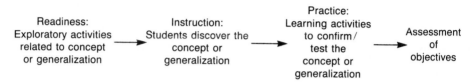

Figure 5.4. An Inductive Lesson

DIRECT VERSUS INDUCTIVE LESSONS

The first type of lesson is the *direct lesson*. The label refers to the fact that, when the lesson begins, you tell the students the concept or generalization to be learned and you lead them through most of the activities. A direct lesson also is referred to as *deductive*.

Direct lessons are deductive because the teacher typically states the instructional objective(s); presents the material to be learned, with examples and nonexamples; provides practice; and assesses students' learning. For instance, if you decided to use a direct approach to teach students to identify examples of figurative language, you would tell them the objective, present the definition and characteristics of *figurative language*, show students examples and nonexamples, engage them in practice exercises, give them feedback and more practice, and then test them. Figure 5.3 illustrates the structure of the direct (deductive) lesson.

In contrast to a direct lesson, an *inductive lesson* begins with exploratory activities and leads students to discover a concept or generalization. In the case of the figurative language lesson, you would begin by giving students several passages containing figurative language. You would ask them to select the most interesting and vivid passages. Next you would ask them to identify the words that made the passages so interesting. Only then would you label these words as examples of *figurative language*, define the term, and describe its essential characteristics. As with the deductive lesson, the final step would be to provide practice exercises and then to assess students' mastery of the objective. Figure 5.4 illustrates the structure of an inductive lesson.

CHECK FOR UNDERSTANDING

To further understand the first two types of lessons, examine the following two teaching episodes involving a sixth-grade classroom. The topic is "honesty."

Lesson 1

TEACHER: Class, I have written the definition of *honesty* on the board. It is freedom from fraud and deception. Does anyone know what *fraud* is? Janet?

JANET: Miss Morrison, I think it means cheating to get something you want from someone else.

TEACHER: Good! Now, what does *deception* mean? Larry?

LARRY: It means using tricks or not telling the truth.

TEACHER: That's right. Now that we have looked at the definition and agreed that honesty requires that you tell the truth and don't use trickery or cheat to get what you want, I would like you to examine these three newspaper stories that I have gathered. Be ready to tell me if the person identified in each story is being honest.

Lesson 2

TEACHER: Class, we are going to examine the idea of *honesty*. I know that many of you know what *honesty* is. In fact, we all have an idea of what it is. However, we each probably have a different idea of its meaning. Instead of writing a definition of *honesty*, I would like you to examine three newspaper stories that I have gathered. I want to know what the stories have in common. Also, be ready to tell me if the person identified in each story is honest.

(Students look at the stories provided)

TEACHER: What do the three stories have in common? (Wait) Larry?

LARRY: The people in each story tell the truth even though they could make more money or be thought of as more important if they lied. In one story, a greeting card company wanted to pay $1,000 for a poem written by this man's great-grandfather to use on a greeting card. They thought it had been written by the man. He told the company the truth even though the company could then use the poem without paying anything for it. In the second story, this woman returned a purse with over $5,000 in it. In the third story, a woman told her daughter that the daughter had been adopted, although the mother could have kept it a secret. They were all honest!

TEACHER: Excellent, Larry! Now, what does it mean to be honest? Lauri?

LAURI: It means to tell the truth, even when the truth hurts!

TEACHER: That's an excellent answer, Lauri. Now let's look at three other news articles and see if the people involved in them are being honest.

Which lesson do you think is direct? Which one is inductive? Why?

Yes, the first lesson was direct and the second was inductive.

What do you see as the advantages and disadvantages of each lesson type? Write your ideas below.

_____

_____

_____

_____

SOCIAL LESSONS

The third lesson type is the *social lesson*. In *social lessons*, students learn together while the teacher acts as the facilitator rather than as the information provider. Rather, information is often provided or experienced by the students themselves. The teacher can move away from the traditional place in the front of the classroom to encourage, assist, and monitor the students as they participate in small groups. In the figurative language–lesson example, students could be placed in small groups to role-play or to read examples of figurative language, they could work together to identify the vivid passages, or they could work in pairs to coach each other during the practice exercises as they prepare for the quiz.

There is one main advantage to social lessons. First, we live in a highly social world. Most work and play is conducted in a social environment. Yet the classroom frequently offers little opportunity for productive, guided interaction among students. Peer teaching, group projects, and role playing all provide experiences in social learning. It is natural for students to learn this way—just watch students on the playground or during free time!

Although we have presented the three lesson categories as discrete entities, they are not necessarily kept separate in daily teaching. It is not uncommon to see them combined or used in sequence in a lesson design. We hope that as you observe and practice teaching, you will be able to identify the lesson categories and to mix and match them yourself.

CHECK FOR UNDERSTANDING

Without reviewing the text on the three lesson categories, write their definitions and describe how they differ from one another. Do your work on the lines below.

_____

_____

_____

_____

_____

Section 3. Direct Lessons

Set Activity

Think of an instructor who uses mostly the lecture method. How long can you listen before your mind begins to wander? What does this teacher do that helps you know what is important? Does the lecturer use visual aids? How does the lecturer check to see if you understand? Write your answers below.

_____

_____

_____

_____

_____

We hope you referred to Chapter 4 for ideas. Remember the importance of appealing to different learning styles, of organizing the information, of allowing students to process information actively, and of clarifying what is most significant.

THE ELEMENTS OF DIRECT LESSONS

The *direct lesson design* presented here is based on research on teaching effectiveness conducted during the 1970s and 1980s (Hunter, 1976; Bloom, 1984; Rosenshine, 1987). These researchers observed teachers, trained them in various methods, and determined that direct teaching tended to produce higher student learning scores on standardized tests in elementary reading and math.

What are the elements of the direct lesson design? The seven elements in a direct lesson are listed below. The elements are clustered to indicate how they fit into the general phases of most lessons:

1. Set	Readiness Phase
2. Objective(s) and purpose	
3. Input and modeling	Information Phase
4. Checking for understanding	
5. Guided practice	Practice/Assessment Phase
6. Closure	
7. Independent practice and reteaching	

When you plan and teach your first lessons, you may wish to use all the elements in the order presented. However, as you gain experience, you do not have to remain a slave to the sequence. Rather, you can develop your own order, bring in other steps, and blend the direct design with elements of inductive or social lessons. Thus any lesson design is not a recipe to be followed exactly. It is best thought of as a road map that suggests alternative pathways—some direct and quick, others less direct but possibly more picturesque.

1. Set

- provides focus (active involvement of learner)
- transfers relevant prior knowledge
- diagnoses appropriate skills as necessary

The *set* activity begins, or introduces, a lesson. You may also use a set after any break in a lesson to focus students' attention. Three aspects of the set are discussed below.

First, a set activity provides a *focus* for the learners' minds by requiring *active involvement* with the content. By *active involvement*, we mean more than passive listening. The active student imagines, writes, pictures, says, or reads, always with some question in mind. For example, one teacher introduced a lesson on creative writing by asking students to imagine a new ending to a story they had just finished reading. Then, after 30 seconds or so, the teacher called on students to share what they were thinking. A set activity is not merely saying to students, "Ok, now we're going to work on math."

In Chapter 4 we described how the sensory memory is the "gatekeeper" for what we remember. If we don't stimulate students to attend to the information we present, they will probably forget it immediately. Thus the focus provided by the set encourages students to pay attention to the lesson so they will remember it.

A second aspect of the set is *transfer*. The set activity should enable the student to relate the new information to something he or she has learned before. In the previous example, the active involvement activity motivated students to relate the new topic (creative writing) to a familiar story. Think about how this example relates to what we learned in Chapter 4. Information is stored in long-term memory in networks of meaning (schemata). New information is more meaningful and more memorable when it is hooked in with relevant information in the brain.

A third aspect of the set activity is *diagnosis*. This step is optional, because you may have recently finished a prior lesson that gave you good information about students' levels of performance. For example, consider a math class that just completed a lesson on dividing single-digit numbers. The next lesson, on dividing double-digit numbers, may not require diagnosis, because you learned how well each student is doing from the previous lesson.

Bear in mind, however, that some information cannot be absorbed unless necessary prior learning has taken place. If students are going to conduct surveys of their neighbors' buying habits, you will want to make sure they have the necessary math skills to summarize their data. Starting the lesson with a quick exercise in basic math facts may provide useful information about who needs a review of the basic skills. Gathering such information is especially important at the beginning of the year when we do not know each child's capabilities.

Diagnosis can also help target those students who already know some of what you are about to teach. For example, in a sixth-grade science class, you probably would want to diagnose students' knowledge before a unit on rocks and minerals if this topic had been taught in an earlier grade. Some students may have had a thorough grounding in the topic, while others may have had very little exposure to it. And students' retention of the information could vary widely. To diagnose students' existing knowledge of rocks and minerals, you can pass around three rocks and have students write what they observe and know about them. In this way you'll find out what is "in their heads" about the topic, and you can tailor the lesson for those who have more or less experience with rocks and minerals.

Set activities are usually short, lasting roughly 3 to 5 minutes. A film or a field trip would not typically be considered a set activity because such an activity might take several hours and would support a variety of topics. You will also want to pick a set that is interesting, but not so engrossing that it distracts students from the activities that follow. As some of us have said, "Don't bring in an elephant to teach the color gray." The main purpose is to focus the students actively, to transfer existing knowledge to the new topic, and, perhaps, to diagnose students' prior relevant skill/understanding.

2. Objective(s) and Purpose

- communicates in student language
- motivates students

Telling the students the *objective* and the *purpose* of the lesson provides further focus as well as that valuable commodity, motivation. In direct lessons, you tell students what it is you expect them to be able to do by the end of the lesson (the objective), how you will evaluate

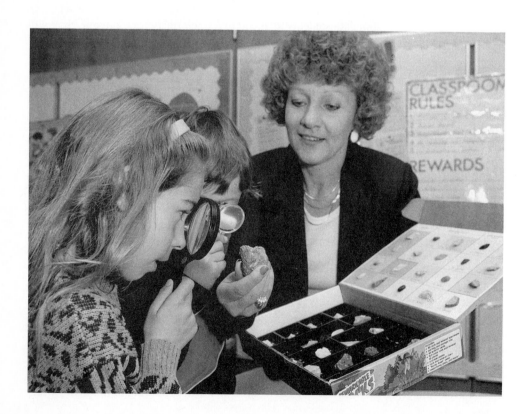

them, and what level of performance you expect from them. Students also want to know why it is important to study the topic and how it will be useful to them—the purpose.

Now you can see why we spent so much time in Chapter 3 on writing clearly stated objectives. They are crucial, not only to help keep your lesson on track but also to motivate students. How will you convey the objective to the students? When you tell the students the objective, you will want to put it in their language, not in the formal way you wrote it when you were planning. So instead of making a statement like "The students will be able to sing accurate half-step intervals 'a capella,' " you would say, "By the end of the week, when I play a note, I want each of you to be able to sing the note that is a half-step up or down, without the aid of the piano." Telling the students, "Today we're going to work on scales" is not an example of conveying the objective because you have not stated any expected *behavior*. The students don't know how they'll be evaluated, nor do they know the learning they'll be expected to demonstrate as a result of the activities.

Telling the students the *purpose* further motivates them. It lets them see how useful the new knowledge, skill, or attitude will be. For example, in the music lesson above, the teacher provides the objective and then says, "It's important for us to hear and sing half-steps accurately because several of our new chorus pieces contain half-step intervals. If we sing them accurately, we'll sound great in the winter concert!"

When explaining to students the objective and purpose of the lesson, it is important to clarify how the lesson relates to the overall unit objectives and purpose as expressed in the unit

rationale. The principle to follow is to relate "this" to "that." Thus, when giving the objective and purpose of the music lesson, the teacher might emphasize that singing half-steps will be combined with earlier lessons on harmonic intervals and that both activities will be important for the larger unit goal of performing a concert.

CHECK FOR UNDERSTANDING

Look back at some objectives you wrote. Pick one that you might have used for a teaching demonstration. Write down two ideas for set activities that will (1) focus your learners actively and (2) encourage them to transfer their existing knowledge of your topic. Diagnose if you think you need to find out what they do and don't know already. Then indicate how you will tell students the objective and purpose of the lesson. Write your answers on the appropriate lines. Share your ideas with a classmate.

Lesson objective: _____

_____

Set (focus/transfer) _____

_____

(diagnosis) _____

_____

Objective told to students: _____

_____

Purpose told to students: _____

_____

3. Input and Modeling (with Checks for Understanding throughout)

- demonstrates topic at hand
- uses variety in presentation
- appeals to various learning styles
- verbal labels point out key elements of examples
- structures information
- involves learners actively

In this phase, you provide the relevant information about the topic at hand. As you present information, you *model*, or demonstrate, it. Periodically, you stop to allow students to summarize or use the material just presented. The process of providing information would include various sources of instruction, not just lectures given by the teacher. Additional sources might be readings, movies, filmstrips, and other media.

When you present information to students, you want to convey the material in a way that will be easiest for them to remember. A long lecture with few visual aids and no breaks for students to digest the information is unlikely to result in long-term learning for most students. The information in Chapter 4 on learning and memory gives us some guidelines to keep in mind during the presentation of information.

First, we must consider *students' individual learning needs*. Recall the various learning styles and needs discussed in Chapter 4. Because of the varied backgrounds and experiences of students in most classes, it is important to appeal to as many learning preferences as possible. This will require, in particular, the application of the learning principle *variety* (see Chapter 4). We'll want to give students the opportunity to encounter the material in a number of ways—for example, through reading, listening, viewing, and touching.

Modeling goes on while you are presenting information. The suggestion is, *Don't just tell it to them; show it to them*. Posters, overhead transparencies, pictures, objects to pass around and explore, demonstrations, chalkboard illustrations—all of these aids help make the verbal information visual and tactile, thus appealing to the variety of learning needs of your students.

Verbal labeling is the technique of pointing out, in words, an idea or element you want students to notice. Verbal labeling of the essential aspects of a visual aid or demonstration is important when you are explaining how to do a project, or how to do a particular procedure. For example, when teachers give directions for an assignment, they might show an excellent example of that assignment on the overhead projector and explain which parts are exemplary.

The verbal labeling is necessary because students may look at the model and not understand which are the most important elements. For instance, a student might look at a poster and assume it's good because of its size, rather than because it conveys the essential information and the colors are vivid. Students need to know what makes an example a "good example." So the teacher should point out and verbally label and describe each aspect of the assignment that makes it exemplary.

Next, we must consider the principle of *organization* and the fact that the memory searches to structure information into meaningful networks. How can you present information in an organized way? First, divide the information into logical chunks in your mind. Outline it or diagram it so that the structure, the generalizations, and the links between the elements of information become clear to you. (Remember the content outline you created earlier [page 57].) Then create a poster, an overhead transparency, or other visual aid that makes this organization obvious to students. The diagram in Figure 5.5 shows the organization of the information in the "Making Choices" unit.

As you are presenting information, refer to the organizational diagram often to let students know how the current pieces of information are related to those that they've already covered and those to come. Have students actively process each chunk after it has been presented. If there are four main points in your lecture, stop after each one and have students summarize what they have learned. If you are showing a long movie or filmstrip, preview it to determine where to stop so students can process the information. In this way, they will solidify their understanding of the material.

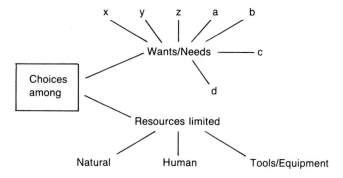

Figure 5.5. Organization of Content

Teacher modeling
an activity

CHECK FOR UNDERSTANDING

Take the objective you used for the set activity you designed on page 172 and outline the essential content. Plan two or three specific ways you could present the information so your students will remember it. How will you appeal to different learning styles? How can you help students organize the information in meaningful ways? Write your answers below. Share your ideas with others.

Objective: _____

_____

Content outline: _____

_____

_____

_____

_____

Ways to make information "stick" (use ideas from Chapter 4):

_____

_____

_____

_____

_____

4. Checking for Understanding

- done during information giving
- students actively process information
- provides information about student learning

We list this as a separate phase of the lesson, even though checking for understanding is interspersed throughout the input and modeling phase (see Figure 5.6). There are two purposes to checking for understanding. The first is to enable students to "digest" the information in small chunks, so that each phase is meaningful to them before the next piece is presented. You probably have had the unpleasant experience of sitting in an hour-long lecture with no opportunity to process, digest, or otherwise interact with the material presented, to "make it yours." When you are given large amounts of complex information without any time to actively process it, you retain little of it.

Recall that short-term memory has a limited capacity—only about seven bits of information can be handled at one time. If we are receiving many pieces of information at once, we overload and begin to forget. Our attention usually wanders. We are no longer learning. Remember the arrow around short-term memory labeled "rehearsal" (see Figure 4.2)? That rehearsal is provided by checking. It keeps information in the memory system and increases the likelihood of transfer to long-term memory.

The checking for understanding phase allows students to actively process information in logical chunks, thus making it more easily remembered. The word *active* is important here. Recall the fourth principle of learning, *active processing* (see Chapter 4). Passive learning is rarely as meaningful as active learning.

One researcher (Rowe, 1974) has suggested the "10-2 rule," which refers to about 2 minutes of active student involvement for approximately every 10 minutes of information presented. For example, if you were teaching a unit on rocks, you might explain the characteristics of sedimentary rocks and model, or show examples (with verbal labeling of essential qualities), for about 10 minutes. You would not go on to explain the second type of rock (igneous rocks) until you had given students a short activity in which they could summarize or apply the information already presented—for instance, classifying examples and nonexamples of sedimentary rocks. Then you would go on to explain and model the characteristics of igneous rocks and again check for understanding. For younger students, more frequent checking may be appropriate. Figure 5.6 illustrates the cyclical nature of this phase of a lesson.

A second purpose of checking for understanding is to find out how well students have absorbed the material. This purpose relates to the concept of continuous assessment we've stressed throughout this book. Without information on students' understanding of the material presented, you would have a difficult time deciding what to do next—go on or reteach.

Often we find that students misunderstood something we said. Or we just didn't explain it clearly enough, or we said something that was downright confusing. When we check for students' understanding, we catch these problems and have a chance to remedy them. Then we can reexplain and model the original information in a new and clearer way because of what we discovered through checking for understanding. Pausing periodically to assess what students are getting out of what we are saying provides excellent cues to help us decide how to proceed.

Staying in tune with what students are thinking also keeps us on our toes. We can think of checking for understanding as "dipsticking," as if we were checking the oil in a car. You may also think of this process as *formative evaluation*—evaluation not for grading but for formulating decisions about where to go next with students.

What activities are useful in checking for understanding? This is where the *active participation* strategies presented in Chapter 4 come in (see page 134). They might include techniques such as having students write a one-minute summary to be read aloud, giving true–false questions that students vote on, or having students think of questions for others to

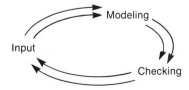

Figure 5.6. Checking for Understanding during Input and Modeling

dipsticking

answer. Usually the least helpful way to check for understanding in most situations is to ask, "Are there any questions?" Many students (especially the shy or less successful ones) do not want to call attention to their lack of understanding. Thus the fact that no one has any questions may reveal little about students' actual grasp of the material.

CHECK FOR UNDERSTANDING

Try this exercise to check your own understanding of this section. In the line after each statement, write **T** if the statement is *true*, **F** if it is *false*.

1. An informational lecture is the opening activity of a direct lesson. _____

2. The best way to model is to state the information. _____

3. Understanding is checked after all the information is presented. _____

4. A movie is one way to provide input. _____

5. It is impossible to check for understanding during a film or filmstrip. _____

The only *true* statement is item 4. Why are the others false?

5. Guided Practice

- activities match the objective(s)
- teacher monitors learning and adjusts accordingly

The purpose of guided practice is to give students an opportunity to practice with the skills or information until they are confident and have mastered the objective. Recall the importance of rehearsal for the transfer of information into long-term memory. The critical aspect here is that there be an opportunity to practice and that the practice be *guided* by the teacher. The teacher constantly monitors to check student progress. If students are in a large group responding to questions with hand signals, the teacher is there to see how students are doing and to correct any misunderstandings. If the students do a few problems or exercises from a book or worksheet, the teacher circulates among students without spending too much time with any one student. In this way, errors can be caught early before they become ingrained by repeated practice. If the teacher finds many students are making the same kinds of errors, he or she adjusts the lesson by reteaching to the whole group in a different manner.

The guided practice activities should follow our principle of *congruence* (See Chapter 4, page 115) by being relevant to the lesson objective. Most practice activities should lead directly to the accomplishment of the objective. For example, if we want students to be able to apply the laws of supply and demand and we ask them to create demand-curve graphs from data in a book, the activity and the objective are closely matched. If, however, we ask students to copy formulas from the book, there may be little match between this rote activity and the higher level objective of applying the laws of supply and demand.

You may ask, What is the difference between a check-for-understanding exercise and guided practice? While monitoring student progress is a key aspect in both phases of the lesson, they differ in purpose and in scope. First, consider the *purpose*. We check for understanding to help students process the information being presented and to find out how they are doing. We provide guided practice to give students a chance, under our close supervision, to gain proficiency by working with the new information. We don't want students practicing mistakes. Guided practice has as its goal mastery of the skill; checking for understanding is merely what it says, finding out if students understand what you present.

The other difference between the two lesson phases is in the *scope*—the amount of information. We check for understanding of the most recently presented chunk of information, not all of the information together. We provide guided practice so the student can put all the chunks together in a practice situation. Guided practice thus encompasses most of the information presented, whereas checking focuses only on the small chunk just presented—the bits and pieces.

Having students do entire worksheets or long assignments from books in class is not guided practice because students may be practicing errors or may become stuck for a long time while the teacher is trying to get around to everybody. If worksheets or book assignments are used, students should work on only a few of the problems or questions before the teacher brings the whole class together to check their success on those few items.

Guided practice may be written or oral; it may include many of the same participation activities referred to in Chapter 4. Throughout the practice time, the teacher monitors, assists, and gauges students' success. He or she decides what will happen next: more practice, or closure, or independent practice.

6. Closure

- ends day's lesson
- gathers information about individual mastery of the objective

There are two ways to think about closure: (1) to close the day's lesson (*closing*), and (2) to assess student achievement of the objective (*closure*). Both are important and should be used when necessary.

1. *Closing: to close the day's lesson.* As we have said, most objectives are not completed in one day. When we finish a part of a lesson, and before we go on to activities related to a different objective, we want students to summarize their own learning. We can do so simply by asking each student to jot down three things they learned this morning. After giving the students "think time," the teacher would call on a few students to answer. This type of closure activity gets students to tie their learning into a neat bundle before leaving the topic. It also gives the teacher information about what students take away from the lesson. An added benefit is that students will know what to say when their mother or father asks, "What did you do in school today?"

2. *Closure: to assess student mastery of the objective.* Another purpose of closure is to find out who has and has not met the objective—a final assessment. A student who cannot perform the skill adequately during guided practice will have nothing but a failure experience when doing independent practice. Closure will show that this student needs more teaching before going on.

Remember, students' correct performance on a guided practice activity does not necessarily mean they can perform well on their own. During the practice, they may have received help from the teacher and/or from their peers. At this point, you will not know which students are capable of succeeding on their own. Therefore, it is important to have a special closure activity that lets you know how well each student can perform *without your help*.

This closure activity may be a quick quiz or a project that students do on their own, such as completing two or three math problems or writing a short poem. Sometimes it is possible to gather enough information about achievement during guided practice so that a separate closure activity is not required. If, however, you skip closure and find that many students are unsuccessful during independent practice, you may conclude that you did not obtain adequate information about who was ready to go on and who wasn't.

What do you do with those students who are still struggling with the guided practice activities? It is a reality of teaching that not all students learn at the same rate. Thus some students may be ready to go on to independent practice while others still need more teacher-assisted practice. At this point in the lesson, you use your closure information to decide who falls into which group.

Notice how each phase of the direct lesson design includes some form of assessment. Continuous assessment is a key aspect to instructional decision making. Excellent teachers collect information, interpret those data, and decide what to do next; then they continue to monitor students' progress and adjust the lesson accordingly. This "monitoring and adjusting" aspect of teaching is critical to success and growth in your teaching career. Continuous evaluation throughout the lesson—during the set (diagnosis), during input (checking for understanding), and during guided practice (monitoring)—gives you valuable information about the students' concerns, misunderstandings, thinking, and prior knowledge. Without this information, our instructional decisions are often misguided and/or irrelevant.

7. Independent Practice and Reteaching

- attends to individual needs by reteaching
- provides further practice to develop fluency/automaticity or extend learning

Through closure, we have determined which students have not achieved the learning stated in the objective. These students need reteaching. The students who were successful on the closure activity will go on to independent practice to develop fluency and automaticity or to extend their learning.

Reteaching is necessary because the first round of set, objective/purpose, input/ modeling/checking, guided practice, and closure did not work. That is, the student has not yet achieved the objective. At this point, it is important to find out where the problem lies. You can look for evidence of misunderstanding in the student's guided practice and closure activities, or you may orally quiz the student. In any case, when you think you have found the problem, you will want to reteach.

Often you will find that several students have not succeeded on closure and need reteaching. If so, you may wish to pull those pupils aside while the other students are working independently. Or you may assign students to mixed-ability cooperative learning teams, in which the misunderstanding must be cleared up before the group proceeds. Another idea is to use peer teaching to help the student master the objective. Finally, individual help before or after school may be useful.

Reteaching usually includes another round of set, objective/purpose, input/modeling/ checking, guided practice, and closure. Reteaching is not just coverage of the content in the same way a second time. Chances are that the first explanation did not sink in. Therefore, you will want to try a different approach this time. Try appealing to a different learning style, or try a different type of guided practice activity. For example, if you presented the information on rocks visually and orally, try, during reteaching, to have your students touch and examine the rocks.

You may be thinking, Is it worth taking the time to reteach? Where will I find the time? Should we be spoon-feeding these kids? In our opinion, it is well worth the effort. Not all students succeed on the first try, and they should have a second chance. Furthermore, research on mastery learning (Bloom, 1984) indicates that, with continuous assessment of student learning and reteaching where needed, students who would normally be near the average of the class can rise to achievement levels typical of the top 10 percent.

Independent practice is designed to increase students' fluency and ability to perform with ease the activity stated in the objective. For example, while some students may be able to do long division correctly, they may need more practice before they can perform the steps quickly and without much effort. Independent practice takes place with little or no teacher guidance. It may be performed in or out of class. Homework is one example of independent practice.

In some cases, more work of the type done in guided practice would seem boring and repetitive to students. For example, after students have shown that they can distinguish a noun from a verb in sentences, having them repeat that activity during independent practice would seem senseless. An *extension* of their learning might be for them to look at magazine articles and find nouns and verbs, or to look for nouns in poetry. They are working with the same skills, but in a different setting, with more complex examples or at a slightly higher level of learning.

While the independent practice activity itself does not have to be closely guided by the teacher, students should receive immediate feedback on their work. Since many students have difficulty working independently, they will also need feedback on how well they work on their own. Thus monitoring or at least visual scanning is a good idea, especially if you are reteaching a small group at the same time.

CHECK FOR UNDERSTANDING

With another student, trade off explaining the terms *guided practice, closure, reteaching*, and *independent practice*. Each of you should write definitions of two of the terms, then exchange your work with your partner's. Try not to look at your notes. Be sure to explain the terms in your own words. Check the accuracy of your understanding by looking back over the previous section.

_____

_____

_____

_____

_____

WHEN TO USE DIRECT LESSONS

The direct lesson is not recommended for every type of content. For example, you might initiate a teaching sequence for some concepts with an inductive lesson and use direct lessons for back-up and practice. Direct lessons tend to be less effective with (1) abstract, fuzzy concepts, such as *majority, equity, justice, discrimination, freedom, ethics, beauty*; (2) content that does not lend itself easily to sequencing of skills (such as reading comprehension and writing improvement); and (3) content that is abstract and includes a high degree of judgment and/or that has a substantial affective flavor—for example, social studies, literature, the fine arts.

Content that has a high degree of structure lends itself well to direct teaching. Examples of such content are introductory sentence, concepts with clear rules, many math and science operations, and foreign language instruction.

Some people think direct lesson design can be used only with lower level cognitive skills (memorization and comprehension). We disagree. Some researchers (e.g., Brown, 1978; Beyer, 1985) have shown success in using direct teaching to enhance students' higher level cognitive skills (e.g., concept learning, comparison, contrast, and analysis). These researchers argue that too often students are given a higher level task without explicit direct teaching on how to attack that task. Many students have not learned such skills on their own and need modeling, explanation, and guided practice before they can operate at the higher levels of thinking. Thus, direct teaching may be used for both lower and higher level cognitive objectives as well as with psychomotor and some affective objectives.

SECTION 3 SUMMARY

Direct lesson design is an efficient way to help students learn well-structured content. It may be less effective with loosely structured, abstract, or affective content. The direct lesson incorporates many aspects of effective instruction: congruence among objectives, activities, and evaluation; organization of content for long-term learning; continuous assessment of the learner; appeal to a variety of learning styles; active student involvement; and rehearsal and practice. While one would not use direct teaching every minute of every day, it is a valuable structure for the design of some lessons.

The following is an example of a direct lesson design on the subject "latitude–longitude." Examine the lesson closely. It will serve as a model while you are beginning to design your own direct lessons.

A Direct Lesson: Latitude and Longitude

Objective (for teacher use):

Given latitudinal and longitudinal readings, students will be able to find a city on a map.

- *Set*
  Teacher holds up flat Mercator projection map. "How are this map and a football field alike? How are they different? Everyone jot down a few ideas and be ready to tell me." Teacher walks around and reads what students write; waits a few seconds and calls on four randomly selected students. (Focus and Diagnosis)

"We studied earlier about the difference between a globe and a flat map. Now we'll learn just a few more details about flat maps." (Transfer)

- *Objective* (Learning Outcome)
  By the end of this lesson, you will be able to use these lines on a map to find cities on the map.
- *Purpose* (Why we're learning this)
  "We're going to be doing a unit on world geography soon, and knowing how to read a map will be helpful to you. It will also help you later on when we take our trip to Canada."
- *Input/Modeling*
  Teacher explains and labels latitude and longitude lines, the equator, the Prime Meridian, and the numbering system used for degrees of latitude and longitude. Points to them on large wall map. Uses a memory aid (mnemonic device): "La*t*itude is *at* the equa*t*or; *long*itude is *long*."
- *Check for Understanding*
  Teacher asks students a series of questions based on information that has been presented. Examples: "What are these lines called?" "What is the Prime Meridian?" (Teacher uses wait time and random selection of students.)
- *Input/Modeling*
  Teacher explains and illustrates how latitude and longitude lines intersect and how to determine north and south latitude, east and west longitude. (Teacher has previously determined by content analysis the order in which these terms and concepts should be presented.)
- *Check for Understanding*
  Teacher asks a few oral true–false questions to which all students respond with an overt signal (e.g., thumbs up or down).
- *Input/Modeling*
  Three latitudinal/longitudinal readings are listed on chalkboard. Teacher illustrates how to use this information to determine which world city is at each of these specific locations. Teacher thinks aloud to illustrate the thinking process and to encourage self-monitoring—metacognition. (*Metacognition* is discussed in Section 4, on inductive lessons.)
- *Guided Practice*
  1. Teacher puts three latitudinal/longitudinal readings on the chalkboard. Gives students 2 minutes to work in groups of three to find the cities. Then the teacher has a few students of varied achievement levels come to the map to identify each city and asks the others if they agree.
  2. Teacher distributes a dittoed copy of a flat Mercator projection map to each student. Teacher has large cards made with a latitudinal/longitudinal reading listed on each card. Holds up one at a time.
     Students may work in pairs if they wish. They determine the correct city for each card according to the information provided and jot down the name of the city on a piece of scratch paper.
     After students figure the answer for each card, the teacher points to the correct city on the wall map and names the city. Students who agree raise hands.
  3. Extra guided practice is planned, but may not be necessary if students are successful. If not used here, it may be used for reteaching or review. It is a worksheet with five latitude/longitude readings. Students work on them with assistance from teacher or other students.
- *Closure* (To make sure every student has achieved the objective)
  Teacher writes two final latitudinal/longitudinal readings on the chalkboard. Each student writes down the name of the appropriate city. Teacher does not provide help at this point. Teacher checks each student's answer individually. Students who do not complete closure correctly are given more guided practice. The others do independent practice.
- *Independent Practice* (This can be done without teacher guidance, perhaps as homework)
  Teacher provides a worksheet that lists 10 latitudinal/longitudinal readings. Students use their

dittoed maps to determine which city is being described and write the name of the city on the worksheet next to its description.

This activity will be followed up with a similar activity the next day. The second step in working with latitude and longitude will be introduced—that is, students determine the latitude and longitude of specific cities. All of these skills, once learned, will be reviewed intermittently. Answers are checked and feedback/reteaching is provided.

Guided Practice Activity A. Using the Elements of a Direct Lesson Design

Create a lesson to meet one of the objectives you have written. Be sure to write your formal objective at the top of the page. Just for practice, include each element of the lesson design as if it were a recipe. Write out all the activities you would do with students. You do not have to write out every word you would say, except when telling students the objective and purpose. After planning for each activity, have a peer or your instructor give you feedback. Compare your lesson with the example lesson.

Independent Practice Activity A. Designing a Lesson to Teach a Cognitive Objective

Design a 10-to-15-minute lesson to meet a lower level cognitive objective. Exclude independent practice. Perform the lesson with a small group of classmates, or in front of a videotape. Have an observer write down what you say or how you perform each phase of the lesson and share the observation notes with you. Write down (1) actions you took that helped student learning and, (2) ideas for improving the lesson. Use the principles in Chapter 4 to help you understand why some things worked well and others did not.

Section 4. Inductive Lessons

Set Activity

Two types of terms are provided below, some with a "yes" beside them, and some with a "no." Examine the items and try to determine what all the "yes" terms have in common. Give them a label. Write in the blank below what you think these common characteristics are.

Madeline Hunter (no)   scientific method (yes)
peer teaching (no)   teacher lecture (no)
figuring out (yes)   hypothesizing (yes)
testing a hunch (yes)   Sherlock Holmes (yes)
drill (no)   deductive (no)

Previously in this chapter we contrasted inductive lessons with direct lessons. That is the point of the list above. All the "yes" terms describe some aspect of inductive thinking. Remember that inductive lessons usually lead learners to discover a definition, concept, or generalization, rather than have the teacher give it to them first. Practice (with monitoring and adjusting) is usually provided after the learner has looked at examples and experimented to figure out the generalization or concept. The advantage and purpose of such an approach are that it stimulates the student to engage in higher level thinking. Students examine information, facts, or data and hypothesize or experiment to arrive at an accurate explanation of the generalization. When a direct method is used, students do not necessarily engage in such higher level thinking.

We present two types of inductive lessons here: *concept attainment* and *inquiry*. *Concept attainment* lessons attempt to get students to discover a concept by looking at examples and nonexamples of the concept, as you did in the Set activity. *Inquiry lessons* attempt to get students to discover a generalization through questioning and hypothesizing. If you are a bit fuzzy about the differences between a concept and a generalization, review the relevant portions of Chapter 2. Can you explain the difference? Figure 5.7 may help to clarify it.

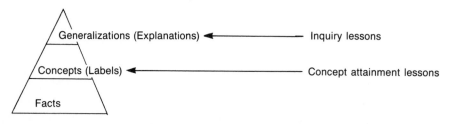

Figure 5.7. Compare the End Product of the Two Types of Lessons

CONCEPT ATTAINMENT LESSONS

Examples of concept attainment lessons are:

- The teacher labels positive and negative examples with "yes" or "no."
- Students categorize critical attributes of "yes" terms.
- Teacher helps clarify questions, presents examples to label.
- Students generate examples.
- Students are encouraged to examine their thinking processes.

In this model, students are presented with words or phrases (*exemplars*). An exemplar is labeled "yes" if it has characteristics or attributes of the concept to be taught (Bruner, Goodnow, & Astin, 1977). An exemplar is labeled "no" if it does not contain attributes of the concept to be learned. By comparing positive and negative exemplars, students begin to form ideas (silently) about the critical attributes of the category. When most of the students think they know what all the positives have in common, some fresh exemplars are presented to them to be categorized as either a "yes" or a "no." Next, they share their ideas and develop labels for the categories. After the teacher gives the technical label (if there is one), students are asked to produce some positive exemplars of their own. Finally, students describe their thinking and how their ideas changed as they moved through the activity.

We know it's hard to visualize how this would work in a class. The following example may help. The teacher wants the students to attain the concept *spicy foods*.

1. Teacher introduces the activity by presenting the following labeled exemplars and asks the students to find what the positive examples have in common. They should use the negative exemplars to help clarify what the concept is not.

tacos (yes)	lettuce (no)	gumbo (yes)
steak (no)	salsa (yes)	cajun (yes)
meatballs (yes)	chile (yes)	chocolate (no)
tortilla (no)	pizza (yes)	cake (no)

2. Students form an idea about what all the "yeses" have in common and write a definition using critical attributes. For example, one guess might be "foreign foods," with the critical attributes that the items come from a foreign country. Students do not share their ideas with one another.
3. Teachers give additional unlabelled exemplars for the students to label as "yes" or "no." For example, rice (no), pasta (no), Tabasco (yes). Teacher calls on students to share their definitions.
4. Teacher names the concept, and restates the definition in terms of the critical attributes. Students are then asked to generate more exemplars. The teacher might listen to the students' ideas and then say, "Yes, the critical attributes of all the 'yes' examples are that they are spicy, that they include many different, strong spices that make the foods hot or strong-tasting. Now jot down one or two more examples that could be considered spicy foods." Students are called on to read their examples, which might be Greek olives, ginger snaps, or curried chicken.

5. Students describe their thoughts, how they formed their definitions and labels, and how they tested them when new exemplars were given. Students might say that they put into one category two exemplars that had a similar quality and then looked at another "yes" food to see if it fit into that category. Then they would contrast those three foods with one of the "no" foods. When a new exemplar was given, they again tested it against the "yeses" and "nos" to see if it fit.

CHECK FOR UNDERSTANDING

Try the concept attainment activity below. Go through steps 1–5 above with a partner, verbally. What did you get out of this exercise that you would have missed if you had been taught the concept using direct teaching?

baseball (yes)	rain (yes)	school (yes)
snow (no)	leaves falling (no)	Passover (yes)
daffodils (yes)	skiing (no)	Thanksgiving (no)

INQUIRY LESSONS

The steps in inquiry lessons are:

- Puzzling event or set of data stimulates students to form questions and to collect additional information.
- Students form, test, and verify hypotheses.
- Students examine and discuss their thinking processes.

Inquiry lessons get students actively involved in discovering a generalization that explains a puzzling event or collection of data. In one popular model (Suchman, 1962), the teacher begins the activity by explaining the inquiry process and the ground rules. Students will not be given any response from the teacher except "yes" or "no" during the questioning period. Next, the teacher presents the puzzling event—something that conflicts with our typical notions of reality. Then the students can ask questions to get more information and to see under what conditions different results would occur. Students, through their questions, begin to isolate relevant variables and to form hunches about causal relationships (hypotheses). Through questions or experiments that test their hypotheses they formulate an explanation for the puzzling event. Finally, the teacher leads students to analyze their own thinking processes.

A concrete example may help you understand how this model of inquiry works.

1. Teacher presents discrepant event (after clarifying ground rules). The teacher blows softly across the top of an 8½″ × 11″ sheet of paper, and the paper rises. She tells students to figure out *why* it rises.
2. Students ask questions to gather more information and to isolate relevant variables. Teacher answers only "yes" or "no." Students ask if temperature is important (no). They ask if the paper is of a special kind (no). They ask if air pressure has anything to do with the paper rising (yes). Questions continue.

3. Students test causal relationships. In this case, they ask if the nature of the air on top causes the paper to rise (yes). They ask if the fast movement of the air results in less pressure on the top (yes). Then they test out the rule with other materials—for example, thin plastic.
4. Students form a generalization (principle): "If the air on the top moves faster than the air on the bottom of a surface, then the air pressure on top is lessened, and the object rises." Later lessons expand students' understanding of the principles and physical laws through further experiments.
5. The teacher leads students in a discussion of their thinking processes. What were the important variables? How did you put the causes and effects together? and so on.

Other types of inquiry lessons do not require a puzzling event and "yes" or "no" questions. Students simply explore data and facts, generate their own hypotheses and generalizations, and test them.

CHECK FOR UNDERSTANDING

Two teachers are discussing a student, John, in the teachers' lounge. John attends class regularly, turns in all his homework, seems to be succeeding on practice activities, but is failing most of the quizzes. This is, indeed, a puzzling set of circumstances! With a partner, working out loud, list four hypotheses that might explain the apparent contradiction. For each hypothesis, give a strategy for finding out if it is true.

Present to another team your hypotheses and strategies for checking them out. Discuss your thinking as you moved through the process.

Assume the correct explanation for John's performance is test anxiety. What did you get out of the exercise that you would have missed if you had been told about John's test anxiety using direct teaching? Discuss this in a group of four.

Independent Practice Activity B. Generating Concepts and Concept Exemplars

1. Generate a concept from your content area. Think of positive and negative exemplars. The exemplars may be words, symbols, phrases, or paragraphs.

2. Describe when you might use this type of approach. Could it be mixed and matched with parts of direct lessons? Which parts?

_____

_____

_____

Independent Practice Activity C. Planning an Inquiry Lesson

1. In your content area, think of a generalization and a puzzling event that illustrates the generalization in action. Then go through the steps of inquiry learning to plan an inquiry lesson. Share your lesson with another student or teach it to a small group.

2. Discuss your concerns about using inductive strategies in your teaching.

METACOGNITION: A BONUS OF INDUCTIVE LESSONS

Before discussing the advantages of inductive lessons, let us examine a bit of learning theory. Researchers studying thinking and problem solving have discovered that it is important for us not only to be able to think but also to be aware of *how* we think. Some researchers (e.g., Brown, 1978) have called this concept *metacognition*—the process of thinking about your own thinking and using this awareness to improve performance. You will read more about this idea in Chapter 6.

Imagine that you are reading a chapter in this book. You turn a page, and you suddenly realize that you have not understood a word of what you read. You are thinking about your own understanding; you are engaging in metacognition! As a result of this insight, you decide to reread the page.

Many students are unsuccessful at learning tasks because they lack awareness of their own thinking or because their preferred strategy is ineffective. To make matters worse, they often lack the tools to examine their own thinking and to generate a more successful strategy.

One part of metacognition is an awareness of one's own *commitment, attention*, and *attitude* toward a task. A second aspect is the exertion of metacognitive control over the learning process: *knowing what information is important, which strategies to use*, and *how to apply a selected strategy*. For example, when writing a science report, a student selects relevant concepts and data. He or she also plans how specific to be, how to organize the data and findings, how to support the main points adequately, and whether to use a graph or figure to support a particular point.

The third aspect of metacognition occurs when the student *monitors* how well the planned strategies are working and *checks progress* made toward the goal. In the science report example, the student keeps track of how well the planned strategies work, whether the report is getting too long, and whether it will meet the requirements (Marzano et al., 1988).

WHEN TO USE INDUCTIVE LESSONS

Now what does this have to do with inductive lessons? Notice that the last step of both the concept attainment and the inquiry lesson is: Thinking about your own thinking. In both models, students explore together how they approached the task, what strategies they used, and how they monitored their performance during the task. Such discussions are especially useful for students who lack adequate planning and self-monitoring strategies; they benefit from their peers' modeling of metacognition.

When are inductive lessons the best choice? Whenever you want students to get practice in inductive thinking (concept formation, hypothesizing, experimenting, critical thinking, and so on), you would select an inductive strategy. We should mention that, in addition to the two strategies presented here, there are other ways to involve students in inductive thinking. Any time you have students figure out a rule that determines whether something fits within a concept or does not, whether something will work or will not, or when you have them design a classification system to organize many pieces of information, or discuss why a literary character did what he did, you are giving students practice in inductive thinking. Instead of doing the thinking for the students and presenting to them packaged information, you are allowing them to generate the information themselves. While inductive lessons may take more time than direct lessons, they have the advantage of meeting two objectives at one time; they teach the content *and* a higher level thinking strategy.

Section 5. Social Lessons

You may have listed students' respect, empathy, cooperation, or caring for others. We all think these values are important. Yet we are often at a loss as to how to teach them in our classes. Many secondary teachers think these goals are appropriate only for elementary levels. We disagree. Given the global realities of the late 20th and early 21st centuries, we think that teaching for cooperation, empathy, and caring is more important than ever.

One way to teach positive values is to model them for students. Many of us tell students our expectations for their cooperation and caring in our classes and give considerable feedback to students. Do certain types of lessons encourage such values? The answer is "yes." Social lessons help students learn to work together while they also meet your other, content-area objectives.

We present two types of social lessons: (1) *role playing* and *simulation* and (2) *cooperative learning*. They may be used for both affective and cognitive objectives.

In *role playing* activities, students take on a role—that is, pretend they are a particular person—to solve a problem or act out a situation. Role playing may be done in small groups or in front of the whole class. For example, students might form pairs to act out effective listening with a partner by reflecting back what has been heard. The role play is usually a brief activity, often completed within a single hour.

A *simulation* is a simplified version of reality in which students take on life-like roles. In contrast to role playing, a simulation usually involves a larger number of students in a larger variety of roles and may extend over several days. In both role playing and simulation, the ultimate outcome of the specified situation is under the control of the students. The activity is not a mere dramatization of an event. Students' actions and decisions may have real-life consequences. For example, students in a class might simulate the creation of a new city; assuming such roles as city council members, homeowners, and so on, they would address various specific dilemmas. If they had made no provision for trash collection in their city, students would soon realize the necessity for such a service as they continue the simulation.

Cooperative learning groups work together to master or process content. An example is to have learning pairs quiz each other to prepare for a spelling test. More detail on each type of lesson follows.

ROLE PLAYING AND SIMULATIONS

Characteristics of role playing are:

- Students take on a role and act it out.
- Students participate in a realistic simulation of an event.
- Students experience and discuss the consequences of their actions.

Set Activity

Imagine you are Millicent Stephens and you are working on the new social studies unit on money management. A science teacher, Jonathan Lopez, comes up to you and tells you that he has been asked to develop a unit for the new health curriculum. He wants to know what steps you went through in designing your unit. With a partner, you are going to act out a 5-minute scene between Millicent and Jonathan. Take 5 minutes to prepare yourselves with questions and answers. Then act out the scene in front of another pair. Then the other pair will act out their scene for you. Afterward, discuss together (1) how you felt in your role, (2) how confident you were in what you were saying, and (3) how this activity helped you assess how well you understand the early chapters of this book.

Role playing and simulation are usually closely related to real-life events—for example, having students become members of the Senate and House of Representatives and go through the process of passing a bill into law.

For role playing and simulation to work, students need very clear directions. (You may have found yourself feeling frustrated during the Millicent and Jonathan scenes because of the brevity of the directions.) The following steps should help you structure role playing for maximum success.

1. Select the roles and the situation. You may have students group themselves in pairs, triads, foursomes, and so on. The whole class may act out the situation together, with you monitoring, or a small group may act out the situation in front of the class. In all cases, students need clearly defined roles and must react to a specific situation. For example, my objective is to teach my junior high school students to refrain from putting each other down. I select two students, Maria and Kirk, to act out a scene in which the characters learn what it feels like to be insulted. In the scene Maria and Kirk are paying for a hamburger. I tell them that Maria makes a mistake and Kirk makes insulting comments to her. In this case, students are given a specific situation to act out. It would be less successful to say, "Have a discussion where you put each other down," because the situation is so vaguely defined.

2. Give the actors time to prepare. To insure productive use of time, establish a time limit and warn students how much time is left. Monitor and coach carefully to be sure students are on the right track. For example, take Maria and Kirk aside and ask what they are going to do. Give feedback.

3. Have the students act out the roles. Monitor and take notes to give feedback. If not all students participate in acting out roles, ask students to be observers and give them specific questions to answer. For example, have students write down the negative comments made by Kirk and describe how the comments made Maria feel.
4. Process and debrief the experience. Ask the actors to describe their feelings and observers to share their insights. This activity may be done in small groups or as an entire class. Focus the discussion on the values, attitudes, and concerns you want to foster. In our example of put-downs, ask Maria to share her feelings too.

Role playing and simulations may be used for both cognitive and affective objectives. Such activities can be a powerful means of developing a deep experiential understanding of content. For example, a history teacher we know has her students divide up into Confederate and Union soldiers to reenact portions of the Civil War. A chemistry teacher has students play the "roles" of various elements as they combine and change in photosynthesis. They follow paths drawn on the floor to indicate how the compounds form and change. While such activities may take a little extra time, they are well worth it. They involve students in tactile, kinesthetic, and physical ways that excite many students who would otherwise be lost and uninterested.

COOPERATIVE LEARNING

Characteristics of cooperative learning are:

- The groups are heterogeneous (mixed).
- Interdependence is fostered among members (sink or swim).
- Individual accountability is encouraged.
- Cooperative skills are taught explicitly, with much feedback.

A *cooperative learning group* is a mixed group that sinks or swims together because each person is responsible for the others' learning. When discussing cooperative learning (Johnson & Johnson, 1987), it is important to contrast it with *individualized learning* and *competitive learning.* In *individualized learning,* students each work on their own to accomplish an objective. Students are not compared with one another; they work to achieve a preset standard. Individual structures are useful when students are well motivated and need little guidance.

Competitive learning is most typical in today's schools. In competitive classrooms, student performance is judged against the average performance of all students. Recall the characteristics of norm-referenced evaluation presented in Chapter 3. If some students succeed, others must be less successful because of the limited number of A grades available. Tests in competitive classrooms are graded on the curve, so the idea is to beat out someone else. The effect of too much competition on students may be low self-esteem, selfishness, and poor communication skills.

Cooperative classrooms are characterized by an attitude of interdependence; the motto is, "We sink or swim together." The students work to help every student on their team achieve the objectives. Each student is held individually accountable for his or her learning and receives an individual score. In addition, teams with a score greater than the minimum level set by the teacher usually receive special recognition or a reward. Students in such classrooms learn to value giving and receiving help. They also learn to work together toward a common goal—a skill that most U.S. companies put at the top of their list for newly hired personnel.

CHECK FOR UNDERSTANDING

Discuss with friends their experience in schools. Do they remember examples of individualized, competitive, or cooperative learning? What was your experience with each type of structure? How did you feel? How did your friends feel? Come to class prepared to discuss your own and your friends' experiences.

The main reason to use cooperative learning, in addition to its obvious social benefits, is that it works. The research on cooperative learning is impressive. Students at all levels who received some cooperative activities (approximately 60 percent of class time, with the balance of time spent in individual and competitive learning) had higher achievement, better retention, more higher level reasoning, greater empathy for those who are different, and higher self-esteem than students who had little or no cooperative learning (Johnson & Johnson, 1987). These are impressive outcomes for such a simple strategy.

How does cooperative learning work? There are four critical components of cooperative lessons: heterogeneous groups, positive interdependence, individual accountability, and cooperative skills learning.

Heterogeneous Groups

Most cooperative groups are mixed in ability or in social make-up. For example, a group of three students may contain one high achiever, one low achiever, and one middle level achiever. Or if social integration is a goal, the groups may be composed of "popular" and less "popular" students. Ethnic and home background may also be the basis for creating heterogeneous groups. Language proficiency and gender may also be taken into account in setting up mixed groups. You may also choose random groupings, where, for instance, all the students with a birthday in May or June join together. Or you could group students by the color of their clothes. Such random groupings make sense at the beginning of the year, when little is known about each student.

When students who don't typically interact with one another are in a face-to-face, interdependent situation, many social barriers are broken down and students learn to value those who are different from themselves. This social integration is particularly important in the adolescent years, when being "popular" is so important. One teacher we know forms groups by having students list the names of three students they would like to have in their group. Then she mixes students who appeared on few lists with those who appeared on many lists.

Group size is also important to consider. As groups become larger, it is harder to get every student actively involved. Therefore, groups of two, three, or four seem to be most productive. It's important that students learn to sit "knees to knees" and eyes to eyes; face-to-face interaction is essential to group learning.

Positive Interdependence

Students need a reason to begin to help each other learn. The fact that the group will sink or swim together creates positive interdependence. How is a sense of interdependence achieved? Typically, group members are made to feel interdependent by limiting the materials (e.g., only one copy of a worksheet or one pencil is given to the group); "jigsawing" the material into sections, with the expert on each piece of the puzzle teaching the other group members; assigning roles (e.g., a checker, an encourager, and a recorder); or by offering group rewards (e.g., if all members succeed, each member receives a privilege or points).

In such interdependent structures, each student must do his or her part in helping the others learn the material or accomplish the task. If one person does not learn, the whole group has failed to help that student. Thus students learn how to help each other learn. One of the simplest ways to use cooperative learning is to have a group of three coach each other for a quiz or test. Then, after assigning individual grades, give special recognition or points to the groups in which every member reached the minimum performance level specified.

Individual Accountability

In individual accountability, each person is responsible for learning the required material. Without individual accountability, groups do not function to the benefit of each member. For example, you may have worked on a group project for which one person did most of the work, and all members got equal credit. This is not true in cooperative groups. For the group to succeed, every member must demonstrate his or her learning.

Accountability may be accomplished by giving students a quiz, with grades recorded in the teacher's book as usual. Or the teacher may rotate among the groups with a clipboard, making random spot checks by asking students questions about material they are supposed to have learned. When students are completing a worksheet together, you may ask all the students to sign their name on the sheet, to indicate that all members agree with the answers and that every student can explain why each answer is correct. Another way to encourage individual accountability within the group is to assign the role of "checker" to a student who is responsible for gauging each person's understanding by asking questions, requesting summaries, and, in general, quizzing the other group members.

CHECK FOR UNDERSTANDING

With a partner, explain how cooperative learning differs from more traditional group work. Be sure to include the three essential attributes of cooperative learning in your discussion.

Teaching Cooperative Skills

Students don't always walk into your classroom knowing how to help other students or how to work in a group to complete a task. Yet such skills are crucial in the workplace (IBM estimates that 90 percent of terminated employees lack such skills). It is therefore our job to teach students how to build and maintain trust, and how to communicate, lead, and manage conflict or controversy. Imagine how successful our relationships with family members would be if we all had such skills!

How are cooperative skills taught? First, a diagnosis is necessary. It is instructive to put students in cooperative groups with a "sink or swim" task and walk around with a clipboard, taking notes on which social skills are present or lacking. For example, you may find that many students do not know how to give each other positive feedback and encouragement. If so, and you think this is an important skill, now is the time to teach it.

Most experts agree that focusing on only one or two social skills per lesson is enough. For example, in an elementary classroom, you might emphasize the skills of sharing materials, being encouraging in comments to others, or listening to others without interrupting. Figure 5.8 provides a list of common social skills. Remember, students will need long-term practice and reinforcement before a social skill will become automatic.

You may use a variety of strategies to teach social skills: direct explanation, modeling, and practice; discovery or inductive activities; or role playing. Of course, the work in cooperative groups provides practice of the skills. This is where monitoring and giving feedback are crucial.

Below are some ideas for teaching cooperative skills:

1. Make sure students know why a particular skill is useful. For example, show students how learning to give encouragement will make it easier for them to get along with their siblings or with other children. Let students know how they'll be rewarded (personally and externally) by using the skill.

2. Help students understand what the desired social skill is. Children cannot comprehend an abstract idea like *encouragement* until they see and hear it in action. Asking specific questions about the behaviors included in the social skill can make it concrete and easier to understand. For example, you may lead students in a discussion, asking "What does giving encouragement look like?" (e.g., leaning forward, smiling, etc.) and "What does it sound like?" (e.g., "Good job!" "That's a good idea.") You may write these behaviors on the board on a "T-graph," as shown in Figure 5.8. You may also wish to have students demonstrate what the skill "looks like" through role playing.

3. Help students practice the skill while they work in groups. You may assign roles ("Today, Joe is the encourager"). Or you may assign a group observer ("Lola, today you put a checkmark next to students' names when they encourage another student"). You may even create a special activity that promotes application of the skill—for example, having students talk in pairs about a hobby while making a conscious effort to encourage the other student to learn the hobby. Of course, you will observe groups and record examples of encouraging behavior on your clipboard. Then you will need to give feedback.

4. Allocate class time to discuss students' use of the social skill. The debriefing may be done within the group ("Lola, show your observation results to the group and have members discuss how well they encouraged each other today"). Or you may give

Social Skills

- Using names
- Contributing ideas
- Praising
- Encouraging others
- Saying "please" and "thank you"
- Paraphrasing
- Respecting other people and property

T-graph on Encouraging Others

Looks like	Sounds like
• Smiling	• "Good job"
• Leaning forward	• "That's a good idea"
• Eye contact	• "Yes!"

Figure 5.8. Social Skills and T-graph

specific feedback to individuals or groups. These feedback and debriefing sessions will take approximately 10 minutes a day at first. Later, you may need to spend only 20 minutes per week to discuss how the desired social skills are progressing.

The following example illustrates a typical cooperative learning lesson for elementary grades. Notice how the objective is specified, and the critical elements of heterogeneous groups, interdependence, individual accountability, and cooperative skills are included.

Cooperative Learning Lesson on Handwriting

Objective: Students will be able to recognize errors in handwriting and provide a corrected example of each incorrect letter.

Group Size: 3 (mixed according to proficiency in writing)

Materials: 3 cards with handwriting errors per group
  1 pencil per group
  1 piece of paper per group

Procedures: Each child in the group will show his or her card to the rest of the group. He or she will explain to the group which letter on the card is incorrect. Then he or she will illustrate how to make the letter correctly on the paper.

Interdependence: Provided by limited materials and job roles that are rotated after each student's turn:
  Writer: Holds card, explains the error, and corrects it
  Checker: Checks writer's correctness.
  Encourager: Provides positive comments.

Individual accountability: Spot-checks by teacher with clipboard to record students' performance and quick individual worksheet the next morning to check students' progress.

Cooperative skills: Encouraging behavior is practiced by each student. Praising is demonstrated and monitored by teacher.

(This lesson was based on one developed by teachers in Clarkston Community Schools, Michigan.)

Guided Practice Activity B. Designing a Role Play or Simulation

Select one attitude or value from your list at the beginning of Section 5. Design a role-playing or simulation exercise to help students grow toward that value. Also think of a role-playing exercise to develop a deeper understanding of your content. Write out your ideas and share them with someone who teaches in your subject area.

_____

_____

_____

_____

_____

CHAPTER SUMMARY

Three types of lesson designs have been described: direct lessons, inductive lessons, and social lessons. All may be used for various types of content and objectives. While direct lessons may be quicker than the other two, they lack the advantage shared by the others. In inductive and social lessons you are teaching not only the content but also the thinking skills or social skills involved. We encourage you to mix and match the lessons when you plan and teach units. The variety will appeal to different student learning preferences and will maintain interest and motivation.

Guided Practice Activity C. Creating a Jigsaw Activity

In your class, count off so that you have groups of four members. Spend 5 minutes getting to know each person (remember his or her name!). Now join with another group of four and pick a partner from the other groups so that you now have four pairs. The first pair will become experts on heterogeneous grouping, the second pair will work on positive interdependence, the third pair will work on individual accountability, and the fourth pair will take cooperative skills.

With your partner, be ready to explain your piece of the puzzle to the others in your original group of four. Create a visual aid to help you convey the information. Prepare for your teaching with your partner for 8 minutes.

Now go back to your original group and have each person explain (and model) his or her piece of content. The others should take notes. To make things interesting, have the person whose birthday is the earliest in the year be the "checker" to make sure each person can explain the section before moving on to the next point. You have 10 minutes to make sure all members of your group can explain all four aspects of cooperative learning. You will be quizzed at the end of this time. (This is an example of the cooperative learning strategy called *jigsaw*.)

Independent Practice Activity D. Designing a Cooperative Learning Activity

With a partner, design a cooperative lesson for content you might teach. Be sure to include the four aspects of cooperative learning in your plan. How will you form groups? How will you create interdependence and individual accountability? Which cooperative skill will you emphasize? Share your written plans with other pairs.

Independent Practice Activity E. Observing a Class

Observe a videotape of a class or visit a class for 2 hours. Take notes on the types of lessons and activities you observe. Write an analysis of which activities helped students learn. Why? What hindered learning? Why?

REFERENCES

Beyer, B. K. (1985). Teaching critical thinking: A direct approach. *Social Education, 49,* 297–303.

Bloom, B. (1984, May). The search for group methods as effective as one-to-one tutoring. *Educational Leadership*, pp. 4–17.

Brown, A. L. (1978). Knowing when, where, and how to remember: A problem of metacognition. In R. Glaser (Ed.), *Advances in Instructional Psychology* (pp. 77–157). Hillsdale, NJ: Erlbaum.

Bruner, J., Goodnow, J., & Austin, G. (1977). *A Study of Thinking.* New York: Wiley.

Hunter, M. (1976). *Rx: Improved Instruction.* El Segundo, CA: T.I.P. Publications.

Johnson, D. W., & Johnson, R. T. (1987). *Learning Together and Alone.* Englewood Cliffs, NJ: Prentice-Hall.

Marzano, R. J., Brandt, R. S., Hughes, C. S., Jones, B. F., Presseisen, B. Z., Rankin, S. C., & Suhor, C. (1988). *Dimensions of Thinking.* Alexandria, VA: Association for Supervision and Curriculum Development.

Rosenshine, B. (1987). Explicit teaching. In D. C. Berliner & B. V. Rosenshine (Eds.), *Talks to Teachers* (pp. 75–92). New York: Random House.

Rowe, M. B. (1974). Wait time, review, and instructional variables. *Journal of Research in Science Teaching, 11,* 81–94.

Suchman, J. R. (1962). *The Elementary School Training Program in Scientific Inquiry.* Report to the U.S. Office of Education. Urbana: University of Illinois.

CHAPTER 6

Teaching to Enhance Thinking

Chapter Overview

During the decade of the 1980s, teaching for and about thinking moved to the top of the national educational agenda. Questions were raised about what constituted "higher order thinking," how best to teach thinking, and how well prepared educators were to teach it. Declining student performance on national standardized tests coupled with predictions that the workplace of the future will require critical and creative thinking added to the level of concern. However, there are many varying opinions on how best to address the problem.

Costa (1985) discusses a three-part program for teaching thinking. He believes that teachers may teach *for* thinking, teach *of* thinking, or teach *about* thinking. Teaching *for* thinking implies teaching in a manner conducive to thinking. In teaching for thinking, the instructor poses problems, raises questions, and establishes a classroom atmosphere in which thinking is encouraged. Teaching *of* thinking involves direct instruction about specific thinking processes—for example, teaching the steps in decision making or problem solving. Teaching *about* thinking entails teaching students about their own thinking and helping them become aware of their mental processes.

In this chapter we will discuss teaching for, of, and about thinking. We will examine a rationale for teaching about thinking, definitions of the term *thinking*, a framework for organizing thinking skills, and activities that promote thinking. Finally, we will discuss difficulties with commonly used thinking skills programs.

Chapter Objectives

After you have completed this chapter, you will be able to:
1. describe why it is important to teach thinking
2. explain the differences among teaching for, of, and about thinking
3. list the levels of Bloom's taxonomy and give examples of questions that you might ask at each level
4. describe teaching behaviors that promote critical thinking, creative thinking, and metacognition

Set Activity

Think for a few moments about two fifth-grade teachers, Corey Garcia and Evelyn Wright. They are each teaching a unit on the westward movement in the 19th century.

In Corey Garcia's class, students use several textbooks, magazine articles, and original source material to discover how the conquest of the West was viewed from Native American and Anglo viewpoints. They see filmstrips, films, and artwork; discuss myths and stereotypes of the West; build dioramas; make relief maps; role-play events and participate in simulations from the 19th century; sing the music of the day; and write essays on what life was like for the people at that time. Students are allowed to work cooperatively for some tasks. At the end of the unit, students write reports on what they learned in the unit and what impact westward expansion has had on life in the United States today.

In Evelyn Wright's class, the teacher presents factual material in lectures, students silently read chapters in a textbook and answer factual questions at the end of each chapter. At the end of the unit, students have a written test on material covered in the textbook.

    1. What are the two teachers' names?

    2. Which teacher do you think is more effective, Corey Garcia or Evelyn Wright? Why did you choose that teacher?

1. Teachers' names _____

    _____

2. I think _____ is   more

    effective because _____

    _____

    _____

    Now think about the structure of the two questions. In what critical way are the two questions different? You may have concluded that in the first question you had only to remember the teachers' names. However, in the second question you were asked to analyze and organize information, make a judgment, and give reasons for your choice. You had to use what is called *higher order thinking*.

Section 1. A Rationale for Teaching Thinking

WHY IS THINKING IMPORTANT?

The United States has moved from an industrial era into an "information age," one in which expertise in the search, retrieval, and transformation of information has replaced industrial know-how as a key to economic success. It is estimated that in fields such as engineering, the information half-life (the time period during which half of the information in a field becomes outdated) is as short as six years (Costa, 1985). Instead of focusing on content or factual knowledge, futurists suggest we must shift our emphasis to teaching students how to problem-solve, make decisions, and think creatively and critically. With these skills, scholars and others who examine educational needs of the next century say, students will be able to "learn to learn," and apply their thinking to many new situations.

THE STATUS OF THINKING AND PROBLEM SOLVING IN THE SCHOOLS

What is the status of thinking in most of America's schools? A research study by Goodlad (1984) indicated that students are especially weak on questions that require thinking. Goodlad's data from over 1,000 classrooms "support the popular image of a teacher standing or sitting in front of a class imparting knowledge to a group of students. Explaining and lecturing constituted the most frequent teaching activities" (p. 105). He found that an average of 75 percent of class time was spent on instruction. Approximately 70 percent of this time involved verbal interaction, with teachers "out-talking students" by a ratio of 3 to 1. Less than 1 percent of such "teacher talk" invited students to engage in anything more than recall of information.

Of course, no one study can reflect conditions in schools nationwide. However, research like Goodlad's has led some educators to suggest that thinking ought to be considered among the basic skills of the future. For example, the National Association of Secondary School Principals, in a chart contrasting emphases for education in an industrial age and in an information society, linked higher order skills with basic skills (Cetron, 1985). The association believes that thinking skills will be among the basics necessary to succeed in our rapidly changing world.

Section 2. What Is Thinking?

DEFINITIONS OF THINKING

If we are to teach students to think, we must first determine what *thinking* is. This is easier said than done. The meaning of *thinking* is elusive and complex, as some aspects of thinking are better understood than others. There are as many definitions as there are individuals writing about thinking. For example, deBono (1985) suggests that "thinking has to do with the way information is arranged and rearranged to make decisions, solve problems, create opportunities, and raise human potential. . . . thinking is the most fundamental and important skill" (p. 203). Perkins (1987) views thinking as an integral part of intelligence. In fact, he defines intelligence as "whatever makes people more effective thinkers" (p. 42).

Despite the variety of definitions, there is general agreement that thinking is a cognitive process, a mental activity by which knowledge is acquired, manipulated, evaluated, and/or created. Thinking entails searching for answers, meanings, or solutions. It involves developing concepts and principles, following logical chains of reasoning, evaluating sources, solving problems, examining multiple solutions, and seeking unusual ideas. A learner who is thinking does not just "soak up" information but tests it, compares it with prior experiences, looks for implications, and uses it in new ways. In order to facilitate these complex behaviors, it is helpful to organize thinking into a framework of components.

A FRAMEWORK FOR TEACHING THINKING

In 1988, the Association for Supervision and Curriculum Development (ASCD) proposed a framework for teaching thinking (Marzano et al., 1988).[1] The ASCD framework represented an effort to develop a common knowledge base and a common language for teaching thinking, in the midst of multiple programs and definitions that each propose varying lists of terminology. Efforts were made to identify fundamental aspects of thinking that students could use repeatedly in the course of learning academic content. While we do not propose the ASCD framework as the only "right" way to teach or study thinking, it does provide an organization that is helpful as we begin our own thinking about thinking.

The five dimensions of the ASCD framework are

- Metacognition
- Critical and creative thinking
- Thinking processes
- Core thinking skills
- The relationship of content-area knowledge to thinking

The five dimensions of the framework do not form a taxonomy, are not discrete, and frequently overlap. In this section we will define the dimensions and examine the relationships among them. In Section 3, we will discuss how the framework can be used in making teaching decisions.

Metacognition

Think about a time you traveled to a new place. Perhaps you were driving and talked to yourself as you tried to remember to "turn left at the drugstore" or "stay in the right lane." Or when doing a math problem, you may have stopped to think "Now, what problems have I seen that were similar to this one? What do I remember about them?" When proofreading a paper you wrote, you may have asked yourself, "What do I really want to say here? Is this the best word to use?" In each of these activities you were aware of your own thinking. You monitored your own performance of the skill or task. Recall from Chapter 5 that this type of "thinking about thinking" is called *metacognition*.

Metacognition refers to the awareness and control of your own thinking, including commitment, attitudes, and attention. It involves active monitoring and consequent regulation and orchestration of the thinking processes. When you are engaged in metacognition, you are aware of what you think as you perform tasks, and you use this awareness to control what you do.

Students can learn that self-monitoring is a valued, high level skill. They can develop commitment, have a positive and personal attitude toward learning, and give attention to introspection and practice. When you help students learn about metacognition or any of their thought processes, you are teaching *about* thinking.

---

[1]R. Marzano, R. Brandt, C. Hughes, B. Jones, S. Rankin, & C. Sukor, *Dimensions of Thinking: A Framework for Curriculum and Instruction.* Reprinted with permission of the Association for Supervision and Curriculum Development and the authors. Copyright © 1988 by the Association for Supervision and Curriculum Development. All rights reserved.

Critical and Creative Thinking

The ASCD framework identifies two basic types of thinking. The first might be exemplified in the decisions you made in planning a unit. You had to think about goals, objectives, and activities. You had to decide which teaching method would be better for your lessons by analyzing your objectives, the students, the content to be taught, and the context in which you were teaching. You weighed the importance of various learning principles examined in this text against other information from other courses and experiences. You were engaged in *critical thinking*.

Critical thinking is defined as "reasonable reflective thinking that is focused on deciding what to believe or do" (Ennis, 1987, p. 10). It involves analyzing arguments, searching for valid evidence, reaching sound conclusions, and making appropriate judgments. To teach critical thinking is to develop students who are fair-minded, objective, and committed to clarity and accuracy. Such students will look for evidence, evaluate sources, and weigh information before taking action or believing new ideas. While good critical thinkers do not necessarily find fault, as in the negative sense of the word *critical*, we must recognize that as we develop thinking ability in students, they will not automatically accept everything a teacher says.

The second type of thinking, *creative thinking*, may be experienced in many different circumstances. Have you ever written an original poem or painted a picture? Did you plan a learning activity for your unit that was different from others you've seen? Have you invented a recipe for Thanksgiving leftovers or created a unique solution for freeing a young child from a locked bathroom? Any of these activities may involve *creative thinking*. *Creative thinking* is "the ability to form a new combination of ideas to fulfill a need" (Halpern, 1984, p. 324) or to generate "original and otherwise appropriate results by the criteria of the domain in question" (Perkins, 1984, p. 19).

Both critical and creative thinking can be used in all academic areas. Critical thinking is generally used to test, refine, and/or evaluate assertions or ideas, while creative thinking usually produces some new idea, product, or way of doing something. However, they are not opposite ends of a continuum, but work together in complementary ways. Critical and creative thinking are both needed to solve problems. For example, if I am planning a story or designing a Halloween costume, I can use creative thinking to generate ideas and critical thinking to make judgments among them. We can teach students *about* critical and creative thinking, to help them evaluate which type of thinking is more appropriate in a specific situation.

CHECK FOR UNDERSTANDING

List two activities you have pursued in the past week that involved critical thinking. Do the same with creative thinking. Write your responses on the lines provided below. Compare notes with a friend. Do you agree on the type of thinking emphasized in each activity?

Critical thinking _____

_____

Creative thinking _____

_____

Thinking Processes

A *thinking process* is a relatively complex sequence of thinking. We use critical thinking, creative thinking, and metacognition in order to engage in thinking processes. Eight processes are considered in the ASCD framework, as shown in Figure 6.1. They are then classified as facilitating *knowledge acquisition* or *knowledge production* or a combination of the two.

Knowledge Acquisition.   The first three processes—concept formation, principle formation, and comprehension—appear to be directed primarily toward knowledge acquisition. *Concept formation* serves as the foundation for the other processes. Recall from Chapter 2 that a *concept* is a category or class of things or ideas that share a common set of critical attributes. Examples of concepts are *address, mail carrier, postage, letter,* and *stamp.* When students learn new content, they must establish essential concepts before they can comprehend more complex information. *Concept formation* is the process of organizing and labeling the category with a word.

Concepts are organized through *principle formation.* ASCD's definition of a *principle* is similar to our definition of a *generalization* presented in Chapter 2. A *principle* is formed when a learner recognizes a relationship that applies to multiple concepts. *Principle formation* is the recognition of relationship between or among concepts. For example, if we were to take all the concepts listed in the previous paragraph (*address, mail carrier, postage, letter, stamp*), we could combine them into a principle such as, "A letter must have an accurate address and sufficient postage in order to be delivered."

In this framework, *comprehension* involves generating meaning or understanding from varied sources by relating newly acquired information to what is known. We do this by observing, reading, and listening. Regardless of the source, when we comprehend, we extract information and integrate it with what we already know in order to generate meaning. We might think of *comprehension* as the process through which newly acquired information is incorporated into existing schemata.

Much of the planning you did in your unit was probably aimed at developing and using the knowledge acquisition processes. You considered the concepts and generalizations (principles) to be developed and the activities you would use to generate meaning (comprehension). In order to facilitate higher level thinking, you will also want to consider what students can do with the knowledge they have acquired. For this task, it is helpful to consider the remainder of the thinking processes, which focus on knowledge production.

Knowledge Production.   The next four thinking processes—problem solving, decision making, research, and composition—build on the acquisition processes through the produc-

- Concept formation ⎫
- Principle formation ⎬ Knowledge Acquisition
- Comprehension ⎭

- Problem solving ⎫
- Decision making ⎬ Knowledge Production or Application
- Research ⎪
- Composition ⎭

- Oral discourse   Knowledge Acquisition and Production

Figure 6.1. Association for Supervision and Curriculum Development Framework for Teaching Thinking

tion or application of knowledge. The final process, oral discourse, is included in this section because it entails both the acquisition and the production of knowledge.

Problem solving is the ability to analyze and resolve a perplexing or difficult situation. Students learn to solve problems by being presented with many different problem types, along with strategies for solving them. Some problems may be considered *closed*, or *convergent*, because there is only one best solution. The distance problems you may have studied in algebra were probably closed problems ("If train A leaves point A at 6 p.m. and travels at 40 miles per hour and train B leaves point B at 7 p.m. traveling at 60 miles per hour, what time will the trains pass each other?").

Other problems are *open-ended*; they have many possible solutions. Planning a successful party, working to combat air pollution, or designing a vehicle that is powered by a mouse trap all involve solving open-ended problems.

There are several models of problem solving, some more appropriate for specific problem types. One commonly used model is the IDEAL problem solving process (Bransford & Stein, 1984). In this model, *I* stands for *identification* of the problem. Sometimes, as in the case of air pollution, a critical step in the process is to recognize that a problem exists. In a math story problem, students must identify the question being asked.

D stands for *definition* of the problem. Sometimes defining a problem may entail restating it or representing it in a new way, such as in a chart or a diagram. In other cases, defining the problem may affect the level of abstraction at which we work (e.g., Is our task really to plan a successful party, or is it to improve staff morale?) or the approach to be developed (Are we concerned with removing pollution from the air or with preventing further pollution?). After the problem is defined, the next step is *E, exploration* of strategies for solution. Many strategies may be considered, depending on the problem type. They range from working the problem backward to using metaphors to brainstorm solutions. While a full discussion of all possible strategies is impossible here, it is important to recognize that problems can be solved in many ways and that we need to match the strategy to the problem (do you recognize the metacognition at work?). After selecting a strategy, problem solvers *act* on their ideas and *look* for the effects (the *A* and *L* steps in *IDEAL*). Was the strategy effective? Is the solution appropriate? These steps can be used to solve problems in content as diverse as planning a simulated trip across the prairie and determining the number of glasses of lemonade one would need to sell in order to buy a baseball mitt.

Decision making, or the ability to select from among alternatives, is so closely related to problem solving that it is sometimes hard to see the differences. In decision making, an individual selects from among competing alternatives relative to some criteria. In problem solving, we do not always have a clear definition of the alternatives or options, or even of the problem itself. An example of decision making is to choose which philosophy from Chapter 2 (essentialist, progressive, or reconstructionist) most reflects your views.

Like problem solving, decision making may be represented by several models. Most models contain some variation of these basic steps:

1. Identify the decision to be made (e.g., Where will we go for our family vacation?)
2. Identify alternatives (Michigan's Upper Peninsula, Disney World, Grandma's house).
3. Identify criteria that will be used to evaluate alternatives (cost, time demands, facilities for pets, family interests).
4. Evaluate each alternative using the criteria.
5. Select the best alternative.

Of course, the process is not always as simple as this step-by-step list might make it seem. Some criteria might be more important than others. If Disney World best meets all the criteria except one, it would seem to be the most appropriate choice. However, if the criterion it does not meet is cost and thus we cannot afford to go to Disney World, it will not be a good choice even if it meets our other needs. Students can practice making simple and complex decisions regarding both practical problems (Which game shall we play during indoor recess?) and academic content (Should Max go back to visit the Wild Things again?).

Research differs from problem solving in that its purposes are to explain and predict rather than to find a correct answer. *Research*, defined here as scientific inquiry, involves both problem solving and decision making. Research is directed primarily toward understanding how something works and using that understanding to predict phenomena.

The steps in research are similar to those described in Chapter 5 as steps in inquiry lessons. In research, investigators observe data, form hypotheses, test hypotheses, and state conclusions. Students studying consumer research, for instance, might design tests to determine the strongest, most absorbent paper towel. Sixth graders considering homework habits might design a test for the hypothesis "Sixth-grade students are more successful in completing math problems while listening to the radio than when working in silence." Second graders studying insects might test hypotheses about the types of food ants prefer. (The latter experiment was actually conducted by a group of second graders, by placing various types of food at equal distances from an ant hill and tallying the number of ants that carried back each type.) In each case, students identified a research question, made hypotheses, gathered data to test their hypotheses, and stated conclusions.

Composition is the process of conceiving and developing a product, which may be written, artistic, mechanical, or musical. When we write, create a dance, a song, a painting, a sculpture, or something mechanical, we are composing. Helping students to learn to compose is not as simple as saying, "Now write about what you did over your summer vacation." For composing to be successful, students need to be taught to plan, implement, review, revise, and evaluate. There is a wealth of literature on teaching the writing process (for example, Proett & Gill, 1986) that is far beyond the scope of this text but that should be part of your preparation in language arts. For this chapter, it is important to recognize that the process of composing is as complex as problem solving or research and represents the recording of an individual's thinking process. If we are to help students compose, we must help them think, recognize their thinking, and plan ways to record their ideas and thoughts. Evaluation of composition must center on success in conveying thoughts. Only when the thought processes are clear, for example, does punctuation become meaningful.

Oral discourse is unique among the thought processes in that it is used both to acquire and to process information. *Oral discourse* is communication (talking) between two or more people. Classroom instruction in oral discourse has implications both in and out of school. Teaching students to be effective in oral discourse entails teaching about listening to and assessing the statements of others, recognizing and respecting points of view, asking for information or clarification, and checking perceptions. Classroom discussions (see Chapter 4) can be fruitful training grounds for oral discourse.

As you can see, thinking processes are complex and diverse. They are not completely distinct from each other; indeed, they frequently overlap. You may decide on the skills and processes you want to stress with your students and incorporate those into your curriculum. After you have planned the knowledge acquisition processes to be used (Which concepts and generalizations will organize this unit?), you may select different knowledge production

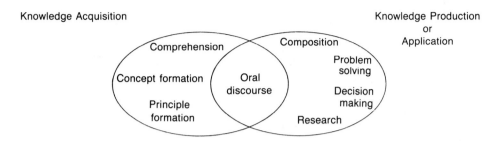

Figure 6.2. Thinking Processes

processes to emphasize in various units. For example, you may wish to emphasize problem solving in a science unit on plants, decision making in a social studies unit on the civil rights movement, or oral discourse in the study of particular works of literature. If you teach students specific steps or skills to allow them to use thinking processes more effectively (for example, teaching the steps in decision making), you are teaching *of* thinking. The processes in the ASCD framework are displayed in Figure 6.2.

Core Thinking Skills

The *core thinking skills* are considered the "building blocks" of the thinking processes. They are relatively specific cognitive operations that are essential for the operation of the other dimensions. They are generally used in clusters and are not as discrete as the list suggests, as some skills build on other skills. They are the following: focusing, information gathering, remembering, organizing, analyzing, generating, integrating, and evaluating. Many of these will be discussed in the section on Bloom's taxonomy. For our purposes, it is most important to remember that the thinking processes, such as decision making, are made up of many different skills.

Relationship of Content-Area Knowledge to Thinking

The final dimension of the ASCD framework concerns the relationship of content knowledge to thinking. Does the amount of prior knowledge affect the way one thinks? Should thinking be taught separately from traditional content, such as math or social studies, or should it be embedded in content? Research on this question is not definitive. While it appears that novices and experts in a particular field think about that field differently (Chi, 1978; Chi, Feltovich, & Glaser, 1981), it is not clear how content affects the way we teach thinking. Some theorists believe that it is best to teach a new skill in content that may already be familiar and is not necessarily part of the regular curriculum. For example, they might teach the steps in decision making while choosing a dessert for lunch. Others believe skills are learned best within a specific discipline (see, e.g., Baron & Sternberg, 1987). Our advice at this point is to keep up to date on your reading as your career progresses, be alert for new research, and, in the meantime, do what seems most effective for your students.

THE CORE THINKING
SKILLS

CHECK FOR UNDERSTANDING

1. What are the five dimensions of ASCD's framework for teaching teaching? _____

   _____

   _____

2. Write a short explanation of the following:

   a. metacognition _____

   _____

   b. critical thinking _____

   _____

   c. creative thinking _____

   _____

3. How could you use the following in a fifth-grade science unit on plants?

    a. concept formation _____

      _____

      _____

    b. principle formation _____

      _____

      _____

    c. problem solving _____

      _____

      _____

    d. composition _____

      _____

      _____

    e. decision making _____

      _____

      _____

Section 3. How Do You Teach Thinking?

At the beginning of this chapter, we said it was possible to teach *for*, *about*, and *of* thinking. Now that we have reviewed one framework for organizing and labeling types of thinking, we will consider ways to use the framework to help students become more effective thinkers. First we will consider ways to teach for thinking—that is, to teach in such a manner that thinking is encouraged and supported. Next we will discuss direct ways to show students how to use thinking skills and processes. Finally, we will examine teaching about thinking, ways to use metacognition to help students learn about their own thinking and the thinking of others.

TEACHING FOR THINKING

Most teachers would say they want their students to think. However, the atmosphere, learning activities, and management strategies used in many classrooms send a different message. If a student asks the teacher to support his or her statements with evidence (or provides evidence to the contrary), invents a solution not found in the teacher's manual, or points out inconsistencies in the teachers' behavior, it is not always easy to welcome such evidence of thinking. However, such are the fruits of a thinking classroom! If we want students to think, we cannot expect them to limit their thinking to neatly prescribed problems during our lessons. Thinking entails patterns of intellectual activity and attitudes of both critical evaluation and open-endedness that must be applied throughout the school day. While many classroom endeavors support thinking, we will consider two main types of suggestions: (1) patterns of classroom interaction and (2) activities for practice in various types of thinking.

Classroom Interaction

As we discussed in Chapter 4, questioning is one of the key strategies for encouraging students to interact with content. Questions can be asked in a variety of settings, including checks for understanding during the presentation of information, class discussions of open-ended issues, or tasks requiring students to put information to use. Unfortunately, it has been estimated that 80 percent of the questions asked by teachers are focused on the recall of specific facts. A helpful model in planning questions that require higher level thinking is Bloom's taxonomy. You may recall that the taxonomy was mentioned in Chapter 2 as an alternative model for planning learning processes.

Bloom's Taxonomy of Cognitive Objectives. Bloom's *Taxonomy of Educational Objectives: Handbook I. Cognitive Domain* (1956) was developed to provide a classification scheme for educational goals and objectives in the cognitive domain. Bloom identified six major hierarchical classes of objectives, or educational behaviors, ranging from simple to complex intellectual abilities and skills. While there are six levels, elements in the categories frequently overlap.

BLOOM'S TAXONOMY

Bloom's taxonomy can be used to study, analyze, and plan questions. It is also a tool to help students to think beyond the level of recall. In addition, questions or activities at many levels help to reinforce the thinking processes and skills that were identified in the ASCD framework.

While the levels are generally thought of as progressing from easy to more difficult, keep in mind that each level represents varying degrees of difficulty.

The six levels of Bloom's taxonomy are the following:

1. *Knowledge*—remembering or recalling previously learned information
2. *Comprehension*—understanding the meaning of information
3. *Application*—using information in an unfamiliar context
4. *Analysis*—taking apart or separating information so it may be more easily understood and remembered
5. *Synthesis*—using information and creating something new
6. *Evaluation*—making a judgment based upon some criteria or evidence

We will present a simplified explanation of the taxonomy.

Knowledge. At this level the student recalls or recognizes specific bits of information. The learner may be required to memorize facts, terminology, or rules for later use, or to sort and retrieve information, but would not be asked to reorganize or apply any of the information. Responses to questions tend to be single-word answers. Answers are predictable and do not require creative thought. However, knowledge is a stepping stone to higher levels of thinking, since information is needed for generating more complex intellectual activity. Examples of questions at this level include:

1. When was the Constitution written?
2. Who signed the Constitution?
3. Recite the Preamble to the Constitution.

Cue words: *Name, complete, select, list, recall, identify, how, what, who, when*

Comprehension. Here students show evidence of understanding and the ability to organize previously learned information. They may interpret by summarizing or by expressing major ideas in their own words. The learner must process the information that was received so that it is not given back in its original form. For example, to check for comprehension, you might ask students to graph population trends in the United States from 1800 to 1990. This task demonstrates comprehension by requiring students to translate newly learned information into another, familiar form. Questions at this level might be:

1. What were the purposes of the Constitution?
2. Paraphrase the Preamble.

Cue words: *Restate, describe, review, relate, give main idea, summarize, tell me in your own words.*

Application. The ability to apply or transfer what has been learned to a new situation is an important goal in education. When students use appropriate concepts to classify new information, they have reached the third level of cognition, application. Students use the knowledge they have acquired in pertinent situations. Thus practice at the application level provides for the transfer of learning. Note the similarity between Bloom's application level and Gagne's concept learning level (see Chapter 2, Table 2.1 and page 49). Questions at this level help with concept formation and principle formation. Examples of questions or activities at the application level are these:

1. Using the commutative property, how would you decide on the answer for 3×4?
2. Here is a case that is before the courts. On which amendment to the Constitution is the defense basing its argument?

Cue words: *Apply, employ, solve, use, demonstrate, show, classify.*

Analysis. At the fourth level of cognition, learners are required to separate information into parts and describe relationships among those parts. This helps students discover how to organize information. Analysis helps learners to reduce the complexities of the information, adds meaning to knowledge, and aids in retention. Questions at this level help with critical thinking, concept formation, and principle formation. Examples include:

1. Compare the Constitution with the Articles of Confederation. How are the two documents alike? How are they different?

2. Compare and contrast the powers of the legislative branch, the executive branch, and the judicial branch.
    Cue words: *Analyze, dissect, compare, contrast, separate.*

Synthesis. Students, using creative and original thinking, must draw upon elements from many sources and put them together into a whole that is new to their experience. Learners are expected to engage in divergent, or open-ended, thinking and produce an original response as they organize elements into new patterns. It is difficult to predict students' responses at this level, since their responses should be unique and varied. Sample activities include a creative endeavor in the arts, such as writing a musical composition, a poem, or story, or changing the ending of an existing story, and the designing of an experiment to test a hypothesis. Questions or activities promote creative thinking. Problem-solving, composition, research, and generating skills are used. Examples of activities and questions are the following:

1. Suppose we had kept the Articles of Confederation. What type of government might exist today?
2. Rewrite the Constitution so that slavery was abolished in 1789. What effect do you think this measure would have had on U.S. history?
    Cue words: *Create, invent, compose, predict, plan, design, improve, what if.*

Evaluation. A learner who makes a judgment based on solid evidence, criteria, or standards is at the sixth level of cognition, evaluation. Evaluation involves having an opinion and making a judgment based on an established standard. This is the highest level of cognition in Bloom's taxonomy. Operating at this level involves a combination of some or all the other levels of the taxonomy. Questions at this level help with decision-making and evaluating skills. Examples are:

1. Which amendment to the Constitution is most important? Why?
2. Here is the Constitution to another country. Here is the U.S. Constitution. Which is better for a republic? Why?

Cue words: *Judge, select, choose, decide, evaluate, critique, justify, debate, verify, argue, recommend.*

It is not always critical to pinpoint the level at which questions are asked; rather, emphasis should be given to questions beyond the knowledge and comprehension levels. Questions at these levels are sometimes called *lower level questions*. They require convergent thinking, thinking that may elicit a single correct answer. Students merely recall or remember information.

Questions that require higher order thinking can yield multiple solutions. Questions at application, analysis, synthesis, and evaluation levels are sometimes called *higher level questions*. They require students to make inferences and interpretations, construct original products, make predictions, or determine judgments. However, it is important to recognize that knowledge, or lower, level questions are valuable as information is needed for students to operate at higher levels.

CHECK FOR UNDERSTANDING

1. Write a brief definition for each level:

   Knowledge _____

   _____

   Comprehension _____

   _____

   Application _____

   _____

   Analysis _____

   _____

   Synthesis _____

   _____

Evaluation _____

_____

2. Match each question with the appropriate cognitive level.
    a. Who wrote *Charlotte's Web?*
    b. Compare your two favorite characters in Charlotte's Web. How are they alike? How are they different?
    c. Compute the area of the barnyard using the formula we learned in mathematics.
    d. Describe Charlotte's appearance.
    e. Which is your favorite book by E. B. White? Why?
    f. Write a poem describing your feelings about the story.
        1. evaluation
        2. synthesis
        3. analysis
        4. application
        5. comprehension
        6. knowledge

Correct answers: a—6; b—3; c—4; d—5; e—1; f—2.

Guided Practice Activity. Developing Classroom Questions

Take a few moments and imagine that you are teaching a unit on the human body to fifth graders. Write two questions that you might ask students at each level of Bloom's taxonomy. Write your answers on the lines provided.

Topic: **The Human Body**

Fifth-Grade Science

Questions:

Knowledge

1. _____

2. _____

Comprehension

1. _____

2. _____

Application

1. _____

2. _____

Analysis

1. _____

2. _____

Synthesis

1. _____

2. _____

Evaluation

1. _____

2. _____

Other Issues in Questioning.   Many of the other techniques for effective questioning discussed in Chapter 4 are also important to consider in preparing activities and questions for higher level thinking. For example, wait time provides students with the time they may need in formulating higher level responses. Probing student answers enables you to understand the reasoning behind a response and may spur students to more elaborate thinking (see pages 221 to 222). Judicious use of praise and acknowledgment of responses can encourage multiple answers. It will take effective application of all you have learned about questioning to prompt maximum thinking in your students.

One issue that deserves special consideration is that of equity. In Chapter 4 we stressed that it is vital to assure that your pattern of questions gives equal opportunities to students, regardless of their gender, race, culture, or achievement level. We would like to reemphasize that it is important to consider equity not just in the number of questions you ask each student but in the types of questions and the degree of probing. If the number of questions is the same, but the higher level questions go primarily to high achieving students (or boys, or any other group), some students do not have the opportunities they need to develop effective thinking. We do not pretend that this balance is easy. But through careful ties to students' prior knowledge, attention to students' strengths, open-ended discussions, and thoughtful probing, you can create a classroom in which students understand that *everyone* is expected to think.

The atmosphere in a "thinking" classroom is affected by factors other than the types and strategies of questions asked. It is necessary to create an atmosphere in which thinking is safe. Students must know that their answers and ideas are respected, even when they disagree with the teacher. They must feel free to ask their own questions, make suggestions, share and compare ideas. Discussions, inquiry, and social lessons are particularly helpful in creating this type of atmosphere. You may even want to consider developing a classroom theme, motto, name, or even a song that lets students know their thinking is important. "Mrs. Jordan's Think Tank" may sound like a different place from "Mrs. Jordan's class." While some people may find such titles silly (or object to a student questioning a teacher), it is important to remember that unless students feel their classroom welcomes thinking, it is not likely that they will think.

Activities for Practice in Thinking

Another way to teach for thinking is to plan activities that are specifically designed to practice various types of thinking. We will consider activities that practice critical thinking, creative thinking, and metacognition. You might also plan activities that practice various thinking skills or processes.

Critical Thinking.   Remember that critical thinking entails careful evaluation of information in order to make judgments regarding actions or beliefs. Ennis (1986) has identified four basic areas of critical thinking: *clarity, basis, inference*, and *interaction*. Activities designed to promote *clarity* would require students to identify the question to be decided and the key arguments presented. Students might be asked to read letters to the editor in a newspaper, identifying the topics of concern and underlining the arguments raised by the writers. They could later apply the standards of a clear topic and identifiable arguments to their own letters on a topic of interest. In math, students might be asked to find the sentence in a story problem that defines the question, or to create a question for a set of numbers.

Activities focusing on *basis* ask students to examine the evidence presented. They might consider the credibility of sources cited and look for signs of bias. For example, advertisements form a ready source of claims for which evidence may be examined. What evidence is presented to suggest that a particular toothpaste whitens better, or a cola tastes better? Do brochures on energy produced by an oil company portray U.S. energy needs differently from those created by the Sierra Club? Why? (This type of question may become increasingly important as more and more companies begin producing educational materials.) For older students, political campaigns are a rich mine of material. What evidence does the candidate present to support his or her viewpoint? It is also possible to look for evidence of bias in historical documents. Might the events at Lexington and Concord have been recorded differently by British and colonial soldiers?

Younger students can examine the effects of point of view through their own experiences or those of familiar characters. How might the three bears feel when they find a strange girl in their house? Is there any evidence in the story to support this? What kind of a girl is Cinderella? How do you know? If two children on the playground both think a particular ball is theirs, how can they decide?

Critical thinking also entails *inference*, or the logical sequence of arguments and generalizations. If our fish prefer a particular brand of food, can we infer that all fish will do so? If all squares are rectangles, are all rectangles squares? Inference can be practiced by analyzing, participating in, and judging debates (perhaps conducted in pairs), examining the logic employed by characters in literature, and working together to solve problems. In fact, all three aspects of critical thinking are used in the fourth area, *interaction* with others. Students may interact in analyzing TV programs for basis or inference, comparing the points of view of historical characters, evaluating options for class activities, seeking examples or principles in their readings, or designing questions necessary to make an informed decision.

Creative Thinking.   Activities designed to practice creative thinking may also center on four areas: *fluency, flexibility, originality*, and *elaboration*. Activities that involve *fluency* require students to generate *many* responses—for example, to list as many problems as they can for which the solution is the number 6. In doing tasks that entail *flexibility*, students are asked to come up with many different types of responses, or responses that suggest several points of view. "How many ways can you use these materials to lift a book from your desk?" is a task that requires both fluency and flexibility. Flexibility can also be used to translate something into a new form—for example, creating a painting to represent a piece of music or an abstract idea like *friendship*. When students are practicing for *originality*, their task is to produce a response that is unique—for example, to imagine how Jack might have traveled home if the beanstalk had broken, or to design a totally new approach for selling sneakers. *Elaboration* entails the addition of details to improve an idea, such as making a jack-o'-lantern so that the entire pumpkin is decorated, or including figurative language to improve a story. Both of those tasks, ideally, should result in original thinking as well.

While high quality creativity also demands critical evaluation, the initial stages of creativity are frequently marked by divergent thinking, risk taking, and open-endedness. Activities designed to practice creative thinking might include brainstorming, creative dramatics, and "what if" questions. What if the Spanish had settled in what became New England? What if you were 1 inch tall? What if all school buses disappeared? What if magnets stuck to wood? Such questions can be used not just to develop creative thinking but to reinforce and elaborate content. "What if" questions can form the basis of class or small-group discussions, creative writing assignments, art projects, or creative dramatics.

Metaphors or analogies can often be used to spur new ideas. Students might be asked what animal reminds them of snow (perhaps in conjunction with Sandburg's poem about fog), how freedom is like a song, or what else is as soft as a cat. A rabbit? A rainy day? How might the concept of supply and demand be portrayed as a photograph? As a dance? Such tasks may appeal particularly to students whose learning style makes holistic, "random" leaps.

Metacognition.   Activities that enable students to practice metacognition help learners become aware of their own thinking. Many such activities require students to verbalize their thought processes. Young students may simply be asked "Why do you like sneakers with Velcro better than sneakers with ties?" "How did you decide to be a pirate for Halloween?" or "Which pieces will you put away first?" Older students may be asked to develop a plan of action before problem solving ("List the steps you will take to complete your group's project") or to write descriptions of the steps they took in order to solve a problem or make a decision ("How did you decide Jane was the thief?"). Paired problem solving (Whimby & Lockhead, 1986) is a particularly effective means of developing metacognition. Students work in pairs, with one student solving the problem while describing his or her thoughts aloud. The second student does not provide the answer but may reflect the first student's ideas, observe strategies, or point out errors. The "listener" also encourages the problem solver to continue to verbalize thoughts, helping both students to become aware of metacognition. On subsequent problems, roles are reversed. Paired problem solving can be used with math problems, logic puzzles, or any type of decision making. It is easiest for students to begin with closed problems, in which their thinking can lead to a correct answer.

Two Cautions.   In considering activities to foster critical thinking, creative thinking, and metacognition, we should keep two cautions in mind. First, we must model the types of thinking we expect from our students by providing an example of the careful weighing of evidence in critical thinking and the risk taking necessary for creative thinking. We must help students understand our own thought processes. For example, we might model metacognition through statements such as the following:

- When I did this problem, I thought about whether to add or subtract. When I saw the key word *difference*, I knew it was probably a subtraction problem.

- When I planned this unit, I knew that spring break would come in the middle of it. After considering several alternatives, I decided to try splitting the unit into two separate sections, one focusing on the geography of the ocean and one on the animals that live there. I am hoping this will make it easier for us to refocus our attention after the break.

We can use metacognition to model other types of thinking as well:

- I knew I wanted an original idea for my poster, so I tried to think of as many different ideas as I could before I selected one. I liked this idea because it used humor but it still made the point.
- Last night when I watched the news, I saw a story that really made me think. It said that people in our city do not favor the building of the new fire station. I wondered how they knew that. I live in the city and no one has asked me how I felt. Do you think *everyone* in the city feels the same way?

Our second caution involves evaluation. Do you remember the principle of congruence, which emphasizes a logical flow from learning goals to activities to evaluation (see Chapter 4)? It is important, but not always easy, to include items involving critical thinking, creative thinking, and metacognition in your evaluation. We, too, have struggled with this dilemma. As we attempt to engage *our* students in higher level thinking and encourage their reflection, we have devised means of evaluation that reflect these goals. It would be much easier, for instance, to ask students to list three components of reflection (a memory task) than to design a task that requires reflection, determine assessment standards, and evaluate it. Nevertheless, if we are committed to higher level thinking as a goal (and we are), it must be assessed.

It is also important to remember that activities designed to assess higher level thinking must ask students to use their thinking in new content; otherwise you may be merely assessing their memory. For example, if students had practiced identifying key arguments by reading a series of letters to the editor, I could not assess their ability to identify key arguments by giving them the same letters. If I did, they would not have to use their higher level thinking to analyze the letters; they could just recall the examples presented in class. Be wary of this challenge, and make sure your evaluation activities reflect those skills you believe are important, and not just those that are easy to measure.

CHECK FOR UNDERSTANDING

Choose a unit topic of interest to you. List two activities you might use to give students practice in each of the following:

Critical thinking _____

_____

_____

Creative thinking _____

_____

_____

Metacognition _____

_____

_____

_____

TEACHING OF THINKING

Teaching of thinking entails explicit teaching of various thinking skills and processes. Some educators (for example, Beyer, 1987) believe that one of the reasons students have so much difficulty with tasks requiring thinking skills is that such skills are seldom taught. We may provide students with a worksheet or activity that asks them to make a decision, without ever providing instructions in how good decisions are made. Thinking processes like problem solving, decision making, and research can be the subjects of carefully designed lessons. It is also possible to design focusing activities, information-giving activities, and practice activities on smaller components of thinking such as identifying bias, looking for different points of view, or using brainstorming to generate many ideas.

If the thinking task we want to teach is clearly defined (if, for example, we wanted to teach the IDEAL model of problem solving), we may choose either a direct or an inductive teaching model. If the task is less clear (for example, could you list four steps for identifying point of view?), Beyer suggests an inductive approach, engaging students in the task (asking them to identify the point of view in a piece of writing, for example) and discussing the steps they used. These steps can then be tested on another piece of writing, as the class defines its own procedure for identifying point of view. The point in either case is that the lesson is focused on the thinking task; the content around which the thinking is organized is secondary. If, for example, your lesson asks students to identify the point of view in an essay about pollution, the focus is not on pollution but on identifying points of view.

After initial teaching, it is important that thinking tasks be practiced in a wide variety of content, and that students be specifically taught that such skills can be transferred to many situations. Without such instruction, it is likely that students will view the skills as linked to particular content and not apply them elsewhere. If, for instance, our lesson on point of view was taught during science as part of our pollution unit, we would first practice the skill in content that is similar to the original lesson. We might look for point of view articles about the danger of oil spills, or in materials provided by the Environmental Protection Agency. Later, however, we would want to teach a lesson transferring the skill of identifying points of view to a very different setting, perhaps in analyzing short stories or in learning to conduct a class discussion. One of the goals in teaching of thinking is that students will use the skills they have gained in many, varied, situations. This transfer is unlikely to occur without our specific attention (Beyer, 1987; Perkins, 1987).

Numerous commercial programs have been developed to teach of thinking, each emphasizing a different set of thinking skills and processes, and organized around different content. Some districts have adopted specific thinking skills programs as their focus for teaching thinking. Commercial programs have the advantage that, in many cases, a carefully sequenced and designed set of skills has already been organized—an advantage that many busy teachers appreciate.

Of course, the parallel disadvantage is that some commercial programs may not fit smoothly into your regular curriculum or would require you to spend extra time or take special training. If your district considers adopting a commercial thinking program, it would be wise to weigh the advantages and disadvantages of many programs before making a decision. A complete treatment of programs for teaching thinking skills is beyond the scope of this text; however, you may wish to explore the topic further as you pursue your teaching career. At the end of this chapter is a brief list of some commercial thinking skills programs.

TEACHING ABOUT THINKING

The final approach to teaching thinking, teaching about thinking, is closely related to teaching of thinking. While teaching of thinking helps students learn the steps in particular thinking tasks, teaching about thinking helps them learn about thinking itself. Most of the activities we discussed regarding metacognition can be used for teaching about thinking. In teaching about thinking, we might give lessons on the various types of thinking (critical, creative, metacognition) and when they might be appropriate. We might study the thought processes of others, reading and interviewing to determine how good thinkers generate, evaluate, and monitor their ideas. As we learn more about brain functioning, we can use this topic, too, to teach students about the processes of their own thinking. If, for example, we learn that mnemonic devices can be helpful in retrieving unstructured information from long-term memory, such information can help students plan their learning more efficiently. All three types of teaching—for, of, and about thinking—combine to provide students with the information, tools, and encouragement they need to become effective thinkers.

CHECK FOR UNDERSTANDING

Define and give an example for each of the following:

Teaching for thinking _____

_____

_____

Teaching of thinking _____

_____

_____

Teaching about thinking _____

_____

_____

Section 4. Issues in Teaching Thinking

The interest in teaching thinking and the proliferation of thinking skills programs have created some problems. Sternberg (1985) has cautioned that in an environment in which everyone seems to be on a thinking skills bandwagon, some important caveats about thinking may become lost among the shouts and applause. First, few commercial thinking skills programs focus much attention on the inherent difficulties in identifying a problem for which students will apply their thinking (remember the *I* in IDEAL?). In the everyday world, recognizing that a problem exists and being able to isolate and describe it is sometimes the most difficult step in problem solving. Anyone who has participated in a group problem-solving activity in the real world recognizes how frustrating it can be to secure agreement that a problem exists, or to reach consensus on the nature of the problem. Sternberg concludes, "In everyday problem solving, it is often harder to figure out just what the problem is than to figure out how to solve it" (p. 196). If we are able to help students become good thinkers, we must attend to problem finding as well as to problem solving.

Second, the majority of problems we face in the real world are messy, ill-structured, and stubbornly resistant to solution. Unfortunately, some thinking skills programs avoid that unpleasant truth by presenting well-structured solution sets, organized into a series of sequential steps. "First you do this, then that, then follow with step 6, and the problem is solved." Consider applying thinking skills to such problems as buying a used car, choosing a career, or finding the right mate. Beyond the obvious considerations, there are multiple paths and sequences that may or may not result in the "right" solution. There often is no single right answer to real-world problems, nor are the criteria for choosing among the alternatives always clear, except in hindsight. Thus if all the problems we present to our students or the thinking activities we plan for them have clear, predetermined answers, our pupils will be short-changed.

Third, in contrast to the exercises contained in many thinking skills programs, life's problems are embedded in the environment and cannot be solved in isolation. Often the factors one must take into account are varied, complex, and confounded. For example, in deciding where to relocate, how much weight should we assign to factors such as climate, population density, distance from family and friends, quality of life, and so on? What may be right in one context may not be right in another, a complexity that may not be recognized in "school" problems.

Fourth, solving real-world problems generates consequences that matter, both in the short term and in the long term. For example, if you have a choice between two jobs, the one that pays better and offers more potential for advancement may require you to purchase an automobile (short-term consequence) and also involve moving away from a close-knit family or life-long friends (long-term consequence). Problems solved in school seldom have significant consequences.

Fifth, thinking skills can only help us confront complex real-world problems; they cannot guarantee clear-cut solutions. In many studies, business executives and political leaders have reported that the formal knowledge and skills they learned in classrooms were not as valuable as the informal knowledge they picked up through experience or through shrewdness, political savvy, or common sense. We must be realistic as to the role of the skills we teach, recognizing the impact of knowledge that will not be acquired in schools.

We believe our teaching principle of experience-based learning, with its emphasis on real-world problems and interaction, can help alleviate some of these difficulties. Students can become involved in working on local environmental problems, school issues, or classroom dilemmas. Establishing or contributing to a recycling program, creating a strategy for dealing with unpaid library fines, planning a simulated Indian encampment, or setting up a classroom reading area are tasks with the complexities and consequences inherent in the real world. We need to teach students to think, not just in textbook-clear experiences but in the fuzzy and awkward problems of the world around us.

CHAPTER SUMMARY

No matter how one views thinking, what definitions are used, what skills are taught, we are faced with the fact that students must attain high levels of knowledge and skills in the various content areas. They need a repertoire of thinking skills to use as they engage in various cognitive processes. They have to develop independence and responsibility for their own learning, be aware of their own thinking, have standards for evaluating what is "good" thinking, and be able to think critically and creatively.

Independent Practice Activity. Designing a Lesson on a Teaching Skill

Choose one thinking skill or process that could be used to enhance a unit of your choice. Design a lesson to teach it. Compare your lesson with that of a friend. Did you find a direct or inductive approach more appropriate?

Programs for Teaching Thinking

1. *SOI*—Guilford's Structure of the Intellect was first used as a measure of intellectual abilities in 1962. Today it is used to:
    a. Teach thinking skills and abilities
    b. Teach creativity (divergent production)
    c. Teach reasoning and higher level critical thinking skills and abilities
    d. Identify SOI learning abilities and teach them to students who have not yet developed these abilities

    This program is based on identifying and teaching highly specific intellectual abilities—for example, the divergent production of symbolic units.
    Address: SOI Institute
              343 Richmond St.
              El Segundo, CA 90245
2. *Instrumental Enrichment*—The core of this program, developed by Reuven Feuerstein, an Israeli clinical psychologist, is a three-year series of problem-solving tasks and exercises that are grouped in 14 areas of specific cognitive development. The exercises are free of any specific subject matter. The goal of the program is to develop, refine, and crystallize functions that are prerequisite to effective thinking. A minimum of 45 hours of inservice training is needed.

        Address: Curriculum Development Associates
                Suite 414, 1211 Connecticut Ave. NW
                Washington, DC 20036

3. *The CoRT Thinking Program*—The goal of this program, developed by Edward deBono, is to teach thinking skills useful to everyone in and out of schools. The program assumptions are as follows:

    a. Lateral thinking (thinking around a problem), unlike vertical thinking, is not necessarily sequential, is unpredictable, and is not constrained by convention.

    b. It is not necessary to be right at every stage of the thought process nor to have everything rigidly defined.

    c. Intelligent people are not necessarily skillful thinkers.

      The program consists of a series of lessons designed to teach "thinking tools"—acronyms such as CAF (consider all factors) that trigger thoughtful responses.

    Address: Pergamon Press
             Fairview Park
             Elmsford, NY 10523

4. *Project IMPACT*—This program, developed by S. Lee Winocur, is designed to improve students' performance in mathematics and language arts by facilitating their acquisition of higher level thinking skills. Activities include a critical thinking component infused into content area lessons through

    a. a sequential and cumulative universe of critical thinking skills designed to help students reason

    b. a model lesson format

    c. 10 teaching behaviors that label and reinforce students' use of thinking in an interactive environment

    Address: S. Lee Winocur, National Director
             Project IMPACT
             Orange County Department of Education
             P.O. Box 9050
             Costa Mesa, CA 92628-9050

5. *Philosophy for Children*—Matthew Lipman developed this program to improve children's reasoning abilities by having them think about thinking as they discuss concepts of importance to them. They do so by reading special novels, followed by teacher-led discussion using structured discussion plans, exercises, and games.

    Address: Institute for the Advancement of Philosophy for Children
             Montclair State College
             Upper Montclair, NJ 07043

6. *Future Problem Solving*—E. Paul Torrance based this program on the work of Alex Osborn and Sidney Parnes. The goal is to develop creative problem-solving skills in students while they learn about the future. Students form teams of four and follow a multiple-step problem-solving process.

    Address: Future Problem Solving Program
             P.O. Box 98
             Aberdeen, NC 28315

7. *Teaching Styles and Strategies*—Published by Hanson, Silver, Strong, & Associates, this program builds on the thinking of Bruce Joyce, Carl Jung, and Muska Mosston. One of the key elements in the Hanson, Silver, Strong program is the use

of questions to evoke higher level thinking. Several of the strategies are based on the work of Hilda Taba. The Hanson Silver Strong Model identifies four distinct learning styles and describes teaching strategies related to each learning style.

Address: Hanson, Silver, Strong & Associates
Box 402
Moorestown, NJ 08057

REFERENCES

Baron, J., & Sternberg, R. J. (Eds.). (1987). *Teaching Thinking Skills*. New York: Freeman.

Beyer, B. K. (1987). *Practical Strategies for the Teaching of Thinking*. Boston: Allyn and Bacon.

Bloom, B. (Ed.). (1956). *A Taxonomy of Educational Objectives: Handbook I. Cognitive Domain*. White Plains, NY: Longman.

Bransford, J. D., & Stein, B. S. (1984). *The IDEAL Problem Solver*. New York: Freeman.

Cetron, M. (1985). *Schools of the Future*. New York: McGraw-Hill.

Chi, M. T. H. (1978). Knowledge structures and memory development. In R. S. Seigler (Ed.), *Children's thinking: What develops?* (pp. 73–176). Hillsdale, NJ: Erlbaum.

Chi, M., Feltovich, P., & Glaser, R. (1981). Categorization and representation of physics problems by experts and novices. *Cognitive Science, 5*, 121–152.

Costa, A. (Ed.) (1985). *Developing Minds: A Resource Book for Teaching Thinking*. Alexandria, VA: Association for Supervision and Curriculum Development.

deBono, E. (1985). The CoRT thinking program. In A. Costa (Ed.), *Developing Minds: A Resource Book for Teaching Thinking* (pp. 203–209). Alexandria, VA: Association for Supervision and Curriculum Development.

Ennis, R. H. (1987). A taxonomy of critical thinking dispositions and abilities. In J. Baron & R. Sternberg (Eds.), *Teaching Thinking Skills* (pp. 9–26). New York: Freeman.

Goodlad, J. I. (1984). *A Place Called School: Prospects for the Future*. New York: McGraw-Hill.

Halpern, D. F. (1984). *Thought and Knowledge: An Introduction to Critical Thinking*. Hillsdale, NJ: Erlbaum.

Marzano, R. J., Brandt, R. S., Hughes, C. S., Jones, B. F., Presseisen, B. Z., Rankin, S. C., & Suhor, C. (1988). *Dimensions of Thinking: A Framework for Curriculum and Instruction*. Alexandria, VA: Association for Supervision and Curriculum Development.

Perkins, D. N. (1984). Creativity by design. *Educational Leadership, 42*, 18–25.

Perkins, D. (1987). Thinking Frames: An Integrative Perspective on Teaching Cognitive Skills. In J. Baron and R. Sternberg (Eds.), *Teaching thinking skills* (pp. 41–61). New York: Freeman.

Proett, J., & Gill, K. (1986). *The Writing Process in Action*. Urbana, IL: National Council of Teachers of English.

Resnick, L. B. (1987). *Education and Learning to Think*. Washington, DC: National Academy Press.

Sternberg, R. J. (1985). Teaching critical thinking: Part 1. Are we making critical mistakes? *Phi Delta Kappan, 67* (3), 194–198.

Whimby, A., & Lockhead, J. (1986). *Problem Solving and Comprehension* (4th ed.). Hillsdale, NJ: Erlbaum.

CHAPTER 7

Teaching for Individual Needs

Chapter Overview

In Chapter 4 we discussed the importance of recognizing individual differences in students and suggested strategies for providing variety in instructional activities. These strategies are helpful in planning lessons that are appropriate for students with a variety of learning styles, interests, and abilities. You will find, however, that in most classrooms there is at least one child whose special needs require more variety and adaptation than most lesson designs provide.

This chapter offers information and techniques to help you plan lessons to meet the needs of gifted and talented students, students with educational disabilities, and culturally diverse and bilingual students. Each of the three sections of the chapter focuses on the characteristics and needs of the type of students discussed, describes teaching strategies appropriate for such students, and explains how those strategies may sometimes be useful for all students.

Set Activity

Diane Lewis, a first-year teacher, sits at her desk at the end of a long October day. So far, she has found fifth grade to be extremely hectic but rewarding. Diane has enjoyed the diversity in her large urban school. Her carefully prepared management system has proved valuable in creating a classroom atmosphere that is warm but businesslike. Although much of the material in the textbooks has been review, Diane is pleased that most of her students are completing their assignments successfully. Best of all, Diane feels as if she is beginning to really know her students—their likes and dislikes, strengths, weaknesses, and interests. Today, however, that knowledge is starting to cause her some concern. The students are all so *different*.

It is easiest to worry about John. Although he is the oldest child in the class, John has the most difficulty learning basic skills. His reading is slow and laborious even in the second-grade reader, and he has not mastered the basic addition and subtraction facts. So far he has not caused any trouble, but his third-grade teacher said he used to get into frequent fights with other children and would not participate in class.

Maria, on the other hand, has caused some problems already. Her ready wit sends the class into fits of laughter, often at the teacher's expense. She is a leader on the playground, devising elaborate games and fantasies for others to play or act out. Her work is erratic. While her creative writing is outstanding, her math and spelling are average at best, and she frequently hands in late or incomplete assignments. Diane often wonders if Maria is really listening to her.

Rosa is another story. Raised in a Spanish-speaking home, Rosa spent her first two years in school in a bilingual program. While she speaks English fairly well, her grammar is weak and her reading not much better than John's. Rosa never volunteers in class, and Diane is seldom sure whether she understands the lesson.

Joe is the star of the class. Whenever a lesson is lagging or a point seems unclear, Diane can count on Joe to come up with the correct answer. His assignments are always complete and accurate. If a topic is mentioned in class, Joe frequently finds a newspaper article or book from home that can serve as an additional resource. Diane has heard other teachers reminiscing about how much they enjoyed Joe in previous years. Diane enjoys him, too, but she continues to have nagging doubts about the work he is doing in class. Is Joe really learning anything? As she thinks about John, Maria, Rosa, and Joe—and her carefully prepared social studies unit on the American Revolution, to begin the next day—Diane wonders how she can ever teach the subject in a way that will reach all her students.

Think for a moment about John, Maria, Rosa, and Joe. What characteristics of each student may have an impact on his or her learning in Diane's class? Write your answers below.

JOHN: _____

_____

MARIA: _____

_____

ROSA: _____

_____

JOE: _____

_____

Diane is facing a common dilemma. While teachers learn important principles of planning and instruction, those principles are always put into practice on a particular day, in a particular lesson, with a particular group of students. The artistry in teaching consists in knowing how to take into account the context of the lesson—in knowing which principles and strategies are most important to emphasize in this set of circumstances.

This chapter will help you adapt your planning and instruction to the needs of students almost every teacher encounters: learners with special needs. The following sections will guide you in planning activities for students like John, Maria, Rosa, and Joe. As you read, remember that none of the special needs addressed are mutually exclusive. A student may be gifted and bilingual; a slow learner may come from a cultural background that affects school performance; and there are, of course, many other combinations. It is important to consider each child first as an individual. Only then is it helpful to consider some of the special needs often found in particular groups of children, in order to give the best possible instruction to each of your pupils.

Section 1. Gifted and Talented Students

Section 1 Objectives

After you have completed this section, you should be able to:
1. describe characteristics of gifted and talented students
2. describe special instructional needs of such students
3. list instructional strategies that are appropriate for gifted and talented students
4. plan lessons in your curriculum area that are adapted for gifted and talented students
5. explain how activities that are appropriate for gifted and talented students may be used in lessons for an entire class

WHAT IS A "GIFTED" STUDENT?

There is no consensus on what constitutes a "gifted" student. Traditionally, giftedness has been identified by a high score on an IQ test, a measurement closely associated with school success. A student who scored in the top 1, 2, or 5 percent of the population (depending on the district)

was likely to be highly adept at school learning and was considered to be gifted. One of the problems with equating giftedness with high IQ is that IQ is not a particularly good predictor of adult giftedness. If we give all our students an IQ test, it will not necessarily identify the next Einstein or Madame Curie or Mozart. Moreover, the information we are learning from studies in human intelligence makes the limitations of IQ tests increasingly clear.

While a complete description of current theories of intelligence is beyond the scope of this chapter, two examples will suffice. Sternberg (1985) has developed a triarchic theory of intelligence. He believes that intelligence includes three basic components: the componential system, or "workings" of the mind in processing information; the response to novelty; and the ability of the individual to interact with the environment—an ability we might call social intelligence, or "street smarts." Individuals who have strengths in one of these three areas might be gifted in very different ways. A person whose componential system is particularly strong might be a whiz at taking in and analyzing information (remember Joe?), while a person who deals well with novelty might come up with original ideas or be an excellent problem solver (perhaps like Maria). And you have probably known someone with particular ability to interact with his or her social environment, someone who knows the right person to call on when there is a task to be done, or who always seems to be at the right place at the right time—someone with social intelligence.

Gardner (1983) believes that we all have multiple intelligences. He has identified seven independent intelligences: linguistic, musical, logical-mathematical, spatial, bodily kines-thetic, interpersonal, and intrapersonal. According to this theory, a person may be gifted in any one of the seven intelligences without being exceptional in the others. For example, a fine dancer might be considered gifted in bodily kinesthetic intelligence but would not necessarily be gifted in math or music. While psychologists continue to disagree as they theorize and investigate the nature of intelligence, they share one idea: Human intellectual activity is complex, much too elaborate to be represented by one number (such as an IQ score).

If we are not to rely on IQ to define *giftedness*, what choices remain? One definition that is used by many districts was proposed by the federal government in 1972:

> The term "gifted and talented children" means children . . . possessing demonstrated or potential abilities . . . in areas such as intellectual, specific academic, or leadership ability, or in the performing and visual arts and who by reason thereof require services or activities not ordinarily provided by the school. (Marland, 1972)

Two important points should be noted about this definition: (1) It broadens the definition of *giftedness* to include abilities other than IQ, and (2) it specifies that students who fall under this definition need services or activities beyond those normally provided by schools. Some districts have set up identification criteria for special gifted and talented programs based on this definition. They attempt to identify students with strengths in each of the areas listed.

Another definition was proposed by Renzulli (1978). His definition might best be understood through the following exercise. Take a moment and think of five people, living or dead, you would consider to be gifted. What do the people you named have in common? If you are like many people, you thought of individuals who developed an important idea, were responsible for a major invention, made a scientific discovery, or created a work of art, literature, or music. One way to describe these individuals is to call them "creative producers"—*producers* of information and art rather than simply *consumers*. Now think about the ways in which we have traditionally labeled students as "gifted." Is the rationale the same? In most cases, students are labeled as gifted because they are skillful consumers of information. They take the input we, as teachers, give them and "return" it to us on our tests, without necessarily doing very much to change or improve it.

Renzulli believes that we have attached the same label, "gifted," to two different types of ability, so he devised two new categories. "Schoolhouse giftedness" is the ability to consume, analyze, and reproduce information, while "creative productivity" is the ability to generate new information. It is important to understand that both schoolhouse giftedness and creative productivity are important. Einstein certainly could not have devised the theory of relativity if he had not consumed his physics! However, schools have traditionally paid much more attention to the consumption than to the production of information. Renzulli's Three Ring Conception of Giftedness was designed specifically to reflect research on creative producers, in the hopes that, if we identified the ways in which giftedness "works" in adults, we might be able to identify or encourage it in children.

The Three Ring Conception of Giftedness (see Figure 7.1) consists of three interlocking circles: above-average ability, creativity, and task commitment. Adult creative producers are of above-average intelligence, but not necessarily from the top 1 percent, or even the top 5 percent, of the population. They also work creatively, and with great commitment to the tasks they choose. Of course, their ability, task commitment, and creativity must be in the same area. If my above-average ability is in math, my creativity is in cooking, and my task commitment is to improving my golf swing, it is not likely that they will produce gifted behavior.

One of the functions of schools can be to help above-average students identify areas of interest and work to develop creativity and task commitment in those areas. We cannot expect even the brightest students to come to school with their abilities, creativity, and commitment already fully developed; that is part of our responsibilities as teachers.

CHECK FOR UNDERSTANDING

List three different ways in which *giftedness* may be defined. Think of someone you know who might be considered gifted according to each definition.

1. _____

_____

2. _____

_____

3. _____

_____

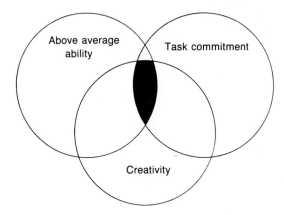

Figure 7.1. The Three Ring Conception of Giftedness. (*The Schoolwide Enrichment Model*, by Renzulli & Reis. Creative Learning Press, 1985.)

WHAT ARE GIFTED STUDENTS LIKE?

The varied definitions of *giftedness* may have given you a clue that there is no simple answer to the question "What are gifted students like?" Some children may be very good at one or more school subjects. Other children may be creative, always ready with a new idea. Some will have a wide variety of interests; others will pursue one specialized area. It is important to recognize that special interests or abilities do not always show up in obvious ways, or even in ways that make our teaching easier. Maria, at the beginning of the chapter, shows creativity in her writing and playground activities, but also in the humor directed against her teacher. Picasso was frequently reprimanded in school because he refused to do anything but paint. He was demonstrating creativity and task commitment, but not in the ways his teachers may have expected.

CHECK FOR UNDERSTANDING

The following list gives characteristics often associated with gifted students.

Large knowledge base
Good memory
Unusually varied and/or intense interests
Highly developed verbal skills
Ability to process information rapidly and accurately
Flexibility in thinking; with ability to see many points of view
Persistence
Awareness of relationships among diverse ideas
Ability to generate original ideas
Enjoyment of abstract ideas

Intense opinions or emotions
Sensitivity to feelings of self or others
Concern for global issues: war, hunger, etc.
Sense of humor

Choose three characteristics and describe how they might be manifested in schools in positive (+) or negative (−) ways. For example, a student with a fine sense of humor may add zest to the class or disrupt lessons with inappropriate comments.

	+	−
1.		
2.		
3.		

Under what circumstances do you think the negative behaviors would be most likely to take place? Although there are many possible causes for negative behavior, bright students who are not intellectually challenged by classwork sometimes find alternate forms of challenge through disruptive activities.

Characteristics of giftedness may also be hidden. It is easy to see evidence of intelligence in a successful student like Joe, but what about Rosa? As teachers, we should look for signs of special interests or abilities in students whose other needs may prevent us from noticing their giftedness. Finally, some students may—consciously or unconsciously—hide their gifts, either because they fear social isolation or because their experience has taught them that good work is rewarded with more work. If most math students are assigned 20 problems and "good math students" are assigned 30, many bright students beat the system by performing like average students.

The assumption that gifted students will make it on their own is a fallacy, especially if by "making it" we mean living up to their potential. Like all learners, bright students need instruction appropriate to their individual capabilities. In some cases districts provide special programs for bright students. Students identified as gifted and talented spend part or all of the day in classes designed to provide challenging experiences. In other cases, resource people assist teachers in planning for gifted students in their classrooms. However, even in districts with special programs, most gifted students spend the majority of their time in regular classrooms, under the direction of a classroom teacher.

BUT WHAT DO I DO WITH GIFTED STUDENTS?

If we acknowledge that giftedness is a complex concept and that identification is not simple, the question remains: What can we do with bright students in our classrooms, regardless of whether they have been officially labeled gifted? One way to approach the task is to recall Renzulli's two definitions and ask, How can I encourage both the consumption and production of information? To answer this question, teachers will have to examine the ways they teach the regular curriculum and make decisions about additional or alternative activities.

Regular Curriculum

One strategy for dealing with the regular curriculum is called *curriculum compacting* (Renzulli & Smith, 1979). In its simplest form, compacting involves diagnosing which of the skills in a particular unit of study some of your students have already mastered. For example, before beginning a math chapter on multiplication, you might give a pre-test covering the main skills in the unit. Some teachers use unit tests for this purpose; others use excerpts from workbooks or worksheets or devise their own tests. If you discover that any of your students have already mastered these skills, it would not be appropriate for them to spend a lot of time practicing or reviewing the same material. In 1888, J. M. Greenwood wrote, "When once a child has learned that four and two are six, a thousand repetitions will give him no new information and it is a waste of time to keep him employed in that manner" (p. 13). Instead, students could "test out" of some material and be provided with alternative activities such as those described below.

In other cases, especially when the instruction deals with concepts rather than skills, gifted students may not have mastered the material yet but can do so much more quickly than other students. For these students you might consider contracts (see Chapter 3), management sheets, or other forms of independent study (Parke, 1989). A contract generally identifies activities that must be completed to help a student master the regular content, as well as related enrichment activities. The contract also specifies how new knowledge and skills will be evaluated. A management sheet may provide direction to a student pursuing self-paced instruction. It is important to remember, however, that the use of independent contracts or management sheets does not release us from responsibility as teachers. While many bright students can master material with much less direct instruction than average students, teachers must still identify areas in which instruction is needed. Sometimes such instruction may be provided on an individual basis, perhaps while other students work on a practice activity, or a student may receive instruction with a large or a small group of students needing to learn the same skill. Periodic individual conferences can be helpful in assessing students' progress, as well as identifying areas of difficulty and planning further activities. The following excerpts are from a sample contract and management sheet.

Social Studies Contract

Required Activities

1. Read pages 69–87 of your text.
2. Complete Check-Up Questions 15 and 28.
3. Choose two blue activities from the Exploration Center. When you complete each activity, record your progress at the center.
4. Complete the unit test when ready.

Optional Activities

1. If you are doing an independent study project, you may work on it during social studies.
2. Research the life of an explorer not discussed in your text. Create a simulated interview with your explorer.
3. Create a song, dance, or play with the theme "exploration."
4. How is exploration in science different from or similar to the exploration discussed in Chapter 8? Read about Watson and Crick's search for DNA. Write an essay comparing their exploration to that discussed in your text.
5. Other activities as negotiated with the teacher.

Math Management Sheet Chapter 5

Page	Instructions	Complete Score	Required Correct	If Not
36	Read top carefully.	Odds, 1–19	8	Evens, 2–20
38		10–15	4	1–9
39	Stop. See teacher for lesson.	Odds, 1–19	8	Evens, 2–20

Alternative Activities

If students' curriculum has been compacted, they will complete the regular assignments in less time than average students. It is necessary to decide how best to use the additional time. One basic decision is between acceleration and enrichment. *Acceleration* is the pursuit of the regular curriculum at a faster pace (for example, going on to the eighth-grade math book while in seventh grade); *enrichment* is the incorporation of activities outside the regular curriculum. It is important to find out your district's policies regarding acceleration and enrichment. Since acceleration affects students' studies years after it occurs, many districts have guidelines for its use. It is likely that much of the planning you will do for gifted students will focus on enrichment.

One type of enrichment can be developed by adapting assignments or techniques in the regular curriculum to provide additional challenge. Many gifted students thrive on inquiry, induction, role playing, simulation, and other activities that encourage higher level thinking

while teaching content. The higher levels of Gagné's learning hierarchy (Chapter 2) or Bloom's taxonomy (Chapter 6) can be helpful in generating ideas for assignments. For example, in Diane's unit on the American Revolution, she may consider assignments that ask students to synthesize information from various sources and then to create a story or art work, or to evaluate the positions taken by the Patriots and the Loyalists. In other cases, students may investigate subtopics or related themes such as the Mexican Revolution, the French Revolution, or even the computer revolution! Lessons from experienced teachers, professional magazines, and commercial materials targeting higher level thinking may be useful in planning such activities.

You may, at times, wish to provide students with a choice of assignments and encourage gifted students to select challenging tasks. Of course, it is important to remember that not all bright students have the same interests and strengths. If we expect students to put forth efforts that are beyond those expected of other students, the tasks must not only challenge them but interest them. You should also make sure that gifted students do not spend too much time working in isolation. If students are able to bypass or condense significant amounts of the regular curriculum, it may be helpful to identify a group of intellectual peers with whom they can work. The students may form a cluster group within one classroom, a group of same-grade students from different classes who come together for instruction or independent work, or a group of mixed-grade students.

CHECK FOR UNDERSTANDING

Choose a unit topic you might teach. Briefly list three enrichment activities that might be suitable for a student who has already mastered much of the unit content.

1. _____

2. _____

3. _____

Did your activities require higher level thinking and/or independent investigation?

Creative Productivity

So far we have discussed ways to adapt the regular curriculum for gifted students, to take into consideration what Renzulli calls "schoolhouse giftedness." What about Renzulli's other type of giftedness, "creative productivity?" How do we encourage students to become producers of knowledge? A popular model designed for this purpose is the Enrichment Triad (Renzulli, 1977), shown in Figure 7.2. The Enrichment Triad includes Type I, Type II, and Type III enrichment.

Type I enrichment consists of general exploratory activities designed to help students identify their interests and to encourage them to investigate these interests further. It includes activities, materials, and resources, such as guest speakers, displays, movies, books, and interest development centers, that extend education beyond the regular curriculum. Any time you set up an interesting display, show a movie expanding the curriculum, or have a guest

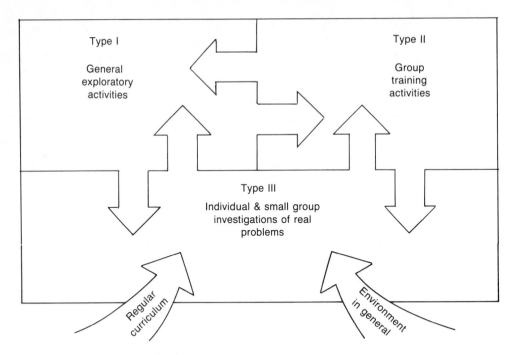

Figure 7.2. The Enrichment Triad

speaker in your classroom, you are providing a Type I activity. The broader the range of topics presented during the year, the better. The key to providing a meaningful Type I activity is the "debriefing" questions that follow. Because a Type I activity is intended to help students identify their interests, the questions should not simply assess whether students understood the material but should raise additional questions, pose problems, and find out which students are interested in pursuing the topic. For example, after an environmentalist has discussed acid rain, you could ask students whether they think there is acid rain in their area, what questions they still have about acid rain and how they could find answers, or if any students would like to learn how to test for acid rain. The most important objectives of Type I enrichment are (1) to expose students to as many varied topics as possible and (2) to encourage them to identify areas of interest and learn more about them.

Type II enrichment is composed of group training activities that can provide students with the tools they need to become independent investigators. (We hope, of course, that you will teach thinking skills to *all* your students.) Some of those skills, like critical and creative thinking, can be taught through the techniques mentioned in Chapter 6. Other activities might include the development of advanced research skills (like using *Readers' Guide to Periodical Literature* or microfiche), data-gathering, or interviewing skills. You may also identify particular skills a gifted student needs in order to investigate an area of interest. If there is a gifted-education specialist in your district, he or she can provide ideas, techniques, and materials. If not, you may wish to consult the professional literature or your state Department of Education for suggestions.

In Type III enrichment, the core of the Enrichment Triad, the students actually function as creative producers. Type III activities are individual or small-group investigations of real problems, selected and initiated by students. What is a real problem? For one thing, it does not have a predetermined answer; if you know the answer, it is not a real problem, even if the student doesn't know. For example, "What are the four food groups?" is not a real problem. "What are the food preferences of fifth graders in our school?" is a real problem that might be answered by a survey. Real problems generally address a social issue, solve a research question, or express an artistic or literary theme.

Learners engaged in Type III activities also attempt to solve problems in a manner that is as close as possible to the way an adult professional might do so. For example, a student interested in the impact of World War II on the town's economy could do oral history interviews, just as a professional historian might. Finally, a Type III has a "real audience." For a first grader, a real audience might be the class next door; for other students it may be more sophisticated. One fifth grader created a child's booklet on local history that went to the local Chamber of Commerce so that new children in town could read it. Other students have pursued projects ranging from the measuring of the acidity of rain in her community (a sixth grader) to the organizing of a townwide celebration of Be Kind to Animals Week (a third-grade group).

A Type III project addresses higher level learning in ways recommended by many of the authorities cited in this text. It requires the problem solving identified by Gagne as the highest level of learning. It provides the fuzzy challenges of real-world problems recommended by Sternberg (see Chapter 6). It certainly utilizes our principle of experience-based learning. However, as you can imagine, a Type III project takes enormous amounts of work, time, and assistance (teachers helping students and/or teachers receiving help). When you have many other teaching responsibilities, the demands of Type III activities can be discouraging. If there is no gifted-education specialist to help you, you might consider two options.

First, you may locate a mentor to assist the student who wishes to pursue a Type III activity. Another option is to consider a Type III project as a class activity. A project like this, initiated by the teacher, is sometimes called a Type II ½! You can plan an activity around a real problem, and encourage gifted students to play pivotal roles.

One third-grade teacher, in the midst of a unit on the community, had her students brainstorm community problems and identify the issue they thought was most critical. As true third graders, they identified the key problem as not having a McDonald's! Undaunted, the teacher asked how the problem could be solved. Data on new housing and roads were gathered, plans for new shopping areas were investigated, graphs were made, and the results submitted to McDonald's. Many students believed that the McDonald's built the next year was a result of their efforts. Older class activities have included the preparation of pamphlets to teach children what to do if they suspect a friend is being abused, living history projects, the creation of school nature paths, historical walking tours, and the establishment of recycling centers.

SERVING MANY STUDENTS

While all students may not have advanced learning abilities, many techniques that are suitable for gifted students can benefit others as well. Many students can be pre-tested for curriculum compacting, especially at the beginning of the year. Recall that in Chapter 3 we encouraged the use of your learning hierarchy to diagnose students' needs. Type I exploratory activities and the higher level thinking provided in Type II benefit all students. While the depth and challenge of Type III projects may not be appropriate for all students, activities that center on real-world problems provide levels of participation suitable for most students. Such activities allow students to develop confidence in their ability to solve problems and have an impact on the world—surely a valuable asset for any child!

Section 2. Students with Educational Disabilities

Section 2 Objectives

After you have completed this section, you should be able to:
1. describe characteristics of students with educational disabilities
2. describe special instructional needs of students with educational disabilities
3. list instructional strategies that are appropriate for such students
4. plan lessons in your curriculum area that are adapted to meet the needs of students with disabilities
5. explain how activities that are appropriate for students with educational disabilities may be used in lessons for an entire class

For much of the history of American education, children with physical, emotional, and mental disabilities were taught in special educational environments by instructors especially trained to teach such children. In the case of a severe disability, the child was taught in a location other than a regular school. If the disability was modest, the child's classroom was typically in a public school, usually in an area set apart from the school's traffic patterns. In either case the children with disabilities were isolated from the regular public education system, and thus from teachers and children in regular classes. However, the second half of the 20th century has seen dramatic changes in the education of such children. Almost every public school classroom now includes one or more students with educational disabilities. While many districts still employ specialists trained in various disabilities, it is essential that all teachers become familiar with the major types of disabilities and strategies for accommodating children with disabilities in the regular classroom.

WHAT ARE EDUCATIONAL DISABILITIES?

A *disability* is a condition that results in a reduced competency to perform some task or behavior, whether the condition is physical, emotional, or intellectual. Disabilities that impede regular educational activities are called *educational disabilities*. Everyone suffers from some degree of disability, in the sense that we all have traits that keep us from performing some tasks at optimum levels. Many people have poor eyesight, or poor color discrimination, or are awkward at sports or shy with strangers. However, these disabilities are mild enough so that we can easily reduce their effects or correct them. It may be useful to think of disabilities as existing within a continuum of competency. For example, consider a continuum of visual acuity, from individuals with excellent eyesight (perhaps those who can read the numbers on the jerseys from the top row of a football stadium!) to those who have no sense of sight. Somewhere in the lower 25 percent of that continuum we would begin to classify persons as disabled. We can sharpen our identification of disability by categorizing the reduced competency as *mild, moderate, severe*, or *profound.*

The major classifications of disabilities include children who are:

1. *Mentally impaired*—Such students function less well than the norm at all levels of learning. In its mild form, mental impairment is often labeled as "slow learning" and the child a "slow learner." In the set activity at the beginning of this chapter, John may possibly be mildly mentally impaired. In its moderate and severe form, intellectual impairment is accompanied by difficulty in adapting to regular classroom expectations and routines and difficulty in getting along with the teacher and other students. Professionals in the field of mental retardation use the terms *educably mentally retarded* to classify mild to moderate impairment, and *trainably mentally retarded* to classify moderate to severe impairment.

2. *Physically impaired*—Such students have disabilities that reduce their capability to perform psychomotor tasks involving small- and large-muscle movement, such as manipulating writing instruments and books, or moving around the classroom. Often the impairment results in reduction in the student's stamina, alertness, and vitality. However, in many cases the physically impaired child has no mental impairment. Common causes of physical impairment are birth defects, disease, and accidents.

3. *Sensory impaired*—Such students have reduced visual or auditory competency. Some teachers have performed a great service for children and their parents by identifying a mild sensory impairment that could be compensated by glasses or hearing enhancements. In more severe cases, the child has limited or no vision or hearing, and individualized teaching must be used to reduce the handicap.

4. *Speech impaired*—Such students have reduced competency in speech communication. A common source of speech impairment is a severe hearing loss that reduces the child's ability to reproduce speech patterns.

5. *Emotionally disturbed*—Such students display repeated inappropriate behavior to the extent that it affects their academic growth, social maturity, and relationships with adults and peers. It is important to distinguish a child who acts out from time to time from the emotionally disturbed child whose inappropriate behaviors are frequent and distinctive. Some emotionally disturbed children are identified because they are verbally and/or physically aggressive, prone to repeated outbursts that upset classroom routines. However, emotionally disturbed children may also be fearful, passive, or withdrawn.

6. *Learning disabled*—Such students demonstrate a reduced competency to perform some behaviors, while performing as well as or better than peers on other tasks. Unfortunately, because of the limited nature of the disability and an individual's efforts to compensate for areas of weakness, learning disabilities may not be identified until many years of schooling have passed. Conversely, some children are wrongly identified as learning disabled when the true cause of disability may be a physical, mental, or emotional impairment. In fact, of all the disability areas, learning disabilities are the most controversial. Because of the imprecise nature of diagnosis, there are major disagreements about the nature of a learning disability and the criteria to be used to classify a child as learning disabled (Wang, Reynolds, & Walberg, 1986, 1988). Varying types of learning disabilities may impair a student's ability to read, attend to stimuli, understand figurative language, or accurately assess spatial relationships.

All of the listed disabilities may occur in a range from mild to moderate to severe to profound. At some level of disability a person loses the capacity to function in society without external assistance. The degree to which individuals are assisted determines the degree of *handicap* they experience. A *handicap* is the disadvantage one suffers from the effects of a disability. The extent to which an individual is handicapped is a result of both the severity of the disability and the degree of assistance offered by society. For example, a physically disabled person in a wheelchair will be handicapped by facilities that are inaccessible, but not in areas designed to accommodate wheelchair access. A student whose learning disability prevents him from reading a science test is handicapped if required to take a written exam. While we cannot prevent all handicaps caused by disabilities, one of our responsibilities as teachers is to do the best we can to minimize the handicapping effects of disabilities in our classrooms. In this case, the teacher could allow the student to take the science test orally. While the student would still be learning disabled, he would not be handicapped in taking his science exam.

EDUCATIONAL DISABILITIES IN SCHOOL

Understanding the relationship between a disability and a handicap is helpful in interpreting the motivation for the events of the late 1960s and 1970s that culminated in the passage of the Education for All Handicapped Children Act, popularly known as EHA or Public Law 94-142. This wide-reaching law, which went into full effect in 1978, required that public schools provide handicapped children a free and appropriate educational program, individually prescribed to reduce their handicap. Indeed, the two key terms in the law are "appropriate" and "individually prescribed." A program is considered appropriate if it places students in the "least restrictive" environment possible, maximizing interaction with nonhandicapped children. Although the law does not use the word *mainstreaming*, that term became popular in describing the shift in emphasis from a policy of housing handicapped children in separate settings, to one in which children participate in many regular educational experiences, in both classroom and extracurricular activities.

In a 1987 review of the impact of the Education for All Handicapped Children Act, the authors concluded that the EHA had been a singular success. They stated that 20 years earlier, most Americans

> would have flatly denied the feasibility of instituting in every school system in the country, a program of individualized education, however imperfect, for 11 percent of the nation's children. Yet, this was done within a few years of EHA's implementation. Regular education teachers, special education teachers, school administrators and others at the local level have demonstrated a remarkable degree of dedication to the law's goals and an equally remarkable willingness to subsidize the program with their own efforts. (Singer & Butler, p. 151)

In fairness, it must be noted that this success was not accomplished without significant problems. Then and now, the sheer size of the change and the number of disability areas created administrative, logistical, clerical, and instructional burdens for the schools. Each disability area has its unique characteristics and challenges. Many physically and sensory impaired children need special equipment, materials, and support personnel. Some children who are classified as disabled qualify for government support because they are also economically disadvantaged; others do not. Some disabilities are hard to identify, particularly in students with multiple disabilities, or students for whom English is not the primary language. However, despite such difficulties, Public Law 94-142 has successfully mandated enormous changes in the education of students with disabilities.

In order to provide all students with the least restrictive environment possible, at least four types of options have evolved, each allowing varying degrees of mainstreaming:

1. *Regular classroom for a majority of the school program.* The student has the support of a resource teacher trained in special education and other professional personnel who specialize in the particular disability involved. The student is with his regular student peers for most of the day but may spend several hours each week in individualized assessment or instruction by a specialist.

2. *Self-contained classroom for a majority of the school program.* The student is taught in a special education classroom and mainstreamed into the regular classroom for varying amounts of time and for appropriate content activities. Such students may join a regular classroom for a limited amount of time each morning or afternoon, or for special subjects such as music or physical education.

3. *Self-contained classroom for the instructional program but within the regular school building.* Placement in the regular building permits the disabled child to participate in individually prescribed experiences and extracurricular activities.

4. *Separate building within an educational campus.* The proximity to the regular building permits the disabled child to participate in appropriate parts of the extracurricular program. (National Education Association, 1978)

It is likely that you will have one or more students in your classroom who will be mainstreamed for all or part of the school day and for whom an individually prescribed program will be required. The individually prescribed requirement of the law is called an *individualized educational plan*, or *IEP*. An IEP must include the following, for each child:

(A) a statement of the present levels of educational performance of such child, (B) a statement of annual goals, including short-term instructional objectives, (C) a statement of the specific educational services to be provided to such child, and the extent to which such child will be able to participate in regular educational programs, (D) the projected date for initiation and anticipated duration of such services, and appropriate objective criteria and evaluation procedures and schedules for determining, on at least an annual basis, whether instructional objectives are being met. (Public Law 94-142, 1975, Sec. 4, a, 19)

In addition to describing the nature of the IEP, the law stipulated that the plan must be cooperatively developed by the child's teacher and the child's parent(s) or guardian, and approved by the designated school administrator or special education supervisor. While the federal law does not do so, some states require that IEPs be prepared not just for students with disabilities but for gifted students as well. If a child in your classroom requires an IEP, a specialist should work with you to plan the individualized program and to clarify your role in carrying out the plan.

Note that the IEP has a similar structure to a unit plan or lesson design. Each is a system beginning with goals that are analyzed and phrased as clearly stated objectives. Activities are designed to help students meet the objectives, and evaluation procedures are used to determine if the objectives have been met. If additional instruction is needed, it is provided. Through-out instruction, there is consideration for students' learning styles, prior knowledge, and experience.

The major differences between an IEP and a unit plan or lesson design are that the IEP is a learning prescription for an individual student and that parents are more directly involved in its preparation and execution. You may also recognize that the IEP rests on criterion evaluation rather than norm-referenced evaluation principles—that is, evaluation is based on a student's achieving a predetermined performance standard rather than on a comparison with the performance of other students. Because of the attractive characteristics of the IEP process, its individual perspective on achievement, the way in which it involves parents, and its systematic structure, many educators have proposed that all students be taught through individualized education plans.

CHECK FOR UNDERSTANDING

Assume that an influential group of citizens recommended that all students be taught through the IEP process. What would be the advantages and disadvantages of that recommendation? Is it a worthy goal? Is it workable and practical? Briefly explain your views. Write your answers below

and discuss the recommendation with others. _____

_____

_____

_____

_____

STRATEGIES FOR TEACHING STUDENTS WITH DISABILITIES

Some general strategies can be employed by the teacher regardless of the nature of the mainstreamed student's disability:

- Learn as much as you can about the disabilities of students in your class. Consult with the special education professional in your building or district to gain additional insights into students' learning styles and strengths as well as strategies to accommodate the disability. For example, a mildly mentally impaired student is likely to be successful if presented with small chunks of information and given considerable reinforcement. A mildly hearing impaired student will benefit from sitting near the speaker, with an unobstructed view for lip reading, while a more severely impaired student may need a translator. You can also use your knowledge of students' interests and strengths to plan individual or class activities particularly suited to their needs.
- Avoid calling special attention to the student's disability. While a matter-of-fact acceptance of a disability is appropriate (you certainly cannot ignore the fact that Paul cannot see the board or Susan cannot read), it is important to relate to students as individuals, not as members of a group. It is no more appropriate to make generaliza-

tions about groups of disabled people than it would be to base broad generalizations on race or sex.

- Do not make assumptions based on the disability. Do not assume that the disabled person is unhappy. Do not assume that individuals with disabilities are disabled in *all* areas, or are less mature than those without disabilities. It is inappropriate to treat a mentally retarded adolescent whose intellectual level is that of a 7-year-old in the way you would treat a typical 7-year-old, or to treat a blind or physically disabled teenager like a small child (Biklen & Bogdan, 1977).

- Establish a classroom environment in which it is a common practice for students of different backgrounds and capabilities to learn from each other. Use the cooperative learning activities from Chapter 5 to integrate students of different backgrounds and abilities so they can teach each other.

- Use a clear management system. Do not accept inappropriate behavior from a disabled child that you would not accept from others. You may choose a less serious consequence, but do not communicate the message to the rest of the class that Paul or Susan can get away with unacceptable behavior. Such inconsistencies may lead to misbehavior or resentment by other students.

- Be enthusiastic and give positive reinforcement in response to the performance of your disabled student. However, as for all children, praise that is repetitious, insincere, or overly broad is not helpful and can be damaging.

- Be sure to have a systematic framework to organize your classroom activity. Some students with emotional, intellectual, or learning disabilities need a carefully established structure in order to work most effectively. Clearly defined objectives, and activities and evaluation procedures that logically follow from these objectives, communicate a sense of security and predictability to all students.

- Consider using a criterion evaluation approach in judging the performance of a student with a disability. Students with disabilities are more apt to be successful if your goal is to move each child to more competence rather than to rate that child in comparison with others.

- You may wish to consider using the IEP format for all your students. Begin with a small portion of your requirements and assess how it works. You may consider individual projects for 10–20 percent of the grade for a particular marking period. You could meet with each student to develop a plan for an individual project. Help each student develop a project goal and transform it into objectives, activities, and a product that can be evaluated to determine if the objectives have been met.

- Finally, become an advocate for the handicapped student. Lobby for alternative learning materials—for example, interesting literature and social studies books for the slow learner that parallel the text for regular students but at a different reading level. Lobby for facilities and materials that can reduce the handicaps of visually and hearing impaired students. See education for children with disabilities as their right as members of society rather than as a privilege granted to them.

RECENT EDUCATIONAL MOVEMENTS AFFECTING STUDENTS WITH DISABILITIES

Two recent movements have sought to increase the integration of children with educational disabilities into regular education classrooms. One involves the integration of severely disabled students into regular classrooms. Severely disabled students include children who are deaf-blind, trainably mentally retarded, profoundly mentally retarded, multiply handicapped, or autistic. Generally the educational programs for severely disabled children center on the development of functional life skills—eating, communication, and hygiene. While such students spend the majority of their time in special education, they are sometimes able to join regular classrooms for appropriate activities.

Research studies have shown that both severely disabled and regular education students benefit from integration. For example, when mixed groups of preschoolers played together, fewer inappropriate play behaviors were observed (Guralnick, 1981). A study of adolescents in an extracurricular activity including regular and severely disabled students demonstrated that many positive verbal and physical interactions occurred (Johnson et al., 1979). School districts in Vermont, New York, and Michigan have created programs in which regular education students serve as peer tutors or "special friends" to disabled students. Both individuals gain from the interaction (Hanline & Murray, 1984). If an integrated program is considered in your school, you may want to encourage your students to participate or devise ways in which your whole class can become involved.

A second movement was triggered by an assistant secretary for the Office of Special Education and Rehabilitative Services, U.S. Department of Education, when she announced that children with mild disabilities would be less handicapped if they were placed in regular education classrooms instead of in special classrooms. She recommended that children with mild disabilities be taught in regular classrooms as long as all the children were instructed through "individualized programs in which momentary learning problems are not viewed as failures but, rather, as opportunities for further instruction and in which special needs students could receive instruction tailored to their needs without suffering the negative effects of social stigma" (Will, 1986, p. 414).

Labeled as the Regular Education Initiative (REI), the proposal was soon followed by recommendations that the best practices from special and regular education be combined in a coordinated system that would allow all students to achieve success in the same classroom. Teaching that enables students with widely differing abilities and achievement levels to work in the same class is known as *adaptive instruction* (Strother, 1985; Wang & Walberg, 1985). In planning for adaptive instruction, the teacher should apply knowledge of individual differences in the classroom when creating units and lessons, including a variety of activities and materials relating to those differences. It is also necessary that evaluation be linked to specific levels of performance, and that intellectual and affective needs of students be systematically assessed throughout instruction. Models of adaptive instruction include the following features (Waxman, Wang, Anderson, & Walberg):

- instruction based on the assessed capabilities of each student
- materials and procedures that permit each student to work at a pace suited to his or her abilities and interests
- periodic evaluations to inform each student of progress toward mastery of the skills being taught
- the assumption by each student of responsibility for diagnosing his or her current needs and abilities, for planning individual learning activities, for pursuing those planned activities, and for evaluating the learning outcome
- the provision of alternative activities and materials to help each student acquire essential academic skills
- choices for students with regard to educational goals, activities, and outcomes
- the involvement of students in helping one another achieve individual goals and to cooperate to achieve group goals

Do these sound familiar? Many aspects of adaptive education parallel the steps that might be taken to provide each student with an individualized educational plan or to implement cooperative learning. Adaptive programs that have been developed, applied, and researched in heterogeneous classes include cooperative learning; peer-mediated teaching; tutoring; and behavior modeling, in which children whose behavior is to be emulated are asked to work with children who are experiencing difficulties. In some cases there is a prescribed academic lesson; in others the model may demonstrate, for example, appropriate playground or lunchroom behavior. In all cases adaptive instruction facilitates the mixing of disabled and regular students, allowing each to learn important lessons.

SERVING MANY STUDENTS

The integration of children with disabilities into regular school classrooms has been a consistent element of local, state, and federal education policy since the 1970s. Under the widely used concept of mainstreaming, the policy has become accepted practice in schools. There are a number of advantages to the practice: the opportunity for cooperative learning; the lessening of isolation experienced by special students; the democratic values that are strengthened; the reduction in stereotypes, prejudice, misconceptions, and outright superstition concerning the disabled; and the promise it holds for the continuation of such values into the adult world.

Drawbacks of mainstreaming include the increased costs of enhanced support needed for educating disabled students in multiple environments, instructional demands on the regular classroom teacher, the possibility for litigation that results when a disabled child is placed in a

less protected environment, and the additional paperwork burden on districts. Most educators believe that integrating a child with disabilities into a regular classroom requires additional effort and commitment on their part. Nevertheless, these same educators are moving toward an adaptive education system, working toward a better way for all children to achieve their maximum potential.

Section 3. Culturally Diverse and Bilingual Children

Section 3 Objectives

After you have completed this section, you should be able to:

1. describe characteristics of culturally diverse and bilingual students
2. describe special instructional needs of each of these groups
3. list instructional strategies that are appropriate for culturally diverse and bilingual students
4. plan lessons in your curriculum area that are adapted to meet the needs of each group
5. explain how activities that are appropriate for bilingual or culturally diverse students may be used in lessons for an entire class

In Chapter 4 we learned that students' home and family backgrounds are important in determining the experiences, attitudes, interests, and beliefs that pupils bring to school. Children come to school with a diversity of languages, cultures, and traditions that affect their school performance. Just as we should know as much as possible about students' learning styles and prior academic experiences, we have to take into account language and cultural differences and consider how such differences may affect students' interactions.

WHAT IS CULTURE?

What do we mean by *culture*? Culture has been defined (Bennett, 1986) as "the learned, shared, and transmitted social activities of a group, the human-made part of the environment that satisfies all basic needs for survival and adaptation to the environment" (p. 7). All cultures share a number of characteristics:

- Language and communication
- A social structure, including family or kinship system, rites of passage, territorial grouping, and systems of rank
- An economic system
- A political system or form of government
- A religious system
- Aesthetic expression (art, music, architecture, costuming)
- Scientific knowledge and technology
- Protection against invasion
- Enculturation (ways of teaching people the accepted standards of the culture)

Children's culture influences their way of perceiving, evaluating, behaving, and doing. It affects the way they speak, the structure of their family, the art and music they value, their social relationships, and many other important factors in their lives. While most of us are aware that students in other countries (say, China or France) have cultural differences that would make their school life different from ours, we should recognize that there are many different cultures *within* our own country that affect students' life styles, values, and school performance.

The dominant culture (*macroculture*) in the United States is Anglo-Western European. Our formal institutions, official language, social values, and other aspects of life in this society were shaped by the experiences of early settlers from Western Europe. For example, the individualism that has been a traditional American value has its roots in Judeo-Christian ethics, and our government was modeled on the English parliamentary system. Yet, simultaneously, microcultures have survived—even flourished—in our society. A *microculture* may be defined as a group of people within a country holding unique cultural patterns. As our nation has grown, many groups of immigrants have arrived, each bringing its own cultural traditions. One of the greatest riches of the United States is the diversity of its people, and the strengths and influences each culture has contributed to the whole.

Unfortunately, the combination of micro and macro cultures has sometimes led to dissension and distrust. At various times in our history, specific cultural groups have been seen as less desirable, less intelligent, or less valued because of their differences from the larger culture. For example, during the late 19th century, the Chinese and the Irish were considered undesirable and subject to social and economic prejudice. Shops seeking employees sometimes posted signs reading, "No Irish need apply." Today, some individuals still judge others by their membership in particular groups. We believe that schools can have an influence in reversing this trend (do you recognize the educational philosophy here?). If we increase our knowledge of the differences among and within cultures, we can better serve the diversity of our students' needs.

CHILDREN OF COLOR

African American, Native American, Hispanic, and other children are sometimes referred to as "children of color," because the color of their skin has influenced the way their cultures have interacted with the American macroculture. Early immigrants from Eastern, southern, and Western Europe were expected to assimilate into American culture by giving up their unique cultural attributes. By becoming part of the American "melting pot," they could identify with the Anglo-Western European culture. However, African Americans, Hispanics, and Native Americans found that because of their skin color, they were unable to disappear into the "melting pot." Instead, many people of color opted for *cultural pluralism*, working to maintain separate identities, traditions, and values within the larger society. Adopting cultural pluralism allowed them to maintain their unique identity while still accepting some attributes of the larger American culture. Native Americans organizing powwows, African Americans wearing traditional African dress, and Hispanic people holding fiestas are examples of individuals and groups encouraging cultural pluralism. However, cultural pluralism is not just a series of activities. An individual's identity as a member of a particular culture affects his or her most basic values, choice of role models, and view of society as a whole.

Unfortunately, cultural pluralism has not been completely accepted in our society. Students who do not assimilate into the macroculture often receive the message that "you are poor, unwashed, unmanageable" (Strong, 1989, p. 2). Judgments about students' abilities, potential, or even interests are sometimes made on the basis of cultural differences. Remember John, at the beginning of the chapter? John had trouble learning basic skills, had been in frequent fights, and would not participate in class. When majority children have such difficulties, the school is most likely to contend that there is a problem with the instruction, or a mismatch between the curriculum and the child's level of development (Hale-Benson, 1986). If John is a minority child, he is 2.3 times more likely to be labeled as educably mentally retarded than a white child (*Status of black children*, 1989). While there certainly are educably mentally retarded students of all races, and such children need special educational support, it is crucial that evaluation of students' abilities be based on their performance on appropriate tasks, not on racial or cultural stereotypes.

Too many students who are African American, Native American, or Hispanic are considered slow and difficult to teach. These *expectations* of inferiority are often passed on to the students, who, by their behavior, turn the expectations into self-fulfilling prophecies. In other words, students tend to behave as teachers expect them to behave. If a teacher labels a student as a low achiever, less is expected and demanded from that student. If the teacher perceives a student to be a high achiever, more is expected and demanded from that student. This view of a student's "expected performance" is communicated to the student by verbal and nonverbal behaviors. Good (1981) cites many ways in which teachers behave toward students they perceive as low achievers. The teachers

provide general, often insincere praise
provide them with less feedback
demand less effort from them
interrupt them more often
seat them farther away from the teacher
pay less attention to them
call on them less often
wait less time for them to respond to questions
criticize them more often
smile at them less

Children who are perceived as high achievers, on the other hand,

are given more opportunities for response
are asked higher level questions
receive more praise and detailed feedback
are given prompts or probes if they seem to be having difficulty
are allowed more time to respond to questions
are provided supportive communications (i.e., active listening, physical closeness, courtesy, acceptance of feeling, compliments)

Students tend to perform at the level expected of them by the teacher. Research has indicated that in classes in which teachers held higher expectations for *all* students, higher general student performance resulted.

TEACHING STRATEGIES FOR CHILDREN OF COLOR

While, like all students, children of color benefit from the general teaching strategies outlined in this text, some teaching and learning activities are particularly important for such children. Strong (1989) has presented a compelling message to be conveyed to all children:

> As your teacher, I will do everything in my power to teach you that effort leads to success, that the circle of poverty can be broken, that education can help break down the color barriers, that what you do now can pay dividends, and that you are Somebody. (p. 2)

One way we can prepare all students for a pluralistic or culturally diverse society is through multicultural education. Multicultural education is designed to promote and value the diversity of cultures in our country, while helping students to see the commonalities in all groups. In a positive multicultural environment

teachers expect all students to achieve, regardless of race, sex, class, or ethnicity

the learning environment encourages positive contact between all students

instructional materials are reviewed for bias

the curriculum includes the historical experiences of all cultures

efforts are made to develop an understanding of, and appreciation and respect for, all cultures

goals and strategies reflect cultural learning styles of all students

time is spent dispelling misconceptions, stereotypes, and prejudices

bulletin boards and classroom exhibits display people of many backgrounds

---

CHECK FOR UNDERSTANDING

1. Write your own definition of *culture*. _____

_____

_____

2. What does culture have to do with teaching and learning? _____

_____

_____

3. Why do you think some cultures have been perceived as superior and others as inferior?

_____

_____

4. What effect have such perceptions had on children of color? _____

_____

_____

5. What effect do these perceptions have on white children? _____

_____

_____

6. How can this cycle be broken? _____

_____

_____

TEACHING STRATEGIES FOR AT-RISK CHILDREN

While schools cannot accomplish everything, Edmonds (1979) reminds us, "We can, whenever and wherever we choose, successfully teach all children whose schooling is of interest to us. We already know more than we need to do that" (p. 24). In addition to general multicultural education, there are specific teaching strategies that seem to be more effective with children at risk of school failure because of cultural differences or varied prior experiences. Instead of focusing on students' deficits, emphasis needs to shift to their strengths and abilities.

Slavin and Madden (1989) reviewed instructional practices that help at-risk students. They define an "at-risk" student as one who is in danger of failing to complete his or her education with an adequate level of skills. They found that the strategies most frequently used were also the least effective: retention of students, pullout programs, and in-class models with aides working in the classroom.

Slavin and Madden stated that the learning deficits that are easiest to remediate are those that never occur in the first place. They suggested that prevention programs beginning in preschool or the early grades are more effective than later efforts at remediation. Intensive intervention in first grade may prevent differences in preschool experiences from causing differences in achievement. The most effective early education programs fell into two categories: *continuous progress models* and certain forms of *cooperative learning*.

In *continuous progress models*, students proceeded at their own pace through a sequence of well-defined instructional objectives. They were taught in small groups composed of students at similar skill levels. They were frequently assessed and regrouped, based on these assessments.

In *cooperative learning* situations, students worked in learning teams to master material initially presented by the teachers. Mixed-ability teams were rewarded according to the individual learning achieved by all team members (see Chapter 5).

Of course, not all children will have access to effective early education programs, and some will still have learning deficits despite their teachers' best efforts. In these cases remedial programs are necessary. Slavin and Madden found that the programs that showed the most convincing evidence of effectiveness for remediation were one-to-one tutoring and computer-assisted instruction.

Other investigators have also suggested strategies for children at risk. According to a report issued in 1989 by the National Center on Effective Secondary Schools, the social-psychological dimensions of schooling for students at risk deserve the most immediate attention. The study stated that many students simply do not try to learn in school because they have experienced almost nothing in previous schooling but failure. They may feel alienated from the mainstream culture and see no hope for advancement in education or employment after school.

Programs that succeeded in reaching such students created an environment that built on students' self-esteem by maximizing student success, responding to students' personal problems outside of school, and connecting the study of school subjects to jobs and practical challenges in the students' lives.

Factors that influence student achievement can be divided into two groups: *affective* and *cognitive* (Beane, 1985). Attention to both cognitive and affective factors can increase the likelihood that all students will succeed.

Affective Factors

Activities focusing on affective factors help build students' self-esteem, develop positive relationships among teacher and students, and demonstrate a positive, caring attitude. Suggestions for such activities include the following:

- Check your perception of students. Ask yourself if you really expect the students to achieve. A study from the University of Chicago found that the major factor in student performance was not parent demography or per-pupil expenditure, but teacher expectations (Kunjufu, 1984). Don't use a student's home environment or social status as an excuse for poor achievement.
- Encourage students to take a more challenging educational path. This will convey the message that you have confidence in their abilities.
- Provide role models with others from the same cultural background. Inform students about opportunities in many fields. Involve community organizations and local businesses and industries. Recruit school graduates to assist in this area.
- Watch the language you use. Grant (Hale-Benson, p. 179) found that social scientists used harsher terms when describing African Americans and more neutral terms when describing whites. For instance, African Americans were seen as belonging to the "drug culture" while whites had a "chemical dependency problem." Blacks had "illegitimate children"; whites chose "single motherhood." Teachers can also be guilty of discrimination in vocabulary.
- Learn about the culture of your students. Understanding their traditions will help you see how students view and interpret their world.
- Let students know that effort is valued. Attribution theory indicates that students' beliefs about the reasons for success and failure can greatly influence their perception of the task and their achievement of a successful outcome. When students believe that they are successful because they have put effort into a task, they experience greater feeling of pride and are more likely to work hard on tasks in the future than if they feel their success was caused by luck.
- Strive to maintain a positive classroom climate. Clear explanations, positive reinforcement, and activities that encourage interaction among students can all contribute to classroom tone.

Cognitive Factors

Activities focusing on cognitive factors work to develop students' knowledge and skills. These activities emphasize high expectations; an enriched, rather than a remedial, program; clear rules and procedures; regular and systematic feedback; and variety in teaching strategies. Specific suggestions for focusing on cognitive factors include the following:

- Check students' prior knowledge. Some students miss the point of a lesson because they don't have the background knowledge that could put the text in context.
- Relate content to students' lives. Knowing about students' interests and backgrounds can help you provide valuable links.
- Provide experiences by including field trips and other enriching activities. If students have not had the experiences necessary for learning a particular subject, you can plan appropriate activities to provide the requisite background knowledge.
- Engage students in meaningful "real world" tasks. When students see that learning has a purpose, they are more likely to stay engaged.
- Use cooperative learning strategies. Many students who do not achieve individually do well with group activities (see Chapter 5).

- Be flexible in grouping students. Heterogeneous grouping is effective. If you do group students homogeneously for some activities, don't always put the same students together.
- Teach students test-taking skills. Practice test-taking environments. Familiarize students with the routines of tests, use practice drills, teach study skills for use in test taking, reduce stress through relaxation skills, and discuss time management.
- Assess students through multiple measures. Allow students to be evaluated through personal interviews, oral tests, and practical assignments.

CHECK FOR UNDERSTANDING

1. What are the two groups into which we can divide the factors that affect student achievement?

_____

_____

2. List three activities for each factor that are particularly appropriate for children of color.

_____

_____

_____

_____

3. Read each of the following examples and tell whether the statement indicates that the teacher has high expectations or low expectations for the student. In the lines at the left, write *H* for *high expectations* and *L* for *low expectations*.

_____ a. "Maria, you always have the answer. Please do number 4."

_____ b. Juan is busily waving his hand. The teacher has not called on him all day.

_____ c. Ann and Heather sit close to the teacher and have many conversations about non-school-related activities with the teacher.

_____ d. "That answer is close, Jim. What if you added another sentence?"

_____ e. No matter what Susan does for homework, her paper never has any useful comments on it.

_____ f. Tony wonders why the teacher doesn't ever look at his area of the classroom.

BILINGUAL STUDENTS

Some students come not only from a culture whose traditions and values differ from those of the mainstream but from homes in which English is not the primary language, or is not spoken at all. Some of these students are truly bilingual—that is, they speak English and their native language; others speak little or no English. In fact, some "bilingual" children have had such limited and/or confusing language experiences that they speak neither language adeptly. While in many districts support is provided for large bilingual populations in the form of special classes or tutoring, many students for whom English is not the preferred language are in heterogeneous classes. In the years 1977–1987, 20 million immigrants entered the United States from Southeast Asia and other parts of Asia, the Middle East, and Middle Europe (Cetron, 1985). Many of the immigrants were children. These students may speak Spanish, Arabic, Thai, Polish, or many other languages. In fact, one of our graduate students teaches in a school that houses students from 27 different countries! In order to serve the needs of this special population, it is important to consider both the characteristics of bilingual students and the strategies that help them succeed in English-language schools.

There is no single profile of a bilingual student. Their behaviors and achievement may vary enormously, depending on their previous educational experiences, familiarity with English, and cultural background. Some bilingual students display low academic achievement, sometimes because of the difficulties in learning created by language barriers, at other times because of difficulties in conveying, in an unfamiliar language, information they learned in school, in their native country, or at home. Still other students feign lack of knowledge in order to avoid embarrassment or questions that they may not understand.

The insecurities that commonly develop from difficult or ineffective communication may be expressed in many ways. Imagine yourself in a foreign country, unable to speak the language in which others are communicating. Those around you think you are ignorant because you express your ideas so poorly, or do not express them at all. How might you react? Some students react to such situations by acting out, sometimes even creating their own cultural stereotypes: We are tough in my country. We do not mix with weaker people. It is much easier to reject first than to feel rejected. Others respond by withdrawing, avoiding any circumstance that might demand communication. Rosa, at the beginning of the chapter, may have chosen this strategy.

Some students, especially as they gain experience in the mainstream culture, can become confused or uncertain about their identity. These students may be unwilling to speak their native language, and reluctant to invite non-English-speaking relatives to school functions or to provide the necessary translation. Lack of self-identity can be particularly acute for students who come from minorities within their native countries, or from countries in which the media are suppressed. Such students have difficulties determining their identity or role in either country.

Depending on the development of their cultural identity, bilingual students may express themselves anywhere along the cultural continuum. Some students find strength in their native culture, wearing traditional clothing and bringing lunches unfamiliar to American students—for example, unleavened bread filled with raw meat. Other students may exaggerate behaviors they associate with American culture. One student brought nothing but Twinkies for lunch, because they are "American food." Choice of hair style and preferences in music and dance are other means by which students from culturally diverse backgrounds indicate their feelings about the macroculture and their native culture.

Some cultures include beliefs about sex roles that affect students' performance or behavior in schools. In some cultures a young girl's honor requires that she remain apart from young men, avoiding American dating customs or mixed gym classes. In others, girls are expected to marry, or at least leave school and wait to marry, in their early teens. Such values create conflict for young women whose identities span two cultures, and for the young men who feel obligated to protect them. Misunderstandings of the dating and courtship patterns of varied cultures can even lead to physical confrontations between different cultural groups. Sex role tensions can also occur when women school personnel interact with students or parents whose traditions preclude females in positions of authority.

Other, less obvious differences in cultures can also cause misunderstandings. How might a student whose culture sees owls as symbols of bad luck view a Halloween sticker on an assignment? How might a teacher for whom eye-to-eye contact is a sign of integrity respond to a student whose culture requires lowered eyes in the presence of authority? Clearly, both language and cultural differences can affect students' interactions in school and, hence, their achievement.

TEACHING STRATEGIES FOR BILINGUAL STUDENTS

Bilingual students will benefit from good teaching and planning, as well as from many of the strategies suggested for children of color. In addition, the following ideas may be helpful:

- Review students' files extensively. Make sure you are clear on the history of the students' educational experiences. A student who was successful in division in her

native country needs different strategies in [...]
division because of language difficulties, [...]
division in English.

- Make and maintain contact with parents. R[...]
  contact the schools because of their limit[...]
  American schools as a threat to their native[...]
  important to convey both your respect for t[...]
  goals.
- Learn as much as you can about the culture[...]
  with parents, local cultural associations,[...]
  specialists in various cultures, and oth[...]
  especially attuned to patterns of communi[...]
- Consider a buddy system or cross-grade t[...]
  assigned to help a bilingual student commu[...] older, successful bilingual student can provide tutoring and can serve as a powerful role model.
- Be cautious about cooperative learning in the beginning. Cooperative learning assumes an ability to communicate and function within an educational system that may not be reasonable for a non-English-speaking student. Avoid putting students in situations they are unable to handle; the results are likely to be a sense of personal inadequacy and a feeling of having let their groups down.
- Present as much material visually as possible. Movies, pictures, filmstrips, and demonstrations can assist students with language development.

T[...]
IMPLEMENTATION: GE[...]
262
- Whenever possib[...]
  with emphasis[...]
  of the contri[...]
  non-Wes[...]
- Be pat[...]
  a ch[...]

...e, share information and positive role models from diverse cultures, ...on those cultures represented in your room. Parent presentations, studies ...butions of varied groups, selection of music, celebrations, and games from ...ern lands all send a message that all cultures are important.

...ent. Adapting to a new language and culture is a long and difficult task, even for ...ild. Time, energy, and genuine affection will be necessary for students to integrate ...at task into the already complex demands of school.

SERVING MANY STUDENTS

It should be clear by now that, as with the strategies suggested for gifted and talented students and students with disabilities, many of the techniques suggested for teaching culturally diverse or bilingual students will benefit all students in your classroom. Positive expectations, attention to individual experiences, and the valuing of diversity should be part of any classroom. In addition, the attitudes and values shaped in a multicultural classroom can prepare our students to live and work in an increasingly diverse society.

CHECK FOR UNDERSTANDING

Imagine that the principal came to your room and informed you that in one week a Polish student would be joining your class. The student speaks limited English and will receive one hour per day of specialized language instruction. How would you prepare for the student's arrival? What strategies might you use once the student has arrived? Write down your ideas; then discuss them with one or more colleagues.

_____

_____

_____

_____

_____

CHAPTER SUMMARY

Throughout this text we have emphasized that learning activities must be planned, carried out, and evaluated according to our knowledge of individual students' needs and abilities. This chapter has focused on the special needs of specific groups of students. Well-thought-out learning strategies geared to their needs are essential if gifted and talented students, students with disabilities, culturally diverse students, and bilingual students are to be successful in your classroom. At the same time, it is vital to remember that each of these groups is made up of many, varied individuals, and that only by knowing the students in your class can you plan effectively. It is also important to keep in mind that many of the ideas and techniques suggested in this chapter will provide benefits to all students, allowing you to meet particular students' needs while creating a more stimulating, responsive, and flexible learning environment for all.

Guided Practice Activity. Adapting the American Revolution

Think back to the students at the beginning of this chapter and to Diane's planned unit on the American Revolution. What advice might you give Diane for activities or strategies that would enhance the unit for the students we described? List at least two suggestions for each student. Compare your list with a friend's. Discuss the characteristics of each student that helped you diagnose his or her instructional needs.

JOHN: _____

_____

MARIA: _____

_____

ROSA: _____

_____

JOE: _____

_____

Independent Practice Activity. Adapting Your Own Unit

Now look at a curriculum unit you have planned or used. List at least two ways you might adapt or add to the unit to meet the needs of the following groups of students:

Gifted/talented students _____

_____

_____

_____

Students with educational disabilities _____

_____

_____

_____

Multicultural or bilingual students _____

_____

_____

_____

REFERENCES

Beane, D. B. (1985). *Mathematics and Science: Critical Filters for the Future of Minority Students.* Washington, DC: Mid-Atlantic Center for Race Equity, American University.

Bennett, C. I. (1986). *Comprehensive Multicultural Education: Theory and Practice.* Newton, MA: Allyn and Bacon.

Biklen, D., & Bogdan, R. (1977). Handicappism in America. In B. Blatt, D. Biklen, & R. Bogdan (Eds.), *An alternative textbook in special education* (pp. 205–215). New York: Love Publishing.

Bloom, B. (Ed.). (1956). *Taxonomy of Educational Objectives: Handbook I. Cognitive Domain.* White Plains, NY: Longman.

Cetron, M. (1985). *Schools of the Future.* New York: McGraw-Hill.

Edmonds, R. (1979). Effective schools for the urban poor. *Educational Leadership, 37,* 15–24.

Gardner, H. (1983). *Frames of Mind.* New York: Basic Books.

Good, T. L. (1981). Teacher expectations and student perceptions: A decade of research. *Educational Leadership 38,* 415–422.

Guralnick, M. J. (1981). The social behavior of preschool children at different developmental levels: Effects of group composition. *Journal of Experimental Child Psychology, 31,* 115–130.

Greenwood, J. M. (1888). *Principles of Education Practically Applied.* New York: D. Appleton.

Hale-Benson, J. (1986). *Black Children: Their Roots, Culture, and Learning Styles.* Baltimore: Johns Hopkins University Press.

Hanline, M. F., & Murray, C. (1984). Integrating severely handicapped children into regular public schools. *Phi Delta Kappan, 66,* 273–276.

Johnson, R., et al. (1979). Interaction between handicapped and nonhandicapped teenagers as a function of situational goal structuring: Implications for mainstreaming. *American Educational Research Journal, 16,* 161–167.

Kunjufu, J. (1984). *Developing Positive Self-Images and Discipline in Black Children.* Chicago: African-American Images.

Marland, S. P. (1972). *Education of the Gifted and Talented: Report to the Congress of the United States by the United States Commissioner of Education and Background Papers Submitted to the United States Office of Education.* Washington, DC: Government Printing Office.

National Center on Effective Secondary Schools. (1989). Newsletter. University of Wisconsin—Madison, *4,* 1.

National Education Association. (1978). *Education for All Handicapped Children.* Washington, DC.

Parke, B. (1989). *The Gifted Child in the Regular Classroom.* Boston: Allyn and Bacon.

Public Law 94-142. (1975). Sec. 4.

Renzulli, J. S. (1977). *The Enrichment Triad.* Mansfield Center, CT: Creative Learning Press.

Renzulli, J. S. (1978). What makes giftedness? Reexamining a definition. *Phi Delta Kappan, 60,* 180–184.

Renzulli, J. S., & Smith, L. H. (1979). *A Guidebook for Developing Individualized Educational Programs for Gifted and Talented Students*. Manfield Center, CT: Creative Learning Press.

Singer, J. D., & Butler, J. A. (1987). The Education for All Handicapped Children Act: Schools as agents of social reform. *Harvard Educational Review, 84*, 409–422.

Slavin, R. E., & Madden, N. A. (1989). What works for students at risk: A research synthesis. *Educational Leadership, 46*, 4–13.

Status of black children. (1989). [Special issue]. *Black Child Advocate*, 15 (4).

Sternberg, R. (1985). *Beyond IQ: A Triarchic Theory of Human Intelligence*. New York: Cambridge University Press.

Strong, L. (1989). The best kids they have. *Educational Leadership, 46*, 2.

Strother, D. B. (1985). Adapting instruction to individual needs: An eclectic approach. *Phi Delta Kappan, 67*, 308–311.

Wang, M. C., & Walberg, H. J. (1985). *Adapting Instruction for Individual Differences*. Berkeley, CA: McCutchan.

Wang, M. C., Reynolds, M. C., & Walberg, H. J. (1986). Rethinking special education. *Educational Leadership, 44*, 27–28, 31.

Wang, M. C., Reynolds, M. C., & Walberg, H. J. (1988). Integrating the children of the second system. *Phi Delta Kappan, 20*, 248–251.

Waxman, H. C., Wang, M. C., Anderson, K. A., & Walberg, H. J. (1985). Adaptive education and student outcomes: A quantitative synthesis. *Journal of Educational Research, 78*, 228–253.

Westling, D. C. (1989). Leadership for education of the mentally handicapped. *Educational Leadership, 46* (6), 19–23.

Will, M. C. (1986). Educating children with learning problems. *Exceptional Children, 52* (5), 411–415.

Classroom Management: Establishing a Positive Environment

CHAPTER 8

Classroom Management: Traditions, Programs, and Research

Chapter Overview

An understanding of effective classroom management is basic to professional practice and should be a significant part of a teacher's preparation. Knowledge of what constitutes sound classroom management can provide answers to a new teacher's numerous questions: Why is there so much concern among teachers about classroom management? How does an effective classroom manager establish an environment that prevents disruption? What are the forces that control a teacher's responses to student behaviors? What programs or strategies have proven to be most workable in classroom management?

In this chapter we describe and contrast the beliefs, guidelines, and practices of three traditions of classroom management—commonsense, behavior management, and humanistic. In addition, we offer insights and practical suggestions gleaned from researchers who observed successful classroom managers in action.

In Chapter 9 we will describe the rational approach to classroom management that we believe blends the best features of the management approaches described in Chapter 8.

Set Activity

You are a new member of the Fairhill Elementary School staff. During a prep period in mid-September, you overhear four teachers discussing a discipline problem. Examine the responses made by Judy, Sandy, and Marilyn to the problem Paul is having with Kevann, one of his students.

PAUL: Kevann disrupts my class every five minutes. It's so frustrating. He is such a sweet child, but I have to tell him to stop talking, visiting, or wandering aimlessly in my class. I plead with him to stop. He stops for a few moments and then he is back disrupting again. I'm at my wit's end.

JUDY: I don't let students out of their chairs until I get to know which children can be trusted. I've learned through experience to be stern for the first month of school and then to loosen up gradually and to become more informal, to let them see that I can smile and enjoy the class.

I also have an arrangement with the principal to send the first two misbehaving kids to her for punishment. It teaches the others an early lesson that I can be tough.

SANDY: Paul, have you taught students your classroom rules and consequences for misbehavior? I spend the first two weeks of class creating an environment in which the students learn that they will receive rewards for positive behavior and punishment for negative behavior.

MARILYN: My approach is very different. I want students to develop self-discipline, to take responsibility for their own behavior, and to realize that when they misbehave, they disappoint me and diminish what we can do together that day. I use group meetings and individual conferences to gain insights about my students' needs and resources and feelings. I find that these practices make it possible for the students to participate in managing the classroom.

Using the information provided, describe the approach to classroom discipline management reflected by each teacher. Write your responses in the space provided below.

Judy: _____

_____

_____

_____

Sandy: _____

_____

_____

_____

Marilyn: _____

_____

_____

_____

The three teachers represent three traditions of classroom management. Judy is identified with the *commonsense* tradition, Sandy with the *behavior management* tradition, and Marilyn with the *humanistic* tradition. These traditions will be discussed in the first section of the chapter.

In nearly every yearly opinion survey between 1973 and 1988, the national Gallup Poll reported that parents, students, and teachers regarded discipline as the most serious problem facing the public schools (Gallup & Elam, 1988). As the case study about Kevann reveals, there are serious differences of opinion about what methods and practices are most effective in addressing discipline and management problems in schools.

As a teacher, you will be forced each day to make decisions on methods and practices to maintain order in your classroom. The achievement of a disciplined and well-managed classroom is not as simple as most packaged, widely marketed discipline programs would suggest. On the other hand, it is not as awesome a challenge as many veteran teachers would have you believe. Reality lies somewhere between the two extremes.

The decisions you make in setting up your room and interacting with students are critical. With increasing numbers of children coming to school from families in which both parents are working, from households headed by a single parent, or from troubled homes and communities, you must be able to enhance a student's personal and social development if you wish to be successful in teaching academic content.

Chapter Objectives

After you have completed this chapter, you will be able to:
1. classify examples of the commonsense, behavior management, or humanistic tradition of classroom management
2. explain the contemporary research principles related to
   a. establishing classroom rules and routines
   b. behaviors of effective classroom managers
   c. preventing classroom disruption
   d. saving instructional time
3. develop classroom rules and routines that are consistent with sound principles of classroom management
4. develop and refine your own philosophy of classroom management

PACKAGED DISCIPLINE

Section 1. Three Traditions of Classroom Management

TRADITION 1: COMMONSENSE

If you were a first-year teacher in 1960, you would have been fortunate if classroom management was a topic covered in your teacher education program. In those days, much of what we know about successfully managing a classroom of children or adolescents came to us by word of mouth passed on from veteran teachers to novices. Often these suggestions were unwritten, or, if written, they were in the form of laundry lists of "do's" and "don'ts."

Unfortunately, commonsense guidelines and practices worked for some teachers, in some schools, with some students, but not in all schools with all students. Thus, the commonsense tradition was seen to possess two serious limitations. First, the reasons why certain guidelines and practices worked better than others remained unexamined and thus were unknown. There was no opportunity to test, revise, and refine them, and consequently no progress was made in improving their effectiveness.

Second, there was no practical way to determine whether a given teacher would benefit from adopting a particular commonsense practice. For example, "Never lose your temper!" was an admonition found in many commonsense lists. Would teachers who often lost their temper but also recovered quickly suffer more harm from a temper outburst than placid teachers who almost never lost their temper? When did "losing your temper" begin to do serious harm to classroom discipline management—after a single outburst or after the fourth or fifth outburst? Since there were no reliable answers to these questions, the commonsense tradition of classroom management lost favor and support in the educational community.

In today's teacher preparation programs and school inservice workshops, guidelines and practices for classroom management emerge from two other traditions. We shall consider the behavior management tradition first.

TRADITION 2: BEHAVIOR MANAGEMENT

The behavior management tradition was based on the behaviorist learning theory of B. F. Skinner—that future human behavior is determined by the consequences that followed past behavior. Behavior learning theory was derived from scientific experimentation, including numerous types of animal studies. It was Skinner who developed layperson language that could communicate the nature of behavior theory to people within the field of education but outside the field of psychology, and, thus, became its primary spokesperson.

Many behavior management programs, although based on behavioral theory, admit to incorporating practices derived from other psychological theories. For example, a behavior management program may include a component that dignifies the importance of student feelings and values, a practice derived from humanistic learning theory.

What are the common elements of behavior management programs? Among the best known of these elements are *contingency management, contracting, noncontingent reinforcement, "catch 'em being good,"* and *rules/reward–ignore/punish.*

Contingency Management

Contingency management, sometimes referred to as an "incentive system," is a widely practiced element in behavior management. It generally involves the use of tangible rewards to reinforce socially appropriate behavior. The basic theme of contingency management is that the worth of a reward you receive in school should be based on the worth of your actions. Often tokens of different values are given and then exchanged for such rewards as books, magazines, free time, or preferred classroom activities. Instead of tokens, play money may be used to redeem desired products from a "student store." In some cases, individual adults and the business community contribute products and services to support the token exchange.

Teachers who employ a "token economy" face some special responsibilities. Established guidelines, scrupulously enforced and followed, help to ensure a fair distribution of tokens. Also, when students are appropriately informed of the system used to earn tokens, they often aid the teacher in maintaining a fair and consistent economy. Before the token economy begins, the parents and the school principal should be informed of the procedures. Teachers must be certain that the token values to be redeemed are adequate in number and are kept in a secure location. A regular time for redeeming tokens should be agreed upon. During the early stages of the program, the redemption period should be short and the reward received soon after.

Contracting

Contracting is a formalized contingency management process usually implemented through agreement with an individual student. The work to be accomplished by the student, the period in which the contract will remain in force, and the reward (reinforcement) to be given to the student after successful completion of the contract are all specified in writing. The teacher and the student sign the contract; in some cases the student's parents do so as well. The legal overtones of the process add a sense of importance and responsibility to the student. Also the strategy is most appropriate for older children and adolescents, who are better able to cope with abstract concepts such as *effort, behavior*, and *achievement*.

Noncontingent Reinforcement

Noncontingent reinforcement, although similar in theme to the previous two elements, has a distinctive difference. Reinforcement takes place without reference to any particular behavior on the part of the student. There is no systematic structure or process, only the teacher's use of a smile, the granting of privileges or special activities, or the giving of gifts such as candy or money to deserving students. When positive noncontingent reinforcement is implemented, students generally behave better even in settings other than the ones in which they received reinforcement. For example, giving a piece of candy on the playground during recess could result in improved student behavior during independent math seat work.

"Catch 'em Being Good"

"Catch 'em being good" is an immediate reward that reinforces a desirable behavior. For example, after a teacher gives an assignment, she may say, "Take out your social studies book and do so without talking to your neighbor. Thank you, Maxine, for being so prompt in getting out your book. You, too, Tanya and Ivan." These students are recognized because they responded promptly and appropriately. The teacher's recognition both reinforces the desired behavior as exhibited by Maxine, Tanya, and Ivan and signals the others that desired behavior will be recognized.

Most educators suggest that this method is most effective at the elementary school level. Certainly, it occurs most frequently at that level. However, we have seen it applied successfully at every grade level, even at the college level. As students get older, they may prefer privately given praise over public praise. We all feel good when we are recognized for doing well, especially when we do not expect it.

Rules/Reward–Ignore/Punish (RRIP)

Some behavior management programs communicate the theme that if "you obey the *Rules*, you receive a *Reward*; if you *Ignore* the rules, you receive a *Punishment*." Referred to as *RRIP*, this approach uses freedom from unpleasant consequences as a form of control. In the RRIP system, logical consequences for misbehavior are given the same status as are rewards for good behavior. In the RRIP system, rules are established to set the limits of behavior. In many cases, students participate in the development of the rules. The teacher then acts as the executor or enforcer of the rules. Students who are compliant get rewarded, and those who are not get punished. Both rewards and punishments are administered with little elapsed time after the behavior that prompted them.

There is a difference in philosophy between two groups of RRIP advocates. One group maintains that certain disruptions, such as soft talking, unobtrusive movements, whispered profanity, and the like should be ignored. The second group cautions that at some point the teacher will have to confront the behaviors that are ignored, because they will increase in either frequency or in intensity. This group charges that ignoring some misbehavior sets up a continuing negative pattern that will be more difficult for the teacher to break the longer it remains in force.

CHECK FOR UNDERSTANDING

1.   Without rereading the text on the elements of behavior management, define the following. Write your definitions below and discuss them with a classmate or a group.

   a.   contingency management _____

   _____

   b.   contracting _____

   _____

   c.   noncontingency reinforcement _____

   _____

2.   Examine the following case study.

   Sam, a third grader, has been absent from school three times within the last month, and each time he comes in, he picks on another student before the day ends. Mr. Griffiths is frustrated by Sam's behavior. He decides to design a behavior management contract for Sam. After analyzing Sam's behavior pattern, he focuses the contract on Sam's habit of picking on his classmates. He discusses the proposed program with Sam and they agree on the following contract:

Contract

On Monday, Sam will sign an agreement that he will avoid using any negative words or actions with his classmates on Monday and Tuesday. At the conclusion of the school day on Tuesday, if Mr. Griffiths has observed no negative incidents, Sam will be allowed to feed the class turtle, George, on Wednesday morning.

1. Review and critique the contract agreement between Mr. Griffiths and Sam.
2. Develop your own contract to deal with Sam's behavior. Share it in a group of three to five persons and come to group consensus about what the contract should contain.

You may have been concerned in your critique that Mr. Griffiths chose to focus on Sam's habit of picking on classmates rather than his absenteeism. We think Mr. Griffiths decided correctly to focus on one behavior per contract, and one contract at a time. This makes monitoring easier for the teacher and enhances the student's likelihood of success. You may also ask why the teacher did not choose to focus on absenteeism as the more important of the two behaviors. As a teacher you will have to make choices about what is most important. Often the decision will not be as clear-cut as in the present case. Mr. Griffiths chose to emphasize safety and the reduction in interpersonal conflict as his first priority—thus the contract to eliminate Sam's picking on other children. We see no reason to dispute that decision.

Assertive Discipline: An Example of a Behavior Management Program

Assertive discipline, a program developed by Lee and Marlene Canter (1976, 1989), is based on the rules/reward–ignore/punish approach. Canter and Canter recommend that teachers create a discipline plan for their classroom with the participation of the parents and the school principal. This system should include the following:

1. A list of rules and a series of lessons to teach the students the difference between acceptable and unacceptable school and classroom behaviors. The result of the rules and lessons should be a clear understanding of which behaviors will result in punishment and which behaviors will reap rewards.
2. A short list of discipline consequences, organized from least serious to most serious, to be administered to students if and when they misbehave. For example, the least serious consequence could be the writing of the misbehaving child's name on the blackboard. The most serious consequence could involve a conference among the teacher, the principal, and the child's parents.
3. A list of rewards to be given to students for acceptable behaviors and especially for those behaviors that contribute to classroom learning success. For example, students could exchange tokens for material rewards, or they could receive verbal praise, written notes of appreciation, or independent reading time.

MEDIA ALERT! STUDENT SIGNS
CONTRACT WHILE PROUD PARENTS
LOOK ON. FILM AT ELEVEN.

4. Procedures that ensure timely and frequent communication with all parents about the classroom rules and consequences of misbehavior. Contacts with parents of particular children whose pattern of behavior warrants it are also made.

An example of an assertive discipline system appears below. The important thing to remember is that students must be taught how to behave. Also, the consequences should be logical—that is, related to the behavior.

Rules

1. Listen while others are talking.
2. Walk quietly in the classroom and halls.
3. Bring materials every day.
4. Respect others' property and bodies.

Consequences

Discipline

1st infraction = warning
    (name on board)

Rewards

Points accumulated until 50 = class party
Positive note to parents

2nd infraction = check by name
    (miss one minute of recess)
3rd infraction = second check
    (miss half of recess)
4th infraction = third check
    (call home)
5th infraction = fourth check
    (see principal)

Free games
Special movie
Computer time
Extra recess
Lunch with teacher
Free time

Letter to Parents

Dear ———,

    I will be your son/daughter's teacher this year. To maintain a positive classroom, we have established the attached rules and consequences. If your child must remain after school, you will be given one day's notice.

    I appreciate your support in upholding this system. Please feel free to call or visit me to discuss anything of concern to you.

Sincerely,

TRADITION 3: HUMANISTIC

Although the humanistic tradition has a long history, its application in classrooms became popular in the 1960s and 1970s. Guidelines and practices can be traced to the work of clinical psychologists, school counselors, and mental health professionals. Humanists hope to create and maintain a classroom environment that emphasizes clear, effective communication, shared responsibility, conflict resolution, and the development of student self-control and need fulfillment. Thus the child's emotional growth and development are highly important in this discipline tradition. Indeed, the teacher often acts as a guide in the classroom rather than as a figure of authority.

    We shall focus our attention on two programs that emerge from the humanistic tradition. Each permits us to explore a different skill area needed by effective classroom managers. The first program, *cooperation through communication* (Ginott, 1972), emphasizes the importance of communication in the classroom.

    The second humanistic program, *reality therapy* (Glasser, 1969), stresses the role of individual conferences and group meetings in establishing a positive environment for learning. We'll discuss the two programs in detail.

Haim Ginott: Cooperation through Communication

Haim Ginott asserts that it is in the teacher's power to establish a classroom and school atmosphere that is evocative of either an exciting and challenging summer camp, or a monotonous and stifling prison camp. Which of the two environments is chosen depends on the teacher's decision to create either a humanizing or a dehumanizing classroom atmosphere.

    Ginott suggests that good behavior is inextricably tied to a good self-concept. The latter is, to a significant extent, built on the messages that adults generally, and parents and teachers specifically, convey to children. In advancing his teacher–student communication model, he focuses on reducing chaos through *congruent communication*, which he describes as a way of sending messages that is honest and in harmony with the needs both of the child and of others (Ginott, 1972). In pursuit of this harmony, Ginott proposes that teachers must (1) express sane messages, (2) deal with feelings, (3) eliminate stereotypes and labels, (4) use praise carefully, (5) build cooperation, and (6) communicate anger. These six principles are the essential building blocks of Ginott's conception of a humanizing, and yet orderly, environment.

Express Sane Messages.   According to Ginott, the best teachers send sane messages, in which feelings are appropriate to the situation and the individuals. He observes that adults are too often predisposed to preach, condemn, force, accuse, threaten, and humiliate, resulting in the dehumanization of young people.

One of the essential principles designed to break this pattern is to separate the child's behavior from the teacher's conception of the child. The child should hear very clearly that "your behavior is unacceptable and will not be tolerated, but there will always be a guaranteed safe place for you in my heart." For example, Leesha, a sixth-grade student, was walking about the room without permission and not writing the assigned essay. The teacher said to her, "You have 10 minutes to finish the essay. Let me see how much you have done." This is a sane message because the emphasis is on the child's "off-task behavior." A different message from the teacher is communicated when she says to Leesha, "Why do you keep walking about? You are always inconsiderate of the others in the room."

Deal with Feelings.   Confronting feelings about self and others is one of the most challenging tasks we face. Ginott counsels teachers that they must help students to sort out their feelings. He suggests that teachers play the role of sounding boards to reflect feelings and ideas expressed by students. For example, students may exaggerate the facts about some situation to impress and to gain attention. Suppose Lauri says to the teacher, "I got all the math problems wrong. I know I am dumb." The teacher may try to prove she is not dumb.

These attempts to argue the logic or dispute the facts may be laudable, but, according to Ginott, a better decision would be to address Lauri's feelings of inadequacy by saying, "That has really made you upset. Well, we all feel that way sometimes. Let's see where you made the mistakes. Understanding that should help you feel better." This demonstrates that the teacher has confidence in Lauri's ability to assess the situation and accepts the child's right to feel bad about her performance in math.

Eliminate Stereotypes and Labels.   According to Ginott, teachers have often used irresponsible labels to describe students. Labeling creates stereotypes for others to apply to the child in future years. It fosters a negative self-image in the student. Labeling, Ginott suggests, is especially dangerous when the teacher, from a position of authority, hardens an attitude into a conclusion about a child's academic and social future. One of us has a good friend whose teacher called her "Pell-mell Pam," to remind her that she was frivolous and often acted without careful thought. Pam struggles with the memories of that label today, some 30 years later.

When students are negatively labeled, their imagination, aspirations, and possibilities for personal growth are disabled to the degree that they accept the label. Thus any conclusion about a child's social or academic standing may become a self-fulfilling prophecy that stifles the child's potential. To avoid negative labeling, it is best to communicate to the class that you identify with your students' expectations and possibilities for the future. Identify their goals and aspirations and use that knowledge to prompt behaviors that will motivate children to work toward their goals. For example, if a student expresses an interest in an educational career, a teacher might say, "So you want to be a teacher. If I can help in any way, let me know." This does not mean that you confirm the student's choice. It only means that you are ready and willing to communicate with the student about the goal.

Use Praise Carefully. Ginott cautions teachers to avoid giving "judgmental praise." Statements such as "Leesha, you are a good student" or "Maria, you are the best student in the class" may make them praise "junkies," dependent on others for self-validation. Praise should be focused on a particular performance "Leesha, I particularly enjoyed the way you used your own experience to show how we can welcome new students in the class" or, "Maria, this is the fourth math test in a row that you have gotten 100 percent. That's the kind of work that makes me confident that you are going to achieve your goal to become a math teacher."

A second caution about the use of praise is the tendency we all have to associate "correctness" with "goodness." A child's ability to do schoolwork correctly is no guarantee that he or she is a "good" child. If the teacher—consciously or unconsciously—connects the two traits, some students may seek to exercise more liberties than are reasonably allowed. Conversely, students whose work does not measure up will arrive at the conclusion that they are "not good."

Third, Ginott suggests that teachers avoid praising minimally acceptable behavior, such as sitting down or working quietly. Instead, the teacher should praise the results of that behavior, as in "I appreciate your working so quietly and hard. We really accomplished a lot today." Praise should be expressed when students behave appropriately in an unusual circumstance: "I really felt good as you solved the problem of who would clean up the spilled milk."

A fourth caution is to refrain from overusing praise, especially when it is not warranted by student behavior. It is tempting to believe that if praise rewards and reinforces behavior, then more and more praise will lead to even better behavior. Unfortunately, students will detect that they are being manipulated and will come to resent it. When they perceive that the praise is insincere, it will lose its positive reinforcement value.

The four cautions are not meant to imply that praise is not worthy and effective. Rather, teachers are encouraged to use praise carefully to avoid the potential pitfalls.

Build Cooperation. Ginott encourages teachers to build an atmosphere of cooperation in the classroom. He suggests that this is most effectively done when students feel a sense of independence and a sense of responsibility for the environment. Conversely, when students are dependent on external authority, their will to strive for self-control is diminished.

He recommends several ways to enhance cooperation through the development of student independence. First, give students alternative ways to solve classroom problems. For example, in the event that room clean-up after art projects has been unacceptable, the teacher can offer the students a choice of selecting a clean-up committee that quits 10 minutes early and cleans up for everyone or of having the entire class end art activities 5 minutes earlier and begin to clean up.

Second, Ginott reinforces the notion that it is more productive to invite cooperation than to legislate it. He encourages teachers to give students opportunities to make decisions about ways to increase cooperation in the classroom. For example, he suggests that when students are off-task, the teacher should reemphasize positive expectations, as in, "Remember, it's Language Arts until 10:20. You should be working on the assignment on pages 27–28." Such a message reminds the students that they have a personal responsibility for what they do during the next 20 minutes.

Communicate Anger.   Lawyers, doctors, construction workers, police officers—in fact, all human beings—get angry in both their personal and their work lives. Teachers are no different. In contrast to those other working people, however, teachers are in physical proximity to those they serve (students) for 5 to 6 hours a day, day after day. It is therefore not uncommon for a teacher's irritation and anger to be fueled by fatigue, student rudeness, classroom emergencies, or disputes with students, parents, or other teachers and administrators. Because the teacher is expected to be warm, gentle, and sympathetic, the public may be surprised when a teacher reveals anger. Yet, Ginott points out, showing anger in front of a class is one of the few times the teacher has the students' full attention.

He advises the use of the *I-message* when showing anger. An *I-message* contains both a description of the behavior that prompted the anger and an expression of how the behavior makes the teacher feel—angry, frustrated, disappointed. The following are examples of effective I-messages:

- The fighting I saw on the playground made me feel sad because it shows that we have not learned our lessons about cooperation.
- Tony, when you use those words in class, I feel very unhappy.
- Sarah, when you interrupt me while I am giving instruction, it upsets me and I become angry.

He contrasts an I-message with a *You-message*, which is much less effective. In a *You-message* the focus is on the child rather than the behavior—for instance, "Stop that fighting. You are making me angry" or "Tony, you must stop saying those nasty words in my class" or "Sarah, you are not to interrupt me again!"

CHECK FOR UNDERSTANDING

Assume that you are an advocate of Ginott's principles of classroom management. Analyze the following case study:

Mrs. Weaver explained to her sixth-grade class that she had to see the principal. "I will be gone for 5 minutes," she informed them. "When I return, everyone working on their assignments and behaving will receive five good-conduct points." She returned in 4 minutes to find most of the class out of their seats, some running, others engaged in a scuffle. She realized that if someone had been hurt, she would have been liable for damages. She clenched her right fist and thumped it into the palm of her hand. Her eyes narrowed in anger. She stood ramrod-straight as the children scurried back to their seats. In a hissed voice forced through clenched teeth, she slowly and deliberately spoke to them:

"I am not going to let myself get mad. I am not going to blame your behavior on your parents and your upbringing. I am not going to let the behavior of some of you ruin the day for me and for the few good students who remained in their seats and continued to do their work. Instead, I am going to calmly ask that you all take your seats and we will continue with class. I trusted you and you responded by being disrespectful."

How well did this teacher follow Ginott's principles of cooperation through communication? What would you have said if you had been the teacher? Write your responses to the two questions in the space provided. Discuss your responses with a classmate.

_____

_____

_____

_____

_____

_____

If you and your classmates decided that Mrs. Weaver was angry but did not express that anger well, you were correct. If you concluded that she really was labeling students by mentioning their upbringing, you are also on target. Finally, her reference to the few "good" students violated Ginott's principle that "correctness" (behavior) should be separated from "goodness" (a person's worth).

If Ginott had observed the scene, he might have suggested that Mrs. Weaver express appreciation for those students who settled down quickly when she entered the room. She would have then told the class that their behavior while she was gone had angered and disappointed her and explained that her feelings were caused by the fact that many of the students had not honored her trust. She should conclude by expressing a willingness to give them a second opportunity soon to show that they can exercise positive classroom responsibility.

William Glasser: Reality Therapy

William Glasser, a psychiatrist, developed his educational program after years of working with troubled youngsters. The basic premise of _reality therapy_ is that a child's past is over and done with. Regardless of that past, whether happy or sad, children make a choice when they select a behavior, whether that behavior is good or bad.

Glasser rejects the idea that the environment from which the child comes determines whether the child will behave well or badly. He is impatient with teachers who find sociological and economic causes to explain or excuse the inappropriate behavior of students. Even though he may concede that these factors may influence behavior, he maintains that teachers should not accept them as justifications for inappropriate behavior.

Glasser places the responsibility for deciding to misbehave squarely on the shoulders of the student. He believes that since human beings are rational beings, they should, therefore, make choices that are conducive to their present and future well-being. The fact that a child becomes disruptive indicates that he or she is not making good choices. The teacher's responsibility is to assist the student to make better choices.

In reality therapy, teachers must help students see the value of desirable behaviors in the classroom. Teachers can also provide opportunities for students to explore alternative approaches to problem solving. To perform these responsibilities, Glasser recommends two activities: _class meetings_ and _individual conferences_.

Class Meetings.   Class meetings, according to Glasser, must be held on a frequent and regular basis. Glasser encourages, as part of the routine curriculum, three types of classroom meetings, named according to the purpose of the meeting. In the first type, labeled as *social conduct problem management*, issues related to school and classroom conduct are discussed and ways to improve them are analyzed and evaluated. Second is the *student progress* meeting, in which the focus is on students' educational progress and ways to enhance it. The third meeting type, *open-ended discussion*, allows the students to make decisions about issues that are important to them.

In class meetings, the emphasis is on the identification of one or more problems affecting the class and on finding solutions to them. Fault finding, assigning blame, and name calling are not tolerated. The teacher's role is to facilitate the discussion while permitting the students to set the direction and the momentum. Glasser recommends that the seating arrangement for meetings be a circle and that the discussion be limited to 30–45 minutes. Before closing, the teacher or a designated student should summarize the findings and recommendations.

Individual Conferences.   Despite the success of class meetings, individual conferences with students about their behavior and school performance may be necessary. Glasser emphasizes that the teacher demonstrate caring to the student during an individual conference. Caring reinforces self-worth, and self-worth produces a belief that the student is successful. Glasser recommends that an individual conference consist of the following eight steps:

Step 1. Individual conferences should stress the student's responsibility for his or her own behavior.

> TEACHER: Newton, why are we meeting?
> STUDENT: I dunno.
> TEACHER: Newton, why are we meeting?
> STUDENT: Because you want to talk to me.
> TEACHER: Why are we meeting for me to talk to you?
> STUDENT: I guess because I would not stay in my seat.
> TEACHER: Right!

Step 2. Have students identify the rule that has been broken and explain why the rule is important to individual and class success.

> TEACHER: Which rule did you break by moving around in class without permission?
> STUDENT: No off-task movement.
> TEACHER: And why do we have the rule?
> STUDENT: Because we would lose too much class time if everyone was moving around the room and disturbing others.

Step 3. Regardless of the student's background or status, accept no justification that will excuse inappropriate behavior.

> TEACHER: OK, Newton. You know and I know there is no excuse for that behavior in this room.
> STUDENT: I know.

Step 4. The student must acknowledge explicitly or implicitly that his or her action was inappropriate.

> TEACHER: So why did you move without permission?
> STUDENT: I can't sit for so long without moving.
> TEACHER: Then we must work out a plan that keeps you on-task.

Step 5. Suggest two or three acceptable alternatives for the student to select from if the urge to move without permission should become irresistible.

> TEACHER: Of the three alternatives I suggested, which one do you think is best for you?
> STUDENT: Number two.
> TEACHER: OK, Newton, when you get the urge again, that is what I expect you to do. Do you need me to remind you when you come to class the first few times?
> STUDENT: It will help.
> TEACHER: Then I will.

Step 6. Logical, reasonable consequences must be communicated and affirmed. The teacher should firmly and consistently administer the consequences if the student chooses an unacceptable alternative the next time he or she moves without permission.

> TEACHER: As you know, if you choose not to do what you promised by informing me that you need to move, you will be isolated from the class for one hour. Neither of us wants that, right?
> STUDENT: Right.

Step 7.   The effective teacher is persistent, never giving up. This may mean repeating the process again with the student, being consistent and patient, and communicating a positive expectation that the student can learn to behave.

> TEACHER: We will talk again at the end of the week to see how well you have done.
> STUDENT: Thank you.
> TEACHER: If you want to talk with me about it before the end of the week, just let me know.
> STUDENT: OK.

Step 8.   The teacher should evaluate at the end of the trial period. Never give up on the student. You may be the student's last hope for a positive future.

CHECK FOR UNDERSTANDING

Now that you have examined the eight steps as advocated by Glasser, summarize each in a word or two. Write your answers on the lines provided. Try to do this exercise without reviewing the steps.

Step 1. _____

Step 2. _____

Step 3. _____

Step 4. _____

Step 5. _____

Step 6. _____

Step 7. _____

Step 8. _____

Guided Practice Activity. Examining Tony's Pattern of Misbehavior

In the first year of your first teaching job at Fairhill Elementary School, you are drawn into a lunch hour conversation between two veteran teachers who are exchanging impressions about Tony, a sixth-grade boy.

> MR. GRIFFITHS: Tony is helpless. He sits and stares. He does nothing. He is just plain lazy. I told him on Tuesday that if he did not change, I was going to get him out of my class.
> MR. HENRY: He is not the only one. Most of the Indian kids learn nothing at home that is helpful in school. They are insolent and lazy. I asked one of them if he was planning to live his whole life on the reservation. He said, "I don't care."

Both teachers turn in your direction, and Mr. Henry says, "Ms. Hoilette, I understand that you did your student teaching on an Indian reservation. What do you recommend we do about Tony and the other Indian kids?" Write a response to Mr. Henry's question. Include at least four principles/ practices found within either the *behavior management* or the *humanistic* classroom management traditions. Also, try to help the teachers develop more appropriate conclusions about the educational potential of Native Americans.

_____

_____

_____

_____

_____

_____

_____

If you began your response by showing respect for the feelings of the two teachers, you have understood what Ginott means about dealing with feelings. Dealing with feelings is necessary with colleagues as well as with students. You may have suggested that your understanding of the Indian culture leads you to believe that group work may produce more learning success and thus help to dispel the stereotype of Indian children as lazy. If you counseled that good people can occasionally behave unacceptably, you will have encouraged the teachers to send sane messages instead of messages of condemnation. These three principles—deal with feelings, eliminate stereotypes and labels, and send sane messages—should be communicated to the two veteran teachers. You may then wish to suggest that they analyze Tony's unacceptable behavior and evaluate his level of ability to accomplish the tasks assigned to him by using a contract.

Section 2. Useful Insights from Contemporary Research Findings

ESTABLISHING CLASSROOM RULES

In preventing minor lapses in discipline from becoming serious disturbances, nothing is as important as the establishment of classroom rules. A *classroom rule* is a statement that informs students which behaviors are acceptable and which are unacceptable in the classroom. Rules are few in number (usually three to seven, for easy recall) and are designed to reduce misbehavior. The relationship between the classroom and the school, the school and the district, the district and the legal system must be understood as the context within which rules are established. The U.S. Constitution provides a framework and the state constitutions provide the authority for the district code of conduct. District policy makes provisions for teachers to develop classroom rules. Consequently, classroom rules must be consistent with the intent, spirit, and substance of district, state, and national policies related to the rights of citizens, the protection of life and property, and the maintenance of order in society.

When developing classroom rules, teachers must be aware that since 1954, the U.S. courts have become active in examining the behavior management of schools and have made student conduct a special area of emphasis. Tension remains between those who would grant wide discretion to schools—a philosophy known as *in loco parentis* that allows teachers and school administrators to act in the place of and with the powers of the parents—and those who wish to restrict that discretion.

Furthermore, there have been disturbing differences in the administration of suspension and expulsion punishments to white and minority students. In 1974, the Children's Defense Fund conducted a large-scale national survey of suspension rates and discovered that minority students were being suspended at twice the rate of white students. Further research sponsored by the Program for Educational Opportunity at the University of Michigan indicated that when teachers failed to communicate rules to students or expressed them in overly broad language and thus permitted teachers a wide latitude in determining guilt, minority students were more severely punished than were white students (Buena Vista Reports, 1979).

Nevertheless, judicial decisions have determined that there are a number of legitimate reasons for the existence and enforcement of classroom rules. First, the creation of a positive teaching/learning environment is essential if schools are to achieve their primary mission, the education of children. Clearly, disorderly or uncontrolled behavior is likely to interfere with the orderly flow of the educational process. Second, rules are made for the safety of everyone in the school community. Rules address such issues as student movement, accident procedures, fighting, and possession of weapons. Third, rules are developed to protect personal and school property from theft and vandalism.

How should school and classroom rules be written? What principles should guide their development? Effective rules clearly communicate the limits of student freedom to do as they please. The following are examples of effective rules:

1. No one is to talk during classroom lessons.
2. There will be no talking in class except when I tell you it is OK.

3. Don't leave your seat while class is in session unless I give you permission.
4. There will be no loud talking or fighting in this room.

These rules are effective because they are

1. *understandable* to the average student
2. *reasonable*, in that they are related to one of the three legitimate reasons for the existence of rules listed above
3. *enforceable* by the teacher

CHECK FOR UNDERSTANDING

Write five rules for your classroom. Make them understandable, reasonable, and enforceable. Share them with classmates and invite suggestions for improvement.

_____

_____

_____

_____

ESTABLISHING CLASSROOM ROUTINES AND PROCEDURES

At this time, we will turn our attention to the establishment of classroom routines. *Routines* are classroom procedures that must be accomplished automatically, with little lost time—for example, lining up for recess or entering the classroom. A procedure for entering class may be: "When you enter class, pick up your folder, go to your seat, and begin to work." When this procedure repeatedly functions without the teacher's verbal intervention, we can say that a routine has been established. As you can see, routines save time and energy—imagine having to direct students to their seats every day, with no time left to speak to an individual student, to take attendance, or complete other necessary start-up activities. In contrast to the three to seven classroom rules, a teacher may have a large number of routines, including how to form classroom groups, pass out material, line up for recess, use the bathroom, and so on.

Some teachers are more effective classroom managers than others, in part because of their development and use of positive and effective classroom routines. The following recommendations for establishing classroom routines have been gathered from a number of research reports. They are presented in two groups—a general list and a list specific to first-week-of-class orientation procedures. Think of how each contributes to an effectively managed classroom.

General Guidelines

1. Greet students on entry to your classroom—meet them at the door, give a pat on the shoulder, shake hands and/or smile. Use your educational philosophy to guide you in developing a greeting style and be consistent and regular in using it.

2. Begin your class promptly with a mental exercise. This exercise may be a review of a homework assignment, a response to something on the chalkboard, or a discussion by pairs of students of some issue. During this time, you may take attendance, deal with an individual student, and monitor the students. Be prepared to actively engage students' minds each day as soon as they enter your classroom.

3. Take time to communicate your objective and purpose for each lesson. Attentive, focused students are less likely to be disruptive. Active involvement of students during lessons also helps to maintain students' attention.

4. Behavior during direct lessons should be based on established routines. Among these are signals for responding to teacher questions, appropriate behavior while someone is speaking, rules for movement in the room, guidelines for pair-sharing and small group work, and so on.

5. Give directions once. Begin training students in the first week to listen carefully. They will learn to listen after two or three days of practice.

6. Expected student behavior at independent work stations or centers should be clarified. Issues related to availability and scheduling, use of resources, and potential problems should be considered.

7. Students should know which legitimate activities they may pursue when their work has been completed. For example, free reading or writing in a journal may be long-term assignments.

8. Establish a routine for ending class. Students should understand the routines for closing, clean up, storage of supplies and equipment, and dismissal.

9. Interruption routines should be developed. Students should be taught what to do if they or the teacher is interrupted. Most students are willing to help develop a list of appropriate activities or behaviors. Let them discuss ideas for staying on-task during interruptions. Crossword puzzles, brain teasers, and word searches may be developed for such purposes.

10. Fire, hurricane, and tornado warnings are not the only emergencies. If there are emergencies (e.g., possession of weapons, fights, someone in danger), what are students expected to do? Plan these routines and train students to behave appropriately.

During the *first week of classes* the knowledge students gain from your orientation activities may be more important than the academic content you impart. During that crucial first week, do not allow students to carelessly wander into the room and just mill around. The first impression students have of you will determine, to a great extent, the way they respond to you throughout the year. Remember the importance we attached in Chapter 5 to establishing a set for each lesson. The classroom management set you create during the first week of class is even more critical to your success as a teacher than your instructional set each day. If the classroom management set is highly negative, students will not give you an opportunity to establish a productive instructional set each day. To make this management set a supportive one, extend your orientation activities across a full week or two.

Guidelines for Beginning the School Year

A. Planning
   1. Establish clear management objectives about what you want to happen in the first class and thereafter. Pay particular attention to the first 15 minutes of class. Anticipate possible external interruptions and determine, ahead of time, responses that will leave in your students' minds the impression that their teacher is businesslike and nice.
B. Setting the Tone
   2. Make sure that your meeting and greeting of students leaves them with a warm and expectant feeling.
   3. Introduce humor into your orientation activities and remarks.
   4. Be authentic. Do not play Dr. Jekyll and Mr. Hyde with the sensitivities of students. Introduce them on the first day of class to the teacher you plan to be for the entire year. Contrary to common wisdom, there is no need to refrain "from smiling until December." Be "firm and friendly" from the beginning (Johns, MacNaughton, & Karabinus, 1989, p. 6).

5. Expose students to a repertoire of reinforcers the first week. Joke, smile, touch, praise, encourage, compliment, use names, incorporate student ideas, and make positive references to the school and the community.

C. Impressions of Students

6. While you try to make a positive impression on students, be equally conscious that you do not develop a negative impression of any students during this first week. Remember that some students will attempt to impress you, others will be fearful, and still others will have had some external experience that will negatively affect their behavior.

7. Develop an awareness of individual students during this first week. Attempt to match them with their level of need. Be especially conscious to establish a climate that meets their physical and psychological safety and security needs.

D. Establishing an Orderly Environment

8. Make sure that on the first day you discuss room arrangements and classroom routines. If there are start-up activities each day, describe and demonstrate them. It is beneficial to have students practice all procedures and to provide feedback throughout the first weeks of school.

9. *Introduce the rules during the first 3 days of class.* Students should understand the behavior rules in your room. Be equally certain to let them know the purpose of these rules, and allow discussions and clarification where necessary. It is your responsibility to enforce rules and to see to it that the rules are focused on learning tasks. Teach the rules each day during the first week at both the memory and the complex cognitive levels of learning.

10. Establish a sense of order by keeping your class together in a large group for the first few days. Allow students to develop a sense of community and to know that you are securely in charge before you break into small-group activities. When you do, teach the rules and routines for small-group activity.

11. Implement initial activities that require a high level of student participation. Such activities should be simple, interesting, pleasant, and guarantee that all students will achieve a high degree of success.

12. Prepare smooth transitions from one activity to the next. This is a time when a classroom routine can be especially helpful. Teaching a classroom procedure by explaining, demonstrating, and rehearsing it greatly reduces transition time. For example, you may teach students how to get quiet when you raise your hand and say "Give me 5." You would practice this and time students each day until the response is quick and automatic.

13. Plan activities to soak up dead time at the beginning and end of class and during transition periods. These activities, often referred to as "sponges," add instructional time and reduce the opportunities for disruption. They should be easy, pleasurable, and relate to valued learning. Brain teasers and puzzles are two commonly used sponge activities.

All these guidelines should be acted upon during the first weeks of school. Begin in the first hour and continue through the following weeks. Reinforce your rules, routines, and expectations throughout the first week, month, and the remainder of the year.

THE EFFECTIVE CLASSROOM MANAGER

Evertson and Emmer developed a series of insights about classroom management gleaned from two research studies, one covering 41 teachers in grades 1 through 6 in 14 schools and a second covering 61 teachers in grades 6 through 8, in 14 schools (Evertson et al., 1981; Emmer et al., 1982). Their studies led them to define *effectively managed classrooms* as those with a high level of student participation and cooperation among the teacher and student peers in class activities. In these classrooms students feel a sense of responsibility for the environment and work willingly along with their teachers and classmates. Tasks were completed ahead of time, and there were few examples of nonproductive or disruptive behaviors.

The question of interest to us is, How did the teachers create such orderly classrooms? Those effective managers considered it their responsibility to *teach* students how to behave in the school and classroom. Those managers did not merely tell students the rules and wait for the pupils to break them, thus forcing the teachers to respond with punishment or verbal tirades. The effective managers were *proactive* rather than reactive. They anticipated problems and gave students practice and feedback on the appropriate behavior.

Evertson and Emmer developed the following conclusions about effective classroom managers in the elementary school setting:

1. Better managers more frequently demonstrated the ability to analyze ahead of time, in precise detail, the teaching and learning tasks during the first few weeks of class. They established routines from the beginning and were specific in providing feedback to students who behaved inappropriately and/or disruptively. They seemed to be clearer about behavior guidelines and required that students function within the borders of that responsibility.
2. Better managers integrated rules as a regular part of the curriculum during these same first weeks. They walked the students through the procedures and held practice exercises as a regular part of the school program. For example, students may be taught three levels of appropriate talk: silence, whisper, and constructive discussion. These would be modeled, demonstrated, and practiced during the first three weeks of the school year.
3. Managers who were better organized were able to prevent disruption by introducing new but essential routines throughout the year. These routines reflected a better understanding of students because the teachers had made an effort to get to know their students.
4. The more effective managers monitored student behavior closely during the first 3 weeks and dealt with problems immediately. They did not ignore deviations from classroom rules and procedures but forthrightly administered appropriate consequences.

Evertson and Emmer arrived at similar conclusions about effective classroom managers in a junior high school setting:

1. The more effective managers integrated rules and procedures into a systematic approach. They were also more successful in teaching and implementing rules and procedures. Better managers were more precise in defining acceptable behavior.

2.   Better managers were more consistent in managing behavior. They were not as likely to ignore disruptive behavior and usually referred to the rules and procedures when giving feedback to students. They generally acted when they noticed a departure from the expected behavior or at least took notice of the infraction.
3.   They expected students to progress and kept track of progress and completion of assigned tasks.
4.   Effective managers presented material and information more clearly. Students had a better sense of the objectives. These teachers were more skillful in establishing task hierarchies in a step-by-step process. They were also more effective in diagnosing the skill levels of students.
5.   The better managers spent more time on the objectives of the lesson and less time on nonrelated activities.

PREVENTING CLASSROOM DISRUPTIONS

Classroom management as we know it today has been greatly influenced by Jacob Kounin (1970). In the late 1960s and early 1970s, he received a grant from the National Institute of Mental Health to undertake several studies in order to improve a teacher's skills in preventing discipline problems. Based on his study of elementary, high school, and college classrooms, he introduced new concepts and terms into the discipline literature. Among the most useful are *overlapping, group alerting, with-it-ness*, and *smoothness and momentum*.

Overlapping

Overlapping is the teacher's ability to attend to more than one event or activity at the same time. Assume the teacher is working with an individual or a small group and a disruption occurs elsewhere in the classroom. The teacher who is able to handle both events without becoming sidetracked is effectively overlapping. For example, the teacher is with a reading group, and a student doing seatwork suddenly throws an object. The teacher asks a question of a child in the reading group, pauses, and attends to the disruptive child. Only 45 seconds later, the teacher's attention returns to the student preparing to respond to the question.

Group Alerting

Group alerting is the technique of keeping students' attention when they have yet to be called on to respond. A helpful strategy is to use wait time—to ask the question, pause, and then orally identify the selected student respondent, by name. Thus you will ensure that all students will expect that they may be called on to respond. By first naming the student to whom a question will be asked and/or by having a predictable pattern of questioning (i.e., alphabetical, or by row and seat).

With-it-ness

With-it-ness is the extent to which the teacher demonstrates an awareness of student behavior in all situations and in all sectors of the classroom. Students believe that teachers who possess with-it-ness have "eyes in the back of their heads." With-it-ness can be measured by the number of times the teacher identifies disruptive behavior as compared to the actual number of occurrences.

Smoothness and Momentum

Smoothness and momentum measures how easily the teacher moves from one lesson to the next without interrupting the instructional flow and student attention. *Overdwelling* is one threat to smoothness and momentum and occurs when the teacher badgers or nags the students about an issue, especially one that is irrelevant to the lesson at hand. The teacher must maintain movement, activity, and attention toward a specific goal. Goal-directedness is essential to smoothness and momentum.

SAVING INSTRUCTIONAL TIME

Jones (1979) developed a training program to help teachers reduce the loss of instructional time resulting from student off-task behavior. He arrived at a set of conclusions about disruptive student behavior from observations in hundreds of classrooms (Cangelosi, 1988). According to Jones, some 50 percent of the available instructional time in the classroom was lost because of disruptive behavior.

Classroom control is strongly influenced by the students' perception of how close the teacher is at any given time. Jones advocates the use of eye contact, facial expressions, gestures, and a "take control" appearance that communicates the message that the schoolroom is a place for work. These so-called low control (or low profile) methods have been identified by other researchers as highly effective in preventing disruption with a minimum of attention and loss of instructional time. For example, the teacher's physical proximity is an effective technique in classroom management. Thus it is recommended that teachers move frequently around and through the classroom.

Jones also examined the way time was allocated in helping students. He reported that teachers believed that they were spending an average of 1–2 minutes with each student who needed help when, in actuality, they spent an average of 4 minutes with each student. Consequently, Jones counseled teachers to be more conscious of the way they distributed time to individuals and the group and to be more equitable in that distribution.

One technique for achieving Jones's goal is called *praise, prompt, and leave* (Jones, 1979). First the teacher approaches the child needing help and *praises* what the student has done on his or her own: "Oh, good! You've got the first problem correct." This reinforces the student's independence. Then the teacher *prompts* the student to make another try by giving a hint or a suggestion: "Number 2 is just like the one on page 16. Try it and I'll be back to check in a minute." The *leave* step is obvious; the teacher leaves, and the student must make another attempt on his or her own. The student has not been reinforced for helplessness by 4 minutes of undivided teacher attention but has been reinforced for independent work and will receive a second praise, prompt, and leave when the teacher returns in a few minutes.

CHAPTER SUMMARY

Since the 1970s, classroom discipline has been identified as one of the most serious problems facing the public schools. Classroom management is a formidable challenge for teachers during their beginning years in the profession. In this first of two chapters focused on the topic, three traditions from which discipline philosophies emerge were discussed—commonsense, behavior management, and humanistic. Programs that fit within the latter two traditions were

discussed, including those of the Canters, of Ginott, and of Glasser. In the second section of the chapter, insights about classroom management were drawn from the work of contemporary researchers. Practice activities focused on your ability to create rules and routines consistent with sound principles of classroom management. You should be able to apply the knowledge from this chapter as you develop your own discipline philosophy. In Chapter 9, we will discuss a rational approach to classroom management that emerges out of our philosophy and represents what we believe is a successful classroom management system.

Independent Practice Activity. Creating a Discipline Philosophy

It is your turn to create your own discipline philosophy, one that best reflects your personality. Consider the three traditions from which classroom management philosophies emerge—*common-sense*, *behavior management*, and *humanistic*—and your own experiences as a student. Be conscious to the extent to which these traditions influence your philosophy about student behavior. As you develop your own philosophy, bear the following generalizations in mind:

1. Disruptive behavior will always occur in the classroom. While you cannot be certain that all students will learn what you teach, you can be sure that on any given day someone will engage in disruptive behavior.

2. What you expect of students is usually what you get from them. If you expect productive behaviors, you will probably get constructive behaviors most of the time. If you expect students to behave poorly, you will set the scene for nonproductive behaviors to follow. Thus, as you write your philosophy, emphasize the positive rather than the negative.

3. Your attitudes toward males and females, toward children from different religious, ethnic, or racial groups, and toward children from different socioeconomic classes will affect the way you interact with members of these groups. It is natural and helpful to know how a group's norms and expectations affect individuals within the group. However, you should always treat individuals as individuals rather than as members of a particular group. All Asians are not young scientists or mathematicians. All males are not interested in football and baseball. More important, in desegregated schools where teachers think minority students can and should behave appropriately, they generally do behave appropriately. Where they are not expected to behave appropriately, they are often perceived as misbehaving.

Write your philosophy in the space that follows. Include a statement about the nature of your classroom and your expectations for student behavior. Be concise and clear. Attempt to keep the philosophy to a paragraph. You may wish to discuss your philosophy with a peer or a group.

_____

_____

_____

_____

_____

REFERENCES

Buena Vista Reports. (1979). Program for Educational Opportunity. Ann Arbor: University of Michigan.

Cangelosi, J. S. (1988). *Classroom Management Strategies*. New York: Longman.

Canter, L., & Canter, M. (1976). *Assertive Discipline: A Take-Charge Approach to Today's Education*. Seal Beach, CA: Canter & Associates.

Canter, L. (1989). Assertive discipline—More than names on the board and marbles in a jar. *Phi Delta Kappan, 71* (2), 37–40.

Emmer, E. T., et al. (1982). *Organizing and Managing the Junior High Classroom* (Report No. 6151). Research and Development Center for Teacher Education. Austin: University of Texas.

Evertson, C. M., et al. (1981). *Organizing and Managing the Elementary School Classroom* (Report No. 6060). Research and Development Center for Teacher Education. Austin: University of Texas.

Evertson, C. M., & Emmer, E. T. (1982). Effective management at the beginning of the school year in junior high classes. *Journal of Educational Psychology, 74* (4), 485–498.

Gallup, A. M., & Elam, S. M. (1988). The 20th annual Gallup Poll of the public's attitude toward the public schools. *Phi Delta Kappan, 70* (1), 33–46.

Ginott, H. G. (1972). *Teacher and Child: A Book for Parents and Teachers*. New York: Macmillan.

Glasser, W. (1969). *Schools without Failure*. New York: Harper & Row.

Johns, F. A., MacNaughton, R., & Karabinus, N. G. (1989). *School Discipline Guidebook*. Boston: Allyn and Bacon.

Jones, F. (1979). The gentle art of classroom discipline. *National Elementary Principal, 58*, 26–32.

Kounin, J. (1970). *Discipline and Group Management in the Classroom*. New York: Holt, Rinehart, & Winston.

CHAPTER 9

A Rational Approach to Classroom Management

Chapter Overview

In Chapter 8 we examined three traditions—commonsense, behavior management, and humanistic—from which classroom management philosophies emerge. The latter two traditions rest on a base of research that lends empirical support to their practices. In the final activity in the chapter, we asked you to write a classroom discipline philosophy that reflects your personality, beliefs, and values. It would not surprise us if your emerging philosophy was a blend of elements taken from more than one tradition. In fact, we believe that the most effective classroom managers are eclectic, in that they select and use the best of the humanistic and behavior management guidelines and practices. We call this the *rational approach* to classroom discipline.

We will describe one example of such a program, the Rational Approach to Practical School Discipline (RAPSD), which was developed by one of the authors and combines elements from the three traditions discussed in Chapter 8. The first section of Chapter 9 will focus on what the teacher can do to prevent disruption. Section 2 emphasizes responses to disruptive students. Finally, Section 3 provides a menu of techniques that are used by the successful rational manager.

Set Activity

Assume you are an advocate of behavior management as an approach to classroom discipline. Based on your knowledge from reading Chapter 8, evaluate Mrs. Henry's responses in the following incident. How would a humanistic manager evaluate the responses? Write your responses in the space provided following the incident.

Leesha is a student in Mrs. Henry's sixth-grade room. In mid-November Mrs. Henry was 10 minutes into a lesson on verbs when Leesha began pulling Tanya's hair. Mrs. Henry said, "Leesha! Pay attention to the explanation being given, dear." Leesha turned her face to the teacher but continued to play with Tanya's hair. Mrs. Henry continued, "I'm waiting." At this point, Leesha let go of Tanya's hair and began playing with Gerald's jacket. Mrs. Henry resumed her explanation of verbs to the class. While looking at the teacher in what seemed like a very attentive manner, Leesha continued to play with Gerald's jacket. After about 6 minutes she initiated a tug of war with Cori over a pencil. Mrs. Henry then told Cori to "watch it."

Chapter Objectives

After you have completed this chapter, you will be able to:

1. describe the rational approach to classroom management
2. analyze examples of student and teacher behaviors using Rudolf Dreikurs's misbehavior classification system
3. discuss and defend student behavior management decisions based on a rational integration of philosophy, attitudes, behavior types, and classroom management techniques
4. demonstrate confidence in analyzing and determining responses to classroom discipline situations by providing a rational base for your choices

DISCIPLINE LEGEND

5. select proactive elements and techniques that are consistent with your management philosophy and teaching style
6. select management elements and techniques that deal effectively with pattern disruption and disrupters
7. respond to classroom disruptions with greater confidence

THE RATIONAL PHILOSOPHY OF CLASSROOM DISCIPLINE: AN OVERVIEW

The rational philosophy is eclectic in that management decisions are guided by sound behavioral and humanistic psychology. In a rational classroom, structure, freedom, and legitimate authority are in balance.

The rational manager takes from the behavior management tradition an emphasis on consequences following positive or negative behavior. The rational manager also believes that the teacher's needs must be met, but not at the expense of the students. External reinforcers are used to emphasize that the student has a choice to behave well and avoid punishment or to behave inappropriately and be punished.

Similarly, the rational philosophy includes some elements from the humanistic tradition. Constructive expression of childrens' wants and desires is supported, self-responsibility is highlighted, anxiety is reduced, and shared authority and a warm environment are advocated. Finally, although the teacher is responsible for selecting and enforcing rules and consequences, he or she is encouraged to involve students in the management of the classroom.

In the rational philosophy, the emphasis is on the classroom as a society in which students and the teacher learn to work together to develop a more cooperative and just community. The rational classroom manager educates children to be accountable for the standards of behavior in the classroom. Thus students are critical about their own behaviors and feel a sense of responsibility to cooperate with the group. This attitude, when held by both teacher and students, works effectively to create a disciplined environment.

Because of the sense of mutual respect built on a belief that all children have equal rights and responsibilities, the rational philosophy can be more responsive to students' cultural, ethnic, and social backgrounds. Nevertheless, the teacher also must be true to the essential management structure that ensures each child a safe, orderly, and cordial classroom environment.

THE RATIONAL APPROACH TO PRACTICAL SCHOOL DISCIPLINE: ITS STRUCTURE

The Rational Approach to Practical School Discipline (RAPSD) was developed by Trevor Gardner at Eastern Michigan University (Gardner, 1989). It exemplifies the rational philosophical approach because it is an eclectic blend of behavior management and humanistic ideas. The RAPSD program has two essential elements.

1. It is proactive in that
   a. both the teacher's and students' needs are considered before classroom rules and consequences are established

    b. the physical organization of the classroom is planned to maximize learning and minimize disruption

    c. understandable, reasonable, enforceable rules, classroom routines, and desirable social behaviors are taught through a discipline curriculum

2. It includes a system for responding to classroom misbehavior. This system

    a. uses Dreikurs's classification system of misbehavior to evaluate the causes of misbehavior

    b. establishes an information system to record student misbehavior

    c. utilizes quality circles to confront disruptive behaviors and disruptive students

    d. implements the positive moments strategy with pattern disruptive students

    e. develops a set of procedures in preparation for classroom emergencies

Section 1. Proactive Strategies to Prevent Classroom Disruptions

The rational manager believes that the management of classroom discipline is divided into two equally important stages. Unfortunately, teachers spend too much of their creative thinking on the second phase—being *reactive* to disruptive student behavior. What will I do if Joanna speaks out in class without permission? How will I respond if Paula threatens my authority in front of the entire class? Should I send Mike to the principal's office if he comes into class late again tomorrow? All of these questions are important. However, teachers would gain greater benefits if they were more *proactive*—understanding teacher and student needs, organizing the classroom to promote learning and prevent disruption, and establishing a discipline curriculum to teach classroom rules, routines, and consequences before disruption occurs.

TEACHER AND STUDENT NEEDS

Keith knocked his pencil on the back of the chair before him. It was the fourth time Mrs. Ronberg had to tell him to stop in the last 35 minutes. When he was not hitting the pencil, he was pulling someone's hair, throwing spitballs, flying airplanes, or talking without stopping until she reprimanded him for his behavior. Even when he stopped after she spoke to him, he was back at it within 5 minutes. "How does one deal with those irritating behaviors?" Mrs. Ronberg asks.

Keith's behaviors express a need. As a teacher, you should spend a significant part of your planning time assessing and predicting student needs as a way to prevent disruptive behaviors and maintain effective management. If you view student misbehavior as the result of a misplaced attempt to fulfill a need, you are more likely to be effective in channeling or changing the behavior. Although there are many theories of need and its relation to human motivation, a brief review of the hierarchical arrangement of needs as developed by Abraham H. Maslow will serve our purposes (1954). Maslow conceived of five levels of need, with the lowest need at the bottom:

Level 5. Self-Fulfillment—Attainment of your full potential, being all that you can be
Level 4. Self-Esteem Needs—Reputation, recognition as a valuable and important person, being your own person
Level 3. Love/Belonging Needs—Acceptance by others, friendship, love
Level 2. Safety/Security Needs—Protection from physical and psychological threats and attacks
Level 1. Physical Needs—The most basic and obvious needs—oxygen, water, food, sleep, sex

It requires little imagination to create a scenario in which a child's misbehavior could be the result of unfulfilled needs at Level 1 (hunger), Level 3 (peer pressure), Level 4 (drive to achieve academic recognition), and so on.

The teacher's needs are also important to consider in classroom management. The emphasis on the teacher's needs by Canter and Canter (1976) is a significant addition to the literature on classroom management (see Chapter 8). When asked by the Canters what teachers want from students, teachers responded with need statements, such as "I don't want hassles from the boys who are trouble makers" (Level 2), "I want them to be good citizens and have positive attitudes" (Level 4).

Although the consideration of the teacher's needs is important, it must be balanced by a concern for the needs of children. Failure to balance these two legitimate needs may result in teacher behaviors that will encourage rather than prevent disruptive student behaviors. Gartnell emphasizes this very point in his critical review of Canter's *assertive discipline* program (Gartnell, 1987). Gartnell believes that children are controlled but do not learn *self-control* if the teacher follows the principles espoused by Canter. The student's sense of responsibility may be neglected in an effort to satisfy the teacher's need to control student actions.

CLASSROOM ARRANGEMENT

The physical arrangement of the classroom has a significant impact on the way teachers manage and the way students behave. Student desks, the teacher's desk, audiovisual equipment, bookshelves, cabinets, learning centers, and other materials and tools must be arranged to maximize instructional results and effective management.

Evertson and Emmer (Evertson et al., 1981; Emmer et al., 1982) identified guidelines for good room arrangements. These primary factors are visibility, proximity, accessibility, and safety. Although we do not believe that there is one right way to arrange classroom furniture, equipment, and materials, these guidelines provide a foundation on which an effective design can be constructed:

1. Students should be easily visible from all areas of the room. (visibility)
2. The teacher must be able, without difficulty, to move close to students during instruction. (proximity)
3. Frequently used instructional materials and supplies should be kept within easy access. (accessibility)
4. Students should be able to see and hear instructional presentations, demonstrations, and displays. (accessibility/visibility)
5. High traffic areas—for example, around pencil sharpeners—should be free from congestion. (accessibility)
6. Arrangement of furniture, centers, and freeways should be designed to facilitate safety in case of emergency situations—fire, accidents, fights, and so on. (safety)

Although, as we noted, there is no one correct pattern for organizing student seating, seating arrangements may be designed according to the six guidelines. The traditional seating arrangement of five rows of six seats, shown as "A" in Figure 9.1, has two disadvantages. First, it affords too little opportunity for eye contact (visibility). Research has documented clearly that in the traditional pattern most of the teacher's attention is directed to the students in the shaded area. Students outside the shadowed area tend to be ignored and are likely to become disruptive. Teachers may compensate for this fact by circulating often among students during instruction. However, during whole-class, direct teaching (especially when teaching at

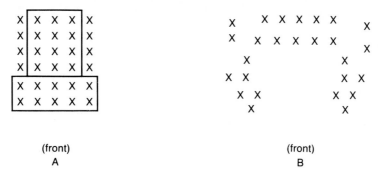

(front)   (front)
A   B

Figure 9.1. Alternative Student Seating Patterns

the chalkboard), it is difficult, if not impossible, to be mobile. A second disadvantage is that it is difficult to get close to students (proximity) when you have to pick your way through rows of desks and chairs.

Because of the disadvantages of the traditional pattern, you may wish to consider alternatives. Many teachers recommend a semicircular or horseshoe pattern such as the one shown as "B" in Figure 9.1. They find that they can maintain eye contact and move quickly and easily among students. Other teachers recommend a three-sided rectangle (one end open for teacher access) or groups of four to five students at desks or table clusters. Whatever seating arrangement you select should be checked for visibility, proximity, accessibility, and safety.

CHECK FOR UNDERSTANDING

Keith is your busy fourth grader. He is constantly moving in your class and always ready to throw spitballs. Although his behavior is not seriously disruptive, it is annoying. He is especially active when he believes that you cannot see him. How can you use your room arrangement to help

solve this problem? _____

_____

_____

_____

_____

The location of the students' desks is not the only concern in planning a room arrangement. The teacher's desk should be strategically placed to facilitate your management style and philosophy. If you plan to offer any instruction while seated at your desk, then it should be placed so that (1) a student can gain easy access and (2) you have visible control over the entire class. If you plan to be up and about most of the time, you'll want to place your desk in an area where you will spend much of your time and close to routinely used materials. As you contemplate a room arrangement for support furniture, equipment, and materials, ask yourself where you will place

1. Learning centers
2. Bookcases
3. Overhead projector
4. Other A-V equipment
5. Students' coats and other clothing
6. Art materials
7. Teacher supplies
8. Aquarium, indoor plants
9. Classroom materials (paper, textbooks, etc.)
10. Costumes
11. Pets, real or stuffed

As you plan the location of your instructional tools and materials, you will want to make sure that each decision is consistent with the guidelines of visibility, proximity, accessibility, and safety. After that, you may consider the aesthetics of the placement. Remember that the ecology of the room arrangement is likely to affect student responses. Some teachers suggest that rooms that are too cluttered may lead students to value disorder and to submit messy work.

Guided Practice Activity A. Designing Your Own Classroom

As a new teacher in the Fairhill Elementary School, you have been assigned a fourth-grade class with 23 students in a room 25 by 30 feet. Design two room arrangements and organize the furniture and space as you would in the week preceding your first day of school. One design should reflect a room with the basics—desks, chairs, bulletin boards, and so on—and the second design should include everything you ever wanted in your classroom. Compare and contrast your designs with others in your class by providing them pages with your design.

Independent Practice Activity A. Evaluating Classroom Arrangements

Visit two teachers' classrooms and evaluate the layout of the rooms on the basis of the four guidelines of successful room arrangement. If it is useful and the teachers are willing, discuss your conclusions with them. Write a brief report to share with your class for discussion. *Caution*: Be prepared to learn from the teachers. If their rooms are not consistent with the guidelines, there may, as we have suggested, be extenuating circumstances.

TEACHING A DISCIPLINE CURRICULUM

Several studies have shown that a teacher's failure to adequately explain and enforce management rules and routines often leads to nonproductive student behaviors. Such behaviors include confusion, incomplete assignments, disruption, frustration, and lower academic achievement (Evertson et al., 1981; Emmer et al., 1982). The process for developing classroom rules and routines together with illustrative examples was presented in Chapter 8.

In large part, the most important rules and routines should enhance a young person's skills as a participant in small and large social groups. Kelly (1982) argued that the development of social skills leads directly to the building of personal relationships. He asserted that the fostering of such skills is critical for children, since they are learning how to get along with others. The degree to which children accept themselves is a significant predictor of the likely strength of their relationships with others. As Matson and Ollendick stated: "A person's ability to get along with others and to engage in prosocial behaviors determines popularity among peers and with teachers, parents and other significant adults" (1988, p. 1).

Inadequate or undeveloped social skills have a recognized relationship to youth delinquency (Roff et al., 1972). Others have demonstrated a relationship between social skills and student dropout rates (Ullman, 1975). The importance of social skills both within and outside the classroom makes it imperative that you accept responsibility to teach them to students.

A curriculum for teaching acceptable social behavior should consist of two units: (1) the teaching of *classroom rules of conduct* and an appreciation of the reasons for rules, limits, and consequences and (2) the development of social skills that lead to *supportive social relationships* among the students and, thus, to a more productive classroom atmosphere.

Teaching Classroom Rules of Conduct

In teaching rules you should follow seven basic steps:

1. Have three to seven rules that cover the essential behavior management needs of your class.
2. Present the rules and consequences to your students on the first day.
3. Be sure that your students understand these rules and consequences so that they can explain them in their own words by the second day.
4. By the third day, provide simulated situations that allow your students to practice appropriate behaviors. Give ample feedback.
5. Continue this practice and feedback until the behaviors are well established. This may take 1–3 weeks.
6. Post the rules in a very visible place.
7. Periodically review and practice the rules to reemphasize their importance and value in the environment.

If a rule says that a student is to sit quietly during independent work, then the teacher explains and models the desired behavior. Then he or she checks students' understanding of the rule by giving examples of and asking students to label appropriate behavior (sitting, feet on floor, eyes on the work) and inappropriate behavior (standing, crowding around the teacher's desk, talking to a neighbor). Then students practice during independent activity while the teacher carefully monitors and gives positive or corrective feedback, perhaps applying rewards or negative consequences later in the week. Before each independent activity the teacher asks the students to state appropriate and inappropriate behaviors and monitors and gives feedback and consequences. Thus, by the end of a week or two, students will have learned how to behave during independent work, and less monitoring will be necessary—for example, during reading groups.

Teaching Social Skills

While one unit of the discipline curriculum focuses on social rules, the second unit emphasizes social skills that help students enhance and strengthen their self-concepts and, thus, their standing in social groups. For example, students should be taught how to avoid being the perennial victim of the class aggressor. To illustrate, consider the following incident:

SARAH: John, you are big, fat, and ugly.
JOHN: I'm not.
SARAH: Yes you are! You're as big as a truck.
JOHN: I'm going to tell on you. You are calling me names.
Sarah gets a parting shot: You are a cry baby too.

John runs to the teacher and reports Sarah's behavior. Too often the teacher will respond by moving immediately to discipline Sarah.

TEACHER: Sarah, how many times must I tell you . . . etc.

A scenario like this is played out in some elementary or middle school classrooms every day. In a rational classroom, however, the pattern is broken by teaching and coaching students to be assertive, poised, and confident in responding to bullies and their verbal taunts. For example, John can learn two simple sentences to use in response to Sarah on subsequent occasions:

SARAH: John, you are big, fat, and ugly. (the aggressor)
JOHN: When you say that, it hurts. (the potential victim)

After that response, most aggressors feel embarrassed and slink away. However, a few will be so hurtful that they may go on to say:

SARAH: I meant to hurt you. You are big, fat, and ugly.
JOHN: Then you succeeded in hurting me.

In most cases the aggressor will apologize and never repeat the performance. Thus strategies that help students deal with difficult social situations not only facilitate individual development but also promote a more positive classroom environment.

The teacher's responsibility is to help students learn assertive responses that build confidence and the will power to confront a bully. Your knowledge about individual children will guide you in shaping the counsel you give to the child who is being victimized. In all cases you inform the victim that a helping adult will not always be ready and available; self-help is the best solution.

The goal is for every person in your classroom to feel responsible for the social environment in the classroom. One technique for achieving cooperation is to urge students to discourage their peers from undesirable behaviors. Some schools teach students how to resolve conflicts with peers. Other social skills might include being supportive, sharing feelings, listening actively, and participating constructively in a group.

Students do not usually learn these skills on their own. Many will need explicit training through a social skills curriculum. This curriculum may be designed specifically for children with social behavior deficits or for all children. The skills should be taught at the beginning of the year and reinforced periodically throughout the year. Role playing, simulations, cooperative learning, classroom meetings, direct and inductive lessons are all appropriate for teaching these crucial social skills.

Guided Practice Activity B. Teaching a Social Rule or Skill

Select a rule or social skill appropriate for a class you might teach. Design a lesson to introduce the desired behavior. Make sure that students understand and practice it. Indicate how and when you will follow up to continue teaching the rule or skill.

_____

_____

_____

_____

_____

Section 2. Responding to Disruption and the Pattern Disruptive Student

DREIKURS'S CLASSIFICATION SYSTEM OF MISBEHAVIOR

In spite of your best efforts to prevent disruptive behaviors by developing effective classroom rules, routines, and lessons, students will misbehave. The students we are concerned with here are those who misbehave repeatedly and often, those we refer to as *pattern disrupters*. Before deciding how to respond to a pattern disrupter, you need to analyze why all students misbehave. One of the best-known theories of student misbehavior is that of Rudolf Dreikurs (Dreikurs, Grunwald, & Pepper, 1982). Dreikurs characterized children's misbehavior according to the goal being sought: *attention seeking, power seeking, revenge seeking*, and *sympathy seeking (inadequacy)*. The child may or may not be conscious of the reason for the misbehavior. However, it is clear that the goals reflect mistaken efforts to fulfill Maslow's Level 3 (Love/Belonging) needs or Level 4 (Self-Esteem) needs.

THE ATTENTION SEEKER

Attention Seeking

As social beings, students share a need to belong and to be accepted by others. Students who lack social skills or who have developed patterns of antisocial behavior still seek to be accepted by their peers. Thus such a student may rise frequently to sharpen a pencil or make unseemly sounds while students are doing seatwork. He or she may ask repeated questions or may blurt out answers during oral exercises—both legitimate answers and silly ones. In each case, the recognition from the class and the teacher reinforces the student in the belief that he or she is an acknowledged member of the group, albeit one who is recognized for the wrong reasons.

An attention seeker legitimately needs attention. However, the teacher should decide the time and the circumstances for giving that attention. Gather enough information to determine the frequency of the inappropriate behavior. When you judge that it occurs often enough to be considered a pattern disruption, decide how and when you will give attention. For example, students who like to talk may be assigned a specific topic, a specific time, and a captive audience. Help them prepare for a 3–5 minute presentation. Most attention seekers will learn that presenting is not as easy as it may appear to be. Those who learn to enjoy it may be granted a few minutes of planned presentation time or be given group leadership work until the need for attention is satisfied and their talking becomes less disruptive.

Power Seeking

Power seeking is a more desperate attempt on the part of the student to be recognized as an important member of the group. The student sees the teacher as a barrier to the goal of achieving power in the classroom. The student's aim is to undermine the legitimate authority

THE POWER SEEKER

of the teacher. When Joan calls you a name in front of the class, she hopes that her friends will admire her for her courage in taking on the teacher. Joan wants other students to conclude that she is free to do whatever she wishes in the classroom.

To confront a power-seeking student, you must decide that you are the legitimate authority in the classroom. Since you are the only professional, there is no need to enter a contest that pits you against a student. If you do, you will rarely come out of the fight a winner. Thus you may consciously decide not to fight. Prepare a series of alternatives to an open war of words. Consider ways to use humor to reduce the level of conflict, invite dialogue, give the student an escape route, or postpone immediate action. In any power confrontation, keep cool. When a student attempts to argue after a reprimand by saying, "I wasn't doing anything. You're always picking on me," don't argue the point, merely repeat the request to get to work or to listen ("Please get to work") each time the student attempts to argue. In this way the student is not allowed to pull the teacher into a power struggle. Some authorities suggest taking deep breaths and saying to yourself, "I'm in charge here" before saying anything to a power seeker. Your calmness and dignity let the class know that the problem is being handled with care and respect. Most students do not relish a fight with a teacher and when given an opportunity to avoid one, they will gladly take it.

Unlike other disrupters, most power seekers seem to be able to do the class work. Therefore, you should use this advantage to find ways to give them legitimate status and prominence. The classroom offers may status-enhancing opportunities for capable students—for instance, to be discussion leaders, run errands, interview important adults and report to class, direct role-playing activities, pass out classroom papers and materials, monitor other students during field trips, and so forth. Students who are granted such opportunities will usually work to preserve the teacher's authority. Although power seekers are typically better than average academically, sometimes less able students exhibit power-seeking characteristics. They should be handled in the same way as more able students.

Revenge Seeking

A struggle for power with the teacher may result in the student's losing face in the eyes of peers. In response, the student may turn to ridicule, taunts, and physical attacks on you and your property to hurt and humiliate the teacher. For example, a student may taunt you with the charge that "you can't even spell right" or ask, "Who sold you that ugly tie?" Personal attacks such as these can be expected. Prepare for them. Respond with humor ("Gee, you're right, my dad has bad taste!") and a willingness to work on the problem. Revenge seeking students expect you to get flustered and defensive. Shock them by not indulging this expectation!

The teacher needs to treat the revenge seeker with care. Instead of your first reaction, probably a sarcastic verbal retort, demonstrate instead that you understand and care. Such a response is more likely to prevent further attacks. It is better to step outside the traditional role of "teacher" and let the revenge-seeking student see you as a humane person. The more belligerent the student, the greater the understanding that is required from the teacher. Find out what things interest the student and initiate a conversation outside class. Positive attention reduces the urge for revenge.

Sympathy Seeking

Barbara spends most of her class time daydreaming. It makes no difference whether the activity is seatwork or direct instruction.

THE REVENGE SEEKER

Ivan's most common statements are "I can't do it" or "I don't understand" or "Will you show me how?"

Kezia is satisfied with a D in spelling. She boasts, "My daddy is a worse speller, but we have a house, two cars, and a boat."

Sympathy seeking students will indulge in one or all of the behaviors illustrated in these examples. They have given up hope that the teacher or their parents will help them. They have given up on themselves, too. They know that you, the teacher, cannot force them to do anything. However, unconsciously they depend on you to keep bugging them. When students whine or complain, there is a tendency to leave them alone. However, you must recognize their behavior as a display of passive resistance, defiance, and personal defeat. Sympathy-seeking students should be told in clear and precise terms what is expected of them. They must experience success at the initial levels of performance. Nothing is more powerful in changing their lowered self-concepts than success in reaching expectations.

In Chapter 8 you were introduced to a strategy for those who try to get you to do it for them called *praise, prompt*, and *leave* (Jones, 1979). The first step is to praise something the student has done on his or her own: "Good, Mary. You've gotten the problem copied." Asking "What's the problem?" only reinforces the student's sense of inadequacy. The next step is to prompt the student's attempt to solve the problem by giving a hint or providing direction: "OK, now look on page 68. It helps you with this part." Finally, the teacher leaves, saying,

"Try that on your own, and I'll be back to check in 5 minutes." Praising, prompting, and leaving, the teacher does not rescue Mary and thus does not reinforce her helplessness. Rather, she is praised for efforts made and "nudged" to try to solve it on her own—a lesson in self-sufficiency.

Table 9.1 displays Dreikurs's four classes of misbehavior, the beliefs that support each misbehavior, an example of a student behavior associated with each type, typical teacher response, and a constructive action guide. To analyze misbehaviors, you must (1) describe the pattern of student misbehavior, (2) classify the behavior into one of the four types, and (3) examine your own feelings and select your response.

Dinkmeyer, in his program *Systematic Training for Effective Teaching*, identified five insights about misbehavior that will, if followed, help make you a more effective manager (Dinkmeyer, McKay, and Dinkmeyer, 1980):

- Misbehavior stems from discouragement.
- Students are usually aware of the consequences of their behavior but unaware of the goals they wish to achieve.
- Students may change goals depending on the situation.
- Students may employ several misbehaviors to achieve the same goal or the same misbehavior to achieve different goals.
- Attention, power, and revenge can be pursued actively or passively in the classroom.

CHECK FOR UNDERSTANDING

Reread the set activity in Chapter 8, in which four teachers—Judy, Sandy, Marilyn, and Paul—discussed the misbehavior pattern exhibited by Kevann. Based on your knowledge of Dreikurs's classification system of misbehaviors, answer the following questions in the space provided:

1. What was the pattern of misbehaviors exhibited by Kevann?

   _____

   _____

   _____

2. Into which type of misbehavior does the pattern best fit?

   _____

   _____

   _____

3. How did the teacher's pattern of responses support your conclusion?

   _____

   _____

TABLE 9.1. Four Classes of Misbehavior

Student Behavior Pattern	Student Belief	Teacher Response	Behavior Type	Constructive Action Guide
Student stops the behavior on teacher command. But soon starts same behavior or another behavior of the same type. Teacher must observe pattern.	Feels that acting out will draw attention of peers or teacher. "I belong only when people are noticing me."	Teacher feels annoyed and frustrated. Wants to coax, guide, and react to student's behavior.	Attention Seeking	1. Resist temptation to coax, guide, or overtly react. 2. Code behaviors to ascertain basic pattern. 3. Formalize process to give attention on your own terms. 4. Reinforce positive behaviors. 5. Give noncontingent reinforcement (see Chapter 8).
Student continues the behavior that the teacher says should stop. May increase intensity of behavior. Seems to ignore teacher although is well aware of command intent.	"I am important and a part of a group only when I control, or when I am proving how strong I can be by standing up to authority."	Teacher feels angry, challenged, provoked, and needs to show who is in charge. Thinks, "I'll show who is boss in this class."	Power Seeking	1. Withdraw from the conflict interaction. 2. Provide students with some control. 3. Teach students how to work for and use power constructively. 4. Use students in meaningful ways in the process of instruction.
Student seeks to hurt teacher or other students physically or verbally. Calls unkind names, tries to ridicule, shows malice, etc.	"I am worthwhile only when I let others feel fearful of me. I do not expect anyone to like me, so I will not be kind to anyone."	Teacher feels hurt and defensive. Desires to retaliate for self or on behalf of others.	Revenge Seeking	1. Do not visibly show hurt. 2. Demonstrate that you care. 3. Be warm and trusting.
Student does not attempt to do work. Always asks for help. Often complains of lack of understanding, although teacher knows student can do the work.	"People will accept me only when they are convinced that I am helpless and unable to do things on my own. My position in the group is enhanced when somebody gets a chance to help me."	Teacher feels despair, discouragement, and helplessness. Will say, "I do not know what else to do with (student)."	Sympathy Seeking (Display of inadequacy)	1. Reinforce your expectation of an assignment at the correct level of difficulty. 2. Do not pity, sympathize with, or criticize. 3. Encourage all positive efforts. 4. Do not be mean but be firm about your expectations.

313

4. Suggest some constructive actions that Paul might have implemented.

_____

_____

_____

If you concluded that Kevann was attention seeking, you are correct. Why attention seeking? First, look at his misbehavior pattern. He initiates a behavior, stops when the teacher commands him to do so, but repeats the behavior or a similar behavior minutes later. Next, what is the teacher's response pattern? Fran feels annoyed and says, "I am at the end of my wits" . . . "so disturbing" . . . "so frustrating." Kevann's behavior has annoyed her beyond composure. The behaviors of both the student and the teacher suggest that the child is seeking attention. Kevann appears to believe that he belongs to the class only when he draws everyone's attention to himself. He is not conscious of the annoyance of his peers at his repeated disruptions. He thinks that no one will remember he is there unless he takes some unusual steps to remind them.

As you decide on constructive actions to change his behavior, you should be certain, first, to document and analyze the pattern of behavior the attention-seeking child exhibits. Second, the actions you select should *not* include coaxing, which only reinforces attention seeking. Third, your selected action should ensure that Kevann receives some legitimate attention. For example, as indicated in Table 9.1, you may use *noncontingent reinforcement*. As you recall from Chapter 8, noncontingent reinforcement is physical or nonverbal attention or other reward given even though the student has not done anything in particular to earn it. It may be a pat on the back, a smile, or a piece of candy. Equally important is *positive reinforcement*—an action the teacher takes immediately after the student has behaved appropriately. *"Catch the attention seeker being good"* whenever possible. In this case, you would give Kevann legitimate attention when he is not deliberately seeking it. (Positive reinforcement and "catch 'em being good" are discussed in Chapter 8.)

Guided Practice Activity C. Analyzing Misbehavior Patterns

To assess your understanding and analysis of the characteristics of Dreikurs's misbehavior classification system, read the following cases and

1. determine the category of misbehavior present in each case
2. Write a response consistent with the recommendations for effective actions on a separate sheet to be shared with colleagues.
3. critique your responses with a peer or with a group
4. be aware of the need to recommend practical actions.

Case 1

Miss Gardner felt that Maxine was the most passive and whining child she has ever had in class. Maxine's mottos were, "I can't do it" "I don't know how," and "Please show me." The school year was 5 weeks old when Miss Gardner walked into the staff room with her hands in the air and in a voice expressing exasperation announced, "I give up." After a moment she addressed a fellow teacher, "Molly, you had Maxine in class last year. How did she do?" Molly replied, "I suspect the same as she does for you. We did not seem to do well together. I wish you good luck."

Assume that Maxine is in your class. Analyze her behavior and plan a course of action.

Case 2

Brian was on top of a desk when Ms. Pettigrew entered the classroom. As he jumped from one desk to the other, she said to him, "Brian, you are not supposed to be on the desk." The rest of the conversation went like this:

BRIAN: I know.
MS. PETTIGREW: Well come down, now.
BRIAN: I don't want to.
MS. PETTIGREW: But you know it's against the rules for you to damage the desk's surface.
BRIAN: I'm just showing them something.
MS. PETTIGREW: Get down, I said.
BRIAN: I'll get down pretty soon.
MS. PETTIGREW: Listen, young man . . .
The dialogue continued for 2–3 minutes while the rest of the class looked on.

If you classified the misbehaviors in Case 1 as sympathy seeking, you were correct. The student's helplessness and the teacher's surrendering behaviors are evidence of a sympathy seeking child.
Case 2 illustrates a power-seeking incident because the student continues his inappropriate behavior as he argues with the teacher.

You should not assume that your days in the classroom will be taken up analyzing student misbehavior patterns. For the most part, you will worry only about the few disruptive students who exhibit frequent and recurring nonproductive behaviors. Distinguishing between incidental disruption and patterns of disruption is important before you select instructional and behavior change strategies. After several class meetings it is usually possible to predict who these pattern disruptive students are. Finally, while there is no magic formula or precise recipe for managing discipline effectively, the approaches presented here can make a significant difference when consistently applied.

ESTABLISHING AN INFORMATION SYSTEM

The second component of a rational discipline system, after you have determined which student behavior is pattern disruptive, is to have an accurate *information system*. The purpose of such a system is to record the nature and incidence of disruptive behavior so that an appropriate response can be made. The system permits the teacher to plot patterns of disruption on a behavior log; the information includes student's name, description of behavior, place, date and time, and teacher responses. Table 9.2 is an example of a teacher's behavior log.

With the availability of menu-driven computer spreadsheets, the recordkeeping, analysis, and retrieval of information can be greatly facilitated if stored on a computer disc. The information in the behavior log helps the teacher detect patterns of student behavior. The identification of these patterns is essential for the teacher to (1) respond appropriately to a pattern disruptive student and (2) communicate the pattern to the student, parents, and

TABLE 9.2. A Teacher's Behavior Log

Student's Name	Student's Behavior	Location	Date and Time	Teacher Response
John Rumfelton	1. Moves out of seat and wanders around room while seatwork is in progress	In math class, 2nd period	5/4 9:30 am	Warns John that if the unacceptable behavior continues, he would be consequenced
	2. Calls two students names of which they disapprove	Math period in class	5/10 9:10 am	Points to logical consequences in rules-teaching week and administers consequences—miss recess
	3. Gets up four times within 30 minutes to sharpen his pencil	In class right after math class	5/20 10:15 am	Administers logical consequences— detention after school.
	4. Calls Sarah a "rag doll who has no brains"	In class during math	5/30 9:35 am	Administers logical consequences— miss recess
	5. Calls the principal a "bag of wind with no direction"	On the playground during recess	5/30 10:30 am	Administers logical consequences— miss recess

Note: This sample of a teacher's log was developed by teachers in an elementary school.

316

administrators. In any case, the RAPSD teacher acts in a consistent manner in administering consequences because decisions are based on informed judgment. The RAPSD teacher makes decisions based on observable patterns of student behaviors.

When a student has been identified as a pattern disrupter, the RAPSD teacher may decide to place the student in a *positive moments* program for a defined period of time. In this strategy, which is discussed in detail below, the teacher blends ideas and practices from the humanistic and the behavior management traditions. Together with an emphasis on individual student differences and an understanding of the social context, the combination of approaches produces what we have described as the *rational tradition* of classroom discipline.

THE USE OF POSITIVE MOMENTS

The time the teacher devotes to a student or a small group of students is related to the students' motivation for academic excellence and constructive social behaviors. A *positive moments* strategy is built on an appreciation of the importance of teacher time spent with two groups—"pattern disrupters" and "cooperatives." The former term refers to students who indulge in social behaviors that are inappropriate in the school environment. The latter refers to students whose behaviors are desirable and, thus, promoted in schools.

The positive moments approach is translated into a set of techniques that classroom teachers use to encourage acceptable behaviors. As you review the techniques, consider how the teacher–student interaction affects both the pattern disrupters and the cooperatives. As a result of the interaction, will the pattern disrupter feel that the teacher knows me, listens to me, helps me, and protects me?

The techniques are organized into logical groupings—those relating to *equity, feedback, rule enforcement, courtesy/caring*. As we examine these techniques, you will be provided with measuring skills and tools that you can use to evaluate yourself on each of the techniques.

Equity

Apportioning Fair Time.   The equitable apportionment of positive time to all students is known as *fair time*. Comments of agreement or encouragement, and expressions of praise and appreciation are examples of *positive time*. Critical comments, commands to desist in disrupting the class, requests for justification, or discussions of tasks that do not result in productive learning are examples of *negative time*. Repeated classroom observations have documented that teachers spend more positive time with cooperatives and more negative time with pattern disrupters. Even when more total time is spent with the disrupters, the major portion of the time is negative.

To alter this relationship, teachers should spend at least *15 seconds of positive time each hour* with the disruptive student. Use those 15 seconds to comment on something good about the student. Things you might mention include behavior change, attendance improvement, pleasant smile, family, favorite sport, favorite subject, and favorite pastime. Fifteen seconds can work miracles in changing student attitudes toward knowledge and constructive social behavior. In about 3 weeks, the teacher is likely to observe an increase in fair time, as more positive time is added to the equation and there is less need for negative time with the student.

Teacher Proximity.   The results of many studies indicate that, in a typical classroom, there are differential attention patterns. In each case, the students nearest the teacher receive more attention than do students in the rear of the classroom or the farthest from the teacher. Students who work at tables get more positive attention if they are in the group of cooperatives. Teachers should consciously spend more time in the proximity of disruptive students. Thus the teacher should review the class seating chart to see where pattern disrupters are seated and adjust seating patterns to focus more positive time on these students.

Distributing Classroom Questions.   As you recall from Chapter 6, Bloom developed a taxonomy of cognitive behavior that included six categories, from *Knowledge* through *Evaluation*. We used the taxonomy to classify classroom questions. In the taxonomy's most basic form, we can divide such questions into two categories: (1) questions that ask only for the recall of information (*knowledge* and *comprehension*) and (2) questions that ask students to use the information (*application* through *evaluation*).

Just as some teachers distribute questions unequitably among cultural groups (see Chapter 7), questions put to pattern disrupters show systematic bias that denies them the opportunity to extend their minds to the thinking level. Teachers have many reasons why they ask the kind of questions they do to different students, but when students become aware that discrimination exists, they will resent it. Feelings of revenge will start to develop. To prevent this discrimination, teachers should

- Ask for opinions from all students
- Ask questions that require students to identify relationships among concepts and generalizations and to organize information
- Use inquiry lessons that have no right answers, to help all students think through puzzling phenomena
- Create a system that ensures a random order of questioning, to eliminate systematic bias and increase classroom attention

The teacher's goal is to distribute low level and high level and convergent and divergent questions equally between pattern disrupters and cooperatives as well as between males and females, high achievers and low achievers and among children from all cultural groups. The reasoning is that all students will then have less time to be disruptive.

Rephrasing/Cuing   When a teacher rephrases a question to make it more accessible to a student or cues a student to assist in the search for an appropriate response, the results are usually positive. Teachers have reported that rephrasing and cuing are made available to a greater degree to cooperatives than to pattern disrupters. Teachers do less probing for the correct answer when questioning pattern disrupters. Whether the teacher fears embarrassing the student or believes that he or she may have failed to teach the material thoroughly, the result is that those who need help the most get help the least.

Feedback

Giving Feedback.   Feedback can be positive or negative, constructive or destructive. Positive feedback may not always be constructive. In the example "Right, Keith, you are always correct," the positive feedback creates an unrealistic pressure on Keith and puts him above other students, who by implication are not always correct. Conversely, negative feedback may not always be destructive, as in "Lara, it is better for all of us if you wait your turn." In this example, the negative feedback is a signal of disapproval; however, the feedback contains constructive advice.

Each student, including the pattern disrupter, should expect and get as much positive validation and correction as other students. In an ideal classroom environment, the teacher promptly affirms and corrects the behavior of each and every student.

Sensitivity to the Ripple Effect.   A response to one student is a response to all students. Kounin, in observations of K–12 and college classrooms, discovered that teacher responses to a single student were perceived by all students as if the teacher were talking to them (Kounin, 1970). When the response was negative, it had a more extended and deeper ripple effect than a positive response. Pattern disruptive students are particularly sensitive to the way teachers speak to others. They consistently compare the teacher's response to others with the way the teacher speaks to them, and they feel resentment when they see themselves as victims of the differences in the two treatments. This may lead to revenge seeking behavior, as described previously.

Giving Praise.   The teacher must find a reason to praise each student, each day. Remembering that praise must be given judiciously, we understand why one clearly recognizable praise statement for each student each day is sufficient. The total amounts to about 7½ minutes out of each day for a class of 30 (15 seconds of praise for each student). Brophy has shown that not enough praise is given to the pattern disrupter who responds with a right or helpful answer (Brophy, 1981). Teachers should be sure that every student receives positive recognition. Bear in mind that students get too much unwarranted praise and too little genuine recognition when they deserve it (Sadker & Sadker, 1985). Consider delaying your praise until you can give it genuinely:

- Praise should express appreciation for achievement, effort, determination.
- Praise must excite. Give it energy!
- Praise must be specific to the event.
- Private praise may be as effective and for some students, more effective than public praise.

CHECK FOR UNDERSTANDING

Think of examples of any positive moments *equity* and *feedback* techniques that have been used in any classroom you have seen. Describe the examples below.

_____

_____

_____

_____

_____

Rule Enforcement

Being Consistent.   The teacher's consistent behavior in enforcing the classroom rules conveys a message of fairness. Regardless of whether the disruption is a minor or major one, the teacher must respond to it in a consistent manner:

- Similar disruptions call for similar consequences.
- Teachers must use care to enforce all rules for every student.
- Establishing too many rules will reduce consistency.

Observing.   A teacher must be observant. Recall the concept of *with-it-ness*, created by Kounin and discussed in Chapter 8 (Kounin, 1970). A pattern disrupter who perceives that the teacher is observing him or her at all times is likely to engage in appropriate behavior. The message is that teachers must remain alert to classroom behaviors, rhythms, and relationships. A behavior that the teacher may find irritating but that does not affect the learning environment should not be made into an overt issue. Instead, teaching energy is best concentrated on pattern disruptions and clearly unacceptable behaviors in an effort to change them. Teachers should

- observe and respond to patterns of behavior—both negative and positive
- demonstrate that he or she also observes effort

Employing Desists Appropriately.   A *desist* is a command that identifies the disrupter and the behavior that is causing the disruption and commands him or her to stop. Since there are no ideal classrooms, desists will be needed. What is crucial is that they be accurately and equitably used.

Courtesy/Caring

Modeling Courtesy.   Visitors from other countries and many U.S. citizens have accused our nation of lacking civility. As we examine the public treatment of the aged, the weak, and the poor, it is not surprising that our schools mirror the lack of hospitality and civility. Teachers should consider ways that respect can be enhanced in such relationships as parent/child, teacher/student, student/student. Teachers must model that respect, especially when conversing with a disruptive student:

- Teachers should use courteous words when speaking to the pattern disrupter
- Nonverbal expression (posture and facial expressions) should show sincerity and an absence of anger.
- Verbal and nonverbal expression should be complementary. On occasion, because of cultural differences, some nonverbal behaviors may be confusing to some students. However, if there is congruence with the spoken words, the true intent will come through.

Exploring Personal Interests.   Students have to be convinced that you are interested in them as individuals. Whatever process you use to help pattern disrupters talk about their lives outside the classroom will be invaluable in promoting their cooperation in school. We all feel respected and worthwhile when other people listen to us and respond to what we say. The personal nature of sharing gives students a sense of importance and belonging, and it permits you to respond as a human being rather than in your role as teacher:

- Find out what you can about student hobbies and relate them in class at appropriate times.
- Ask students to share their experiences.
- Give writing assignments that require the integration of personal experiences and show interest in the revelations from pattern disrupters.

Listening.   Students who listen learn. Teachers who listen also learn. The art of listening may be one of the teacher's most important assets. Listening is essential for justice, for appropriate response, for gaining time, and for thinking in the classroom. As students talk, the teacher should be sensitive both to what they are *saying* and to what their words indicate about their *feelings*.

For example, Joseph is yelling and speaking abusively to another student. Let him finish. Extract the essentials from what he said. Respond to those essentials in a constructive manner. If your response is disapproval, take time to make him aware that your disapproval is of his behavior and not of him as a person. It is important that you listen not only to what is said, but also demonstrate an understanding that the student is hurting.

To listen completely, teachers should remember the following:

- Listen for feelings as well as for facts.
- Recognize all on-task contributions.
- If you must interrupt a student who is speaking, acknowledge the interruption.

Touching.   Babies in a crib move toward a corner, a doll, a blanket—any object with which they can feel contact. The desire to be physically close to another human being is instinctive in children and in adults. As a teacher, look for the appropriate opportunity to touch a student and when it comes, take advantage of it.

Touch can be a useful management technique in the classroom. A firm, friendly touch can dissuade a student from engaging in disruptive behavior. The teacher must, however, be careful when touching a student to make it a brief encounter and be confident that the student will not see the gesture as a threat. Tapping the student on the shoulder or upper arm may be sufficient to gain attention. In case of a violent incident, the firm touch should have immediate and commanding effect.

Some school districts expressly forbid the touching of students. The teacher should know district policies on such matters and adhere to them. Because touching for some students may help focus their attention but, for others, may be a bewildering or frightening experience, it is essential that both the nature of the situation and the student's likely response guide the teacher's decision.

Students from Southeast Asia, Hispanics, or African Americans may have a different response to being touched than other Americans. You should explore the differing cultural reactions with your class. Do not show shock or disdain if you are touched by a student. Evaluate the intent of the touch. Demonstration of disapproval to a kindly, innocent touch may permanently distance some students and cause them to distrust you.

Be aware that the pattern disrupter is less likely to be touched by adults, in school and at home. You should not touch a student in the midst of an argument or if the student is angry at you. If the student's anger or disruption is directed at someone or something else, approach from the front and try to accompany the touch with eye contact or words that inform the student that it is the teacher who is touching.

Following are two examples of how touch may be effectively used as a classroom management technique:

David was reading a comic book during Ms. Sand's class. Ms. Sand had assigned an exercise. David continued to read the comic book. She calmly approached his desk, touched his hand, and then, while facing him, placed her hands on his desk and pointed to the exercise that had been set. She looked him in the eyes for the count of 3 and left.

Cindi and Mike are talking "about life" as Mr. Francis gives a dictation. As he continues to dictate, he moves to the desk closest to Cindi's and grasps her shoulder gently but firmly. As she looks at him, he makes eye contact with the second student and points to their books. He leaves as quietly as he came. His touching was timed to coincide with the end of a sentence. They will begin to write on the next sentence.

Remember:

- Teachers should touch.
- A touch may be a pat on the shoulder or a gentle nudge.

Accepting Feelings.   Dealing with feelings is one of the most mysterious areas of human behavior. Goodlad's research reported in *A Place Called School* suggests that classroom tasks are accomplished in a bland environment "with little emotion, from interpersonal warmth to hostility" (Goodlad, 1983, p. 230). To help overcome the sense of emotional sterility, teachers should be alert to ways of generating feelings in students. Teachers who are able to do this mobilize positive feelings among students and possess the skill to control negative feelings. Our general belief, based on years of teaching experience, is that students, especially pattern disrupters, learn more in classrooms in which teachers are apt to accept, encourage, and validate student feelings.

Guided Practice Activity D. Selecting Positive Moments Techniques

   1. Summarize each of the four categories of *positive moments*. Give an example of each in your own words.

_____

_____

_____

_____

   2. Select five techniques for implementing a positive moments strategy that you could use in your next teaching assignment. Briefly explain how you would use the techniques.

_____

_____

_____

_____

IMPLEMENTING POSITIVE MOMENTS: A SUMMARY

The following list summarizes the key suggestions involved in the implementation of a *positive moments* approach in your classroom.

Preparation
1. Select two students with disruptive behavior patterns.
2. Establish a baseline frequency (how many times the misbehavior occurred) for 2 weeks before implementing your positive moments approach with the two students.

Implementation
1. Every classroom hour, include 15 seconds of positive time with each student.
2. Touch each student three times each week.
3. Administer consequences when one of the students breaks a rule.
4. Praise each student at least once a week.
5. Give feedback about inappropriate behavior. Clearly articulate that the behavior is unacceptable and explain why it is unacceptable. Reinforce acceptable behavior.
6. Stand close to the students in a friendly way at least twice each week.
7. Use *Quality Circle* meetings to explore alternatives to disruptive behavior (see below).
8. Place the two students in a visible location at all times.
9. Plan and implement a strategy that will encourage the students to tell you something about themselves.
10. At the end of each week inform the two students that you have been pleased with their improved behavior and/or mention three or four specific good things they have done.
11. Call or write to the parents of the two students and tell them something good about each child.
12. Give each child a responsible task each day for the first week and one each week thereafter.

If the First Approach Fails
1. If you do not observe a 30 percent reduction in disruption in 3 weeks, move to the establishment of a contract with the student and shake hands on it.
2. Ask the student, "What rules have you been breaking?" "What have you been doing that breaks these rules?"
3. Ask, "What are your plans for stopping what you have been doing?" (Work toward a goal. Help the student be realistic.)
4. Ask, "How do you plan to reach the goal?" (Work to develop a plan.)
5. Ask, "How long will it take before I see a change?" (Work toward a specific and realistic time period; the shorter the time interval, the better.)
6. Ask, "How can I help you achieve the goal?" (You may even suggest a way to help.)
7. At the end of the agreed-upon period, assess, praise, and/or guide to another contract; reduce or lengthen the time period as necessary. (The goal is to get one week of nondisruptive behaviors. Be realistic, as this may not happen until the third or fourth week.)

ORGANIZING AND CONDUCTING QUALITY CIRCLE MEETINGS

A common activity in a RAPSD classroom is the use of meetings called *Quality Circles*. Based on Glasser's *classroom meetings* (see Chapter 8), Quality Circles are used to reinforce personal and group responsibilities, to process the causes of and the alternatives to misbehavior, to recommend changes in past behavior, and to discuss community issues that affect school life. In a Quality Circle the group helps the disruptive student to acknowledge the behavior and to plan ways of reducing the severity and incidence of the behavior. A Quality Circle is an example of a social lesson, as discussed in Chapter 5.

Public disclosure is excluded during a Quality Circle. That is, the student whose behavior is being discussed is not publicly identified with the disruption. Rather, each student discusses what he or she would do if faced with the situation that led to the disruptive behavior. The disruptive child listens to the discussion of the problem, without being referred to in person, and privately or publicly decides what changes will be made. In this approach, the problem, not the person, is the focus.

The seating arrangement should be a closed circle, with the teacher seated as a group member. Although misbehavior should always be discussed in the third person, the issues and concerns can be discussed either in the first person or the third person, depending on individual choice. No names should be used except when giving positive reinforcement. The teacher's role is to be a facilitator. Students should be allowed freedom to initiate issues that they believe are affecting class behavior and performance. In closing a Quality Circle session, everyone is encouraged to summarize what occurred, but no one is required to speak.

When a case of disruptive behavior is being discussed, the teacher will usually close by asking, "What should be done if circumstances create a similar situation that caused the disruption?" This strategy embedded in a Quality Circle is called *decision therapy* (DT). The focus of DT is to have pattern disrupters make decisions about what they will do in the future. The DT rationale is that each time a pattern disrupter hears or states a positive, constructive action, it reinforces the chances that the appropriate behavior will be selected on future occasions.

RESPONDING TO EMERGENCIES

The RAPSD model also recommends that the teacher develop a set of predetermined procedures in the event of a classroom emergency. For example, what will you do if two students begin a fight in the classroom or on the playground? If a student brings in a toy gun or knife, what action will you take? If a student uses expletives or physical or racial slurs to describe you or another student, what will be your response? What will the administration do in any of these emergency cases? Since emergencies are handled in different ways in different schools, you must be prepared for them. Four factors you should consider when developing an emergency procedure are

1. *Personal Behavior*
   - Be firm and consistent.
   - Developing a disciplined life is not a dramatic event; it's putting a series of correct social habits together progressively.
   - Focus your actions on improving your relationship with the disruptive student(s).

2. *Incentives*
   - Use an incentive system as a first step to prevent emergencies, but incentives should be soon phased out. Students should be taught to find value in a disciplined environment rather than to behave to secure token rewards.
3. *Standards*
   - Teach students what is the socially acceptable behavior in your classroom.
   - Be sure that students know what behaviors are unacceptable in your classroom.
   - Don't permit students to escape the acceptance of responsibility and the consequences of their actions.
4. *Analysis*
   - The rational approach emphasizes low rather than high control management.
   - Keep Dreikurs's four types of misbehavior in mind as you analyze what the disruptive student did to create the emergency.

What specifically should I do if a fight breaks out in my classroom or near me on school property? Even when you are at your best, a fight places you in a tense, irrational, and potentially dangerous situation. Expect to make mistakes in judging who started the fight and what proportion of the responsibility each combatant should be assigned. Be cautious in judging and avoid, if you can, the role of fight arbitrator. To help you prevent mistakes, we shall recommend two things you can do when facing a student fight.

First, when encountering a fight, decide whether it is an individual or a group fight. In individual fights there are only two combatants. Other students may be encouraging the fight, but each of the two combatants represents social, racial, ethnic, or other subgroup in the class merely by chance. When you investigate, the noncombatants are willing to assign blame to each of the combatants.

In the case of an individual fight, send the two fighters to a different corner of the room or to different locations in the playground. Reconstruct the incident as accurately as you are able. If possible, have each combatant write out what happened. Bring the students together and inform them that there is only one story you wish to hear and that it is the correct sequence of events. Let them tell their version to each other without interruptions. After the facts have surfaced, expose and explore feelings, before, during, and after the fight. In most cases, the students will agree on what occurred, thus avoiding the necessity for you to be the judge. Try to avoid identifying a "winner" and a "loser." Even if there is an admission of guilt, let the "guilty party" leave feeling a winner because you recognized the honest and cooperative behavior.

A group fight can be inferred if (1) three or more students are involved, (2) social, racial, religious, ethnic, or other identifying group epithets are heard, (3) there have been rumors about conflicts between groups, (4) there has been a previous history of group divisiveness, and (5) the atmosphere becomes a tomb of silence as soon as you attempt to investigate what caused the fight. In the case of a group fight, divide the class into the respective groups and let each group list all the things the other group has done to cause harm. Let each group review the other's lists and correct inaccurate perceptions. Facilitate an open dialogue to restore a community atmosphere and positive attitudes. Have students discuss what should happen if the situation becomes ripe for a repeat fight.

Second, and most important, students should be taught that a fight is the responsibility of both parties. The only excuse for fighting is for the protection of life and limb. A student who is attacked should feel safe in reporting the incident to the teacher and expecting that something appropriate will be done about it.

Guided Practice Activity E. Planning for an Emergency

Create a plan of action to use if you found three students fighting in the hall. Use the ideas presented in this section.

_____

_____

_____

_____

_____

Section 3. Additional Management Techniques

The techniques that follow are used by effective managers to maintain order in the classroom. The rational management approach recommends and makes use of all of them. Consider which ones are most consistent with your discipline philosophy and give you the most confidence as a classroom manager.

NONVERBAL CLASSROOM MANAGEMENT TECHNIQUES

The teacher continuously communicates in every classroom through verbal and nonverbal messages. These messages, conscious or unconscious, purposeful or inadvertent, prevent, help, control, or encourage discipline problems. The following represents a sample of the nonverbal management techniques organized within each of the major sources of nonverbal messages.

Teacher Attire

There are significant data from the business world, from observers of fashions, and from the social science literature to substantiate the effect of dress on people's behavior. Thus it is not surprising that the way the teacher dresses affects the responses of his or her students and helps set the tone for classroom control.

As a teacher, your dress communicates your attitude toward order, neatness, and appropriateness of behavior for different settings. It conveys a message about your feelings toward societal standards. The community in which you teach has determined acceptable dress standards for teachers. Do not be enslaved by these standards but do respect them. The teacher's attire, therefore, should be professionally appropriate for each occasion: gym, science class, picnic, and so on. If the teacher's choice of dress is of the stiff collar and tie fashion, the hidden message may be one of an exacting and uptight individual—a headmaster/headmistress with little room for understanding. Sloppy clothes, on the other hand, may indicate sloppy attitudes toward students, academics, or order in general.

If colors are always dark and drab, the teacher may seem unexciting, and the classroom atmosphere will reflect this feeling. The use of flashy jewelry can invite ridicule and disrespect, depending upon the individual teacher. The same holds true for overuse of colognes and perfumes. Dress as the professional person you are. Be conscious of the image you desire to project. Modesty should be the goal of the rational manager.

Eye Contact

Eye contact may be the most potent nonverbal management technique available to the teacher. Teachers who develop the skill of doing periodic sweeping surveys of their room usually control marginal problems by that means alone. An eye survey may be slow and deliberate with no specific student as a target, or it may be swift and certain in order to jog memories that the teacher is still there and in charge.

Eye contact with an individual says something different from what eye contact with a group says. The situation and severity of the behavioral problem will dictate the method of eye contact that the teacher uses. Look at the individual or visually roam around the group so it is obvious who the target is. Expressions of approval and disapproval may be communicated in brief flashes of eye contact. A look must always be purposeful, certain, and timed—not so quick that the student loses the impact, and not so slow that the student believes the teacher is deliberately trying to cause embarrassment. Practice using your eyes as a discipline technique; they will serve you well.

Facial Expressions

Intentional or unintentional facial expressions make a difference in the way students respond to the teacher's management. Teachers should use facial expressions appropriately to show impatience, or warmth, concern, and patience, in an effort to prevent discipline problems or to maintain an air befitting the classroom situation. Facial expressions can indicate concern or anger, in order to give students the opportunity to change their behavior before the teacher must resort to verbal cues (spoken anger, for instance). Anger may be demonstrated by slanting the brows inward and downward, close to the eyes, with the lips firm.

The knitted brow can express concern rather than anger. The forever stern look (taut cheek, downtrend of the corners of the mouth) can mean there is no room for tolerance. Be careful not to show mocking smirks. Students are quick to pick these up, unless they are intended in good humor and the students clearly understand that.

Smiles can be a powerful means for showing approval and be much more personal than verbal cues, particularly in some cultures. In short, it can be both a help and a timesaver to use nonverbal rather than verbal cues and make requests with a smile.

Movement in the Classroom

A teacher must be at ease in the physical setting of the classroom. Teachers should move in a manner that is purposeful, deliberate, and self-confident. Too often, teachers' movements are unrehearsed, haphazard, thoughtless. Such movements can have disruptive effects on the classroom environment.

Control of movement as a form of nonverbal communication is an important aspect of the disciplinary encounter. Fast attack-like motions in response to minor offenses can result in much more severe behavior if a student becomes defensive. A teacher has to make a quick appraisal of the problem and decide on its potential to erupt into something more serious. This decision will dictate the urgency with which the teacher moves and the subtlety or the obtrusiveness of the movements.

Most classroom situations are not emergencies. Thus teachers should not overreact to the particular circumstances or students. Finally, don't turn away from the class for a long time, as this may indicate lack of communication and invite talking or other behavior that is irrelevant to the lesson.

Using One's Hands

The appropriate use of the teacher's hands is a highly effective management technique. Hand messages can be as precise as verbal messages. Hands can point out a particular student, draw attention, signal silence, and so on. For example, after Mr. Roshaw established eye contact with the three girls in the back row, his hand pointed at Cindy and his index finger signaled a "no," to cue her to stop stuffing paper down Todd's shirt. The gesture communicated to Cindy the teacher's disapproval of a potentially disruptive behavior without interrupting the class. Cindy quickly stopped, to avoid drawing negative attention to herself.

Finally, do not be tempted to use hands to maintain control in a threatening fashion, as the hands may elicit a physical reaction.

The Power of Posture

The teacher's posture affects classroom management as much as—sometimes more than—the posture of students. Standing tall (straight posture) during the execution of a discipline procedure may suggest command or superiority. On the other hand, slouched shoulders may indicate defeat and hopelessness and lead to challenge by some students or fear by those who feel that the teacher is not in control.

The examples that follow illustrate some effects that posture may have on management success:

> Leaning over them from the waist to supervise students' work or social behavior is more threatening than stooping.

> Moderately slow, deliberate steps, with upright frame, indicate that the teacher is in command.

If your authority is challenged by a student exhibiting a defiant posture, do not back down. Move close enough, after you have given a reasonable direction, so that you are about two long steps away. Look directly at the student. Repeat your command slowly and maintain a comfortable stance. Wait. Maintain eye contact. If and when the student breaks eye contact, acknowledge the response and return to the lesson.

CHECK FOR UNDERSTANDING

Assess yourself on each of the six nonverbal techniques. Which one(s) will you need to work to improve?

	OK	Needs Work	Not Sure
Attire			
Eye contact			
Facial expression			
Movement			
Using your hands			
Posture			

VERBAL CUES IN MANAGEMENT TECHNIQUES

As nonverbal techniques may be called the "silent treatment," verbal cues may be thought of as the "audible treatment." Verbal cues may consist of complete sentences, phrases, exclamations, grunts, laughter, and so forth. The sensitivity of the teacher toward the student and toward the situation will dictate what verbal response is selected. Verbal cues stand as good a chance of being misinterpreted as nonverbal cues. Quite unconsciously, a teacher may use a word that is loaded—culturally, sexually, or racially. Care in the choice of verbal cues is especially crucial at the beginning of the term, because the students and the teacher do not know each other.

When properly used, verbal expressions can open doors of communication. What a teacher says, how it is said, when it is said, and to whom it is said are all significant elements in a verbal management technique.

Voice Is the Crucial Element

The teacher's ability to manipulate the voice is an essential skill in controlling a classroom. Through tone and volume, voice communicates meaning during an interaction, particularly in a stressful, disciplinary situation. The tone and volume of the voice can create, increase, or lessen stress.

Teachers must enunciate clearly. When commands are given, they should be brief and specific. "John, please be quiet." Sharp, short phrases may be sufficient for reprimands or for attracting students' attention. You may calmly say to students who are talking: "Trevor. Marge." The voice should reflect calm and assurance. Pause long enough for them to regain composure and proceed with the lesson.

Speak distinctly, in a pleasant, friendly voice. Students will listen more attentively and be more likely to ask questions spontaneously if the sound effects are pleasant and harmonious. Tape recording a few lessons and playing the tapes can reveal to the teacher poor speech habits, such as lack of tone variation or too many "uh's," that detract from the presentation and interaction.

The teacher who yells is likely to find that students will yell back. If the teacher yells, "John! Be quiet!" the student is likely to shout back, "I'm not talking!" or "OK!" or "I'm not making any noise!" or "What for?" In such a situation, no matter what is said, the result may be anger, threat, defensiveness, or a contest for power. The teacher's tone often sets the tone for the student's response.

Feelings, such as disapproval, annoyance, and anger, should be carefully expressed with appropriate voice tone and volume. Know your students. Some are very sensitive, while nothing seems to bother others. Some students are just beginning to experiment with the expressions of their own feelings. Others have had disapproval expressed to them in a destructive manner all their lives. Teachers must learn to recognize these feelings in students' voices and modulate their own voices accordingly.

Content and Control

The content of verbal communication can become the essence of a teacher's management technique. The message should not be focused on personal approval but on *task* accomplishment. Instead of saying, "I don't like it when you keep rapping on the desk," the teacher might say, "We will never finish learning how to do fractions if the noise continues" or "It is more difficult for us to understand fractions with the continuous rapping." A statement like the first example can be used, but it depends on the relationship of teacher and students for its effect. The latter two examples are task-oriented, and students respond more appropriately to such messages.

Verbal commands such as "Hey, stop that!" have minimal effect in controlling a situation. To maximize the effect of a command, the teacher should be sure that it helps the student involved and the other students who are aware of the situation. Give a clear message: "Mike, stop playing with that car, and start writing your essay." When teachers increase the clarity of verbal desist messages, students are less likely to become disruptive.

Threats are bad management techniques. For example, some teachers often say things such as, "If you do that again, I'll deal with you," or "If you don't stop, you will see what happens." The use of threats will not lessen the chance that the disruption will be repeated. In fact, it may encourage such behavior.

The credible use of a "threat" should be more appropriately called a "warning." For example, you might say: "John, this is the third time you have shouted without reason in this class. When you choose to do that again, you will miss your free time." Leave it right there. Do not wait for a response. Continue the academic task at hand.

The teacher's message should be delivered with firmness. You are more likely to achieve control if you use a businesslike tone of voice, walk closer to the disrupter, and/or continue to look at him or her as you go on with the lesson. These actions, when judiciously undertaken, convey to the students the professional quality of your teaching. "I wish you people would pay attention" is what the teacher who expects to lose control would say. Your message should have *power*. "You have to master letter-writing skills in order to enhance your job-marketing skills, so let's stick to it." Such a statement demonstrates power accompanied by respect and expectations. Power is in the implication that the teacher has information to give. Respect and high expectations enhance power by establishing a relationship between effort and the achievement of a worthwhile goal.

Responding to Student Blockers

"I Did Not Do It."   "I did not do it" is a response common to most students. Many teachers unwisely try to use logic in proving to students that they did do what they were accused of doing. That is precisely what the students want the teacher to do. Teachers should resist the temptation to justify a reasonable action each time one is taken. For example, if you are *sure* that James behaved inappropriately but he denies it, go ahead and administer the logical consequence you normally use. Do not provide an opportunity for the student to lie. Close the dialogue after the first denial with "James, I know you did it. I saw you do it, and you know that such behavior is unacceptable."

"I Did Not Know."   In the rational classroom management program, it is unlikely that a student will say, "I did not know." The teacher would have spent the first weeks of school explaining which behaviors are acceptable and which are not. Therefore, students will have had opportunities to explore both the behavior examples given in class and unfamiliar examples that may emerge later. However, as much as a teacher prepares, a few students generally end up saying, "I did not know." Your response is to affirm the rule that was broken, in the context in which it was taught. Be calm and professional in the process. You may respond by saying, "Let me remind you of when and how we covered this incident." Administer the consequence that had been agreed upon earlier. In most cases, the student is prepared to accept it. "Now that you know, I'm sure we will never have to deal with this again from you." Return to your academic instruction.

"I Was Not the Only One."   Another comment students will make is, "I was not the only one doing it. Why are you picking on me?" The teacher should firmly but quietly reply, "Vonda, I'm sorry. You are the only one I saw, so right now I can only deal with you." The logical consequence should be administered. Be very careful that you are not being unfair to the student. Some students develop a reputation for being disruptive, and it becomes easy for others (students and teacher) to see them as the disrupter in any situation. Be sure that social and cultural stereotypes are not predisposing you to "pick on" certain students unconsciously. For example, if you believe that students from a particular minority group are usually more disruptive than other students, you may, without being aware of doing so, pick on such students disproportionately. However, once you have examined your motive, your judgment, and your decision, and are confident that you are being fair and equitable, go ahead and do what you have to do without fear.

"You Are a Racist."   Students may say, "You are the man," "You are for the man," "You have forgotten your roots," "You yell at us but not at them," and a host of other statements that may be summed up in one sentence: "You are a racist." Statements like these are used by both the dominant and the minority student cultures in an effort to make the teacher feel guilty. Teachers of all races often find themselves defending their actions to prove that they are not what they are made out to be. Some teachers unwisely try to explain how much they have

worked for or supported desegregation efforts. You must remember three points in responding to such accusations:

1. The students know you, and if you are racist, there is nothing you can say at this point that will disprove that belief. If you are not, they know that and are merely trying to anger you.
2. The students' main objective is for you to feel guilty and begin to defend yourself.
3. When you begin to put up a defense, you are responding to students' manipulation and they have you beaten.

Instead of offering an explanation, say, "You know that what you did was unacceptable. The consequences are . . ." Repeat the statement as many times as you deem necessary as you administer the consequence.

Guided Practice Activity F. Assessing the Ideas

In Section 3, nine additional techniques were presented that have been used by rational managers to assist them in responding to disruptive students. Which three or four of the nine were the most meaningful to you? Why? Write your response on the lines provided. Be prepared to share your list with classmates.

_____

_____

_____

_____

_____

CHAPTER SUMMARY

Maintaining an environment conducive to learning is a primary responsibility of the classroom teacher. You must believe that you have the power to manage a classroom of students. Even if you have the management skills but do not use them with the confidence advocated in this chapter, you may end up as a frustrated manager.

The rational manager formulates policies to communicate reasonable expectations, disciplinary practices, and consequences, both positive and negative, that create a constructive environment in the classroom. We recommend that you integrate essential elements from the behavior management and humanistic philosophies that best fit your personality and style. The blending of the two philosophies into the Rational Approach to Practical School Discipline (RAPSD) results in a proactive position that will earn the respect of students, parents, and administrators. Adopting this approach is the first constructive step of the rational manager.

The second step taken by the rational manager is to build a predictable, comfortable, and secure learning environment in your room. Creating that environment requires that you teach collective responsibility for managing the classroom, for helping peers stay on-task, for sharing, for safety, and for respect, within the first weeks of school. Furthermore, your prudent integration of rules, routine procedures, and management techniques will promote positive individual and group behaviors. Your efforts to be consistent, to respect the civil rights of students, and to prevent rather than punish will be well received.

However, in spite of your best efforts as an effective discipline manager, conflicts and other disruptive behaviors will occur in your classroom. Your knowledge of the causes of misbehavior combined with your use of Quality Circles and positive moments strategies will enable you to be as rational in response to discipline situations as you are in creating a classroom environment in which many discipline situations fail to develop.

Independent Practice Activity B. Responding as a Rational Manager

Return to the set activity at the beginning of this chapter. In that activity you were asked to respond both as an advocate of behavior management and as a humanistic manager. How do you think Mrs. Henry would have responded if she were a rational manager?

_____

_____

_____

_____

_____

Independent Practice Activity C. Reflecting on What You Learned in Chapter 9

What concepts and techniques did you learn in Chapter 9 that will help you prevent discipline problems from surfacing in your classroom? What did you learn that will help you respond in a discipline situation?

_____

_____

_____

_____

_____

Independent Practice Activity D. Comparing Classroom Discipline Philosophies

What are the essential differences among the three major discipline strategies discussed in Chapters 8 and 9?

_____

_____

_____

Independent Practice Activity E. Revising Your Classroom Discipline Philosophy

Examine the discipline philosophy you wrote at the conclusion of Chapter 8. What characteristics of the rational approach to classroom management can you use in revising your philosophy? Think specifically of the proactive elements—teacher and student needs, physical organization of the classroom, the use of a discipline curriculum—and the elements in a system to respond to discipline situations: Dreikurs's classification system of misbehavior, an information system, Quality Circles, positive moments, and procedures for responding to classroom emergencies.

_____

_____

_____

_____

_____

REFERENCES

Brophy, J. E. (1981). Teacher praise: A functional analysis. *Review of Educational Research, 51*, 5–12. Washington, DC: American Educational Research Association.

Canter, L., and Canter, M. (1976). *Assertive Discipline:* A Take-Charge Approach to Today's Education. Seal Beach, CA, Canter & Associates.

Dinkmeyer, D., McKay, G., & Dinkmeyer, D. Jr. (1980). *Systematic Training for Effective Teaching.* Circle Pines, MN: American Guidance Services.

Dreikurs, R., Grunwald, B., & Pepper, F. (1982). *Maintaining Sanity in the Classroom.* New York: Harper & Row.

Emmer, E. T., et al. (1982). *Organizing and Managing the Junior High Classroom* (Report No. 6151). Research and Development Center for Teacher Education. Austin: University of Texas.

Evertson, C.M., et al. (1981). *Organizing and Managing the Elementary School Classroom* (Report No. 6060). Research and Development Center for Teacher Education. Austin: University of Texas.

Gardner, T. (1989). *Rational Approach to School-Wide Discipline*. Manual. Ann Arbor, MI: Pedagogic Press.

Gartnell, D. (1987, January). Unhealthy for children and other living things. *Young Children Journal*. pp. 10–11.

Goodlad, J. I. (1983). *A Place Called School*. New York: McGraw-Hill.

Jones, F. (1979). The gentle art of classroom discipline. *National Elementary Principal, 58*, 26–32.

Kelly, J. A. (1982). *Social Skills Training: A Practical Guide for Interventions*. New York; Springer.

Kounin, J. (1970). *Discipline and Group Management in the Classroom*. New York: Holt, Rinehart & Winston.

Maslow, A. H. (1954). *Motivation and Personality*. New York: Harper & Row.

Matson, J. L., & Ollendick, T. H. (1988). *Enhancing Children's Social Skills*. Elmsford, NY: Pergamon Press.

Roff, M., Sell, B., & Golden, M. (1972). *Social Adjustment and Personality Development in Children*. Minneapolis: University of Minnesota Press.

Sadker, D., & Sadker, M. (1985). Is the o.k. classroom o.k.? *Phi Delta Kappan, 66*(5), 358–361.

Ullman, C. A. (1975). Teachers, peers and tests as predictors of adjustment. *Journal of Eduational Psychology, 48*, 257–267.

CHAPTER 10

Looking Back and Looking Ahead

Chapter Overview

Throughout this text we have discussed a variety of decisions you will make as a teacher. We have considered planning, in which you select and analyze instructional goals and objectives and develop activities based on the subject matter, your educational philosophy, your knowledge of child development and learning principles, and the needs of your particular students. We described the teaching of units and outlined three categories of lessons— direct, inductive, and social. We also considered teaching for higher level thinking and the ways in which lessons may be altered to best serve students with special needs. Finally, we examined various approaches to classroom management and presented our suggestions for creating a successful classroom discipline system.

In this chapter we will consider you, the teacher, the one who must bring it all together. Where will you go from here? What roles will you be playing as a professional in education? We offer three visions of your role. First, we see you as a decision maker, using the information from your college courses and teaching experiences to forge your own success. Second, we see you as a continuous learner, becoming wiser and more successful each year as you learn more about teaching and learning. Finally, we see you as an educational change agent, helping form an exciting and productive future for education in your school, district, and state.

Chapter Objectives

After you have completed this chapter, you will be able to:
1. describe the major themes and the decision-making model presented in this book
2. present a plan for your own continuing development as a teacher
3. explain some of the themes that hold promise for improving education in the future
4. describe actions that you might make to contribute to the future of the profession

Section 1. The Teacher as Decision Maker

REVIEW OF THE BOOK'S STRUCTURE

We have divided this book into three large topics—planning for instruction, instructional implementation, and classroom management. The following outline illustrates how the chapters are organized:

Planning for instruction
- Choosing and analyzing classroom goals—Chapter 2
- Writing instructional objectives/evaluating results—Chapter 3
- Selecting learning activities—Chapter 4

Instructional implementation
- Designing and presenting units and lessons—Chapter 5
- Teaching to enhance thinking—Chapter 6
- Teaching for individual needs—Chapter 7

Classroom management
- Classroom management: traditions, programs, and research—Chapter 8
- A rational approach to classroom management—Chapter 9

As we plan for instruction, we usually think of two kinds of planning, long-range ("How will I organize the next unit of information?") and short-range ("What am I going to do tomorrow?"). In Chapter 2, we presented ways to choose long-range goals and analyze content that is related to those goals. We noted a variety of factors that should be considered when making decisions about goals. As we continued with long-range planning, in Chapter 3, we examined the importance of clearly stated instructional objectives and evaluation procedures to assess students' attainment of those objectives. Finally, in Chapter 4, we discussed factors to consider when planning activities and guidelines for commonly used teaching techniques.

When we put our plans into action, we should consider the units of instruction and the types of lessons we will present. The organization of units and alternative lesson types were presented in Chapter 5. We also need to make decisions about how to promote higher level thinking (Chapter 6) and how to meet students' individual needs (Chapter 7). As we implement our lessons, we are constantly monitoring students' responses and making adjustments in our plans. Many of these changes are made "on our feet"—that is, spontaneously. Other changes are made as we more thoughtfully reflect on the day's lessons and prepare the next day's plans.

Classroom management decisions must be made during both planning and implementation of instruction. In Chapter 8 we discussed three traditions from which classroom discipline philosophies emerge, along with commonly used programs and research. While the choice of management philosophies and programs is up to you, we suggest the eclectic method described in Chapter 9, the Rational Approach to Practical School Discipline.

THE DECISION-MAKING MODEL

A key goal of this book is to give you workable techniques and principles to enable you to make intelligent teaching decisions that will help your students succeed. We hope that you will not merely follow the textbook, as many teachers do. We encourage you to act as a "designer" of units and lessons, drawing on a variety of resources and activities that lead to your main objectives.

The decision-making model presented in this book is illustrated in Figure 10.1. In the center are listed the factors to consider when you make any teaching decision and when you interpret the effects of your decisions. The three phases of teachers' reflective thinking are shown as a continuous process of decision making: (1) pre-teaching decisions for action, (2) teaching action, modifications, and observation of their effects, and (3) post-teaching reflection and predictions about future actions. We will deal with each area below.

Pre-Teaching Decisions for Action

When we are planning a lesson or a sequence of lessons, we take the factors listed in Figure 10.1 into consideration by asking:

What's important to me in this lesson?
What are the key concepts, generalizations, and facts to be communicated?
What is the appropriate depth and scope of this material for students?
Which students will need special attention?
Which activities will help the students meet my objectives?
How will I organize the materials and the students for a productive learning
    environment?
What conditions can I anticipate that may influence the outcomes of the lesson?

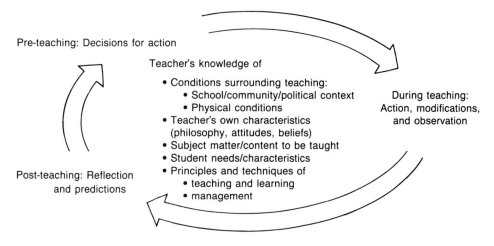

Figure 10.1. Factors Considered in Teaching Decisions and Reflections

When we answer these questions, we feel confident that we have thought through the important decisions. Then we prepare to put these decisions and plans into action. Just before we teach the lesson (perhaps that morning), we look over the plans one more time and ask ourselves the pre-teaching reflection questions listed below:

What student objective(s) am I hoping to achieve today?
What activities have I planned that will lead to these outcomes?
What type of lesson(s) will I use?
How will I know when students have achieved the objective(s)? What specifically am I looking for?
Is there any particular aspect of teaching that I am working to improve today?
Is there some way I can gather evidence on how well I'm doing in that area (e.g., have a friend or student observe, make a tape recording, make notes on my behavior, etc.)?
Are there any problems I'm anticipating, and have I planned strategies to avoid them?
Have I considered the factors in Figure 10.1 in my plans?

Teaching: Action, Modifications, and Observation

During the act of teaching, you will be making many decisions each minute. The process can be mind-boggling, especially if you have not spent enough time analyzing your plans. The payoff for careful and thorough planning is realized during the actual teaching. Because you have already done considerable pre-thinking about the activities, students, conditions, your own needs, and potential problems, you are not surprised when plans have to be modified. In many cases, you have visualized the potential problems and have backup plans ready and waiting. Without pre-planning, teachers can be frozen into confused inaction (or stunned into inappropriate overreaction) when things do not go as planned.

STRESSFUL LESSON

During your interaction with students, you are making minor changes and adjustments to your plans. These are based on the information you gather as you teach and observe how students are responding. If they are not successful and interested, modifications need to be made. If the appropriate action is not taken, student misbehavior and poor attitude may result.

Sometimes a lesson just does not go well. In such cases, it is important to observe your students carefully. You will find that the information you obtain from observation will be useful as you analyze the lesson. While you may not have enough time to think the problem through in the heat of the moment, you will have time later. You will want to analyze what went wrong, and why. Without this knowledge, how will you be able to prevent the same thing from happening again? Your observations are also crucial when things are going well. Later you'll want to think about why your lesson went particularly well so that you can build on those elements in future lessons.

Post-Teaching: Reflection and Predictions

After teaching, it is advisable to take time during planning period, lunch break, after school, or before school the next day to reflect on the lesson. You might use the following questions as a guide:

> How did the lesson go? What happened as I hoped it would? What didn't?
>
> What do I know about teaching and learning that might help me explain why the lesson turned out the way it did?
>
> How well did the students do in accomplishing my stated outcome? What evidence did I see that led me to this conclusion?
>
> What things did I change in the lesson? Why?
>
> How did I do in the area of teaching I chose to work on? What does the information I gathered show?
>
> Were there any conditions that played a role in the outcome of the lesson (e.g., student needs, physical factors, school context)?
>
> If there's anything I'd like to change in the lesson, what would it be?
>
> What alternative activities or approaches might be more successful? What has worked well in similar situations? Why? Which alternatives will I try next time?
>
> Are there any puzzling questions that remain in my mind that I find myself mulling over during the day? How could I find answers to those questions?

As a result of these reflections, you will plan your next actions.

CHECK FOR UNDERSTANDING

Imagine that you have taught a lesson on the correct use of semicolons. You told the students they were going to work on semicolons. You showed them a few examples on the board and gave them a worksheet with exercises on it. But students had little success on the worksheet and were frustrated and negative by the end of the lesson. You are now in the work area after school, reflecting on your actions and the students' responses. On the lines below, write several questions you would ask yourself that might help you figure out what went wrong. Compare your list with another student's list and come up with suggestions for improving the lesson. Be sure you can explain why your revised plans would help students succeed.

_____

_____

_____

_____

_____

Ways to Improve Our Own Decision Making

Clearly, there is a good deal to think about before, during, and after teaching. Keeping a *journal* to help you reflect on your own teaching experience may be a helpful way to improve your own teaching. Or you may prefer to discuss your experiences with a trusted colleague. If you do ask another teacher to discuss your teaching with you, pick someone who is competent, positive, and willing to be helpful, and who will keep information about individual students confidential.

    Peer coaching can be of immense help when you are trying to learn more about teaching. Peer coaching in its simplest form occurs when you visit another teacher's classroom, or that

PEER COACHING

teacher visits yours. You may ask the colleague to look for something specific (for example, whether you are giving all students attention and response opportunities). Or you may just want the teacher to help you examine your entire lesson from a different perspective. If you feel hesitant about having a friend observe you, you may wish to begin peer coaching by observing another teacher, especially one who is strong in an area you need to learn more about. Later, you can ask a trusted colleague to observe you.

Our advice to you is to find ways to examine your own decision making and the effects of your actions on students. The next section examines your role as a continuous learner—the essence of a true professional.

Guided Practice Activity. Planning for Decision Making

Write below three specific actions you will take during student teaching or during your first year of teaching that will help you grow in your decision making. Think of these as New Year's resolutions.

1. I will _____

_____

_____

2. I will _____

_____

_____

3. I will _____

_____

_____

Section 2. The Teacher as Continuous Learner

Your role as a professional decision maker will continue throughout your career. If you are to learn and grow as an educator, it is important that you gain information that will contribute to your effectiveness in the classroom. Because knowledge about teaching and learning is increasing rapidly, teachers must make an effort to stay current on trends in educational research. Review the research carefully and look for ways to put the new principles and ideas to use in your classroom. We are not suggesting that you jump on every educational bandwagon that comes along—far from it—but we do hope that you recognize that the information in this textbook is just a beginning.

We authors have gained a significant amount of knowledge and insight throughout our own teaching careers; much of this information simply was not available when we started. We encourage you to do the same. Subscribe to professional publications, join educational organizations, and continue to study through graduate and inservice education. As you do so, view the information you learn critically. See how new ideas fit in with tried and true principles. Don't be afraid to experiment and, conversely, to retain ideas you find effective and appropriate. Very few educational trends need be swallowed in their entirety. Your professional judgment will allow you to choose what is best for your students and what fits your personal philosophy and values.

You have the opportunity to begin the process of continuous learning as you observe teachers in your pre–student teaching or student teaching experiences. We encourage you to enter each situation thoughtfully. The examples you see in those classrooms will have an enormous impact on the way you teach a class of your own. Watching experienced teachers can give you a chance to learn the practical ins and outs of teaching. It can help you understand how the instructional techniques and principles in this book can be applied with a variety of students in a variety of situations. On the other hand, no teacher is perfect, and no two individuals' educational philosophies and values are identical. Therefore, don't be afraid to question, to consider alternatives, or even to say to yourself, "This is something I'll do differently in my own class." You may find, in the end, that your view changes and you decide to adopt a technique you had earlier rejected. Or you may decide that just because something "works" for one teacher does not mean it is the best way, or the way that fits with your personal values.

You will find many opportunities for professional growth through workshops offered during student teaching and your first years of teaching. We urge you to take advantage of these opportunities for learning new ideas and gaining new perspectives. It is in such settings that we can sit back and reflect on our own practice. We receive support for change and experimentation. And, finally, we have the comfort of hearing that other teachers struggle with the same issues that puzzle us! As each year of teaching goes by, you will feel more confident, more comfortable with what you are doing, and clearer about your goals and accomplishments. As you enter your third or fourth year of teaching (sometimes earlier), you may find that you have the inclination and energy to look outside your classroom to become involved in educational issues in the school and in the district. The next section discusses your role in the larger arena of education.

Section 3. The Teacher as Educational Change Agent

A HISTORICAL PERSPECTIVE

The 1980s will likely be known in educational history as a period of intense educational reform. During that decade a score of reports were written and presented in the media, beginning with *A Nation at Risk* (U.S. Department of Education, 1983). These reports contained hundreds of recommendations for changing teacher certification, school organization, curriculum, and teaching methods. There were recommendations to require more math and science courses in high school, to extend the school day or school year, and to require a stronger liberal arts preparation for future teachers.

Unfortunately, few of the recommendations involved the most important element of the learning process—the interaction between the student, the teacher, and the home environment. And glaringly missing were suggestions for strengthening the role, outlook, and behavior of the teacher (Maeroff, 1988). It is our view that until the role, responsibilities, and rewards of teaching are redefined and enhanced, the recommended reforms will fail to produce the educational improvement that we all desire.

To illustrate the present state of teaching, consider the following comments written by two veteran public school teachers:

> Yet, I love to teach. I love working with youngsters, watching independence develop, seeing eyes light up with understanding, nurturing excitement about learning, empowering students to believe in themselves, and encouraging self-discipline. (Wheatley, 1988)

> In a typical school you are isolated, cut off from everyone, the rest of the culture outside the school doesn't give a damn about you or about the kids you are trying to teach. The school system itself almost regards you in that way. You are in the place where the bells are ringing, but the people who are calling the signals for the schools are in places where they can't even hear the bells. (Maeroff, 1988)

Consider the rewards and benefits expressed in the first account—developing understanding, promoting discovery and excitement, nurturing independence and self-discipline—

all worthy goals that draw teachers to the calling. And there are schools in which all this and more is possible. Yet there are also many places in which the downside of teaching is painfully obvious to teachers, as seen in the second account.

The second teacher alludes to three enduring unpleasant facts of teaching life encountered by many idealistic public school teachers: (1) the feeling that your life is controlled by others—by people who don't walk in your shoes and who don't understand your needs, feelings, and problems (Rand Corporation, 1978), (2) the isolation that prevents teachers from sharing their ideas and solving mutual problems, and (3) the fact that curriculum decisions about what is to be taught are too often made by supervisors and textbook writers (Ohanian, 1985; Komoski, 1985; Edmonds & Pasch, 1974). These realities become clear to the insightful teacher when the challenge and novelty of the early years of teaching wear off, usually between the third and fifth years (Sarason, 1971).

LIBERATING EDUCATION FROM PAST LIMITATIONS

Although the identification of the teacher's worklife ailments is relatively easy, there are no simple solutions. To illustrate the difficulty, imagine that the solutions to these problems are locked in a safe that can be opened only by three different locks, each with its own combination. To make the situation more difficult, imagine that each of the necessary combinations is in different hands.

THE TIME LOCK IMPRISONING THE TEACHER IN AN UNPLEASANT WORKLIFE

Because of the attention given to educational reform during the 1980s, we believe the time is right to open this safe and solve the worklife problems of teachers. Recent surveys indicate that taxpayers are willing to spend more for education if our schools can demonstrate the ability to educate all children in the most basic skills so that achievement (especially in math and science) is competitive with other countries (Gallup & Elam, 1988).

What are the combinations to the three locks that will open the safe? The *first combination* opens the lock that has kept schooling and teachers imprisoned in a portrait from the past. The image society has of education must change from the early 20th-century depiction of schools as garment factories in which the worker (teacher) fashions a salable product out of the raw material (student). This image portrays the teacher, like the garment worker, laboring under difficult conditions—crowding, few breaks, noise, isolation. Just as garment workers had no say in the management of the workplace, so decisions about students, schedules, and materials are too often handed down to teachers, with little opportunity for their input. And, again like the factory workers, too many urban teachers are plagued by outdated equipment and limited materials, even basic necessities such as pencils and paper (Carnegie Foundation, 1988).

The U.S. public needs to change this factory worker image to one of an autonomous professional working in desirable conditions, able to make appropriate decisions. In this new view of the teacher, collegiality would replace isolation, shared decision making would replace autocratic administration and supervision, and modern facilities would replace unpleasant, outdated schools and equipment. Teachers would feel empowered to make decisions about the hiring of new faculty, textbook selection, curriculum, and instruction.

The *second combination* releases the lock that gives teachers too little time—too little time to plan teaching units and lessons, create materials, organize resources, evaluate instruction, meet with colleagues, revise plans, inquire into the effects of teaching, work with small groups and individual statements, consult student records, meet with parents, and mentor future and new teachers.

It may surprise you to know that the average elementary teacher has 45 minutes (or less) for lunch and 20 minutes of time during the day when students are at special activities (e.g., art). This leaves little time for the tasks listed above, so most teachers squeeze in a few of the most important activities (e.g., planning) before or after school. Much of the "extra" work is done at night or on weekends.

One of the authors of this textbook was lucky enough to teach during the 1960s in a school in which each teacher had 150 minutes of unscheduled time each day. The time was used for the more professionalizing activities referred to above: planning, problem solving, creating new understandings, and sharing with colleagues. It is our belief that teachers will have little opportunity to grow professionally without more unscheduled time during the teaching day. If it was possible then, it can be accomplished in the 1990s!

The *third combination* opens the lock that makes possible the reform of teacher education. In the past, preparation and training did not adequately prepare teachers for the complexities of the work. Perhaps it is impossible for any sequence of courses and practice teaching experiences to equip a newcomer to deal with such a difficult job. It is our contention, however, that much can be done to improve teacher preparation.

First, teachers need to know the technical skills of teaching—how to ask questions, lecture, and so forth. But they also need to have an opportunity to experiment with these skills in a variety of settings, to observe their effects on students and others, and to interpret their experience in terms of relevant theories and principles. Thus we suggest a combination of theory, skills, and practice, with many opportunities to reflect on their interaction within the particular teaching situation. The components of a teacher's preparation are the tools to assist in decision making; they are not rules to be followed blindly.

For this final lock to be sprung open, teacher education should be seen as a collaborative effort between schools and universities. Professors and teachers must join together to determine the skills, concepts, theories, and other elements necessary for a professional decision maker. Professors can no longer remain isolated in the university; every effort must be made to help upgrade teacher education.

HOPEFUL TRENDS IN EDUCATION

Fortunately, you are entering education at a time when there are major movements to open all three locks—professional image, time, and teacher education. These movements combine to offer hope and direction for much-needed changes in education. They are known as *teacher empowerment, school restructuring*, and *inquiry-oriented teacher education*.

Teacher empowerment refers to the process of giving teachers more control over their own and their students' destiny in schools. Empowered teachers participate in school-based management decisions regarding materials, staffing, students, scheduling, and so on. Empowered teachers also participate in school improvement projects, in which a leadership team composed of the principal, teachers, and, perhaps, parents follow a systematic procedure to solve a school problem or fill a need. All teachers and staff contribute ideas to the team as they assess needs, plan and implement improvements, and evaluate the effects of the changes.

Such school-based management and school improvement plans require that schools be organized differently from the way they are now. This leads us to the idea of *restructuring*. Many schools are experimenting with ways to create the time for teachers to participate in school management, professional development, and school improvement efforts. In addition to using daily substitute teachers, some districts have provided highly trained full-time substitutes in classrooms of teachers who spend an entire semester at a professional development academy to upgrade their planning and teaching skills. Many schools offer teachers released-time or team-teaching situations so they can participate in management or improvement activities.

Finally, schools of education and district staff development offices are coming to see that teachers' continuous learning need not be mandated from above by rigid evaluation systems and prescribed curricula and teaching methods. The movement is toward *inquiry-oriented growth activities*, in which teachers participate in peer observation and colleague coaching, action research (investigations of the effects of our teaching on our students), peer evaluation, self-directed learning at workshops or conferences, and mini-grants for development of units and materials.

In short, the days of "Thou shalt teach using only these techniques, and we're going to evaluate you on them" are quickly fading. And the sky is sunny for the teacher who wishes to take charge of his or her professional development by joining with others to learn more about the mysteries of teaching and learning.

HOPEFUL TRENDS IN EDUCATION

YOUR ROLE IN THE FUTURE OF EDUCATION

You may have been thinking, "What does all this have to do with me? I'm just going to go and teach my students, and stay out of this whole mess." Yes, that is what you will need to do your first few years of teaching. You will have your hands full in your own classroom. But soon you will become more aware of possible shortcomings in your school's policies, the curriculum, the district's policies, and so on. As professionals, we are never in total agreement on anything. You will begin to see changes that should be made in your school or in your district. This is when you move into your role as change agent.

What do we know about change? How can teachers bring about change? What is your role in your school or district as changes are made? We encourage you to be a proactive and vocal agent for positive change in your school and district. As you notice major problems, speak up! Instead of just joining teachers' lounge or lunchroom gripe sessions, tackle major problems by forming a task force with the help of the principal to investigate the problem or issue and propose a solution to the staff.

You'll be surprised at how easily things can be changed when a few people are willing to do the footwork to find and implement a solution. One of the authors worked in a school that had the ugliest teachers' lounge we had ever seen. We got together and put on a teachers' play, charged admission, and raised enough money for new carpet, drapes, and furniture. That experience made us all feel proud that we could improve our own environment. That all-too-common attitude of powerlessness and hopelessness disappeared.

When you have a desire to seek solutions to a problem in the school, you can offer to join the school leadership team. This team will be assisted by the principal in helping the staff find and attack persistent problems. Serving on such a team is hard work, but participation builds a sense of cooperation and high morale among teachers.

Another way to become involved in providing direction for the profession is to become active in your local teachers' union or association. The two teachers' organizations—the National Education Association (NEA) and the American Federation of Teachers (AFT)—offer many opportunities for members to have a say in proposed changes. Political decisions regarding funding, teacher evaluation, and pay have a profound influence on a teacher's daily worklife. Teachers' associations provide a vehicle for promoting desired outcomes in the profession.

Curriculum design is another area in which there is opportunity for input and professional growth. Many schools and districts ask teachers to help create new units of study; the assignments are often with pay, during the summer. Such a professional activity can be renewing and can provide a service to other teachers in the district.

You may be asked to share your curriculum materials with other teachers during a workshop or during individual consultation. When you do so, you become a teacher of teachers. As you take on this role, it is important to remember that reform comes slowly. You will need great patience in your role as change agent. We all go through predictable stages as we are asked to adopt new and unfamiliar ideas or procedures. In teaching, the earlier stages usually have to do with the need for information and concerns about personal competence. For example, as you begin your teaching experiences, your initial concerns are likely to center on issues such as "How do I keep control?" "What are the lunchroom procedures?" or "What am I supposed to teach about World War II?" Later, as the procedures become more familiar, you may begin to focus more on the effects on student learning (Hall & Loucks, 1978). As you become more familiar with school routines and basic teaching techniques, you will feel freer to

consider the effects of specific techniques on student learning, the variety of student needs, and ways in which you can improve and elaborate upon your ideas.

These natural stages of development can be frustrating for individuals acting as change agents. You can imagine how it might feel when you have designed a technique to help students learn more effectively, and the people you share it with are concerned chiefly about their own ability to use the materials and where they will come from! Change is slow and occurs most successfully in an atmosphere of low threat, frequent teacher sharing, and safe experimentation (Sparks & Simmons, 1989).

It is important to keep these stages of concern in mind as you go through changes in your own teaching, as well as when you share information with others. Research indicates that teachers may remain personally threatened and clumsy with the new practices for the first year or two of use (Hall & Loucks, 1974). Patience and persistence are the keys to change and improvement. Try to focus on the progress made toward the long-range goal and avoid comparing the current situation with the ideal image. Such an attitude will add to your sanity as you try to implement reforms in your school or classroom.

A final idea about taking an active role in shaping the future of education—consider becoming a leader in a professional organization. There are groups for teachers of particular subjects (e.g., International Reading Association), organizations related to curriculum and supervision (e.g., Association for Supervision and Curriculum Development), service organizations (e.g., Special Olympics), special interest groups (e.g., National Association for Gifted Children), and general organizations for teachers (e.g., Phi Delta Kappa). These groups

offer exciting growth and leadership opportunities for teachers. And most of them have state or local subsidiaries.

You may choose to serve on a committee to help plan a conference, or you may decide to write an article to be published in a journal sponsored by one of the groups. You may run for an officers' position in one of them. There are a variety of opportunities for leadership on the national, state, and local levels. We encourage you to seize the opportunity to make a contribution to your profession!

Independent Practice Activity. Planning for Professional Growth

Write five ideas for your own professional growth. Be sure to include ideas for professional contributions in your area of interest.

A FINAL WORD

In Chapter 1 we said that we wrote this book to help you become the best teacher possible: an empowered educator capable of making thoughtful and appropriate instructional decisions. There is no single path or easy prescription for this goal. We have provided information, tools, and guidelines to help you begin. But the art and science of teaching demands not just the best of our learning, intellect, and decision making; it also requires insight, sensitivity, persistence, humor, patience, stamina, and joy in the process of learning. While the goal may seem daunting, there is no profession with greater potential to communicate, to make change, or to touch individual lives. John Steinbeck tells of a teacher who touched his life, as we hope you will touch the lives of your students:

Like Captured Fireflies

In her classroom our speculations ranged the world.
She aroused us to book waving discussions.
Every morning we came to her carrying new truths, new facts, new ideas
Cupped and sheltered in our hands like captured fireflies.
When she went away a sadness came over us,
But the light did not go out.
She left her signature upon us
The literature of the teacher who writes on children's minds.
I've had many teachers who taught us soon forgotten things,
But only a few like her who created in me a new thing, a new attitude, a new hunger.
I suppose that to a large extent I am the unsigned manuscript of that teacher.
What deathless power lies in the hands of such a person.

California Teachers Association Journal, *October 1957*

REFERENCES

Carnegie Foundation for the Advancement of Teaching. (1988). *An Imperiled Generation: Saving Urban Schools*. Princeton, NJ.

Edmonds, V., & Pasch, M. (1974). Teacher: Consumer or designer. *Educational Technology, 1*, 50–51.

Gallup, A. M., & Elam, S. M. (1988). The 20th annual Gallup Poll of the public's attitudes toward the public schools. *Phi Delta Kappan, 70*(1), 33–46.

Hall, G. & Loucks, S. (1978). Teacher concerns as a basic for facilitating and personalizing staff development. *Teachers College Record, 80*, 36–53.

Komoski, K. P. (1985). Instructional materials will not improve until we change the system. *Educational Leadership, 47*(7), 31–37.

Maeroff, G. I. (1988). *The Empowerment of Teachers: Overcoming the Crisis of Confidence*. New York: Teachers College Press.

Ohanian, S. (1985). Huffing and puffing and blowing schools excellent. *Phi Delta Kappan, 66*(5), 316–321.

Rand Corporation. (1978). *Implementing and Sustaining Innovations*. Santa Monica, CA.

Sarason, S. B. (1971). *The Culture of the School and the Problem of Change*. Boston: Allyn and Bacon.

Sparks, G., & Simmons, J. (1989). Inquiry-oriented staff development. In S. Caldwell (Ed.), *Staff Development: A Handbook of Effective Practices* (pp. 126–139). Oxford, OH: National Staff Development Council.

Steinbeck, J. (1957, October). Like captured fireflies. *California Teachers Association Journal, 7*, 5.

Wheatley, A. (1988, May 16). It's becoming harder to teach at elementary schools [Letter to the editor]. *Ann Arbor News*.

U.S. Department of Education. (1983). *A Nation at Risk: The Imperative for Educational Reform*. Washington, DC: Author.

Index